Oliver O'Donovan's Moral Theology

T&T Clark Enquiries in Theological Ethics

Series editors
Brian Brock
Susan F. Parsons

Oliver O'Donovan's Moral Theology

Tensions and Triumphs

Samuel Tranter

t&tclark
LONDON • NEW YORK • OXFORD • NEW DELHI • SYDNEY

T&T CLARK
Bloomsbury Publishing Plc
50 Bedford Square, London, WC1B 3DP, UK
1385 Broadway, New York, NY 10018, USA
29 Earlsfort Terrace, Dublin 2, Ireland

BLOOMSBURY, T&T CLARK and the T&T Clark logo are trademarks of Bloomsbury Publishing Plc

First published in Great Britain 2020
This paperback edition published in 2022

Copyright © Samuel Tranter, 2020

Samuel Tranter has asserted his right under the Copyright, Designs and Patents Act, 1988, to be identified as Author of this work.

For legal purposes the Acknowledgements on p. vi–vii constitute an extension of this copyright page.

All rights reserved. No part of this publication may be reproduced or transmitted in any form or by any means, electronic or mechanical, including photocopying, recording, or any information storage or retrieval system, without prior permission in writing from the publishers.

Bloomsbury Publishing Plc does not have any control over, or responsibility for, any third-party websites referred to or in this book. All internet addresses given in this book were correct at the time of going to press. The author and publisher regret any inconvenience caused if addresses have changed or sites have ceased to exist, but can accept no responsibility for any such changes.

A catalogue record for this book is available from the British Library.

A catalog record for this book is available from the Library of Congress.

ISBN: HB: 978-0-5676-9459-1
PB: 978-0-5676-9641-0
ePDF: 978-0-5676-9460-7
eBook: 978-0-5676-9462-1

Series: T&T Clark Enquiries in Theological Ethics

Typeset by Deanta Global Publishing Services, Chennai, India

To find out more about our authors and books visit www.bloomsbury.com and sign up for our newsletters.

Contents

Acknowledgements		vi
Introduction		1
1	Groundwork: 'The Natural Ethic'	13
2	Topography: *Resurrection and Moral Order* – 'The Objective Reality'	35
3	Contour: *Resurrection and Moral Order* – 'The Subjective Reality' and 'The Form of the Moral Life'	99
4	Territory: *Desire of the Nations* and *Ways of Judgment*	163
5	Remapping: *Ethics as Theology*	191
Conclusion		227
Postscript: The end of ethics		233
Appendix: Cartography with O'Donovan and friends		235
Bibliography		243
General index		267
Index of scripture references		273

Acknowledgements

Gratitude, as I seem to recall Barth said (if he didn't, he should have), is the ground of the Christian ethos. This project, as a faltering attempt to sketch some part of that ethos, ought to be grounded in the same doxological way:

> Blessed are you, O Lord, the God of our ancestor Israel, forever and ever. Yours, O Lord, are the greatness, the power, the glory, the victory, and the majesty; for all that is in the heavens and on the earth is yours; yours is the kingdom, O Lord, and you are exalted as head above all. … And now, our God, we give thanks to you and praise your glorious name. But who am I, and what is my people, that we should be able to make this freewill offering? For all things come from you, and of your own have we given you. (1 Chron. 29.10b-14)

Tracing the story of how this book came to be, I want to now record my gratitude to those teachers at Aberdeen who nurtured my interest in theology and ethics, and with regard to this study, particularly Prof Brian Brock, Dr Mike Mawson and Prof Phil Ziegler (under whose supervision it got going as a master's dissertation).

This research subsequently proceeded as doctoral work at Durham University, generously funded across three years by the Arts and Humanities Research Council. The final form is only slightly modified from the thesis, for good or ill. My PhD studies were supervised by the ever-kind and wise Prof Robert Song, who contributed much more to what was a wonderful three years in the North East than simply keep an eye on my writing. (I remember a prospective initial discussion of this research with Robert, at the dinner table of the annual Society for the Study of Christian Ethics conference. After an encouraging conversation I emerged from the dining hall only to notice a scurrying in the bushes by the door. I thought it was some kind of vole, but Robert observed – correctly – that it was, in fact, a hedgehog. I have not since quite managed to be either a 'hedgehog' or a 'fox', in Isaiah Berlin's terms, but Robert has been gently helping me avoid mistakes ever since.)

The Ayres family – Lucy (Aithne would want Lucy to be first), Iain, Thomas, Anna, Medi and Lewis – also did much to make our time in Durham hospitable and interesting. To Lewis, I owe special thanks for taking the time to make sense out of some of the worst passages of my prose – if not, yet, of the undoubted missteps in my thought.

The final stages of preparing the manuscript for submission as a PhD and then publication as a book took place far from Durham: first, during a year in South East Asia (among wonderful colleagues, students and friends to thank, I mention here only the treasured encouragement of Dr JHW Chan); and then in the quite different surrounds of Bolton, Greater Manchester (thanks to Mum and Dad, for your love in things great and small) and occasionally in Ahoghill, Co. Antrim (thanks to Dessie and Eleanor, as supportive of a son-in-law's strange career choice as one could hope). I am also thankful for those institutions that have allowed me to take my first steps in teaching, including Lindisfarne College of Theology and St Hild College of Theology.

Many other teachers, colleagues, friends and church communities have taught and sustained me through the writing, from its beginnings in Aberdeen to its main progress in Durham and beyond. Among those who have contributed more or less directly to the thoughts behind this book, I would like to thank not least (in some sense of alphabetical and chronological order): from Aberdeen, Joy Allan, Matt Burdette, Kevin Hargaden and James King – and generous readers Amy Erickson and Kevin O'Farrell; from Durham, Pete Baker, Ben Coleman, Ed Epsen, Tim Escott, Ross Jesmont, Jenny Leigh, Richard Rohlfing, Francis Stewart and Matt Williams (plus all the rest of the brilliant Dun Cow folks); and from elsewhere, David Bartram Torrance.

In addition, I am grateful to Brian Brock and Susan F. Parsons for extending the invitation to place this work in their excellent series, and to Veerle Van Steenhuyse, Anna Turton and their colleagues for their work in bringing it to published fruition.

All that said, it is to my wife AVM – true travelling companion in this earthly *peregrinatio* – and to our daughter Aithne Clare – who was born in our second year in Durham – that I dedicate this book, such as it is. Aithne: this part of the book is like where Mr Silly puts his friends inside his book, except that my book, which is already too big, isn't big enough to actually fit anyone in.

All scriptural citations in this book are from *New Revised Standard Version Bible*, copyright © 1989 National Council of the Churches of Christ in the United States of America. Used by permission. All rights reserved worldwide.

Introduction

This study offers a sustained engagement with the thought of the major contemporary Anglican theologian Oliver O'Donovan (1945–).[1] As an exploration of O'Donovan's extraordinarily wide-ranging work, it is itself necessarily broad in scope. However, inasmuch as it represents an assessment and not simply a rehearsal of his moral theology, a particular thread of critical reflection runs through this book, tying its treatment of diverse texts and themes together – namely, the question of the relationship between eschatology and ethics.

That this question can be asked of O'Donovan's thought is, I hope, not arguable. 'Every Christian ethics', as Jürgen Moltmann writes (and more of Moltmann later), 'is determined by a presupposed eschatology'.[2] Yet left unelaborated, that is a somewhat uninteresting claim. We could equally observe that every Christian ethics is determined by its presupposed doctrine of creation, providence or salvation, or by its ecclesiology or its theological anthropology; all dogmatic *loci* bear upon moral theology in some way (or ought to). So too do a whole host of other factors, not least philosophical and sociological assumptions. However, Moltmann's claim becomes markedly more interesting when we begin to suspect that there is an 'eschatological squeamishness among many Christian ethicists'. (So David Elliot, in his recent book *Christian Ethics and Hope.*)[3] It becomes yet more intriguing when we realize that the field of Christian ethics has recently seen a renewal of attention given to the doctrine of creation, typically unmatched by any comparable recommitment to thinking through the moral implications of Christian teaching about, say, the kingdom of God, or other

---

[1] A biographical note: Revd Prof Oliver M. T. O'Donovan FBA FRSE. Tutor, Wycliffe Hall, Oxford (1972–7), Assistant then Associate Professor of Systematic Theology, Wycliffe College, Toronto (1977–82), Regius Professor of Moral and Pastoral Theology and Canon of Christ Church, Oxford (1982–2006), Professor of Christian Ethics and Practical Theology, Edinburgh (2006–13), and Professor Emeritus (2013–). Now, in addition, Honorary Professor, St Andrews, Canon Provincial and Provincial Theologian of the Province of York in the Church of England. Past President of the Society for the Study for Christian Ethics. For a list of his publications see *The Authority of the Gospel: Explorations in Moral and Political Theology in Honor of Oliver O'Donovan*, ed. Robert Song and Brent Waters (Grand Rapids: Eerdmans, 2015), 285–91. The sheer number of pages it takes to catalogue such output (and more items could be added from the last few years) says much about O'Donovan's ability to consistently produce work of the highest order: fifteen books, eight ethical booklets, thirty-eight contributions to collections, forty-one journal articles and seventeen magazine articles; and all this, on top of the teaching and supervision of students, university administration and ecclesial service.
[2] Jürgen Moltmann, *Ethics of Hope*, trans. Margaret Kohl (Minneapolis: Fortress, 2012), 9. Moltmann's own typology (9–41) of different constellations of eschatology-in-relation-to-ethics does not seem to me particularly accurate. Issuing from a similar context but generally more reliable, I think, is Gerhard Sauter, *What Dare We Hope? Reconsidering Eschatology* (Harrisburg: Trinity Press International, 1999).
[3] David Elliot, *Hope and Christian Ethics* (Cambridge: Cambridge University Press, 2017), 1.

eschatological affirmations. There are probably many reasons for this state of affairs, and many of the reasons are good; plenty will become evident in what follows. But they do not seem to me sufficient cause for the relative neglect of this important aspect of systematic and moral-theological reflection. Still, if Moltmann's general point raises the possibility that the question of eschatology and ethics may be asked, and Elliot's suspicion of contemporary squeamishness further spurs us on to actually ask it, we have not yet established why this enquiry might be especially rewarding to pursue in relation to O'Donovan's work. It is so, I suggest, for at least three reasons.

First, and most obviously: in O'Donovan's writing, the more-or-less direct question of eschatology and ethics is rarely far from the surface. Its appearances amount to no small collection of material, covering as they do more than four prolific decades. Second, besides that fact, on my reading, O'Donovan's response to this question also plays a significant role in sculpting the theological foundations that undergird the many topical edifices of his moral and political thought. Finally – and this is the precise critical point that it is the burden of this study to prove – I believe that the place of eschatology in the foundations of moral theology is an area of tension across the entire span of O'Donovan's published work.

The theological foundations are worth paying attention to. While O'Donovan, having pursued a vocation as a professional practitioner of Christian ethics, is justly known in part exactly for his topical forays, he has also always been 'a theologian at heart' (as he described his own teacher Paul Ramsey).[4] Accordingly, O'Donovan has much to say about the doctrinal bases of moral theology. In addition, careful consideration of the form of his doctrinal commitments promises to make the topical forays more intelligible. Any serious attempt to reckon with O'Donovan's arguments about matters as diverse as just war, biotechnology or ecclesial disagreement over sexuality requires patient reflection on the detail of these theological commitments, along with the ways they play out. Just so, the performance of ethical judgement about 'issues' illuminates the antecedent theological convictions. Conversely, by saying 'antecedent', I do not wish to give the misleading impression that the traffic all runs one way. Not at all – in sometimes more and sometimes less methodologically acknowledged ways, the peculiarities of contextual discernment shape the deployment of O'Donovan's theological convictions and the convictions themselves. Their mutually conditioning character is a feature of his moral theology (as any other moral theology) that I try to remain alert to throughout this exploration.

That the question of the relationship between eschatology and ethics is one that can be asked of O'Donovan's thought should now be clear. But why a book should devote so much space to O'Donovan, taking his work as its central and organizing concern, may not seem self-evident to some readers. In response to this point, it may be worth sharing two motivations, one of which is academic and one of which is autobiographical, though the two are hardly separable. The strictly academic rationale should become clear in the summary of my argument, which follows in a moment, and will be more fully displayed as the study progresses. For now, perhaps, reason enough

---

[4] O'Donovan, 'Paul Ramsey: 1913–88', *Studies in Christian Ethics* 1, no. 1 (1988): 82–90.

can be supplied by quoting Rowan Williams: 'Oliver is a difficult, enriching writer, the stimulus of whose work is exceptional for all those who have engaged with it.'[5]

I would add to Williams's commendation a complicating factor. Despite the exceptional stimulus that engagement with O'Donovan represents, it has apparently proved difficult for those who have engaged O'Donovan's work to place his powerfully idiosyncratic contributions into conversation with other voices. This difficulty surely accounts for what is, relatively speaking, a wider lack of critical engagement with O'Donovan's work (especially when compared with, for instance, his contemporary Stanley Hauerwas).[6] It may also partly explain a feature of the contemporary appropriation of O'Donovan's thought that I investigate in this study, wherein some Christian ethicists adopt O'Donovan's *doctrinal* formulations wholesale, and perhaps uncritically, besides taking up the judgements of his moral and political thought. It may sometimes seem, then, as though those who appreciate O'Donovan tend simply to reproduce his thinking as a component part of their own projects, whereas those who are not so appreciative simply leave his work unremarked. (Again, a contrast might be drawn with Hauerwas: those who have demurred from Hauerwas's approach often write as though they have felt that they have to interact with it – if often in unfortunately caricaturing fashion.) With this twofold situation in view, the aim of

---

[5] Rowan Williams, foreword to *The Authority of the Gospel*, viii. O'Donovan's thoughts on Williams' thought can be gleaned in 'Archbishop Rowan Williams', *Pro Ecclesia* 12, no. 1 (2003): 5–9; the foreword to *On Rowan Williams: Critical Essays*, ed. Matheson Russell (Eugene: Wipf and Stock, 2009); and the interview with O'Donovan and his wife Joan Lockwood O'Donovan in Rupert Shortt, *God's Advocates: Christian Thinkers in Conversation* (London: Darton, Longman, and Todd, 2005), 248–72, at 267–8.

[6] The literature on Hauerwas is extensive, including the following: Arne Rasmusson, *The Church as Polis: From Political Theology to Theological Politics as Exemplified by Jürgen Moltmann and Stanley Hauerwas* (Notre Dame: University of Notre Dame Press, 1995); Samuel Wells, *Transforming Fate into Destiny: The Theological Ethics of Stanley Hauerwas* (Carlisle: Paternoster, 1998); Emmanuel Katongole, *Beyond Universal Reason: The Relation between Religion and Ethics in the Work of Stanley Hauerwas* (Notre Dame: University of Notre Dame Press, 2000); *Faithfulness and Fortitude: Conversations with the Theological Ethics of Stanley Hauerwas*, ed. Mark Nation (Edinburgh: T & T Clark, 2000); R. Scott Smith, *Virtue Ethics and Moral Knowledge: Philosophy of Language after MacIntyre and Hauerwas* (Aldershot: Ashgate, 2003); John B. Thompson, *The Ecclesiology of Stanley Hauerwas: A Christian Theology of Liberation* (Burlington: Ashgate, 2003) – and Thompson's subsequent books; John Swinton, *Critical Reflections on Stanley Hauerwas's Theology of Disability: Disabling Society, Enabling Theology* (Binghamton: The Howarth Pastoral Press, 2004); *God, Truth, and Witness: Engaging Stanley Hauerwas*, ed. L. Gregory Jones, Reinhard Hütter and C. Rosalee Velloso da Silva (Grand Rapids: Brazos, 2005); *Unsettling Arguments: A Festschrift on the Occasion of Stanley Hauerwas's 70th Birthday*, ed. Charles Pinches, Kelly S. Johnson and Charles M. Collier (Eugene: Cascade, 2010); Mark Ryan, *The Politics of Practical Reason: Why Theological Ethics Must Change Your Life* (Eugene: Cascade, 2011); Miika Tolonen, *Witness Is Presence: Reading Stanley Hauerwas in a Nordic Setting* (Eugene: Resource, 2013); Nicholas M. Healy, *Hauerwas: A (Very) Critical Introduction* (Grand Rapids: Eerdmans, 2014); Adrian W. Baan, *The Necessity of Witness: Stanley Hauerwas's Contribution to Systematic Theology* (Eugene: Pickwick, 2015); *The Difference Christ Makes: Celebrating the Life, Work, and Friendship of Stanley Hauerwas*, ed. Charles M. Collier (Eugene: Cascade, 2015); Robert J. Dean, *For the Life of the World: Jesus Christ and the Church in the Theologies of Dietrich Bonhoeffer and Stanley Hauerwas* (Eugene: Pickwick, 2016); Brian Brock and Stanley Hauerwas, *Beginnings: Interrogating Hauerwas*, ed. Kevin Hargaden (London/New York: T & T Clark, 2017); Silje Kvamme Bjørndal, *The Church in a Secular Age: A Pneumatological Reconstruction of Stanley Hauerwas's Ecclesiology* (Eugene: Pickwick, 2018); and finally, David B. Hunsicker, *The Making of Stanley Hauerwas: Bridging Barth and Postliberalism* (Downer's Grove: IVP Academic, 2019). I hope the point is clear.

the present book is to remedy a lack of critical engagement with O'Donovan's thought, providing an interrogative re-description of his moral theology and attempting to offer a modest evaluation of it. Moreover, since the particular task of tracing eschatology's place in O'Donovan's thought proves to be one that enables us to entertain a number of diverse discussions in contemporary theology and ethics, I also hope in a focused way to contribute to broader conversations.

The autobiographical motivation behind this study will no doubt also become evident throughout – whether intentionally or not – but I will make one direct comment addressing it. My church background, like O'Donovan's, is British Anglicanism of a largely evangelical cast.[7] Discovering his work a little way into my first studies in theological ethics, I found a project that appeared against this formation both familiar and strange: a peerlessly sober and sophisticated expression, perhaps, of my tradition's convictions, wrought specifically in moral-theological conceptuality, yet an expression seemingly underdetermined by some of that tradition's characteristic commitments.[8] Though other traditions have since informed my own theological instincts besides evangelical Anglicanism (itself composite), and though others also inform O'Donovan's – I engage in a little *Quellenforschung* in what follows – my impressions about some tensions in his thought have not entirely shifted. This study is, therefore, the occasion for me to dwell with those puzzling features awhile, in order to see what clarity might be found. If the predominant mode in what follows is therefore extended critical engagement, it should be taken as a kind of serious acclaim: appreciation shown not merely by reproducing a masterpiece, but by contemplating what the qualities and limitations of its palette are, alongside the works of others.

Summary

Chapter 1 lays out the basic moral-theological vision of O'Donovan's early (1978) article 'The Natural Ethic', which I argue expresses a number of fundamental convictions with signal intent.[9] I relay O'Donovan's criticism, there, of what he regards as Protestant ethics' besetting errors: the confusion of ontology and epistemology, and the parallel confusion of creation and redemption. I also lay out his proposed solution. With an unsatisfactory then-contemporary polarization into 'creation ethics' and 'kingdom ethics' in view, O'Donovan suggests that balance should be struck between creation and redemption, and, correlatively, between nature and history. Seen in context, O'Donovan's proposal was a uniquely brilliant attempt to 'let the fly out of the fly bottle',

---

[7] For details, see Shortt, *God's Advocates* (265), and those relayed in Timothy Dudley-Smith's two-part biography of John Stott, O'Donovan's childhood pastor at All Souls, Langham Place: *John Stott: The Making of a Leader* (Downers Grove: IVP, 1999), 255; and *John Stott: A Global Ministry* (Downers Grove: IVP, 2001), 95.

[8] In what follows, I use the terms 'Christian ethics', 'theological ethics' and 'moral theology' more or less interchangeably, though aspiring to some degree of sensitivity to the ways the terms are used variously across theological traditions.

[9] O'Donovan, 'The Natural Ethic', in *Essays in Evangelical Social Ethics*, ed. David F. Wright (Exeter: Paternoster Press, 1978).

addressing seemingly intractable debates that roiled evangelical theology. He sought to honour all that must legitimately be honoured, but still managed, in so many words, to say 'Perhaps you could think of it this way.'[10]

Yet for all its bold insight and real promise, 'The Natural Ethic' does not itself achieve the balance it proclaims, because, as I show, the doctrine of creation is afforded much more weight than is redemption, or eschatology. Indeed, the title suggests as much. Eschatology's entry into O'Donovan's thought is therefore ambivalent, and I illustrate how in this article it gets caught up in a critique of historicism; eschatology is presented as the cause of moral-theological distortion, as much as anything positive. The 'natural ethic' O'Donovan proposes, then, places strictures upon eschatology at this point, and I argue that they are worth noticing because they are never sufficiently overcome in O'Donovan's work, despite his later attempts at amelioration. The strictures are present, I argue, due to three closely connected factors: (a) O'Donovan's sense of the priority of creation over redemption in Christian confession; (b) his discernment of the broader cultural milieu and the necessary Christian response to it (a discernment I locate also in *Begotten or Made?*); and (c) his construal of salvation as restoration.[11]

To be sure, the shortcomings of 'The Natural Ethic' highlight a difficulty that is not peculiar to O'Donovan – to do justice to the full scope of Christian doctrine is a constant struggle for anyone writing Christian ethics. Indeed, O'Donovan's article actually ends by asking a question that seems to admit the challenge and to gesture beyond its own conclusions: 'If we cannot *balance* creation ethics and kingdom ethics, what can we do with them?'[12]

Chapters 2 and 3 of my study take a lead from this significant early question, following the lines of enquiry that chapter 1 established through O'Donovan's 1986 book *Resurrection and Moral Order*.[13] I argue that what 'The Natural Ethic' announces in brief compass, this first major statement now declares in essential continuity but more expansively, offering a comprehensive and influential position encompassing each main topic of Christian ethics and indeed the Christian life. *Resurrection and Moral Order*, therefore, rewards extended attention, which I divide as follows, in chapters that represent the nub of my investigation.

Chapter 2 focuses largely on what O'Donovan terms 'the objective aspect'. It considers, first, the notion of moral realism and its anchoring in a particular conception of the created order. In so doing, I seek to situate O'Donovan's position within debates concerning natural law. Informed by this analysis, the chapter then examines O'Donovan's doctrine of creation and his choice of the resurrection as theological ethics' principal motif. As I see it, with this choice – and the book's programme as a whole, rigorously ordered by it – O'Donovan attempts to answer the question with

---

[10] These two sentences borrow Bishop Robert Barron's commendation of the writing of Edward Oakes on nature and grace (the 'fly' image is Wittgenstein's). So Barron, 'Foreword' to Oakes, *A Theology of Grace in Six Controversies* (Grand Rapids: Eerdmans, 2016), xi.
[11] O'Donovan, *Begotten or Made?* (Oxford: Clarendon Press, 1984).
[12] O'Donovan, 'The Natural Ethic', 35. Italics original: as in every quotation throughout this study, unless noted otherwise.
[13] O'Donovan, *Resurrection and Moral Order: An Outline for Evangelical Ethics*, 2nd edn (Leicester: Apollos/Grand Rapids: Eerdmans, 1994).

which 'The Natural Ethic' concluded. The structure and content of O'Donovan's answer turn on what he understands to be the resurrection's two aspects, one that looks 'backwards' to the past restoration of created order, and another that looks 'forwards' to its future transformation.

Both aspects are, in a sense, 'eschatological'. In the final analysis, however, it seems to be the 'backwards look' that determines the fundamental basis of O'Donovan's ethics, at times effectively subsuming the more strictly eschatological 'forwards look' under what can appear a somewhat monolithic account of created order. To adopt T. S. Eliot's turn of phrase in *Four Quartets*, if the two aspects might be presented as follows: 'Without elimination, both a new world | And the old, made explicit', then O'Donovan's proposal sometimes seems to resolve into an affirmation of 'the old, made explicit', at the expense of 'a new world'.[14]

It is particularly noteworthy that the resurrection is interpreted primarily as – and this is a key phrase – the 'vindication of created order'. Although I explore the merits of the concept, it often seems to produce a pattern whereby O'Donovan effectively announces eschatology, only to expound creation.[15] Moreover, the particular notion of vindication, and its companion term 'restoration', understood in a certain way, does not only account for O'Donovan's way of understanding the 'backwards look', which invites the concern that it involves an over-realized eschatology. It also affects the 'look forward', which is often described in terms of the very strong eschatological continuity of the created order. It is true that a more transformative, discontinuous eschatological element is also attested, but accent upon that aspect is sometimes qualified by reference to the notion of the created order's already-achieved restoration, besides an inference that O'Donovan draws of the unshakeable perdurance of this order – seemingly much as it now exists. A vital element of my argument at this point is that I find O'Donovan's particularly confident case for the stability and therein direct normativity of the natural order partly dependent on soteriological and eschatological conclusions that may not be quite as dogmatically self-evident as the book's argument intimates.

All told, *Resurrection and Moral Order*, like 'The Natural Ethic', may fall short of its integrative ambitions. Ultimately, eschatology's reappearance is augmented, but still a touch ambivalent. Again, I believe that its place is unduly hindered by O'Donovan's valid but disproportionate recoil from historicism, the details of which this chapter assesses. A final section of Chapter 2 attends to three challenges to O'Donovan's position: the first concerns the question of creation and covenant; the second addresses the ways in which eschatological notions of restoration and transformation can and cannot be thought compatible; and the third introduces Gerald McKenny's reading of O'Donovan's thought as it pertains to the evaluation of developments in biotechnology – specifying it further in light of my earlier analysis, and conveying the mixed implications for appropriation of O'Donovan's moral theology.

---

[14] T. S. Eliot, *Four Quartets* (London: Faber and Faber, 2001), 5.
[15] Transposing here Eugene Rogers's description of Barth, announcing pneumatology only to expound Christology. Eugene Rogers, *After the Spirit: A Constructive Pneumatology from Resources outside the Modern West* (Grand Rapids: Eerdmans, 2005), 27.

Having examined *Resurrection and Moral Order*'s topography of the metaphysics of morals in Chapter 2 and having found both much to learn from and yet an overdetermination by the groundwork of a natural ethic, Chapter 3 fills in some of the contours of this text O'Donovan calls an *Outline for Ethics*. Largely assessing what he terms 'the subjective aspect' of his account, I observe continued tensions and work to shed light on them by employing the categories established by the previous chapter. Nevertheless, I also now focus more on interpreting passages that might be thought to represent ideas to be appropriated more straightforwardly, and in particular might help us towards a constructive articulation of eschatology's place in ethics. A wide range of the book's other themes are treated here, including related claims about freedom, love and authority, about sin and knowledge, and about the moral implications of historical novelty. Consideration is also given to the relationship between the divine command and the order of creation, and to the ethical corollaries of the dogmatic relationships between pneumatology and Christology, and between eschatology and ecclesiology. I also explore O'Donovan's imagination of the moral life, particularly his understanding of conversion and the development of character, and of obedience's texture in light of the cross and the resurrection. Again, I survey each of the themes in conversation with an ecumenical cast of interlocutors.

Though I have queries to raise about O'Donovan's account of some of these themes, I do find that O'Donovan begins to develop more of the present moral import of eschatology here, especially as the pneumatological determination of the Christian life comes to the fore. I argue that the benefits of this approach start to be seen in the emerging descriptions of human agency, and of ethics' ecclesial dimension. After this set of thematic explorations, I investigate *Resurrection and Moral Order*'s final, directly eschatological flourish, including its promising invocation of the great Pauline triad: faith, hope and love. These features are certainly welcome, yet O'Donovan's appeal to them curiously straitens the role of hope, inhibited by a familiar reticence.

Chapter 4 focuses on O'Donovan's mid-career theo-political writings, especially the important monographs *The Desire of the Nations* and *The Ways of Judgment*.[16] These books put O'Donovan's basic theological commitments to further work, and indicating this, I observe a similar explication of the resurrection's moral import in terms of the 'vindication' of created order (here, again, rendered as the concept of 'Restoration'), even as other aspects of redemption are also found corresponding, but lesser, practical import. Furthermore, I return to the question of how O'Donovan's discernments of sociopolitical context affect the shape of his theology – and vice versa. In particular, I reflect on what seem to be oversights about issues, such as poverty, that afflict what O'Donovan calls 'Northern democracies' as well as the Global South, and seek to establish how these oversights might be complexly related to theological resources employed – or neglected. My suggestion in this chapter is, therefore, that both exponents and critics of 'O'Donovanian' political (and moral) theology would do well to attend carefully to the symbiotic relation between his contextual judgements and his theological presuppositions, which determine and are determined by them.

---

[16] O'Donovan, *The Desire of the Nations: Rediscovering the Roots of Political Theology* (Cambridge: Cambridge University Press, 1996) and *The Ways of Judgment* (Grand Rapids: Eerdmans, 2005).

Chapter 4 also shows, in O'Donovan's maturing ecclesiological meditations, a continued development of eschatology's subtly specified connection to the church. This development can be seen to impact upon a pair of concepts important for O'Donovan's theo-politics – judgement and the secular – and also upon both the earthly limitations of justice in this realm and the leavening of eschatological witness within it. The chapter concludes by touching on debates surrounding O'Donovan's post-lapsarian grounding of political authority. I seek to offer a small contribution showing how eschatology, besides creation and providence, figures differently in his theo-political thought than in his moral theology. For if the tone of O'Donovan's ethics is set by an interpretation of the resurrection as created order's already-achieved vindication – allied, perhaps, with an assured expectation of that order's perdurance in the eschaton in whole and in part – then the tone of the political theology is set by other doctrinal emphases, among them a quite different eschatological consideration. Aside from the articulation, in *Desire of the Nations*, of an ecclesial ethic oriented to the recovery of creation, the more austere atmosphere of the theo-political vision is produced by a conviction about the provisionality and penultimacy of the present order. If the mood of the earlier work was set in part by its eschatology's 'realized' character, the eschatology that colours these later works lends a more apophatic sensibility, not least owed to a certain awareness of the horizon of the Last Judgement.

My final chapter, Chapter 5, chases a number of the foregoing leads through O'Donovan's recent trilogy *Ethics as Theology*, bringing the treatment up to date.[17] I propose that we understand these three books as a recalibration of O'Donovan's fundamental moral theology.[18] And, as regards our subject of the tension surrounding eschatology in his thought, I suggest that we particularly appreciate the amplified part hope now plays in a fuller treatment of the Pauline triad, along with a concomitant phenomenological meditation upon the temporal reality of the moral life. Taking stock of where our exposition has brought us so far, I note that up to this point we have found in O'Donovan's eschatology a past element (the resurrection's vindication of created order) and a pair of future elements (confident ascription to the eschaton of the total restoration of created order, and more apophatic ascription to the eschaton of judgement and transformation). With the reconfiguration of *Ethics as Theology*, however, more space than before seems to have been made for extended and substantive exploration of eschatology's direct bearing on the moral life in the present.

However, it is therefore disappointing to find that in the first and second volumes, *Self, World, and Time* and *Finding and Seeking*, there seems to be a continued cordoning off of eschatology from moral reason – sometimes this demarcation is stated even

---

[17] O'Donovan, *Self, World, and Time: Ethics as Theology vol. 1* (Grand Rapids: Eerdmans, 2013), *Finding and Seeking: Ethics as Theology vol. 2* (Grand Rapids: Eerdmans, 2014), *Entering into Rest: Ethics as Theology vol. 3* (Grand Rapids: Eerdmans, 2017).

[18] The last of these books was published as my study was already well underway, and had the timing been different, I think I may have written a differently proportioned book, with the centre of gravity lying less in the treatment of *Resurrection and Moral Order* and shifting a little towards the most recent publications.

more baldly than before. I suggest that one of the reasons for this is O'Donovan's concern for the distinction between dogmatics and ethics, which is expressed in *Ethics as Theology*, and which I trace as it recurs in his earlier thought up to this late point. Though I will go on to trouble the manner of the distinction O'Donovan draws, I observe first that his intentions in drawing this distinction are laudable on at least two counts. On the one hand, O'Donovan seeks to preserve a fitting sense of Christian doctrine's doxological excess over practice (a sense that is especially apposite as it relates to eschatology). On the other hand, O'Donovan's description of the dialectical movement of Christian ethics between the poles of generic moral thought and theology proper can be seen to possess an apologetic bent, aiming to show how moral reason, though possessing its own shape and logic, necessarily opens up to a word of revelation (including the disclosure of eschatological reality). Nevertheless, I trouble the way in which O'Donovan often draws the distinction so as to emphasize the formal ethical import of eschatology while marginalizing its material impact. I worry that it tends to side-line what scripture and tradition understand as eschatology's structuring of ethical discernment, in concert with other elements of Christian teaching. While O'Donovan elucidates, exquisitely, how we might understand the formal aspects of hope to open up the present moment of deliberation-to-action, we find that he seems to have little time for the ways others have understood how hope in the kingdom of God also directs our attention and conduct concretely.

The critique of Jürgen Moltmann in *Finding and Seeking* – for confounding hope and anticipation – is a case in point. Despite its general perspicuity, O'Donovan's critique betrays the oversight as it evinces a marked failure to sympathize with the priorities of Moltmann's eschatological ethics. That oversight, as I present it, is one reified in the omissions in *Finding and Seeking*'s treatment of the epistle of James; here, the particularity of moral responsibility in light of the kingdom of God is simply skipped over – a particularity again expressed in that epistle in terms of responsibility towards the poor.

These oversights stand in some tension with those parts of O'Donovan's work that show that eschatological imagination can, and should, inform moral reasoning in thoroughgoing fashion. Chief among them is, in fact, the final instalment of the trilogy, *Entering into Rest*. Quite self-consciously with this volume, O'Donovan arrives at the moment of exposition that allows more space for eschatological themes that were curtailed earlier. Again, he does so especially in relation to the ecclesial dimension of ethics, beyond its generic dimensions. Despite and perhaps because of these developments, however, one is left wondering whether the earlier strictures – even or especially in the first two volumes of *Ethics as Theology* – were entirely coherent or legitimate, theologically.

The main chapters of the study, which offer a reading of O'Donovan's chief works, therefore, conclude with a great deal gleaned from O'Donovan along the way, yet without arriving at an unqualified affirmation of any of his works as regards specifically the handling of eschatology's moral import. I close the argument by crystallizing the book's constructive intimations, won from the engagement with O'Donovan. In short, I affirm the value of 'hope in action', and I make some modest constructive proposals for speech about the relation of eschatology and ethics, beyond the inhibition that I worry affects parts of O'Donovan's thought.[19]

Finally, lest it be thought I am arguing that eschatology be regarded as merely so much grist for the mill of practical policies – or metaphysical cipher for them – a postscript, 'The End of Ethics', indicates what might, beyond ethics, be called eschatology's properly doxological or contemplative excess: an inassimilable 'more'. The appendix, 'Cartography with O'Donovan and Friends', is a kind of schematic follow-up exercise to the main chapters of the book, employing the hyper-systematic schema from David Kelsey's *Eccentric Existence* to chart O'Donovan's position alongside a handful of other prominent contemporary Protestant perspectives. These include those of Kathryn Tanner and Gilbert Meilaender, as well as emerging schools that have been given the names 'apocalyptic' theology and 'Erlangen' Lutheranism.

A note about reading and writing

Before we begin, I want to record a pair of general features of O'Donovan's work and, in so doing, help to explain further why my study has turned out the way it has. It verges on the platitudinous to say that a particular author possesses a singular style, or that an audience's experience of reading that author's singular style will affect the reception of the ideas so expressed. But both really are true and really are important to note in O'Donovan's case, and this leads to the first point. If you are going to read O'Donovan, or read about O'Donovan, you need to know what you are in for.

John Milbank, not himself a theologian renowned for accessibility, writes that O'Donovan possesses a 'characteristically elusive profundity'.[20] 'No one', some of O'Donovan's American admirers acknowledge, 'has ever accused O'Donovan of writing too simplistically, and his impact has been, so far, perhaps unduly limited by the impression of rebarbative indirectness and obliqueness that marks his prose'.[21] As Michael Banner puts it, most frankly:

> O'Donovan's work is intensely focused and concentrated, and makes few concessions to the neophyte. O'Donovan reaches the mountaintop without seeming even to pause to catch a breath and from there surveys the terrain with magisterial scope and authority. The rest of us will likely be struggling up, very far behind, and even at base camp may have a touch of altitude sickness.[22]

---

[19] 'Hope in action' should not be misunderstood as suggesting that the object of our hope is action – that is the wrong way around; rather, because 'we have such a hope, we act with great boldness' (2 Cor. 3.12). I take the phrase from Steven Rodenborn, *Hope in Action: Subversive Eschatology in the Theology of Edward Schillebeeckx and Johann Baptist Metz* (Minneapolis: Fortress Press, 2014).
[20] From the dust jacket recommendation to O'Donovan's *Church in Crisis: The Gay Controversy and the Anglican Communion* (Eugene: Wipf & Stock, 2008).
[21] Philip Lorish and Charles Mathewes, 'Theology as Counsel: The Work of Oliver O'Donovan and Nigel Biggar', *Anglican Theological Review* 94, no. 4 (2012): 717–36, 721.
[22] Michael Banner, review of *The Authority of the Gospel*, *Theology*, 119, no. 3 (2016): 208–9, 208.

Yet those same American admirers see in O'Donovan's mode of communication something deliberate, proposing that it may be precisely here that he has most to teach us: '[W]e anticipate that the slowness of ... impact – in recent years, however, gathering steam – is due more to the impact it is designed to make than to any failure on his part to communicate. For his aim is not simply to give us *content*, but to introduce us to a way of thinking.'[23]

That may be so. O'Donovan's 'dense prose' doubtless results 'in a great deal of elegance in expression and conceptualisation', as Lewis Ayres says.[24] Still, as Ayres continues, 'there are ways in which his use of this style hinders clarity, not least that 'it is often extremely difficult to discover O'Donovan's sources or particular engagements'; O'Donovan sits light to academic conventions to an extent that in 'a less well-known author ... might simply be thought a nuisance'.[25] And, to be quite honest, where footnotes do appear in O'Donovan's texts, they can themselves be daunting, exhibiting astonishing breadth of erudition besides astonishing linguistic prowess. In *Ways of Judgment* alone there are engagements in Hebrew, classical and *Koine* Greek, and citations in Latin, French, German, Italian and Irish.[26]

The second point is that, besides his actual prose, O'Donovan's mode of argumentation is not always easy to settle into. Quite often he approaches topics dialectically, considering two or more distinct trends of thought on a particular matter – only occasionally personified – before presenting his own solution. Real strengths inhere in this style, not least the ability to consider questions in the round, turning them this way and that. A related merit is that O'Donovan is able to unearth the genealogical roots of moral positions more or less patiently and sympathetically. When the critique of any position is dispensed, it is thereby regularly acute. However, at least one danger is attendant upon O'Donovan's approach. I say attendant, because I take it that the main risk is one for his readers, and even more so for second-hand readers, as much as it is one that affects his own conclusions. To render it in Banner's imagery, the danger is this: if the reader does not try to struggle up the slope for themselves, they can seem to arrive so easily with O'Donovan at the mountaintop (some readers seem to begin there!) that they might be given to assume that the terrain he sketches from the top has been covered with consistent evenness and impartiality. But to achieve both sweeping overviews and exhaustive treatment of all relevant particulars is simply impossible for anyone, and I do not doubt that O'Donovan is well aware of the impossibility; responsible appropriation of his thought needs to recognize it, too. Neither beginning from the mountaintop nor only following in his footsteps, we will

---

[23] Lorish and Mathewes, 'Theology as Counsel', 721.
[24] Lewis Ayres, 'In the Path of thy Judgments', *Reviews in Religion and Theology* 4, no. 4 (1997): 25–34, 25–6.
[25] Ibid., 34.
[26] Worth noting here, variously, is that O'Donovan studied classics at Oxford; that while he was brought up in England, his father was the major Irish writer known as Frank O'Connor (O'Donovan's mother Joan Knape was also a poet); and that he has published English translations of significant philosophical works written by Robert Spaemann – from the German – and Jean-Yves Lacoste – from the French. I note the details of the respective translations later, as each become materially relevant.

instead need to struggle up, very far behind, working carefully to see where we might have to forge our own paths.

I should make a third and final point, which derives from the first two. This third challenge is not so much about O'Donovan's work as it is about responding to it in one's own. In view of his prose style and his dialectical argumentation, writing fairly with accuracy regarding O'Donovan's thought is no easy endeavour. It is because of this that I take time with the texts, sometimes quoting at length, seeking to acknowledge as many of his complex manoeuvres as I can. There are, I grant, an overwhelming number of these twists and turns in O'Donovan's writing, and each of them that I neglect could be cited in response to any one of my lines of critical enquiry. Yet my critical enquiry does itself put forward the contention that being able to point out that a thinker at some point treats every element deemed necessary does not necessitate assent to the relative weight given to each element overall, or to the particular role that each element is allotted. It is not nothing to show how a particular swing of the dialectical pendulum can be problematic: especially if the counterpoise is regrettably remote or muted. To put it more bluntly: just because you can find everything you think is right somewhere in O'Donovan, it does not mean that O'Donovan says everything just right.[27]

These three points are so much as to say: O'Donovan is difficult to read, difficult to understand well and difficult to write about – especially analytically. Still, the wager of this book is that these tasks are worthwhile.

---

[27] To be clear, I would argue that this is true of any major theologian, let alone the rest of us; that is why the critical tasks of reception, interpretation and appropriation are unavoidable.

1

Groundwork

'The Natural Ethic'

Introduction

I begin my exploration of O'Donovan's writings with an early article entitled 'The Natural Ethic', which originated in a paper given at the 1978 National (UK) Evangelical Conference on Social Ethics. The piece might be regarded as juvenilia (O'Donovan was still in his early thirties when he wrote it), and it is true, as we shall see, that O'Donovan's thought will gain a high degree of subtlety that is not especially evident here. But the argument of 'The Natural Ethic' is one possessed of a serious constructive ambition and prosecuted with confidence; it has been described with some credibility as 'a manifesto for his later work'.[1] On my reading, the way O'Donovan puts together an account of moral theology in this essay is essentially constitutive of the way he will continue to do so throughout his career – or at least until the partial recalibration of the late trilogy *Ethics as Theology*. Furthermore, 'The Natural Ethic' commends itself as a place to start because, among the constellation of ideas introduced as basic to O'Donovan's thought, we find eschatology occupying an ambiguous position. The article captures a kind of 'freeze-frame' moment, then, which represents an initial stage in a decades-long wrestle with creation and redemption, their relation and the implications for morality.

This chapter examines O'Donovan's assured early statement in some detail. First, it introduces his presentation of three rival traditions of moral theory, exploring his account of the decline of the third of these – the 'natural ethic' – and the results of that decline within Protestant thought. Protestant thought, O'Donovan claims, habitually confuses ontology and epistemology, imputing sinful disorder to nature where it ought not, and – relatedly – misapprehending the relationship between creation and redemption. This Protestant error is the backdrop against which he wishes to retrieve an ethic oriented to natural order. Next, I observe eschatology's curious entry into O'Donovan's argument. Caught up in a critique of historicism, eschatology appears at times to be tarred with the same brush, and portrayed as a cause of ethical irresponsibility. Nevertheless, O'Donovan does make a formal proposal that

---

[1] Luke Bretherton, *Hospitality and Holiness: Christian Witness Amid Moral Diversity* (Farnham: Ashgate, 2010), 89, n.16.

balance should be struck between nature and history, and just so between creation and eschatology. And notably, this proposal is designed to overcome the polarization of 'creation ethics' and 'kingdom ethics' that vexed evangelical moral and political discussion (and perhaps Protestant theology more widely).

I will argue, however, that 'The Natural Ethic' itself struggles to achieve that balance. The doctrine of creation seems to be afforded substantially more weight than eschatology; the article's title suggests as much. This disparity may not, in itself, represent grounds for criticism. Despite the formal affirmation of balance, it seems that balance is not what O'Donovan ultimately wants to espouse. (Intriguingly, in the questions for discussion that accompany the paper in its published form, we will find what appears to be an acknowledgement of that fact.) Nonetheless, O'Donovan appears to place limits on the positive ethical import of eschatology as a result of this imbalance, and that seems to me a mistake.

Accordingly, I probe the reasons for the weighting of 'The Natural Ethic' and propose three contributing factors: first, O'Donovan's sense of the priority of creation over redemption in Christian confession; second, his discernments regarding the pressures of the broader cultural milieu and the basis of a faithful Christian witness within it (a judgement similarly expressed, as we shall see, in O'Donovan's slightly later *Begotten or Made?*); and, third, a notion of salvation as being principally the restoration of creation. Again, none of these features are necessarily problematic, intrinsically. But when they are understood in such a way as to diminish the moral significance of Christian teaching about eschatology, then a wrong implication has been drawn, and suspicion will wrongly be cast upon much that is theologically defensible – even upon that which, arguably, is imperative on the basis of the gospel.

Three rival traditions

O'Donovan begins the article with an account of three traditions of philosophical thought and their differing ways of conceiving moral disagreement.[2] In the first place is one – we may call it rationalist, and O'Donovan gives as example the utilitarians – which 'thought that moral judgement was essentially a matter of accurate prediction: '[I]f one could know exactly what consequences would follow from each of the alternative courses of action, one would be in no doubt as to which to follow.'[3] But this perspective is found wanting: '[T]he most profound and terrifying moral controversies resist this kind of rationalization.'[4] A second tradition – we may call it emotivist, though O'Donovan names no exemplar here – has by contrast 'represented moral disagreement

---

[2] The brief presentation O'Donovan offers is not entirely unlike a compressed version of Alasdair MacIntyre's later typology in *Three Rival Versions of Moral Enquiry* (London: Duckworth, 1990), though perhaps the third (that is, winning) version in O'Donovan's case – the natural ethic – may represent a differently inflected sort of Thomistic answer than the winning version in MacIntyre's – 'tradition'. Or, at least, the preferred versions are directed to answering slightly different questions.
[3] O'Donovan, 'The Natural Ethic', 19.
[4] Ibid.

as a function of inscrutable personal commitment'.[5] Again, this perspective misses crucial aspects of morality: 'Moral judgements, unlike personal choices, belong to the public domain of reason.'[6] It is, then, to neither of these traditions, but to a third, that O'Donovan invites us to turn in search of a more satisfying explanation:

> The natural ethic offers us this account of moral disagreement: that when men look on the world as a whole they see different things. On the bare facts they may agree; but the structure of reality behind the facts they see quite differently, and this affects the way they describe and understand the facts. Is there such a thing as 'food', or only market produce? Is there rule and obedience, or only a social contract? Is there free gift, or only subtler forms of exchange? Are there natural ties, or only voluntary associations? At this metaphysical level many of the most profound and painful moral disagreements arise.[7]

Stated like this with its sequence of paired interpretations, the natural ethic seems to be attractive first of all because of its theoretical sensitivity to possibilities of divergence in the morally freighted interpretation of reality. But it will become clear that for O'Donovan, this tradition of moral reasoning is taken up because of its assistance in answering ethical questions coherently by supplying an encompassing metaphysics, besides explaining disagreement about them. Surely it is because he sees in 'natural teleology' the ability to illumine the structure of reality behind the facts and therefore to suggest an answer one way or the other – and in each of these cases we may guess the natural ethic would support the first of the two options given – that O'Donovan will seek 'to make a case for' it, in response to those 'who have wished to deny it'.[8]

The neglect of the natural ethic

Though there are now those in both science and theology who would deny it, the natural ethic was 'the accepted view of mediaeval Christianity, which got it from Platonic and Aristotelian philosophy'.[9] But for the audience, O'Donovan thinks, it may be unfamiliar, even unpalatable, not least because this tradition 'has had little favour in Protestant cultures'.[10] That O'Donovan imagines his hearers might find the proposals disagreeable, though, is not simply because they are Protestants but more profoundly because they are people of modernity. As people of modernity, they inhabit a moral imaginary constructed after the collapse of the earlier consensus, and, on O'Donovan's analysis, this collapse has had grave results for moral theory. If ethics formerly possessed a unified conception of nature, in which nature bears moral significance because it is conceived of as possessing kinds and ends replete with natural meaning,

---

[5]   Ibid., 20.
[6]   Ibid.
[7]   Ibid., 21.
[8]   Ibid.
[9]   Ibid.
[10] Ibid.

then that is now denied. His case thus rests on the claim that confidence in the inherent order and moral normativity of nature has been undermined, and ought to be urgently recovered.

The revolutionary movement that bequeathed the legacy of a disintegrating metaphysics, O'Donovan explains, consisted in a potent combination of two philosophical innovations: voluntarism and nominalism. Voluntarism suggested that moral value is ultimately decided by God's will, not God's intellect, *contra* the classical tradition: 'Nature, as the expression of God's mind, was value-free; questions of good and evil turned on what it was God's will from time to time to command.'[11] The sundering of fact and value followed. Nominalism, for its part, expressed the sceptical assessment that language of natural 'kinds' is creative rather than empirical, and introduced in its place a metaphysics of singulars.

Now, it is not O'Donovan's gestural metanarrative as such that I want to draw attention to. It bears family resemblance to prominent approaches such as Charles Taylor's and Alasdair MacIntyre's – though note its early date.[12] It is O'Donovan's theological gloss on voluntarism that merits closer attention: 'Another way of expressing it [voluntarism] would be that God's purposes are to be known only in his providential work in directing history, not in his creational work which precedes history.'[13] Here we already find *in nuce* O'Donovan's acute sensitivity to the danger of neglecting the doctrine of creation, and his inclination to view that neglect as the root of many modern moral ills. (More complexly, we also find the insightful suggestion that it is possible for forgetfulness of creation to coexist with putative remembrance of providence.)

The besetting error of Protestant ethics

The philosophical innovations of voluntarism and nominalism fostered scientific thought – O'Donovan's comments on this aspect of its heritage need not detain us[14] – and they also inspired the Reformers, lending 'tools' with which 'to attack the

---

[11] Ibid., 22. Andrew J. B. Cameron draws upon this article's account of voluntarism in *Joined-up Life: A Christian Account of How Ethics Works* (Nottingham: IVP, 2011), 150 – an Australian introductory book demonstrating wide familiarity with a range of O'Donovan's texts.

[12] O'Donovan addresses 'modernity critique' directly throughout his work. See *Common Objects of Love: Moral Reflection and the Shaping of Community* (Grand Rapids: Eerdmans, 2002), 46–8; comments in Shortt, *God's Advocates* (251); and *Ways*, where he speaks of 'that flurry of intellectual restlessness and suspicion variously called "post-liberal", "post-modern", or "modernity-critical"' (174). 'Modernity', he writes in its final chapter, is 'that great carcass around which a shoal of shark-toothed narratives forever wheels and hovers'; nevertheless, there he makes another attempt to trace modernity's origins, which he argues (incisively) are tied up 'in part' with 'the fate of the spiritual tradition' (298).

[13] O'Donovan, 'The Natural Ethic', 22.

[14] Not because they are uninteresting, but because of space. The understanding of science O'Donovan sets out in major monographs and in topical studies could fruitfully be brought into conversation with the metaphysically ambitious engagements with natural science written by theologians associated with Radical Orthodoxy (Conor Cunningham, Simon Oliver, and Michael Hanby). No less interesting to compare is Gerald McKenny's *To Relieve the Human Condition: Bioethics,*

Thomist epistemology which allowed that in principle (and in fairness to St Thomas one should stress the phrase "in principle"), natural man might perceive natural values and natural meanings without the aid of revelation'.[15] The Reformers responded with a 'powerful and authentically Christian stress on the decisiveness of revelation', encapsulated in their Christocentrism.[16] Now for O'Donovan, it was apt for them to emphasize what might have been occluded: that 'the bestowal of meaning is part of God's saving work in history'.[17] Erroneously, though, Protestantism took as corollary of this that 'in nature man can discern no meaning'.[18] It has therefore frequently focused solely upon 'revelation in history', which, while 'certainly the lynchpin of Christian epistemology', is not the only legitimate concern of ethics.[19] In doing so, 'making the epistemological issue supreme over the ontological', Protestantism 'has often tended to upset the balance that the Fathers struck'.[20] And the imbalanced position, mistaking epistemological challenge for ontological deficiency, produced a misattribution of some consequence: 'God's creation should not be held responsible for a fragmentation which is really due to the problem of *knowledge* in fallen mankind'.[21]

Having identified these confusions, O'Donovan offers some semantic clarification. He argues that in Christian theology, 'nature' as a concept can properly be used to denote two things. Either it can be 'contrasted with "revelation" as an epistemological programme, or contrasted with "history" to make an ontological distinction'.[22] Clarifying this renders pellucid what Reformational instincts blurred:

> The important epistemological points that the Reformation had to make must not be allowed to shelter a destructive and semi-Christian ontology. It is one thing to say that until the Word became incarnate, man could discern no meaning in nature; quite another to say that until the Word became incarnate nature had no meaning. Revelation is the answer to man's blindness, not to nature's emptiness. True, man's blindness is itself part of a disruption within nature, which we call the fall. But the very fact that nature can be called disrupted and disordered shows that it cannot be inherently meaningless.[23]

Technology, and the Body (Albany: SUNY Press, 1997), especially the book's account of modernity's technological 'Baconian project' and its distorting pressure on understandings of medicine.

[15] O'Donovan, 'The Natural Ethic', 25. Assessment of these claims, of course, is immensely complex. They are contested on a number of levels. For up-to-date references to the relevant literature, if what seem to me somewhat unconvincing conclusions, see Silvianne Aspray, 'Louis Bouyer and the Metaphysics of the Reformation', *Modern Theology* 34, no. 1 (2018): 3–22.
[16] O'Donovan, 'The Natural Ethic', 25.
[17] Ibid.
[18] Ibid.
[19] Ibid., 25, 26.
[20] Ibid., 27.
[21] Ibid., 34. O'Donovan's language is often unreconstructed. We read of 'mankind', 'man' and the moral theologian as 'he'. He defends the former pair of constructions in *Finding and Seeking* (62ff.), by which time I think he should have known better. I have not redacted any quotations, but try to avoid the same usages myself.
[22] O'Donovan, 'The Natural Ethic', 26.
[23] Ibid., 26–7.

The article's postscript on '"The Natural" in Theology' further elaborates these distinctions. Reiterating the two proper uses, O'Donovan addresses a third sometimes found in theology, in which 'natural' stands for 'fallen'. This he finds inadmissible. Here also he recognizes that the second use of 'natural' he has permitted – where nature names our ontological context – is contested, but, interestingly, he defends it against the counter-proposal that the category of creation is more fitting for this purpose.[24] Key to the defence is a contention that God's preserving and sustaining work, besides creation's initial establishment, must be likewise affirmed in a wider concept: 'We need a term broader than "creation", one which will include also what has commonly been designated in Christian theology as "providence"'.[25] O'Donovan's category of nature, then, contains the idea of 'a natural order' that incorporates assumptions of 'providential dispositions' for creaturely life, 'the political realm, for example'.[26] (We should mark this early mention of the providential character of political order, because bearing in mind the way it is formulated vis-à-vis notions of 'nature' and 'creation' will help us when in Chapter 4 we turn directly to O'Donovan's theo-political work and interpretations of it.) Put differently, the 'natural' does not refer simply to features of an Edenic scene but also to provisions that are post-lapsarian but are nonetheless built into the very fabric of things with which morality has to do. And for O'Donovan, a particular error issues from failure to speak of the natural order in this more expansive way, namely, the constructivist assumption that 'these secondary forms of natural existence' – by which he presumably means the 'providential dispositions' for fallen humanity – are the products of human invention, an incorrect, 'quite untheological' conclusion.[27]

So much for a sketch of the article's initial assertions. Let us turn to the way eschatology features in the argument, ambiguously introduced into the narrative I have just relayed.

Ambivalence about eschatology

The paragraphs that come under the heading 'History – Revelation and Eschatology' are somewhat difficult to parse, and the ambivalence of eschatology in O'Donovan's argument owes partly to this section's lack of clarity.[28] Here O'Donovan continues

---

[24] By using the term nature in this way, O'Donovan makes a similar affirmation to conservative Catholic moral theologians. Consider for instance Romanus Cessario, who argues thus on the basis of a doctrine of creation (no mention here of providence, though it is implicit): 'Because the believer knows that God created in wisdom and love, no Christian should engage in the popular suspicion about the reliability of nature as a theological category … despite the strong prejudice found in many modern theologians against using nature as a theological category, contemporary Catholic thought reaffirms the classical natural law tradition'. Cessario, *Theology and Sanctity*, ed. Cajetan Cuddy (Ave Maria: Sapientia Press, 2014), 181. Confidence in the notion of nature based on affirmation of the doctrine of providence marks some recent Reformed retrieval of natural law reasoning – see Chapter 2.
[25] O'Donovan, 'The Natural Ethic', 32.
[26] Ibid., 33.
[27] Ibid.
[28] Ibid., 25.

to paraphrase the Reformers' stance, affirming some elements while delineating the problematic effects of others, and he intimates something of his own perspective. I will quote three of the paragraphs in full. They follow immediately after a sentence quoted already, about the Reformers' (alleged) conviction that meaning is bestowed as 'part of God's saving work in history, for in nature man can discern no meaning':

> What the Christian doctrine of revelation does for natural meaning, its eschatological expectation does for natural purpose. Within Christianity one cannot think or speak about the meaning of the world without speaking also of its destined transformation. The problem of evil is met, not by asserting a profound cosmological order in the present, but by confident announcement of God's purposes for the future. He who has come to earth as the meaning, has come also as the Purpose or Fulfilment. To understand the first coming of Christ it is necessary to expect the second coming.
>
> There are, of course, notoriously, two ways of living in expectation. We can believe in the value of intermediate transformation, 'preparing the way of the Lord', and so commit ourselves to a life of activity; or we can feel that the ultimate transformation renders all penultimate change irrelevant, and so resign ourselves to a life of hopeful suffering. But what these two attitudes have in common is far more important than what differentiates them. They both take a negative view of the *status quo*. There is no natural purpose to which we can respond in love and obedience. The destiny of nature has to be imposed on it, either by our activity or by God's. The purpose of the world is outside it, in that new Jerusalem which is to descend from heaven prepared as a bride for the bridegroom.
>
> This description of the Christian impact on the natural ethic would meet with fairly wide acceptance, among those who deplore it as well as among those who welcome it. Yet I am bound to think that there is much of importance that it leaves out.[29]

I grant that for the first and second of these quoted paragraphs, O'Donovan is ventriloquizing and then criticizing theological positions that are at variance from his own. But I am still inclined to suggest that here and in wider passage, the register in which each point is made is not transparent and that this particularly muddies the treatment of eschatology. Its appearance as a theme here is followed immediately, as though explicating the prior paragraph, by the aside elucidating two modes of eschatological anticipation that, note, are both deemed problematic. What we find – and if I am right, this may exemplify a troubling pattern in O'Donovan's thought – is that aspects of eschatology often feature prominently as beliefs constitutive of positions under critique. At worst, these elements of eschatological expectation seem to be quickly placed under suspicion as a cause of moral irresponsibility. Their perceived threat serves as a theological foil for O'Donovan's retrieval of the natural ethic, just as rationalism and emotivism are introduced as philosophical foils.

---

[29] Ibid., 25–6.

Thankfully, O'Donovan does come back around to his own constructive point, and to affirm the place of Christian eschatology, which 'has to be seen in the light of the doctrine of creation':

> Christianity is an eschatological faith, having as its central theme the experience and hope of redemption from evil. But this redemption is not to be understood dualistically as the triumph of a good redeemer-god over an evil creator-god. It is because God is the creator of nature that he does, and will, redeem nature from its state of corruption. He who is the Saviour of the world is also the 'Logos', 'through whom all things were made'. He is the Second Adam, restoring that which the First Adam lost. Creation and redemption are not in hostile antithesis, but in complementarity, each providing the context in which we understand the other.[30]

The positive integration of eschatology, then, is part of O'Donovan's account of the importance of balance in theological understanding – between ontology and epistemology, creation and redemption, and nature and history.

Balance

What is required, O'Donovan goes on to argue, is 'Balance between Nature and History'. There is a particular 'Christian balance' between the two, for which it is imperative to recognize both 'meaning given in the natural order' and 'meaning revealed in the course of history'.[31] Failure to do so results in mistaken approaches on either side, which he calls 'static naturalism' and 'an indeterminate belief in progress', respectively.[32] I will examine each in turn.

Static naturalism

Static naturalism issues in an ethic 'with which Christianity can have nothing to do'.[33] From a theological perspective, 'respect for given orders can easily become a form of idolatry'.[34] And there are all kinds of 'givens' that may falsely 'command our love and allegiance …. Much has been honoured as "natural" that is purely conventional, the product of certain passing historical circumstances, and in this way great oppression has been laid on the souls of men'.[35] Though O'Donovan does not explicitly distinguish between them, according to his analysis, naturalism makes two main errors. One allows

---

[30] Ibid., 27.
[31] Ibid.
[32] Ibid.
[33] Ibid.
[34] Ibid.
[35] Ibid., 27–8. Comparable here are the kinds of natural law reasoning John Bowlin distinguishes from his own much more recent proposal, in 'Notes on Natural Law and Covenant', *Studies in Christian Ethics* 28, no. 2 (2015): 142–9, 144.

'respect for given orders' – genuinely given natural orders, that is – to inflate to the point that they become controlling absolutes. The other perceives natural orders where there are none, venerating as divinely created that which is humanly constructed, and in so doing, it esteems the transient as though it is eternally binding.

As we may expect, though, given the article's purpose as a defence of 'the natural ethic', O'Donovan is keen to distance his critique of static naturalism from more thoroughgoing scepticism. To this end, his second postscript engages 'The Views of T.F. Torrance':

> Torrance's objection to natural teleology is that it fails to distinguish the creation from the creator, an objection which is valid against some, but certainly not against all versions of the theory. In return we must object that the value supposedly conferred upon nature by divine grace is a mere abstraction unless it can be recognised, with or without the help of revelation, in the purposive interconnectedness of kinds. Only so can we see that the universe is an 'order', and affirm, with the creator, that it is 'very good'. Without the possibility of this discernment, the doctrine of creation is destined to drop out of sight, and man's autonomous will-to-mastery must take over, imposing human purposes where God apparently omitted to impose divine ones.[36]

O'Donovan, then, argues that the ontological distinction between Creator and creature is not correctly applied if its result is the scouring of the concept of nature of its classical teleological implications. Still, we have seen that the effort to distinguish his natural ethic from pure naturalism does somewhat nuance O'Donovan's approach. In making the distinction, he observes two further obstacles for any 'natural ethic'.

First, nature's claims may appear 'generic' in form, even in situations where they are rightly discerned. We may therefore find ourselves obligated by multiple natural 'is-ought' demands. O'Donovan acknowledges, then, that should we centre our ethics on natural givens, moral difficulties would still present themselves. If the force of his case for the natural ethic sometimes seems to rely on minimizing just this complication, we can be glad of the admission here that the plurality of possible moral goods that confront ethical deliberation can seem cacophonously, incoherently diverse. Crucially, the point O'Donovan derives from this acknowledgement is that resolution of this difficulty demands that moral reasoning receive guidance from another source. A circumscribed problematizing of static naturalism thus opens the door for a circumscribed embrace of history. In a moment, we will turn to the distinction he makes between that embrace, on the one hand, and historicism, on the other. Before that let us consider the other obstacle O'Donovan envisages for a purely natural ethic: fallenness.

No doubt to the relief of many in his audience, O'Donovan now observes that 'in our actual situation in salvation history, we are dealing as fallen men with a fallen nature'.[37]

---

[36] O'Donovan, 'The Natural Ethic', 34.
[37] Ibid.

> Both we and nature come under the judgement of the God who created us, and that judgement is reflected in an ascetic series of duties and vocations which stand in paradoxical relation to natural goals and functions. Thus we are required to 'hate' our father and our mother, our wife, children, brothers and sisters, and even our own life, in order to be Christ's disciples. Allowing for the element of rhetoric in this, we must still recognise a demand which falls quite outside the scope of the natural order, and, because the natural order itself is in rebellion against God, runs counter to it. Again, there is the possibility of a calling to singleness, 'making ourselves eunuchs', as Jesus puts it, for the kingdom of heaven's sake; and here too we have to recognise an eschatological demand which runs counter to the course which nature indicates.[38]

The complexity of this passage again underscores the challenges of O'Donovan's article, and the sense in which he is already seeking to reckon with a range of theological considerations in articulating his moral ontology. The way the argument seems to run here invites two sets of observations.

First, it is welcome, in an essay that earlier developed without any positive account of living in eschatological expectation, that there is here an acknowledgement of the vocation of singleness. (I hope it inarguable that singleness can, however else it might be analysed, be fittingly understood as a correlate of eschatological reality.) And it is welcome that the demands of discipleship are testified to here in their disruptive quality in relation to 'natural goals and functions'. Still, absent that more substantive argument for the eschatological witness of the moral life, might leading with the sense in which ascetic duties reflect God's judgement upon rebellious nature, and then seeming to connect it with those vocations that derive from 'an eschatological demand', risk conceiving them as chiefly an infralapsarian counterweight?[39] I am not sure whether O'Donovan is imagining singleness in that way, but he seems to court that inference here.

What we can notice here, and will explore throughout this study, is that a certain delicacy of treatment is needed when we articulate the place in redemption history of any aspect of creaturely life that Christian ethics deals with (here kinship, marriage and singleness). The salvation-historical emplacement of each reality is contested, of course, but also I think on any good account that emplacement will be complex. For instance, it would not be untrue to say that the celibate state 'for the sake of the kingdom' embodies by extension a critical verdict on the claims of natural affinities under fallen conditions, so long as we also remember to say what is surpassingly true of this vocation – that it embodies a witness to the life of Christ, his church and his coming kingdom. To give a complementary example: neither is marriage in this time purely correspondent to natural goals and functions, since while not at all untouched by the fall, it perdures through creaturely rebellion due to providential grace, is refigured in the advent of Christ, and – as O'Donovan indicates – is ascetically disciplined in light

---

[38] Ibid.
[39] The sense in which singleness 'embodies a judgment against the limitations of familial affinities' is developed in Brent Waters, *The Family in Christian Social and Political Thought* (Oxford/New York: Oxford University Press, 2007), 237 – originating in a DPhil thesis supervised by O'Donovan.

of the coming kingdom, at the fulfilment of which, it seems, those who were married will live 'like angels in heaven'.[40]

It would be a mistake to allow a theology of calling, and especially of the most plainly eschatologically oriented vocations, to be governed rather than inflected by *topoi* of corruption and corruption's judgement. Again, I am not sure whether O'Donovan courts that inference here. But if he does, it would be out of keeping for a theologian so concerned otherwise to present morality first in relation to the prior goodness of divine gift – usually the gift of creation, of course, but I see no reason why that principle would not hold as regards the 'grace upon grace' of reconciliation and redemption, from which derive the vocation of singleness and the demands of discipleship.[41] I have reflected in some detail on these questions here, partly because this allows us to table some considerations that we will carry with us throughout this study, and partly because I wonder whether O'Donovan's treatment of the radical demands of discipleship and the vocation of singleness suggests an unresolved grappling with creation, fall, salvation and consummation – and perhaps a struggle to satisfactorily render eschatology's import for the moral life.

The second observation is that the passage's mention of the fallenness of the natural order is welcome, since in O'Donovan's writing, this is relatively rare. (A helpful earlier description states that 'the world was an ordered creation tragically spoiled'.)[42] Welcome, too, is the suggestion that nature must stand under divine judgement – presumably 'nature' strictly in the sense of 'fallen' nature, since the two, he has said, should not be taken as synonymous. This does reveal that O'Donovan in fact accepts the problem of the fall as more than solely epistemological; if nature must be judged, surely humankind's inability to see and implement nature's claims aright is not the only morally significant effect of sin.

Yet this remains another area of tension in 'The Natural Ethic', and, I believe, continues to be unresolved in O'Donovan's thought. 'The Natural Ethic' does not explain what exactly might be fallen and thereby judged about the natural order, or how this fallenness and judgement might relate to the primeval divine pronouncement of its goodness. That is understandable; it is a short piece. Nevertheless, once more the important questions that arise at this point should remain with us throughout

---

[40] Mt. 22.30 (NRSV – as all scriptural citations in this book). For an account sensitive to the way Augustine's views on these matters are informed by his understanding of salvation history see Jana Marguerite Bennett, *Water Is Thicker Than Blood: An Augustinian Theology of Marriage and Singleness* (Oxford/New York: Oxford University Press, 2008), originating in a PhD thesis supervised by Hauerwas. Waters suspects Bennett of stretching the concept of household too far, and thus of muting 'the witness of marriage and family to the goodness of God's creation', which he characterizes as 'providential witness' in contrast to the church's 'eschatological expectation' (Review, *Modern Theology* 29, no. 2 (2009): 341–3). That kind of suspicion typifies O'Donovan's worries about Hauerwas; equally, Hauerwas' worries about O'Donovan would be typified in the suspicion that could be raised of Waters' book from Bennett's perspective – that it has too optimistic and undialectical an understanding of the natural order's normativity. I return to both books later.

[41] Jn 1.16. In this study, I make direct recourse to the biblical text from time to time – an approach held in common with O'Donovan, who I consider a wonderful exegete, and for which I make no especial apology besides that of being no academic specialist in biblical studies. 'Here, in this life', wrote Yves Congar, 'all that we can do is to rely on Scripture and stammer a few sentences'. (*I Believe in the Holy Spirit*, trans. David Smith (New York: Herder and Herder, 2015), 2.68).

[42] O'Donovan, 'The Natural Ethic', 27.

this study. Are the structures of created order in some way compromised, as these sentences just quoted might suggest, or are they simply now opaque to us, which seems to be the force of sentences such as the one I quoted earlier: 'God's creation should not be held responsible for a fragmentation which is really due to the problem of *knowledge* in fallen mankind'? Or again, is the reality to which our action ought conform without remainder the self-same reality as pre-lapsarian created order? If the rhetoric typically suggests that it is the same reality, O'Donovan has already given hints that it is not. Providential ordering, he says, is ingredient in the 'natural order' in addition to the protological fundament, and we ought to recognize providence's 'secondary forms' as morally binding. Furthermore, the 'eschatological demand', as O'Donovan understands it, seems to be more than the restatement of a mandate native to Eden, even as it appears for him to be principally a judgement on creatures' failure to fulfil that mandate. So the moral order depicted in O'Donovan's natural ethic may seem to be moving towards becoming a more multifaceted reality than it at first seemed.

Any 'natural ethic' will surely have to answer questions from Christian theology like those stated earlier, as well as more epistemological questions, about the degree of self-evidence the natural order has for us and – critically – what it might then mean to claim that this order might function normatively. We will have the chance to address them in Chapters 2 and 3, but they need to be acknowledged even before we consider further questions that must be added about how *eschatological* goods might be discerned, by whom, and with what authority – and about these goods' relation to created goods. O'Donovan is not innocent of these challenges, as the rejection of 'static naturalism' shows. Nevertheless, with 'The Natural Ethic', he commits to establishing the place of 'the natural' in moral reasoning prior to such concerns, following an order of exposition more familiar to Thomists than Barthians, and in so doing tends to downplay their consequence.

Still, O'Donovan is clear in his disavowal of static naturalism, and indicates that naturalism as such cannot claim Christians' sole allegiance. His thinks that the Reformers were accurate in their critique of Thomist naturalism (though truly sub-St Thomas) on the grounds that the critique was motivated by their desire to be thoroughly theological in their moral reasoning. And insofar as they were correct, O'Donovan suggests, we must follow suit: 'We cannot allow ourselves, then, to champion an ethic in which everything is given in nature, nothing is to be revealed in history'.[43] The antidote to static naturalism is clearly not flight from nature into an unbridled historicism. The article is entitled 'The Natural Ethic', after all, and a sharply critical appraisal of historicist thought follows the assessment of naturalism.

Historicism

Eschatology reappears in this appraisal, for the 'other route' historicism represents on O'Donovan's account involves 'abandoning altogether the given values in favour

---

[43] Ibid., 28.

of a solely eschatological outlook'.[44] 'Belief in progress', he says, 'can be thought of as "salvation history" without salvation'.[45] Such belief generates optimism about history's direction, but it lacks another vital salvation-historical sensibility: an understanding 'of history as the restoring of what was lost, the recovery of things as they were always supposed to be'.[46] These dense lines elicit two comments.

First, I worry that describing historicism as 'a solely eschatological outlook' seems again to risk insinuating that eschatology itself is responsible. O'Donovan is not alone in reading the doctrinal category 'eschatology' onto secularized philosophy in this way, of course; it is a widespread and plausible interpretation.[47] It yields a valid judgement upon the a-theological or partially theological character of modern philosophies of history and – the issue in question – upon their denial of nature. But the way O'Donovan puts it seems to invite misunderstanding. And if my hunch is correct, we will find his arguments typically more careful in distinguishing doctrines of creation from secular or quasi-theological ethical naturalism than they are in distinguishing doctrines of eschatology from historicist moral thought.

Second, the statement that 'history' is 'the restoring of what was lost, the recovery of things as they were always supposed to be' raises significant considerations for our enquiry. We will find that much in O'Donovan's thought depends on this idea that the movement of salvation history is above all one of restoration. In the next chapters, I will examine this notion in some detail and will seek to distinguish between possible positions. For now, let us raise some questions regarding which the disagreements may come in: *what* is restored – and *when*? This pertains both to epistemological aspects and to ontological aspects: it is about how God heals the vision of human creatures who cannot see clearly – though who continue to see 'in a mirror, dimly'; and about whether we are to presume the restoration of natural order in this time between the times.[48] And it pertains to the temporal and eschatological fulfilment of God's work in Christ and by the Spirit: it is about how we speak well respectively of the 'once for all', the 'more and more', and the 'yet to come' of God's work of restoration. (Finally, it will also be about the aspects of salvation that are not well captured by the idea of restoration, and how they relate to it.)

This may seem like a further question for purely doctrinal elaboration, rather than one directly pertinent for moral theology, but I think that it has moral implications that are perhaps surprisingly near-at-hand. Differing judgements about these implications will have consequences for myriad areas of Christian ethics. Doctrinal decisions about

---

[44] Ibid.
[45] Ibid.
[46] Ibid.
[47] The classic account is Karl Löwith, *Meaning in History* (Chicago: Phoenix Books, 1949). Contestation of this diagnostic coupling of the structure of Jewish and Christian eschatology with secular notions of progress can be found in Hans Blumenberg, *The Legitimacy of the Modern Age*, trans. Robert Wallace (Cambridge: MIT Press, 1985). For current research along the lines of Löwith, see the work of Judith Wolfe. Henri de Lubac's vast, untranslated studies of Joachim of Fiore and Joachim's legacy offer a grand narrative. For English-language reception, see Joseph S. Flipper, *Between Apocalypse and Eschaton: History and Eternity in Henri de Lubac* (Minneapolis: Augsburg Fortress Press, 2015), and Cyril O'Regan, 'A Theology of History', in *T & T Clark Companion to Henri de Lubac*, ed. Jordan Hillebert (London/New York: Bloomsbury T & T Clark, 2017), 301–6.
[48] 1 Cor. 13.12.

the relation of creation, sin, providence, salvation and consummation determine moral decisions about the normativity of nature (and history), affecting how one thinks about questions of technology, sexuality, ecology, politics and more besides. O'Donovan does not yet adumbrate the ethical consequences of his understanding 'of history as the restoring of what was lost' – apart from the indication that political authority is to be comprehended as rooted in divine dispensation.

Ambiguities aside, O'Donovan's reflections on historicism are already insightful. He argues, for instance, that historicism makes genuine hope impossible. While 'hope requires some point of identification between the thing hoped for and the one who hopes for it', in the historicist imagination, the ineluctable drive of progress means 'the future is known only as the negation of what is ... not as the more profound affirmation of its true structure'.[49] What is to come, therefore, cannot be the object of hope, only of existential fear or dread. I am not sure whether this is an accurate claim as regards historicist self-understanding (it seems to me that historicism also seeks to secure itself against the future, trying to outflank anxiety by replacing hope with ironclad certitude).[50] But it is certainly an interesting claim about the experience of living one's life according to that philosophy of history. And it is historicism's moral results, as he understands them, which particularly trouble O'Donovan. When the givenness of nature is discarded, we are told: 'Value and meaning now arise from the very fact of transformation itself; there is no other criterion, other than the simple fact of change, by which we can judge good and evil'.[51] The forward thrust of 'progress' must therefore separate those on the 'right' and 'wrong' sides of history, with pejorative labels attached to those opposing change and badges of honour to those engineering it: '"Progressive" and "reactionary" become the standard terms of praise and blame'.[52]

While 'The Natural Ethic' eschews both pure naturalism and historicism, it is clear that O'Donovan considers this progressivism to be the era's regnant attitude, and I think at this point we discover the rationale for what, despite claims of parity between nature and history, appeared to be a lack of even-handed treatment of creation and eschatology. 'The Natural Ethic' is intended to serve as a corrective for an audience who, it is presumed, tend towards the progressivist historicism that is fashionable – a tendency he described theologically as a 'solely eschatological outlook'. The final section of the conference address explores the foregoing argument's 'bearing on a disagreement which has disturbed our own small circles in recent years'.[53]

---

[49] O'Donovan, 'The Natural Ethic', 29.
[50] Cyril O'Regan describes Hegel's conception of providence to this effect, 'a proposal in which knowledge has been substituted for faith, certainty for hope, absolute transparency for the ambiguity of history'. O'Regan, 'On Hegel, Theodicy and the Invisibility of Waste', in *The Providence of God: Deus Habet Consilium*, ed. Francesca Aran Murphy and Philip G. Ziegler (London/New York: Bloomsbury T & T Clark, 2009), 76. It is this historicist attitude to the future, I think, which O'Donovan describes in *Begotten or Made?* (see the discussion later in this chapter), and elsewhere.
[51] O'Donovan, 'The Natural Ethic', 29.
[52] Ibid.
[53] Ibid., 30.

'Tensions in evangelical ethics'

Though O'Donovan has a clear sense that of these mistaken positions just sketched, the historicist position is more likely to be held by his contemporaries than pure naturalism, he again sets up the question in terms of balance. He is anxious that if creation and redemption are not thought together, misguided attempts will be made to develop Christian positions from either pole. This situation is not merely a theoretical or typological possibility but is exactly the bifurcation of ethical programmes that O'Donovan indicates has caused the 'tensions in evangelical ethics'.[54] There are those 'who urge upon us a "kingdom" ethic and those who support a "creation" ethic'.[55] Both are lopsided: 'Neither kingdom nor creation can be known independently of each other. He who is called the King of kings is also called the second Adam: nature and history in him are not divided. We would be foolish to allow ourselves to be polarised in this way'.[56] He also proposes his audience would do well not to map 'kingdom ethics' and 'creation ethics' onto political clichés of 'left' and 'right'.

O'Donovan is, nevertheless, mindful of the potential pragmatic reasons 'naturalist and historicist camps' have formed:

> We have to proclaim the gospel in different cultural and philosophical contexts. Many of us have deep sympathy with the problems of the Third World, tyrannical regimes, oppressive family and tribal structures, maldistribution of resources, and so on, and, speaking authentically to the static naturalisms which have produced and aggravated such problems, will talk eschatologically of transformation, even with a daring but possible expropriation of language, of 'revolution'. Others of us are concerned chiefly with the problems of the Western world, the abuses of technology, the threat to the family, the dominance of financial power, and so on, and find themselves needing constantly to point to the *data* of created nature. No doubt there is a temptation here: it is easy for the one group to think of the other as 'conservative' or 'radical'. But whenever we do this we exclude one side of the nature-history balance, and condemn our own stance to being less Christian for lack of that balance.[57]

---

[54] Ibid.
[55] Ibid. For background, see Chris Sugden and Oliver Barclay, *Kingdom and Creation in Social Ethics: Grove Booklet E:79* (Bramcote: Grove Books, 1990) and Robin Parry, 'Evangelicalism and Ethics', in *The Futures of Evangelicalism: Issues and Prospects*, ed. Craig G. Bartholomew, Robin Parry and Andrew West (Leicester: IVP, 2003). For context see the longer tale as pertains to Anglicanism in Jonathan Chaplin, 'Evangelical Contributions to the Future of Anglican Social Theology', in *Anglican Social Theology: Renewing the Vision Today*, ed. Malcolm Brown (London: Church House Publishing, 2014), and Jeffrey P. Greenman, 'Anglican Evangelicals on Personal and Social Ethics', *Anglican Theological Review* 94, no. 2 (2012): 179–206 – the conclusion of which begins by quoting *Resurrection and Moral Order* as the baseline for Anglican evangelical ethics. More broadly see Nigel Biggar, 'Evangelicalism and Social Ethics', in *Evangelical Anglicans: Their Role and Influence in the Church Today*, ed. R. T. France and A. E. McGrath (London: SPCK, 1993). Biggar writes: '[C]ontemporary evangelicals are much more inclined than their Victorian predecessors to conceive of economic and social life as the proper objects of divine redemption ... indicated by their appeal to the incarnation as the basis of Christian social involvement, and by their emphasis on the social nature of the kingdom of God' (108).
[56] O'Donovan, 'The Natural Ethic', 30.
[57] Ibid., 31.

This passage is especially instructive, further contextualizing O'Donovan's thought. It places the question of doctrine's import for ethics parallel to a broader one about discernment of the times. It is thoughtful in its appreciation for the contextual concerns that lead Christians to draw forward certain aspects of the gospel in their thinking and speaking.[58] Moreover, it points to a somewhat reductionistic explanation of the ethical 'use' of particular doctrines, though I wonder if it might at the same time threaten to reify it. Either way, at root, O'Donovan's intention is to urge his contemporaries into a deeper understanding of the theological framework that can shape moral action; in the final line of the address, he enjoins his hearers to 'grasp the Christian metaphysic in its wholeness and realise its significance for ethics'.[59] ('Realize' here could coherently be taken both in the sense of cognisance and of actualization, both comprehension and the carrying through of this comprehension in a theological ethics shaped by the whole.) But it is also clear that O'Donovan thinks such deeper understanding will yield the natural ethic. And that, it seems to me, already grants privilege to one contextual discernment over another – even on the article's own terms.

For confirmation that O'Donovan's discernment of the times produces a moral theology that appears to stack the deck in favour of creation, we need only consult 1984's *Begotten or Made?*, in which a number of parallel judgements emerge as foundational for the more particular ethical argument.

Case study: *Begotten or Made?*

The theme of nature's givenness features prominently here, too. Acknowledgement of this givenness is contrasted with our technological culture's construal of all activity as making. That construal, O'Donovan argues, 'imperils what it is to be human ... deprives human existence itself of certain spontaneities of being and doing, spontaneities which

---

[58] What difference would outliers make to the typology – 'conservative' eschatological ethics or 'progressive' creation ethics? Recognition of these possibilities might strengthen O'Donovan's case inasmuch as he troubles neat mapping of 'left' and 'right' onto particular doctrinal concentrations, albeit would necessitate more typological sophistication. In some circles, both Catholic and evangelical Protestant, those who emphasize creation's moral import *are* thought 'progressive' over against an escapist eschatologically driven conservatism reducing matters of faith to thinly conceived spirituality or soul-saving for heaven. The picture is complex in this sense, which O'Donovan recognizes when he criticizes dualisms. *Resurrection and Moral Order* has been taken up with relish by some evangelicals as offering the possibility of positive theological accounts of worldly activities like work and politics, and broader definitions of mission – even ecological concerns. I have no desire whatsoever to disparage this, nor such readers of O'Donovan, from pursuing a reading of him to that end. In their case, they may be reacting not so much to *kingdom* ethics but to a purportedly eschatologically based rationale for what is really *anti*-ethical quietism. My hope is only that asking the question of Christian ethics' relation to doctrine with some latitude from this pressing contestation is of scholarly and long-term ecclesial benefit, and might ultimately allow one to come to slightly different conclusions, without denigrating the real gains afforded to more thoughtful evangelicals by O'Donovan's work. If my reading is at times critical, it is sympathetic in hoping to articulate a place for eschatology in a thoroughly Christian moral metaphysics that can help evangelical ethics transcend its perennial pendulum swings.

[59] O'Donovan, 'The Natural Ethic', 31.

depend upon the reality of a world which we have not made or imagined, but which simply confronts us to evoke our love, fear, and worship.'[60]

I suggest that the genealogical sketch in *Begotten or Made?* also ratifies my reading of 'The Natural Ethic'. Its aim is the depiction of the 'Liberal Revolution', then thought to be approaching its zenith in the late twentieth century. Given the work's precipitating bioethical topic – artificial human fertilization – the story is primarily narrated so as to unearth cultural shifts disturbing medical self-understanding and practice, though O'Donovan is, as ever, tracking political consequences. He describes the shifts in modernity as a 'revolution', and his defence of the designation 'revolution' for these changes epitomizes his sense of the danger inherent in historicist talk of the future: 'revolution' is appropriate because it denotes 'a community [seeking] to act together *en masse* in such a way as to fashion its own future'.[61] O'Donovan detects in the phrase 'fashion the future' the relinquishment of belief in divine providence. To seek to fashion the future is 'to refuse to let one's act go ... to strive to extend one's control even to directing the stream of history ... to assume a totalistic responsibility for what will happen, to treat the whole course of events as an artifact which one can mould in one's hands'.[62]

In order to respond to this disturbing cultural attitude, O'Donovan turns directly to theological resources, namely, the doctrines of creation and providence:

> Christians should at this juncture confess their faith in the natural order as the good creation of God. To do this is to acknowledge that there are limits to the employment of technique and limits to the appropriateness of our 'making'. These limits will not be taught us by compassion, but only by the understanding of what God has made, and by a discovery that it is complete, whole and satisfying ...
>
> Secondly, Christians should at this juncture confess their faith in the providence of God as the ruling power of history. To do this is to acknowledge that there are limits to man's responsibility with regard to the future, to deny that it can be an artifact which we can mould in its totality. This would be to recover the possibility of 'acting well', of contributing to the course of events a deed, which, whatever may become of it, is fashioned rightly in response to the reality which actually confronts the agent as he acts.[63]

These discernments may have been accurate – and may still be. But reading *Begotten or Made?* alongside 'The Natural Ethic' shows unmistakeably that the prominence of creation and providence in O'Donovan's thought is tied to these discernments. That is emphatically not to say creation and providence are not appropriate remedial resources with which the church should respond to its context. My point, rather, is

---

[60] *Begotten or Made?* 3. *Begotten or Made?* originated in O'Donovan's 1983 London Lectures in Contemporary Christianity (a series instituted by John Stott a decade earlier).
[61] Ibid., 7.
[62] Ibid., 7, 8.
[63] Ibid., 12–13. For a later topical work deploying the insights of *Begotten or Made?*, see Brent Waters, *Reproductive Technology: Towards a Theology of Procreative Stewardship* (London: DLT, 2000), especially 48–9, 89.

that this close link does unsettle any impression that the programme announced in 'The Natural Ethic' is the free-standing expression of balance that it seems at points to present itself as. That impression is further disturbed by what we read at the end of the published article.

A twist in the tale

'The Natural Ethic' is accompanied in its published form by four 'Questions for Discussion', presumably supplied by O'Donovan himself:

1. Are there matters of fact which carry with them a moral demand?
2. Is scientific description bound to over-simplify the truth?
3. Is what we see through Christ in nature different from what we would see otherwise?
4. If we cannot *balance* creation ethics and kingdom ethics, what *can* we do with them?[64]

The fourth is especially relevant. Its phrasing may strike us as curious – it seems as if O'Donovan has been advocating precisely for balance in the article, expending much energy extolling it as the prime virtue of a theological metaphysics of morals.[65] The expressed goal of his narration appeared to be balance between nature and history, and his sense of the need for both 'creation' and 'kingdom' perspectives in Christian ethics suggested as much. While we have found that he is clearer about what happens if a doctrine of creation is lacking, he has shown keen awareness of the pitfalls awaiting those who slough off either pole. For good reason Sean Doherty is able to report, when drawing on 'The Natural Ethic' in a subsection of his book entitled 'Should Social Ethics Be Based on Eschatology?', that 'O'Donovan's solution is a "balance" between nature and history, between creation and eschatology'.[66] Yet with the concluding question of 'The Natural Ethic', it seems like O'Donovan gestures towards an account that integrates the concerns of creation and kingdom ethics without balancing them – without simply adding so much of one and an equal amount of the other.

To make sense of this, and to discern the emerging shape of the ethic being proposed, we need to realize that O'Donovan's interest in the balance between his subjects is not at all indifferent to the conceptual relationship that obtains among them. Though there might be a certain abstract formal quality to the way the paired

---

[64] O'Donovan, 'The Natural Ethic', 35.
[65] The pursuit of balance is often ascribed to Anglican theology, and there is certainly something of that Anglican disposition in O'Donovan's writing. But of course the ascription does not yet tell us much materially or evaluatively until we look much closer at what the component parts are taken to be and how they are being synthetically combined. Only then is it possible to say whether any particular *via media* is a 'strikingly balanced witness' – as Michael Ramsey described Anglicanism in *The Gospel and the Catholic Church*, 2nd edn, repr. (London: SPCK, 1990), 220 – or not.
[66] Sean Doherty, *Theology and Economic Ethics: Martin Luther and Arthur Rich in Dialogue* (Oxford: Oxford University Press, 2014), 162.

terms operate, he does not intend to place nature and history squarely side-by-side, as if taxonomically coeval. The corresponding terms creation and redemption (or eschatology) indicate the ordered salvation-historical relationship between the two, and their mutually interpreting character. For O'Donovan, though nature 'is not a part of salvation through Christ, neither is it opposed to it, for it is the work of the same God, the creator and sustainer of all. In either case the natural is presupposed by, and redeemed through, the work of salvation: natural knowledge is restored by revelation, the natural order of things by saving history'.[67] Recall what was said earlier, to the effect that 'Christian eschatology … has to be seen in the light of the doctrine of creation'.[68]

There is evident theological good sense in this stipulation, which as a refrain in O'Donovan's thought I will revisit in subsequent chapters. The familiar, valuable point made about the self-identity of the God who acts in creation and redemption sets bounds responsible theology should operate within. Nevertheless, with an eye to later arguments, I want to stress already that those bounds do not in themselves necessitate one or other particular account of the relationships between creation, reconciliation and eschatological consummation – though they may rule some out – nor one or other account of the moral import of those relationships. We have already seen that while the notion of redemption-as-restoration that O'Donovan invokes again here by proposing that 'natural knowledge is restored by revelation, the natural order of things by saving history' is potentially unobjectionable on its own, there are grounds for discussion of what that restoration might mean, and when.

Yet if for O'Donovan a conception of consummation as the completion of restoration might sometimes appear to follow seamlessly, his mention of eschatology's present moral demands did seem to point to an additional element of eschatology with more disjunctive ethical significance for the here and now. Whether this loftier understanding would, if developed, unsettle the strongly continuous creation-redemption scheme that licenses a particularly untroubled appeal to the moral normativity of nature is not clear. Furthermore, it does imply that the doctrinal argument for the 'natural ethic' may not be as secure as O'Donovan makes out. In the next chapter, I will pursue these questions much further. By interrogating the particular shape of O'Donovan's theological ethics, I aim at the same time to show that theological latitude is available to answer faithfully in a different way. A more extensive consideration of eschatology's significance beyond the notion of the recovery of natural order does not by definition endanger a unified doctrine of God, the presupposition of the goodness of creation, or practical moral responsibility in our (or any other) time.

There is another way in which paying attention to O'Donovan's convictions about *taxis* aids us in understanding his moral theology – and leads us to ask another critical question of it. Noticing his sense of the interrelation of doctrines also helps explain the reticence exhibited about the natural order's fallenness, and alerts us that it may be funded in part by a classical theological principle. As traditionally conceived – the view

---

[67] O'Donovan, 'The Natural Ethic', 32.
[68] Ibid., 27.

is often described as 'Augustinian'[69] – speech about the fallenness of nature is in a sense irreversibly secondary, a subset of the more fundamental confession of the goodness of creation. Good and evil are neither temporally nor ontologically equiprimordial. They are categorically asymmetrical, and evil is understood as privative – as parasitic. Though not all Protestant theology has always remembered to state it,[70] meaningful speech about creation's condition *post lapsum* must therefore presuppose the world's created goodness, an origin and status illustrated by the very fact of its existence. Nonetheless, if this principle (and, for Protestants, the reminder) is legitimate, it does not yet tell us how to assess the depths and details of sin's effects on the current order. Therefore, while the principle should underpin all moral enquiries in Christian ethics, and may supply the theological perspective that helps to resolve some, it should not be hastily applied to foreclose any.

At any rate, these considerations of *taxis* have helped us to see both the logic and the tensions of what O'Donovan is straining to do in this early work, and the sense in which he seems both to aim at balance and then to realize that the goal ought to be something beyond it.

Conclusion

'The Natural Ethic' does, I think, already attempt an integrative account in trying to seek balance under the aegis of a natural ethic, entertaining creation *and then* eschatology, rather than any artificially schematic, neutral combination of both. (Or creation and providence, and then eschatology.) It is clear that O'Donovan could not as easily imagine incorporating his contemporaries' concerns under the heading 'The Historical Ethic'. That alone may engender suspicion in, for instance, more radical Barthian quarters, where it might be suspected that O'Donovan has surreptitiously tipped the scales towards creation at the expense of new creation. We are certainly still searching for an adequate treatment of the significance of eschatology for the moral life.

I have established that the imbalance (and if we read the article through the lens of its closing question, then to say 'imbalance' is not necessarily to criticize) is caused by a sense of creation's logical priority over redemption in Christian confession, and by another related sense that contemporary ethical challenges require primarily the recovery of creation. O'Donovan's sensibility is formed by both judgements, and each appears symbiotically to determine the other. Strengthening the doctrinal conviction of creation's priority is a second – that redemption is in a strong sense restoration. This

---

[69] The thought is not restricted to St Augustine. See, for example, Michel René Barnes, 'Privation: Out-Narrating Evil' in 'Ebion at the Barricades: Moral Narrative and Post Christian Catholic Theology', *Modern Theology* 26, no. 4 (2010): 511–48, which mentions Gregory of Nyssa's comparable understanding.

[70] I would suspect that this is far less acute an issue for mainstream Protestant theology now than it was when O'Donovan was writing 'The Natural Ethic'. Whether this would be as true of evangelical Protestant piety, I am not so sure. Equally, I am sure that much contemporary mainline Protestant theology and practice could do with a recovery of the doctrine of sin.

reinforces the imbalance, but is also the catalyst for a presentation of Christian ethics that 'does' something with creation and kingdom ethics other than balance them. For if 'restoration' is the definitive eschatological act, or at least conveys eschatology's *moral* meaning, then O'Donovan's own recognition and integration of kingdom ethics would seem largely to entail the restatement of creation ethics. Despite all the insights O'Donovan wins for us, that particular conclusion seems to me unsatisfactory, in the light of scripture and tradition. But as we are about to see, it is arguably the settlement that underlies *Resurrection and Moral Order.*

2

Topography

Resurrection and Moral Order – 'The Objective Reality'

Introduction

We turn now to *Resurrection and Moral Order* (first edition 1986). It is a demanding book, and such is its significance for my study that I devote two chapters to examining salient features. O'Donovan's preface to the second edition (1994) suggests that the book has 'three principal orientations':

> Purposeful action is determined by what is true about the world into which we act; this can be called the 'realist' principle. That truth is constituted by what God has done for his world and for humankind in Jesus Christ; this is the 'evangelical' principle. The act of God which liberates our action is focused on the resurrection of Jesus from the dead, which restored and fulfilled the intelligible order of creation; this we can call the 'Easter' principle.[1]

My reading, mindful of each orientation but animated by the question at hand, divides its attentions as follows.

This chapter focuses in its first part on analytical discussion of major aspects of the argument. These are largely concentrated in Part One of the book, concerning 'the objective reality', but where relevant material from later sections is drawn upon too. Initially this chapter addresses moral realism and the idea of created order. It then considers the motif of resurrection, first in its relation to the created order and human agency, and second in its relation to eschatology – the place for which is found to be expanded but still ambivalent. Again, to see the shape of O'Donovan's argument, we need to explore the book's (developed) critique of historicist thought. Finally, I show how *Resurrection and Moral Order* is an attempt to answer the concluding question of 'The Natural Ethic': 'If we cannot *balance* creation and kingdom ethics, what *can* we do with them?' In the second part of the chapter, I assess three challenges to O'Donovan's

---

[1] O'Donovan, *Resurrection*, ix. All references to the second edition. As will become evident, 'Easter' is a leitmotif in O'Donovan's thought, a metonym for all that salvation signifies. The title of an introduction to Christian ethics produced by O'Donovan's student Stephen Holmgren exemplifies this: *Ethics after Easter* (Lanham, MD: Rowman and Littlefield, 2000).

argument: one that queries the place of covenant besides creation; a second that tests the compatibility of eschatological registers of 'total restoration' and 'transformation' (both found in O'Donovan), and their implications for ethics; and a third that probes the feasibility of O'Donovan's position on the stability of the natural order in view of 'the ingenuity of art'.

Having explored the book's foundations in Chapter 2, Chapter 3 for the most part takes up its other major subjects topic by topic, evaluating passages particularly germane to the issue of the moral import of eschatology. Beyond this, a subchapter directly examines the work's eschatologically oriented final chapters, before a section of concluding analysis addresses *Resurrection and Moral Order* in its entirety. As I alluded to in the introduction, my sense is that in this book, O'Donovan continues to grapple with some of the same tensions evident in 'The Natural Ethic', marshalling considerable resources in the attempt to craft a definitive statement that will effect their resolution. It is a major contribution to moral theology. Yet, as I also suggested and intend now to demonstrate, some of the same tensions do not by this point seem too much closer to being resolved.

Before we begin, let me note that in trying to offer an interpretation of this important book, I have found comparison especially helpful with a number of O'Donovan's roughly contemporaneous publications: the monograph *The Problem of Self-Love in St. Augustine* (1980), which presented doctoral and postdoctoral research; a work of historical and doctrinal theology, *On the Thirty-Nine Articles* (1986); an article, 'Evangelicalism and the Foundations of Ethics' (1993); and a collection of his Oxford sermons, *The Word in Small Boats*, which encompasses this period as well as including later sermons.[2] I draw on each of these from time to time, periodically interleaving resonant quotations (other relevant passages that I am unable to review are recorded in footnotes). Besides these, the moral theology outlined in *Resurrection and Moral Order* is also foreshadowed – and re-inscribed – in discrete treatments of particular ethical issues that O'Donovan made around the same time. In much the same way I took up *Begotten or Made?* briefly as a case study in Chapter 1, I take up *Church in Crisis* as a case study in this chapter. Nevertheless, these topical works are not my focus in this study, though I hope the exposition here could serve to contextualize them for a reader.[3]

Moral realism and created order

The subject of moral realism and created order in O'Donovan's thought merits substantial reflection in itself. As Chapter 1 indicated, a cluster of questions unavoidably

---

[2] O'Donovan, *The Problem of Self-Love in St. Augustine* (New Haven/London: Yale University Press, 1980), hereafter *Self-Love*; *On the Thirty-Nine Articles: A Conversation with Tudor Christianity* (London: SCM, 2011), hereafter *Thirty-Nine Articles*; 'Evangelicalism and the Foundations of Ethics', in *Evangelical Anglicans*, hereafter 'The Foundations of Ethics' – an essay substantially similar to *Resurrection* that does not actually engage any evangelical Anglicans, instead presenting O'Donovan's own position; *The Word in Small Boats: Sermons from Oxford*, ed. Andrew Draycott (Grand Rapids: Eerdmans, 2009), hereafter *Small Boats*.

[3] A full list is found in *The Authority of the Gospel*.

ramifies from commitments like his, and it is necessary to say something about all of that here, though much of further interest will necessarily be left for another day.

However we interpret the details of *Resurrection and Moral Order* (various interpretations will be assessed in what follows), it seems to me that the book occupied a singular position in respect to these subjects. O'Donovan is apparently well acquainted with both Thomist affirmations of natural law and Barthian rejections, but his own account is not easily classifiable as either.[4] Certainly, plenty of commentators have noted an affinity with natural law modes of moral reasoning. The Catholic moral theologian Jean Porter, a painstaking historian and prominent contemporary advocate of natural law's Thomistic expression, notes in her book *Natural and Divine Law* – a book O'Donovan himself calls 'admirable'[5] – that 'a growing number of Christian ethicists' are taking up 'the problem of the moral significance of human nature', and counts O'Donovan among these congenial figures.[6] O'Donovan, Porter writes, 'recently argued that an evangelical theology is not at variance with, but to the contrary implies an attentiveness to the natural order as the basis for Christian ethics'.[7] (More recently still, she writes that her own 'overall theological approach to creation and redemption is indebted to O'Donovan ... in particular *Resurrection and Moral Order*'.)[8]

Another Catholic theologian, Fergus Kerr, when tracing 'recent theological accounts' of something like natural law, finds O'Donovan's book 'one of the most interesting'.[9] In a similar vein, David McIlroy argues that another scholar 'is right to describe [O'Donovan] as presenting "the most theological view possible of the doctrine of natural law"'.[10] Yet it is also true, as McIlroy perceives, that O'Donovan 'is so chary of the overloaded meaning of "natural law" that he tries to avoid using the term'.[11] For Philip Lorish and Charles Mathewes, it is no wonder, then, that to 'innocent readers' *Resurrection and Moral Order* appears 'a curiously compound work, at times highly scriptural, at other times verging on sounding like a work in natural law'.[12] That impression, too, is surely right – though both the presentation of natural law that Porter

---

[4] See O'Donovan, *Resurrection*, 85–7.
[5] Review, *Theology* 104, no. 817 (2001): 60–1.
[6] Jean Porter, *Natural and Divine Law: Reclaiming the Tradition for Christian Ethics* (Grand Rapids: Eerdmans, 1999), 27.
[7] Ibid. Earlier, Porter wrote: '[S]urprisingly, the neo-orthodox theologian Oliver O'Donovan admits that nature may offer a limited but real source of moral guidance'. *The Recovery of Virtue: The Relevance of Aquinas for Christian Ethics* (Louisville: Westminster/John Knox, 1990), 27. She refers to *Resurrection and Moral Order* in both cases. Porter's description of O'Donovan as neo-orthodox is forgivable, if amusing, especially given his comments on neo-orthodoxy, cited in Chapter 5. This mis-description betokens misunderstandings that sometimes still characterize Catholic interaction with Protestant ethics, and *vice versa*, as is her reference to 'liberal evangelism' (presumably meaning evangelicalism, in the sense of Protestantism) in comments on neo-orthodoxy's rejection of virtue ('Virtue Ethics', in *The Cambridge Companion to Christian Ethics*, 2nd edn, ed. Robin Gill (Cambridge: Cambridge University Press, 2012), 97.
[8] Jean Porter, *Ministers of the Law: A Natural Law Theory of Legal Authority* (Grand Rapids: Eerdmans, 2010), 57, n.110.
[9] Fergus Kerr, *After Aquinas: Versions of Thomism* (Oxford: Blackwell, 2002), 102.
[10] David McIlroy, 'What's At Stake in Natural Law', *New Blackfriars* 89, no. 1023 (2008): 508–21, 514.
[11] Ibid. This is also true of some proponents of 'creation ethics' (e.g. Oliver Barclay, 'Creation and Providence', in Sugden and Barclay, *Kingdom and Creation in Social Ethics*, 6 – who also prefers 'creation ethics' to 'common grace').
[12] Lorish and Mathewes, 'Theology as Counsel', 723.

finds in scholastic theology and, as we shall see, the presentation that O'Donovan offers ground a Christian defence of a 'natural ethic' in an appeal to scriptural bases. The matter is evidently not straightforward. Let us try to characterize O'Donovan's view.

The place to begin, plainly enough, is 'Part One' of the book, entitled 'The Objective Reality', which can be seen to revisit and develop themes 'The Natural Ethic' introduced. Gerald McKenny summarizes the basic argument of this section well:

> O'Donovan articulates the norm of conduct in terms of a metaphysical order of natural kinds and teleological relations while arguing that the privileged disclosure of this order is found in biblical revelation. The moral order is cosmic: O'Donovan does not understand it in terms of human nature or reason; rather, he understands human nature and reason in relation to man's ordering in the cosmos. Still, the norm of human conduct lies in this natural order even if its knowability as well as its normativity are ultimately grounded in Christ.[13]

As this distillation suggests more precisely than Porter's comments, O'Donovan's moral realism concerning the natural is primarily cosmic before it is anthropological, though without doubt it also includes claims about the normativity of human nature.[14]

On my reading, O'Donovan's basic sensibility owes more to a Reformed disposition of wonder at the ordered beauty of God's creation than to a more circumscriptive concern for the morally significant features of human nature (such as human reason).[15] Now, it may seem strange to describe his sensibility as 'Reformed', given that I suggested earlier that creation's prominence in O'Donovan's project is partly his response to Protestant neglect. 'The Natural Ethic' did lament the proclivity inherent in Protestantism for allowing the doctrine of creation to be eclipsed by the doctrine of the fall, and the same complaint is made in his book *On the Thirty-Nine Articles* with regard to Cranmer's document and later Protestant piety.[16] However, there Calvin is excused. And on at least one telling of Calvin's ethics, O'Donovan's basic kinship with

---

[13] Gerald McKenny, *The Analogy of Grace: Karl Barth's Moral Theology* (Oxford: Oxford University Press, 2010), 138, n. 37.

[14] On moral realism in conversation with O'Donovan see Rufus Black, *Christian Moral Realism: Natural Law, Narrative Virtue, and the Gospel* (Oxford: Oxford University Press, 2000) – originating in a DPhil thesis supervised by O'Donovan.

[15] Here an instructive comparison might be made with James Gustafson. In profession also Reformed, and extremely worried about anthropocentrism, Gustafson seems to resolve these anxieties differently, in a troublingly less-and-less Christological way. Reviewing Gustafson's *Theology and Ethics*, O'Donovan wrote: 'The search for a natural ground of ethics has thus led him into paths far removed from the traditional Christian humanism of natural law, to an austere religion where the fabled cold wind of Reformed fatalism blows with a keener edge.' *The Journal of Theological Studies* 35, no. 1 (1984): 275–9, 277. Besides Christology, Gustafson's so-called 'theocentric' ethics was 'prepared to jettison traditional eschatology', as P. Travis Kroeker notes in 'Eschatology and Ethics: Luther and the Radical Reformers', now republished in Kroeker, *Messianic Political Theology and Diaspora Ethics: Essays in Exile* (Eugene: Cascade, 2017), 98, n. 5. We should prefer O'Donovan's theological ethics on both counts.

[16] See O'Donovan, *Thirty-Nine Articles*, ch. 5, 'The Concealment of Creation'. Compare Dietrich Bonhoeffer, 'Natural Life', in *Ethics*, DBWE 6, ed. Clifford J. Green (Minneapolis: Fortress Press, 2005). E.g. 171, 173: 'The concept of the natural has fallen into disrepute in Protestant ethics ... the concept of the natural must be recovered from the gospel itself.' (N.B. *Resurrection* does not engage Bonhoeffer at any point).

Reformed thought in terms of the significance of nature for morality can be confirmed. Guenther Haas writes:

> The foundational theological doctrine for understanding Calvin's view of Christian ethics is creation. In the act of creation God brings into existence, not only all creatures, but also 'the very order of things' directing them. This ordering is the means by which God governs all of his creation. Creatures in their diversity obey God by submitting to the 'order of nature' that he has determined for them. This is also the case for human beings. Though ... distinct from all other creatures in that they are made in the image of God, their lives are still governed by the order of nature. It prescribes their relations to God, to one another, and to the rest of creation. The entry of sin and evil into the world has not changed that.[17]

Indeed, Rowan Williams describes O'Donovan's thought as 'one of the most eloquent and compelling restatements in the modern age of a classical Reformed divinity which, like Calvin's own thinking, is imbued with the insights of the patristic age as well as the results of painstaking scriptural exegesis'.[18]

Within his astonishingly wide-ranging scriptural engagement, germane to our present theme is one line in the Psalms' theology of creation that O'Donovan appears particularly to cherish, quoting it often: 'The world is established, it shall never be moved' (Ps. 96.10, also 93.1).[19] I believe this kind of biblical affirmation does much work in O'Donovan's thought. It is the bedrock of a robustly realist ethics, which reminds us that moral reflection is not undertaken in a vacuum: true moral judgements 'are founded on reality as God has given it'.[20] But if there is now a more explicit layer of scriptural reasoning supporting his moral realism, O'Donovan again makes much of the kinship of his moral realism with classical ethics, finding in this 'a point of agreement with ... Plato, Aristotle and the Stoics [who] treated ethics as a close correlate of metaphysics. The way the universe *is*, determines how man *ought* to behave himself in it'.[21] Ethics must take account of the givenness of things.

---

[17] Guenther Haas, 'Calvin's Ethics', in *The Cambridge Companion to John Calvin*, ed. Donald McKim (Cambridge: Cambridge University Press, 2004), 93. I am no expert on Calvin or the shifting sands of interpretation in recent times. However, I note that Haas's own perspective is informed by O'Donovan's *Resurrection and Moral Order*, as well as a range of neo-Reformed thinkers I mention below. See Haas, 'The Significance of Eschatology for Christian Ethics', in *Looking into the Future: Evangelical Studies in Eschatology*, ed. David Baker (Grand Rapids: Baker, 2001).

[18] Williams, 'Foreword', vii. In a review of John Milbank and Adrian Pabst's *The Politics of Virtue – New Statesman* (18 October 2016) – Williams notes that Milbank and Pabst view the rise of Protestantism as a 'fall' moment, and regrets their lack of effort in interacting with political theologians such as O'Donovan or Jacques Ellul, whose modernity critique is coupled with Protestant commitment. https://www.newstatesman.com/culture/books/2016/10/liberalism-and-capitalism-have-hollowed-out-society-so-where-do-we-turn-now (accessed 8 October 2019).

[19] O'Donovan, *Resurrection*, 61. Cf. O'Donovan, 'The Foundations of Ethics', 99, *Desire*, 40. Also important for O'Donovan in this regard is the Creator's answer in Job 38–41. See e.g. O'Donovan, 'Where Were You ... ?' in *The Care of Creation: Focusing Concern and Action*, ed. R. J. Berry (Leicester: IVP, 2000).

[20] O'Donovan, *Resurrection*, 17.

[21] Ibid., 17.

Created order, then, names 'the structure of the world in its objectivity, which includes ... its authority to evoke our action'.[22] And if response to this created order constitutes fitting moral action (in O'Donovan's thought, created order is often synonymous with '*moral* order'), then moral reason should not be thought of as essentially creative, as *poeisis*. Living well, O'Donovan wants to show us, is not a primarily a constructive undertaking; rather, as he writes later in the book, it involves discerning 'the good of human action which conforms to the truth of the created order'.[23] But imagining the moral actor as principally *homo faber* is exactly what, in his view, modern philosophy has tended to do. Conceiving subjective dimensions of human morality as the most important ethical realities,[24] freedom has often been posited as existing over against nature's given contours, rather than as expressed in conformity to them. As we saw in *Begotten or Made?* and will see again, O'Donovan believes that this modern self-understanding is causative of much moral disarray.

O'Donovan is not alone in this diagnosis, of course, nor in turning to a notion of created order, or something like it, as a cure. In our time, the quest for the prized meta-ethical possession of an objective referent in nature – or the assertion of it – seems to be energized for some Christians (and others) by concerns that contemporary culture is afflicted by the radical subjectivism and relativism of militant secularism. I have already made the link to some Catholic moral thought (though ultimately Jean Porter's account of natural law yields different results than O'Donovan's as regards some contemporary ethical questions), and O'Donovan saw in some of John Paul II's pronouncements a kindred spirit. In a response to *Veritatis Splendor* entitled 'A Summons to Reality', he wrote of their shared opposition to a modern view that stresses 'the innovative powers of human resolve and will to mould and shape reality'.[25] In terms of Protestant thought, we have seen a remarkable return to natural law reasoning in American Reformed precincts.[26] I am not entirely unsympathetic to these concerns, but I hope that there is more involved that the simple abutment of a predetermined culture wars agenda; this is the suspicion raised of his fellow Protestant natural lawyers from the quite different perspective of John Bowlin.[27] A further study of the relation of these projects to O'Donovan's would be worthwhile, but for now I suspect that O'Donovan, despite some formal similarity and some similar instincts, is not to be too quickly associated with their endeavour.

The best way to see how O'Donovan upholds his particular claims, and in so doing to begin assessing whether they are vulnerable to theological critique, is to pause

---

[22] Ibid., 191.

[23] Ibid., 125.

[24] The strong rejection of a kind of 'Cartesian' solipsism that O'Donovan shares is, I take it, more common in theology now than it was in parts of the twentieth century. We probably have Fergus Kerr among others to thank for that.

[25] O'Donovan, 'A Summons to Reality', in *Understanding Veritatis Splendor*, ed. J. Wilkins (London: SPCK, 1994), 43.

[26] The relevant literature includes Stephen J. Grabill, *Rediscovering the Natural Law in Reformed Theological Ethics* (Grand Rapids: Eerdmans, 2006), and David VanDrunen, *Natural Law and the Two Kingdoms: A Study in the Development of Reformed Social Thought* (Grand Rapids: Eerdmans, 2010). Again I am no expert as regards this literature.

[27] See John Bowlin, 'Contemporary Protestant Thomism', in *Aquinas as Authority*, ed. Paul van Geest, Harm Goris and Carlo Leget (Leuven: Peeters, 2002), 251.

and trouble *Resurrection and Moral Order* with a question that should be pressed of any Christian ethics built upon what might seem to be general claims about nature's normativity: What is *Christianly intelligible* about this kind of moral realism? O'Donovan anticipates the question. We might even think he begins to respond to it with the title of the book. You can legitimately place 'moral order' next to 'resurrection', he seems to say; the two concepts are not contradictory. And the bold claim that the book makes is that a moral realism based on created order is not just potentially intelligible in light of the gospel but demonstrably implied by the theological commitments that derive from it. O'Donovan's natural ethic, then, is intended to be a thoroughly theological ethic.

A theological ethic

That O'Donovan intended to make a defence of his ethics in 'properly' theological terms might seem barely worthy of comment. But it cannot be taken for granted when we recall when this book was written. Considered against the backcloth of the approaches that must have been presented as viable options in his early reading in the field, O'Donovan's ethics has an unashamedly doctrinal and even confessional character.[28] Early readers were evidently struck by it, and among them, some, like James Gustafson, were unsettled by its theological self-confidence. We will return to

---

[28] I do not mean to be uncharitable, or to imply that the state of Christian ethics was entirely parlous. Figures faded from memory quickly become totemic of a bygone age's foolishness (Joseph Fletcher is a prime example). But evidence from both Catholic and Protestant quarters is sufficient to assume that things were not as healthy as they might have been. Potted histories of twentieth-century moral theology are supplied, by-the-by, in lots of works concerning specific aspects of Christian ethics, as well as in many introductory books, and in the likes of *The Oxford Handbook of Theological Ethics*, ed. Gilbert Meilaender and William Werpehowski (New York/Oxford: Oxford University Press, 2005) – especially Part IV, 'The Structure of Theological Ethics: Books that Give Shape to the Field'. These histories tend to be written by Americans, telling stories about American Christian ethics. Stanley Hauerwas's is delightfully polemical – found, among other places, in 1983's 'Keeping Theological Ethics Theological', reprinted in *The Hauerwas Reader*, ed. John Berkman and Michael Cartwright (London/Durham: Duke University Press, 2001). This essay can profitably be read alongside Hauerwas's 1997 sketch of the discipline's longer history, 'How "Christian Ethics" Came to be', reprinted in the same volume, originating as 'Doctrine and Ethics', in *The Cambridge Companion to Christian Doctrine*, ed. Colin Gunton (Cambridge: Cambridge University Press, 1997). Long-form, though no less partisan, narrations include Gary Dorrien, *Social Ethics in the Making: Interpreting an American Tradition* (Chichester: Wiley-Blackwell, 2008), and James Keenan, *A History of Catholic Moral Theology in the Twentieth Century: From Confessing Sins to Liberating Consciences* (New York: Continuum, 2010). On the Protestant side, D. Stephen Long, 'Protestant Social Ethics', in *The Cambridge Companion to Christian Political Theology*, ed. Craig Hovey and Elizabeth Phillips (New York: Cambridge University Press, 2015), and Brian Brock, 'Christian Ethics', in *Theology: A Thematic and Historical Introduction*, ed. Kelly Kapic and Bruce McCormack (Grand Rapids: Baker Academic, 2012), both put Hauerwas himself into the story. On the Catholic side, the Belgian Dominican Servais Pinckaers presents another account of Catholic moral theology's fortunes (closer to the magisterium's view, one suspects, or at least those of Popes John Paul II and Benedict XVI). See *Morality: The Catholic View*, trans. Michael Sherwin (South Bend: St. Augustine's Press, 2001), which presents accessibly the findings of Pinckaer's magnum opus, *The Sources of Christian Ethics*, trans. Mary Thomas Noble (Washington: Catholic University of America Press, 1995). So too does a scholarly work made possible by Pinckaers: *The Ethics of Aquinas*, ed. Stephen J. Pope (Washington: Georgetown University Press, 2002), especially Part Three, 'The Twentieth Century Legacy'.

Gustafson's comments later.[29] Gene Outka wrote – I presume positively, though perhaps ambiguously – that *Resurrection and Moral Order* 'is an unapologetic restatement of orthodox Christianity and the shape ethics must take if such orthodoxy is to govern'.[30] In it, suggested Timothy Sedgwick, 'the logic of Christian moral concepts is given in the theological use and understanding of those moral concepts so that the meaning of the concepts is grounded in reality itself. The shape of Christian ethics is, therefore, determined first of all by systematic theology'.[31] Alister McGrath commended the book in glowing terms for its conviction that ethics 'rests upon doctrine', finding especially agreeable the idea that 'Christian ethics rests upon a proper understanding of the objective order imposed upon creation by God'.[32] (Indeed, McGrath has taken up O'Donovan's particular articulation of created order repeatedly in his own work.)[33]

O'Donovan himself gives an insight into the self-consciously theological determination of his proposal, observing that many theologians had become content to leave the field of ethics to philosophers' 'great formal theories' (a criticism still made in more recent years by Michael Banner).[34] It is in response to this retreat, O'Donovan writes, that he constructs a theological base prior to a more strictly ethical treatise, itself organized theologically.[35] Whatever we make of the constructive proposals of O'Donovan's book, in terms of seeing his accomplishment, it is worth recalling that many mainline Protestant moralists operated with diluted theological presuppositions and that despite 'the rediscovery since the 1970s of the long obscured place of social ethics in evangelicalism',[36] there was at this point little scholarly evangelical ethics to speak of. If one of the contributions of O'Donovan's teacher Paul Ramsey to moral theology was 'to follow Karl Barth and make room for the truth of Christian doctrine as that which would once again render intelligible the moral good', then it can be

---

[29] James Gustafson, review of *Resurrection*, *The Journal of Religion* 68, no. 1 (1988): 131–3.
[30] From the first edition's dust jacket.
[31] Timothy F. Sedgwick, review of *Resurrection*, *Journal of the American Academy of Religion* 57, no. 2 (1989): 419–21, 419. Cf. Maurice Reidy's review of *Resurrection*, *Scottish Journal of Theology* 42, no. 1 (1989): 131–4, 131.
[32] Alister McGrath, 'Doctrine and Ethics', *Journal of the Evangelical Theological Society* 34, no. 2 (1991): 145–56, 145.
[33] See e.g. Alister McGrath, *Scientific Theology: Nature*, vol. 1 (London/New York: T & T Clark, 2002), 217–18; *Science and Religion: A New Introduction*, 2nd edn (Chichester: Wiley-Blackwell, 2010), 89–90.
[34] O'Donovan, *Resurrection*, 181. See Michael Banner, *The Ethics of Everyday Life: Moral Theology, Social Anthropology, and the Imagination of the Human* (Oxford: Oxford University Press, 2014), which provides a dose of acerbic commentary on Christian ethics' dependence on moral philosophy, though does not engage too much with contemporary Christian ethics. Banner's earlier work is premised on a similarly lugubrious diagnosis of 'the state we're in', but does not yet make the additional remedial prescription of a turn to ethnography. See *Christian Ethics and Contemporary Moral Problems* (Cambridge: Cambridge University Press, 1999), especially the first chapter 'Turning The World Upside Down and Some Other Tasks for Dogmatic Christian Ethics', and *Christian Ethics: A Brief History* (Chichester: Wiley-Blackwell, 2009), especially the final chapters. For discussion, see Samuel Tranter and David Bartram Torrance, 'Ethnography, Ecclesiology, and the Ethics of Everyday Life: Introducing Michael Banner', *Ecclesial Practices* 5, no. 2 (2018): 157–71, and *Everyday Ethics: Moral Theology and the Practices of Ordinary Life*, ed. Michael Lamb and Brian A. Williams (Washington: Georgetown University Press, 2019).
[35] O'Donovan, *Resurrection*, 181.
[36] Parry, 'Evangelicalism and Ethics', 165.

argued, as D. Stephen Long does, that nobody has 'developed Ramsey's insights better than ... O'Donovan'.[37]

The situation in Catholic moral theology does not seem to have been any better. Magisterial pronouncements had begun to urge that the 'theological disciplines be renewed through a more living contact with the mystery of Christ and the history of salvation', and that among them, moral theology ought to be 'nourished more on the teaching of the Bible'.[38] But there was no consensus whatsoever about how ethical discourse should reflect this renewal, and the distinctiveness of Christian ethics was an especially live question in the decades immediately succeeding the Second Vatican Council.[39] I mention this because O'Donovan, clearly familiar with the work of Protestant ethicists – as well as Anglican predecessors like Kenneth Kirk and Lindsay Dewar – tracked Catholic debates carefully too. A little later, I note his interaction with the 'new natural law' of John Finnis and Germain Grisez, which garnered some attention from Protestant theologians, but O'Donovan also engaged Karl Rahner, Josef Fuchs and John Mahoney.[40] If another of Paul Ramsey's achievements was his pioneering ecumenism – at the time of Ramsey's passing, he was 'arguably the only example ... yet ... of an ecumenically eclectic Western Christian moralist' – then O'Donovan took up Ramsey's mantle in this respect, too.[41]

In *Resurrection and Moral Order*, to return directly to the point, we should expect to find a *theological* account of nature's normativity (indeed, one enriched by a wider and longer tradition than twentieth-century Protestant social ethics), and should expect that this account can itself be evaluated on theological terms. As the denial of pure naturalism in 'The Natural Ethic' already suggested, the ethic advocated for here will not be intended as merely positivistic or unhermeneutically naturalistic. Christian ethics, O'Donovan announces in one of *Resurrection and Moral Order*'s most quoted statements, 'must arise from the gospel of Jesus Christ'.[42] This assertion illumines the particular semantics of the book's subheading – *An Outline for Evangelical Ethics* – and his wider project's claim to be 'evangelical'. As he explains in an article from around this time, that term is nearly always meant in the etymological sense:

The word 'evangelical' is used as the adjective corresponding to the noun 'Gospel'; so that 'evangelical ethics' ... is all Christian ethics as it understands its relation

---

[37] D. Stephen Long, 'Moral Theology', in *The Oxford Handbook of Systematic Theology*, ed. John Webster, Iain Torrance and Kathryn Tanner (New York: Oxford University Press, 2007), 465.

[38] *Optatam Totius* (1965), 16. To the same end, in *Veritatis Splendor* (1993), John Paul II encourages moral theology's 'close and vital connection with biblical and dogmatic theology', as well as 'Christian ascetical and mystical theology' (111).

[39] See e.g. *Readings in Moral Theology*, vol. 2: *The Distinctiveness of Christian Ethics*, ed. Charles Curran and Richard McCormick (New York: Paulist Press, 1980).

[40] O'Donovan, *Resurrection*, xii, 50. Cf. O'Donovan's pointed reviews of volumes by Fuchs, a thinker deeply critical of what he called 'the false Christianising of morality' undertaken in the Council's name (*The Journal of Theological Studies* 40, no. 1 (1989): 331–7); and Mahoney (*The Journal of Theological Studies* 39, no. 1 (1988): 348–50), showing familiarity with Bernard Häring's work, too.

[41] O'Donovan, 'Paul Ramsey', 84. Besides engagements with Catholic theologians and Papal documents in print, note O'Donovan's service from 1983 to 1994 as member of, then consultant to, the second round of Anglican-Roman Catholic dialogue (known as ARCIC II).

[42] O'Donovan, *Resurrection*, 11.

to the Gospel correctly, not the concern of a single movement or party within the church. I have no objections, of course, to the use of the term to designate such a movement by those whose business it is to chart the ecclesiastical currents through which we sail; nor do I resist being counted in, if those whose business it is to judge that I belong to it. But I must insist, it is not *my* business![43]

Resurrection and Moral Order is 'evangelical' in precisely this sense, then: it envisages the starting point of ethics as nothing other than the proclamation of the prophets and apostles. To paraphrase O'Donovan's contention, the gospel is not tangential to the sphere of human striving and struggling, but has something vital to say to it. Thus when the church raises its voice to proclaim the evangel in the realm of morality, it does not speak in another register, one more severe or prohibitive. Its tenor remains that of glad tidings.[44]

Having established O'Donovan's own claims for the theological grounding of his natural ethic, we can press our question again, this time more precisely, and ask what is good news in particular about his elucidation of objective reality and thereby moral realism. Ultimately, O'Donovan gives us an answer by speaking of the impact of the *resurrection*, and assessing the adequacy of that proposal is the burden of the rest of this chapter. But before progressing to that consideration I want to highlight the significance of an answer that is implied within and presupposed by it, namely, that the *doctrine of creation* is already good news for ethics. Creation is, as we have already realized, O'Donovan's supreme doctrinal commitment. However we evaluate his articulation of the other moments of the divine economy, it is clear that his case for the objective basis of ethics is underwritten by an appeal to creation; if the moral order's objective reality is revealed as created, then the ordered form of creaturely existence tells us of its Creator's purposes.[45] If creation is still good, just as was identified by the divine pronouncement, then nature is reliable as a foundation for the moral life. From these affirmations, a more detailed picture unfurls, which we can now survey.

---

[43] O'Donovan, 'How Can Theology Be Moral?' *Journal of Religious Ethics* 17, no. 2 (1989): 81–94, 94, n. 2. The article was part of the journal's profile of 'evangelical ethics'. Even in O'Donovan's article 'Evangelicalism and the Foundations of Ethics' the word is more-often-than-not meant like this. Alongside other surveys cited in this study which place O'Donovan in the context of evangelical thought, see Dennis Hollinger and David P. Gushee, 'Evangelical Ethics: Profile of a Movement Come of Age', *The Annual of the Society of Christian Ethics* 20 (2000): 181–203. Jonathan Chaplin's editorial in the April 2017 issue of *Crucible: The Journal of Christian Social Ethics* – an issue entitled 'Evangelical Social Ethics' – describes O'Donovan as 'the most significant and original British evangelical social ethicist (and moral theologian) of our generation' (5).

[44] O'Donovan, *Resurrection*, 12. O'Donovan commends *Veritatis Splendor* for shaping 'the moral discourse of the Church as an evangelical proclamation'. O'Donovan, 'A Summons to Reality', 42.

[45] O'Donovan uses the language of creatureliness less than might be expected, at least for someone influenced by Barth. My treatment of *Resurrection*, however, draws heavily on this helpful vocabulary.

Creation

Consequent upon the conviction that creation is not formless or void, but good and ordered are the account's most important details, which, as McKenny's summary already began to lay out, seek to outline creation's definite, definitive characteristic. At the outset, O'Donovan analyses two classical ways of characterizing natural order.[46] Platonic conceptualities, first, are found hierarchical in a way inimical to Christian understanding. They are not wrong to understand the world as teleologically ordered, but their ontological schemas overemphasized 'higher' and 'lower' distinctions among forms, establishing teleological relations between them without regard for the true creatureliness of the very least. The Aristotelian version O'Donovan reviews more favourably, though he deems taxonomies concerning genus and species overdetermined. But it is a broadly Aristotelian framework that makes it through the analysis, with some Platonic supplementation. As McKenny says, *Resurrection and Moral Order*'s moral universe contains 'a metaphysical order of natural kinds and teleological relations'. By receiving the two classical elements into a theological approach, he self-consciously follows the lead of scholastic theologians, whose achievement he sees as integration of Aristotelian insights with Platonic teleology beyond the natural. (We are thinking here of the texture of creation, but notice that in keeping with this, in O'Donovan's idea of right moral reasoning, the consideration of kinds – which correspond to generic relations – and of ends – which correspond to telic relations – is imperative.)

In preserving a place for supernatural teleology alongside immanent teleologies of created order, we might expect O'Donovan's moral vision to possess at this point an overtly eschatological dimension. That dimension, we might anticipate, would see human creatures as always embedded within the world yet most basically longing for more, and creation as a whole directed by its final (supernatural) cause towards its ultimate end. To put it that way is to employ an idiom, I think, O'Donovan would be content with: in *Self-Love* he writes that for Augustine, the 'teleological thrust reaches its term in God alone'.[47] And *Resurrection and Moral Order* certainly shares this understanding. Nevertheless – and here is what I want to notice – any inclination to develop this dimension (might we call it transcendent?) is repeatedly controlled by reminders that humankind's progress 'towards a life which goes beyond this world' does not negate this world.[48] Our 'pilgrimage' to that 'supernatural end' is conducted here, in 'the reality of creation'.[49]

It is because of the strength of his this-worldly conviction, I think, that when O'Donovan defines teleological ethics, while acknowledging its reliance on 'the ontological conception of God as the *summum bonum*', he places the accent elsewhere.[50] For him, the tradition of teleological ethics is valuable predominantly as an approach 'in which it was the task of moral reasoning to recognise and respond to the ordered

---

[46] This paragraph paraphrases O'Donovan, *Resurrection*, 73–5.
[47] O'Donovan, *Self-Love*, 41.
[48] O'Donovan, *Resurrection*, 15.
[49] Ibid., 123.
[50] Ibid., 138.

structures of being and good'.[51] In the final instance, he does share teleology's interest in the eschatological *telos* of consummation to which creatures are drawn, but in his appropriation of teleology, Christian ethics is left – oddly – somewhat as it would be without the full extension of Christian theology's eschatological dimensions. That this can be the case, I argue, is explained by a particular type of eschatological commitment that O'Donovan holds besides this other, more transcendent one: a commitment we shall find instantiated in his all-determining interpretation of the resurrection.

The choice of resurrection

An observation by McKenny again serves to introduce our present theme: 'Moral theologies can be identified in part by the aspect of Christology they take to be fundamental for ethics, and debates in moral theology often turn on claims made for the centrality to ethics of the incarnation, the cross, or the resurrection.'[52] Identifying O'Donovan's moral theology according to these kinds of distinctions is largely straightforward, and among other early readers, James Gustafson did just that:

> For all of its 'orthodox Christianity', *Resurrection and Moral Order*, like any systematic account, bears the distinctive stamp of its author. One could have quite orthodox Christian ethics in which the crucifixion rather than the resurrection is featured (crucifixion is absent from this book), in which a divine command theory of ethics is defended, in which the historical ordering is more positively stated than is the created order, and so forth.[53]

Now, the question of historical ordering in relation to created order has been touched upon in Chapter 1 and will be returned to shortly. Moreover, there certainly is present an element of divine command theory – an abstract term, as O'Donovan would maintain.[54] And crucifixion is not absent from the book, as we shall see. But it is true that the resurrection is central, and O'Donovan does clarify his claim regarding its centrality, in view of other considerations, much like those Gustafson raises (evidently not all readers paid much attention to a small-print section where O'Donovan sets about that task).[55]

The centrality of the resurrection, explains O'Donovan, is a 'theological proposition since it cannot be substantiated directly by quoting from the text of the New Testament':

> Looking elsewhere we can find other 'ifs' that reinforce our commitment to the moral life. ... In ... the New Testament there is great freedom in reaching for aspects of the Christian kerygma that will afford us a motive for Christian

---

[51] Ibid.
[52] McKenny, *The Analogy of Grace: Karl Barth's Moral Theology*, 10.
[53] Gustafson, review of O'Donovan, *Resurrection*, 133.
[54] I say a little more below about divine command theory and natural law in O'Donovan, locating him within some recent work.
[55] O'Donovan, *Resurrection*, 13.

obedience. The advent of Christ, his death, resurrection and ascension, his sending of the Spirit and his expected return to judge, all these can and do incite believers to ethical seriousness. Even the simple example of Christ can incite us to imitate him. ... We are not attempting to deny the richness of the New Testament's ethical appeal; but it is the task of theology to uncover the hidden relation of things that gives the appeal force.[56]

O'Donovan pre-empts readings like Gustafson's with these and other comments (and he also redoubles his effort in the preface to the second edition). He is not unaware that things could have been otherwise. Each aspect of Christian proclamation attracts systematic theological reflection; none are ethically irrelevant. But for O'Donovan, the other moments orbit the resurrection as the kerygmatic lodestar, because he takes as his express focus the disciples' testimony that it changes everything.[57]

Or, rather – with more accuracy as regards O'Donovan's own sense of the resurrection's supremacy – what this seems to mean is not so much that it changes everything but rather that everything *hinges* on it. In the book's term of choice, the resurrection is a 'vindication' of creation.[58] Because we can confidently identify the God who raises Jesus from the dead as the Creator of the world, the event of Christ's resurrection reaffirms the given order of creation against dissolution; it stands against any and all corrosive effects of creaturely rebellion. Put together like this, we see 'the hidden relation of things that gives the appeal force', that it 'is the task of theology to uncover'.

But even if O'Donovan here describes that judgement as the task of theology as it reads and draws out the logic of Scripture, it could be argued that his case for the resurrection's centrality is *moral-theological* as much as, or before, it is a dogmatic one. What I think O'Donovan locates as especially valuable in the theme of the resurrection is the claim, condensed and made portable in his leading concept of vindication, that this order is proved to be beyond the jeopardy that it seemed to have been in. The proclamation of the resurrection bespeaks, for him, the restoration and fulfilment 'of the intelligible order of creation'.[59] In this, moral realism can lay claim to being good news: '[T]he gospel ... is God's last word about man's ambiguous relation to the created good.'[60] The ethical implications follow on in train, for if the resurrection is a resounding restatement of the divine intention that the created order be good (and stable), then it ought no longer be a matter of doubt that we must take heed of its structure in our moral deliberation. Questions concerning epistemology and sin that we carried from

---

[56] Ibid. We might add the transfiguration, following Orthodox thought; or the election of Jesus Christ from all eternity, following Barth; the teaching of Christ, following the Anabaptists; or the Exodus, following liberation theology.
[57] Cf. O'Donovan, *Thirty-Nine Articles*, 27. That book may be 'a work of high catechetics rather than scholarship' as O'Donovan suggests humbly in his preface to its second edition – no doubt wary of trespassing upon the territory of historical and dogmatic theologians – but its 'confident and voluble voice' (vii) allows readers useful insights into his doctrinal instincts at a similar time to O'Donovan, *Resurrection*.
[58] Drawing in this paragraph largely on O'Donovan, *Resurrection*, 13–15, but the theme recurs.
[59] O'Donovan, *Resurrection*, ix.
[60] Ibid., 178.

'The Natural Ethic' rightly resurface in relation to this account of created order and its vindication, but we must postpone investigation of them to Chapter 3. The point to grasp at present is that O'Donovan suggests moral theology should above all pay attention to God's faithfulness to creation, the chief moment of which faithfulness is Christ's resurrection.

One question we can raise directly now is about the repeated use of the term *vindication* as a consistent cipher for the redemptive act of God. It is a strong, imaginatively captivating motif that captures something of Scripture's dramatic presentation of salvation. Other moral theologians have picked it up in the wake of O'Donovan's use (for a worked example see the discussions of Joshua Hordern's work in Chapters 3 and 4).[61] But it would be valid to ask whether employing vindication as a controlling concept can obscure as well as clarify. At risk of reciting a truism, shorthand terms for salvation inevitably foreground certain aspects of God's work of grace over others. There are two features of O'Donovan's use of this term that I wish to highlight.

First, the term 'vindication' itself would normally seem to be used in connection with, say, vindication of the Psalmist, of Israel, of the oppressed, of the servants of the LORD, and of the LORD himself.[62] In other words, never directly in relation to the order of creation. That is not to say that such an association is illicit. But it may signify O'Donovan's tendency to show salvation's import for the natural order before its import for God's people, and it invites the query of whether this adequately reflects the way the words run, scripturally speaking.

Second, to use vindication as a soteriological motif, in the manner O'Donovan does, seems initially to suggest God's refusal of our refusal of the goodness of creation. Whether it suggests more than that I am not sure, but those who have taken it up have seen it, I think, as a comprehensive term. And O'Donovan himself does seem to use it in that way, for instance writing that the resurrection 'vindicates the created order in this double sense: it redeems it and transforms it'.[63] We therefore need to consider, going through, how 'vindication' might relate to those other concepts that O'Donovan makes use of, not least restoration, renewal and transformation. I will return to address this question in some detail at the end of the chapter. While it is always difficult to discern the pressures that influence an author's choice of vocabulary, nevertheless, 'the problem has a far greater fascination than if it were merely a matter of sighing over terminological loose ends in the work of a single theologian' (as O'Donovan wrote himself about Augustine's use of the language of self-love).[64] It is of great moment for

---

[61] See e.g. Gilbert Meilaender, *The Freedom of a Christian: Grace, Vocation, and the Meaning of Our Humanity* (Grand Rapids: Brazos, 2006), 39; Andrew J. B. Cameron, 'How to Say YES to the World: Towards a New Way Forward in Evangelical Social Ethics', *Reformed Theological Review* 66, no. 1 (2007), 23–36; and John Wyatt, 'The New Biotechnology', a chapter added in the fourth edition of John Stott, *Issues Facing Christians Today* (Grand Rapids: Zondervan, 2006). Stott himself draws on O'Donovan in earlier chapters of that widely influential book. I am not necessarily raising a critical point about any of these uses – simply observing a sample of O'Donovan's influence in this respect, from the United States to Australia and the United Kingdom.

[62] See e.g. Deut. 32.36; Ps. 24.5; 37.6; 98.2; 103.6; Is. 61.1–2; Jer. 51.10; Mic. 7.9.

[63] O'Donovan, *Resurrection*, 56.

[64] O'Donovan, *Self-Love*, 1.

how we think of creation and eschatology in theological ethics. At any rate, noticing how essential to his project this piece of O'Donovan's vocabulary is, I submit, shows as clearly as any quoted sentence can that O'Donovan's case for the centrality of the resurrection is at its heart ethical: what is vindicated in the created order is morality's objective basis.

That the case for the resurrection's centrality is moral-theological is equally evident from O'Donovan's argument that implied in the vindication of objective order is the concomitant vindication and reaffirmation of *human agency*. This chapter has focused first on the objectivity of created order in which and with which we find ourselves,[65] and I take up the theme of agency in Chapter 3. But we should already note the close link in *Resurrection and Moral Order* between objectivity and moral agency. O'Donovan sees the goodness of given order not just in that creaturely things are ordered generically and teleologically but also in that our actions have kinds and ends, and that our reasoning-to-action can be orderly. According to Andrew Errington, the 'notion of generic kinds of action is the most important goal of O'Donovan's account of created order'.[66] I have drawn attention to other goals of O'Donovan's account that I take to be prominent, but Errington's insight is astute, and if other goals are as important, they are mutually implicating.

Reflection upon human agency is the task that O'Donovan proposes as paradigmatic for ethics as a discipline. And if the Christian ethicist characteristically searches for a properly theological footing for this endeavour, O'Donovan understands himself to be offering resolution by making the resurrection his focal point: the resurrection can anchor an account of moral agency because it represents the moment that freedom was secured once and for all.[67] If morality is 'participation in the created order', 'Christian morality' is 'glad response to the deed of God which has restored, proved and fulfilled

---

[65] By 'with which' I denote, e.g. our somatic form, as well as the nature of other creatures. O'Donovan's conviction about the givenness of bodies is applied in his *Transsexualism and the Christian Marriage* (Bramcote: Grove Books, 1982), also published in the *Journal of Religious Ethics* (1983) and reissued in 2007. For three different responses to this book ranging from broadly sympathetic to extremely critical, see Brian Brock, *Christian Ethics in a Technological Age* (Grand Rapids: Eerdmans, 2010), 331–5; Robert Song, 'Bodily Integrity Disorder and the Ethics of Mutilation', *Studies in Christian Ethics* 26, no. 4 (2013): 487–503 (reprinted in *The Authority of the Gospel*); and Gerard Loughlin, 'Being creature, becoming human: Contesting Oliver O'Donovan on transgender, identity and the body', *ABC Religion and Ethics* (5 September 2018), https://www.abc.net.au/religion/being-creature-becoming-human-contesting-oliver-odonovan-on-tran/10214276 (accessed 26 September 2019).

[66] Andrew Errington, *Every Good Path: Wisdom and Practical Reason in Christian Ethics and the Book of Proverbs* (London: T & T Clark, 2020), 150. This excellent study includes more detailed treatment of O'Donovan's account of action than is presented here. I concur with the recommendation of Daniel Westberg, when in a list of desirable features for a renewed moral theology, he writes under the heading 'Catholic and Evangelical' that 'O'Donovan, as an Anglican, provides a clear model (and challenge) in keeping before us the call to be evangelical and christocentric, but at the same time to have the patience to work through the details of practical reasoning and the analysis of action associated with Roman Catholic ethics'. *Renewing Moral Theology: Christian Ethics as Action, Character, and Grace* (Downers Grove: IVP, 2015), 27–8. For O'Donovan's most direct account see 'Christian Moral Reflection', in *New Dictionary of Christian Ethics and Pastoral Theology*, ed. David J. Atkinson and David H. Field (Downer's Grove: IVP, 1995), 122–8. In particular, its perspicuous formulation of the two complementary movements of 'moral reflection' and 'moral deliberation' has gained currency.

[67] O'Donovan, *Resurrection*, xviii.

that order, making man free to conform to it'.[68] This account is not unpersuasive. It is both theologically substantial and conceptually elegant. Its merits notwithstanding, however, in later chapters I will raise the suspicion that O'Donovan may presume, *a priori*, the task of vouchsafing free human action to such an extent as to subtly distort the proportions of his theology. As a result, some moral implications of eschatology and sin – each of which may shape quite dramatically a theological narration of human action – can seem to be shirked. But at this point, we should continue to address *Resurrection and Moral Order*'s claims about human action on their own terms.

Paramount in the illustration of O'Donovan's understanding of the resurrection's significance for ethics are the figures of the first and second Adam. The resurrection's meaning 'is that it is God's final and decisive word on the life of his creature, Adam': God's 'No' to Adam's decision that left humankind mired in sin and destined for death, encompassed by God's 'Yes' to created order. Humankind's rebellion against God and God's world has not been allowed to win out, but has been overcome by Jesus Christ, the second Adam. This recapitulatory divine action unerringly restates the Edenic orientation of the Adamic – towards life. There is not space to explore O'Donovan's implicit Christology in depth here, but we will get the gist of it (and its power) if we understand that at its heart lies a Pauline, patristic, and Reformed understanding of *representation*.[69] The key point of this understanding to fathom for his moral theology – there are ramifications in the theo-political work, too[70] – is this. It was possible, before Christ's resurrection, to wonder whether 'creation was a lost cause', whether 'God's handiwork was flawed beyond hope of repair', because of the creature's consistent effort 'to uncreate itself, and … the rest of creation'.[71] But Christ has been raised, and 'in the second Adam the first is rescued'; he 'has not been allowed to uncreate what God created'.[72]

That Christological – and, just so, soteriological – image of representation is therefore important for O'Donovan's theological anthropology and its relation to his cosmology (for want of a better term). To further appreciate the significance of this nexus, we need first to note his anthropology's pivotal thesis. Both Eastern and Western Christian traditions, O'Donovan argues, emphasize the existence of a specific human nature, established in the act of creation, and replete with native excellences and virtues.[73] He deliberately enlists this traditional principle in preference to what are castigated as the 'ectoplasmic' formulas of modern attempts to detail humanity's

---

[68] Ibid., 76.
[69] For confirmation of the Reformed idiom, see O'Donovan, *Thirty-Nine Articles* (78–9), and 'Oliver O'Donovan-Moral Reality', in *Being in Christ: A Biblical and Systematic Investigation in a Reformed Perspective*, ed. Hans Burger (Eugene: Wipf & Stock, 2009).
[70] See e.g. O'Donovan, *Ways*, ch. 9 (149–63, especially 157–8 for the theological element).
[71] O'Donovan, *Resurrection*, 14.
[72] Ibid. Murray Rae takes up these passages appreciatively, but seems to entertain more seriously than O'Donovan the challenge that 'considered in itself' history 'is left with that verdict'. Rae's account of how 'the alteration to history' effected in the resurrection manifests itself in the world today focuses on themes of witness and intercessory prayer. Behind this subtly different sensibility is, I think, a different (more Kierkegaardian) judgement about the relationship of faith and history. Rae, 'Salvation and History', in *God of Salvation: Soteriology in Theological Perspective*, ed. Ivor J. Davidson and Murray Rae (Farnham: Ashgate, 2011), 97, 100–3.
[73] O'Donovan, *Resurrection*, 17.

definitive character.[74] Taking 'radical freedom' as one such nebulous hypothesis, O'Donovan is caustically sceptical about any such bid to discern and describe the nature of humanity without reference to circumambient natural realities. Instead, we should recognize that humankind finds its dwelling within a broader universe of fellow creatures, from which the concept of humanity is 'actually inseparable'.[75]

For O'Donovan, the redemption of humankind is likewise inseparable from the redemption of the rest of creation. Because Christ represents Adam and his kin, and in and with them the whole created realm that they represent, the restoration of humankind entailed in the resurrection is also the inexorable vindication of the order of things in which humankind took its place and in which it continues to exist. The moral pendant of this particular Christological metaphysics is once more the reaffirmation of the created order as the place of our moral action; redeemed creatures no less than pre-lapsarian ones live and move and have their being in that ordered world.

That, I think, is how the pieces of O'Donovan's basic argument fit together. We are now in a position to make an initial comment upon it. We may expect that talk of the resurrection would go on more predominantly in an eschatological register than O'Donovan's here. (That is not to say that language of future hope, of transformation and so on are absent – we shall see that in due course.) But in the first movements of *Resurrection and Moral Order*'s argument, that kind of language seems to be more-often-than-not indexed to the language of vindication. Formally, this is simply because – like 'The Natural Ethic' – O'Donovan's presentation moves carefully and sequentially from one affirmation to another. Again, like the earlier article, the way the sequence plays out seems to prioritize the affirmation of nature. Materially, we have seen that the variety of moral realism espoused by *Resurrection and Moral Order* adjudges the resurrection massively significant, but that it registers that significance initially in relation to existing order.

It seems to me that there are at least two noteworthy implications. First, it follows from O'Donovan's perspective that the objective referent of Christian ethics is in the most basic sense no different than the one that confronts humankind in general.[76] This raises important questions concerning the universal and the particular dimensions of Christian ethics. Second, and somewhat counter-intuitively, gauged from the angle of the book's basic claims, while the resurrection seems to be a symbol of vast importance for how we conceive of the reality with which morality has to do, at times on O'Donovan's account, the resurrection itself may appear to be of primarily epistemological consequence. Let us explore each implication in turn.

Universal and particular

First, on O'Donovan's understanding of the resurrection, the reality that has been vindicated is the world that all of us bump up against. Christian ethics can thus speak

---

[74] Ibid., 18.
[75] Ibid.
[76] See O'Donovan, *Resurrection*, 17.

about the natural order not merely as a niche intellectual discipline but as a discourse with universal reach: 'The summons to live in it is addressed to all mankind, because the good news that we *may* live in it is address to all mankind.'[77] One does not 'opt in' to this tradition of inquiry and its way of seeing the world; it spans all things in their deepest reality, potentially illuminating the widest range of moral circumstances.

This set of claims are made by moral theologians in different ways, and it is worth considering, briefly, how O'Donovan's argument might be situated in relation to one or two others. Among proponents of natural law, Herbert McCabe provides the most memorable – if characteristically hyperbolic – articulation of the universality claimed by this approach:

> There is no such thing as Christian ethics. There is just ethics. Christians may have contributed quite a lot towards our understanding of ethics (as well as contributing a certain amount to our misunderstanding), but ethics, like all other human knowledge, belongs to mankind. It cannot be the secret doctrine of a sect. This, incidentally, is what Catholics are talking about when they speak of natural law: they want to emphasise that ethics a matter of our common humanity, and not of some esoteric teaching.[78]

In just this way, natural law is thought to be attractive in its latitude, its relevance to the entire sphere of human affairs. McCabe and O'Donovan clearly share an instinct here, and their arguments seem to be motivated by similar doctrinal commitments. True, natural law claims – including McCabe's, if we read beyond this quotation – are typically based directly on creation without the kind of refraction through resurrection that is O'Donovan's presupposition. But it is not immediately apparent what difference O'Donovan's starting point makes.

Nonetheless, the instinct about universality McCabe expresses with deflationary intent can sometimes sound much more aspirational, even emphatic, when made by O'Donovan.[79] One reason for this is that his approach to ethical universality is at times of a more explicitly Christological cast than that of McCabe (and, to a greater or lesser extent, those of perhaps almost all other natural lawyers). If McCabe wishes to remind Christians that when they 'do' ethics, they are participating in a common human endeavour, O'Donovan wishes to remind Christians that the gospel they proclaim addresses human morality as such, given the claims it makes about the realities of creaturely life in the world. Again, for some, natural law is especially appealing because in enables attention be given chiefly to the rational evaluation of intra-mundane goods, and it may thereby be thought to offer grounds for moral agreement across traditions – but this goal does not seem to be the one motivating O'Donovan's argument for a natural ethic. His fundamental moral theology is, I think, less about establishing

---

[77] Ibid.
[78] Herbert McCabe, *God Matters* (London: Bloomsbury, 1987), 19. Cf. Victor Lee Austin, *Christian Ethics: A Guide for the Perplexed* (London: Bloomsbury, 2012), 36–9.
[79] Evangelical 'creation ethics' seems to have been in part motivated by intentions similar to natural law reasoning, if more combined with expressly apologetic aims – see e.g. Barclay, 'Creation and Providence', 6.

common grounds than it is about putting Christian ethics on the front foot; even less is his intention levelling the playing field.

We might say that *Resurrection and Moral Order* tries to hold together universal claims with those of a more particularist (it could be said, post-liberal) character. This lends a certain complexity to O'Donovan's thought that can make it difficult to classify. For instance, Samuel Wells and Ben Quash place O'Donovan, alongside Hauerwas and Milbank, in their (favoured) category 'Ecclesial Ethics', distinguished – for pedagogical purposes at least – from 'Universal Ethics' and 'Subversive Ethics'. However, they note that because, for O'Donovan, 'the sources of Christian ethics are available to everybody and binding on everybody … yet they are derived from authorities only Christians recognise … O'Donovan is a kind of bridge figure between ecclesial ethics and universal ethics'.[80] In a compelling recent essay, Nicholas Townsend suggests that O'Donovan's bridge position – and that of Nigel Biggar – actually indicates a flaw in Wells and Quash's typology.[81] Descriptively that is surely true, but given that their own perspective seems contentedly 'ecclesial', I wonder whether their acknowledgement that O'Donovan's thought in certain respects reaches across to a 'universal' perspective is a tacit criticism of its coherence. Might it imply that the bridge is in truth sometimes shakier than it seems?

On my reading, O'Donovan often attempts to hold together universal and more particularist claims this by funnelling the former through the latter:

> In the sphere of revelation, we will conclude, and only there, can we see the natural order as it really is and overcome the epistemological barriers to an ethic that conforms to nature. This nature involves all men, and indeed … does include a certain 'natural knowledge' which is also part of man's created endowment. And yet only in Christ do we apprehend that order in which we stand and that knowledge of it with which we have been endowed.[82]

I will touch on the epistemological question shortly, and Chapter 3 will afford a closer look at epistemological issues, with the chance to plumb what that 'in Christ' might mean for morality. But for now let us consider the way O'Donovan draws a distinction on similar grounds between his approach and an approach in ('new') natural law that was then particularly influential:

> The difference between Finnis and myself, then, seems to amount to this: while I believe that a distinct behaviour is demanded by the resurrection of Jesus, he believes that the same behaviour is demanded which was demanded anyway, but that the demand is clearer and more cogently perceived.[83]

---

[80] Samuel Wells and Ben Quash, *Introducing Christian Ethics* (Chichester: Wiley-Blackwell, 2010), 191.
[81] Nicholas Townsend, 'Should Jesus Christ Be at the Centre of Introductions to Christian Ethics?' *Studies in Christian Ethics* 33, no. 1 (2020): 95–106, 101.
[82] O'Donovan, *Resurrection*, 20.
[83] Ibid., ix.

The position that O'Donovan stakes for himself is appealing. But from what we have read, it has seemed like the resurrection's impact is precisely to make 'the demand' of the created order 'clearer and more cogently perceived'. To be sure, *Resurrection and Moral Order* like 'The Natural Ethic' will subsequently allow for the possibility of 'distinct behaviour … demanded by the resurrection of Jesus'. It would therefore be more accurate to say that O'Donovan seems to believe *both* what he attributes to Finnis here *and* what he attributes to himself. At this stage, though, it is not clear what that 'distinct behaviour' might be, and how it figures in the Christian moral life alongside that 'which was demanded anyway'. I suggest that O'Donovan's whole position is probably quite well summarized in claims set out not by O'Donovan himself, but by Gilbert Meilaender:

> The God who commands at Sinai has created a world with a morally coherent shape and form – a shape that is knowable, at least in part, by those who have not yet found themselves in covenant with Israel's God. … Israel's God does not, however, leave his people to their own inadequate attempts to discern this order embedded in the creation. He is gracious enough to speak, to command … . We know, of course, that in the history of redemption the incarnate God himself must finally vindicate the moral order of creation in the face of human failure and disobedience. Moreover, we who in our baptism have come to name Jesus as Lord, are called not just to discern the shape of creation or listen for the commands of Torah, but also to understand the moral life as discipleship, as following Jesus in his obedience to the Father.[84]

The meaning of the resurrection

Second, to repeat, gauged from the angle of the book's basic claims, while the resurrection seems to be a symbol of vast importance, it appears sometimes to be of primarily epistemological consequence. This may seem a strange comment, given O'Donovan's strong commitment to the implications for morality of reality beyond the human mind. Yet in his book's first strand of argumentation, the resurrection does not seem to change reality but – in Christ – to reaffirm it, and to redirect our moral gaze towards it. Its significance does not appear necessarily to be in, say, its commendation of a new order that norms our action, but in its function as the noetic condition of possibility for true comprehension of an existing order. The resurrection is a sovereign gesture of re-presentation, of re-authorization; in it God commends the creation to us. 'We must speak about creation', writes O'Donovan, 'because in Jesus' resurrection God has given back the created world'.[85] (Robin Parry's laconic summary of the argument of *Resurrection and Moral Order* expresses just this idea: 'A gospel ethic is a resurrection ethic, which is a renewed creation ethic.')[86]

---

[84] Meilaender, *Freedom of a Christian*, 39.
[85] O'Donovan, *Resurrection*, xvii.
[86] Parry, 'Evangelicalism and Ethics', 187. Parry regards this as O'Donovan's achievement – see further below.

To be clear, if I have called the resurrection a symbol of vast importance for O'Donovan, I do not at all mean by this that his understanding of the resurrection as an event represents a symbolic understanding of a Schleiermacherian, Bultmannian, or Tillichian kind (granting that none of these are straightforward). If we set aside the moral dimensions of O'Donovan's understanding for a moment, we will find that O'Donovan's understanding of the resurrection is squarely realist, as located in the context of twentieth-century theological discussion. In the terms of David Fergusson's heuristic of types within this debate, it is surely 'traditional' rather than 'radical' or 'liberal'.[87] On George Hunsinger's more recent typology, O'Donovan's understanding would likely be placed at the antipode of that space Hunsinger populates with Schleiermacher, Bultmann and Tillich; it would sit with the 'second type', represented by Pannenberg and N. T. Wright – two figures with whose work O'Donovan is familiar, as we shall see in more detail later.[88] O'Donovan holds, for instance, that 'the authority of God is not incommunicable, interior and removed from public view, but is located in the public realm in an event of history which may be told', namely, the resurrection.[89] In *Thirty-Nine Articles*, he explicitly cautions against 'giving the resurrection a merely noetic or explanatory function … at the cost of overthrowing the character of redemption as history'.[90] Wells and Quash, then, are not wrong to characterize O'Donovan's view of the resurrection as 'normative' (in contrast to Bultmann's 'illustrative' view), or to say that on the 'normative' view, the implications for ethics are 'enormous, perhaps definitive'.[91]

The critical claim I am making operates on something of a different level, though it carries its own provocation. It unspools as follows. O'Donovan's historical realism indubitably licences (and perhaps implies) attribution of significant ontological gravity to the resurrection: it really happened, and it really had an effect. Yet the ontological aspect is couched so much in terms of continuity that the only thing that could possibly be new about the resurrection would seem to be its efficacious work in securing knowledge where there was doubt.[92] In this scheme, the resurrection makes possible right apprehension of what was obscured but has always been there just the same. In other words, O'Donovan's presentation of the resurrection *is* at risk of giving it 'a merely noetic or explanatory function' when considered in its implications *for the determining metaphysics of morals*.

Though this is the claim I wish to defend, a bolder, more provocative one could be made. Raising it may help us see some of the distinctions at stake. Might O'Donovan

---

[87] David Fergusson, 'Interpreting the Resurrection', *Scottish Journal of Theology* 38, no. 3 (1985): 287–305.

[88] George Hunsinger, 'The Daybreak of the New Creation: Christ's Resurrection in Recent Theology', *Scottish Journal of Theology* 57, no. 2 (2004): 163–81. Hunsinger considers these theologians' approach laudable, but as 'elevating history at the expense of transcendence' (163). Moltmann, Hans Frei and Barth comprise Hunsinger's favoured third type.

[89] O'Donovan, *Resurrection*, 141. Though note in a different context O'Donovan's critique of Pannenberg's historicism, mentioned below.

[90] O'Donovan, *Thirty-Nine Articles*, 28.

[91] Wells and Quash, *Introducing Christian Ethics*, 19.

[92] Here, too, a comparison with Wright may be apt. See, critically, Samuel V. Adams, *The Reality of God and Historical Method: Apocalyptic Theology in Conversation with N.T. Wright* (Downers Grove: IVP Academic, 2015), 153–6.

sometimes write as if Christ's resurrection is not just the first fruits of but has already effected the cosmic renewal traditionally counted among the 'Last Things'? Consider again a line from the book's preface, which when speaking of 'the resurrection of Jesus from the dead', continues in the past tense that it 'restored and fulfilled the intelligible order of creation'.[93] Or another we have already quoted, which states that the resurrection 'restored, proved and fulfilled that order'.[94]

We might also pause over these sentences from 'The Foundations of Ethics', an article that condenses the argument of *Resurrection and Moral Order*:

> The resurrection of mankind in Christ is the reversal of that slide from created order into dissolution that began in Adam's disobedience. The resurrection of the race means that we may live, but not merely live in our disordered state but live in a renewed order. Renewal is not hope for isolated individuals alone; it means participating in a world that has been renewed.[95]

I grant wholly that the image of representation that is operative here appropriately allows one to speak in the present tense of the 'resurrection of mankind in Christ'. The sense of participation it carries does even allow us to speak in a meaningful way of the 'resurrection of the race' as already accomplished, though stated alone that might mislead (we await the general resurrection, after all). It might also be possible to speak fittingly in the present tense of 'a renewed order', if by that we indicate the proleptic anticipation of new creation – perfectly in the life of Christ, falteringly in the life of his church. But to speak of 'participating in a world that has been renewed' in the strong sense that O'Donovan sometimes appears to imply seems to go further towards the completion of 'reversal' than the sense of inauguration we might expect. To make sense of it we would seem to need to understand as already realized the fulfilment and perfection of creation that scriptural authors seem to await as the future manifestation of Christ's achievement; 'salvation ready to be revealed in the last time' (1 Pet. 1.5).[96]

I do not think O'Donovan wants to say this. Sometimes he is much clearer: 'The resurrection of Christ ... is the promise, but not the fulfilment, of a world-redemption yet to be completed; the order there renewed and vindicated in principle still awaits its universal manifestation.'[97] And I concede that ambiguity concerning the temporal reference of soteriological and eschatological claims is to a point the result of tensions created by biblical testimony (and by the ineffability of the mysteries to which Scripture witnesses). In view of those tensions, it is difficult to avoid parsing the 'now' and 'not yet' of eschatology – the 'already' and 'still more'[98] – with a degree of obscurity unhelpful in the depiction of the Christian life. On the other hand, if we read the repeated past

---

[93] O'Donovan, *Resurrection*, ix.
[94] Ibid., 76.
[95] O'Donovan, 'The Foundations of Ethics', 97.
[96] See also, classically, Rom. 8.18-25. O'Donovan does at times recognize this; in *Resurrection* (243), he speaks of 'the non-human creation await[ing] its redemption' in Christ, but the point is typically made to highlight the scope of redemption in terms of the natural (indeed cosmic) order, rather than its futural element.
[97] O'Donovan, *Resurrection*, 22.
[98] So Martinus C. de Boer, *Galatians: A Commentary* (Louisville: Westminster John Knox, 2011), 34.

tense of O'Donovan's descriptions as indicating the over-realization of eschatological fulfilment, then, for the sake of the orderly depiction of that life, O'Donovan seems to assume a degree of clarity that we are not given to confess.

What we seem to find is O'Donovan risking the implication *either* that created order has not been marred by sin in any significant manner, *or*, that if it was, it has already been restored in an overt sense. In the first case, the resurrection means epistemic rectification: the decisive declaration that creation is good, to the falsification of human pretensions (and it would be pretence rather than capacity) to have effectively tampered with it. In the second, the resurrection also already effected an ontological restoration.

However, I submit that perhaps the more modest account we should charitably understand O'Donovan to be making – or, if he is not, the one we might make instead – is something like the following (and here I will quote other theologians in order to make it). The Christian, believing in the resurrection as 'the already commenced and yet-to-come restoration of Creation as Creation', being freed from conformity to the disorder of sin, lives 'as if' that restoration was already fully actualized.[99] Thus, in hope, the Christian 'reaches towards the coming consummation and glorification, acting in and upon the world as the reality which it will be'.[100] And we must recall, to complicate matters appropriately, that living 'as if' in witness to creation's eschatological consummation involves inhabiting 'as if not' the world in its current state.[101] To see why O'Donovan is led to such a strong and sometimes overstated defence of the integrity of the created order – an overstatement that seems to affect the way eschatology is articulated – we need, as in Chapter 1, to consider his reaction to historicism.

---

[99] John Milbank, 'Can Morality Be Christian?' in *The Word Made Strange: Theology, Language, Culture* (Oxford: Blackwell, 1997), 229. The passage reads as follows:

> To believe in plenitude is to believe in the already commenced and yet-to-come restoration of Creation as Creation. ... This belief is belief in resurrection. As resurrection cancels death, and appears to render murder non-serious, it restores no moral order, but absolutely ruins the possibility of *any* moral order whatsoever. That is to say, any reactive moral order, which presupposes the absoluteness of death. For the Christian, murder is wrong, not because it removes something irreplaceable, but because it repeats the Satanic founding of *instituting* death, or the very *possibility* of irreplaceability, and absolute loss. But in the resurrected order there need be no law even against such Satanism, because it is so manifestly senseless, because this possibility occurs to no one, because here the only law is that of *nature*, that of *life*, but specifically human life which consciously partakes of the creativity of God. Here, at last, in the Resurrection, there is only natural law (and in *this* sense I concur with Oliver O'Donovan). For in the resurrected order, in the life of our vision of God in his final Christic manifestation, the occasion for the exercise of death-presupposing virtue (as Paul says) drops away, and only charity – gift and counter-gift – remain.

> Milbank himself is not particularly clear about the temporal reference of his statements, for instance the 'Here, at last' – but we should take them as having present *moral* implication as the phrase 'as if' indicates a little higher on the same page, before the quoted sentences.

[100] John Webster, 'Hope', in *The Oxford Handbook to Theological Ethics*, ed. Gilbert Meilaender and William Werpehowski (New York/Oxford: Oxford University Press, 2005), 291–306, 304.

[101] 1 Cor. 7.29. Cf. Kroeker, 'Living "As If Not": Messianic Becoming or the Practice of Nihilism', in *Messianic Political Theology*, 15–33.

Against historicism

The section of *Resurrection and Moral Order* entitled 'Eschatology and History' does return us in part to the pattern of exposition in 'The Natural Ethic'. The bones of the account are already there in the earlier piece, and O'Donovan's criticism of historicism in the later book is similarly assertive, such that Gustafson can write that 'on the basis of his argument for the moral order and its knowability' O'Donovan 'fulminates against "historicism" ... in a quite unnuanced way'.[102] Without doubt, O'Donovan's treatment has not yet developed the nuance achieved in *Ethics as Theology*. There are critical questions to be asked about the relation of the moral order to history, too, some of which are pursued in the following. But here we do find a more detailed depiction of historicism than in 'The Natural Ethic', along with a longer catalogue of its ethical effects and many constructive comments about Christian ethics. Understanding why O'Donovan lands the way he does on contemporary moral questions requires understanding of this depiction and catalogue as much as anything else. This subchapter of my study is intended to aid the reader to that end.

The occasional rhetorical flourish of O'Donovan's 'fulmination' in various passages *adversus* historicism does produce a set of memorable characterizations. Among them is the succinct definition of historicism as an attitude for which 'all teleology is historical teleology'.[103] Occasionally, however, the overdrawn way in which historicism

---

[102] Gustafson, review of *Resurrection*, 132. On the shifting attitude to natural universality and historical particularity in Gustafson's own work, see Stanley Hauerwas, 'Time and History in Theological Ethics: The Work of James Gustafson', *Journal of Religious Ethics*, 13, no. 1 (1985): 3–21. Besides Strauss, George Grant and Hannah Arendt inform O'Donovan's thought – see O'Donovan, *Resurrection*, 67. Joan Lockwood O'Donovan doubtless contributed much to the understanding of Grant in particular. See her monograph *George Grant and the Twilight of Justice* (Toronto: University of Toronto Press, 1984). Grant's critique of technological modernity has, like those of Jacques Ellul and Leo Strauss, certainly influenced O'Donovan deeply. For more on Grant in this respect, see Brian Brock, *Christian Ethics in a Technological Age* (Grand Rapids: Eerdmans, 2010), especially 66–101. Cf. Robert Song, *Christianity and Liberal Society* (Oxford: Oxford University Press, 1997), a work originating in an Oxford DPhil. supervised by O'Donovan.

[103] O'Donovan, *Resurrection*, 58. Worth comparing is a programmatic article published slightly earlier by Timothy F. Sedgwick: 'Revising Anglican Moral Theology', in *The Future of Anglican Theology*, ed. M. Darrol Bryant (New York: Edwin Mellon, 1984). Sedgwick employs Bernard Lonergan's account of 'The Transition from a Classicist World-View to Historical Mindedness' to draw a contrast between a prior 'intellectualist framework' which 'assumed that values are objective, that ... stand for qualities or relations that are independent of us, and which we as rational beings are then able to grasp universally', and 'the alternative claim that values are human symbols which express the evaluative understanding which persons have made. Values arise historically and so express a particular historical understanding and vision'. Post-Oxford Movement Anglican moral theologians like Kirk, he says, followed Thomist rationalism, but we – following developments post-Vatican II – ought to embrace this alternative claim, viewing the self 'in terms of responsibility': 'Morality is a human creation that expresses our developing identity' (136–9). O'Donovan by no means simply avows that Thomism, but he usually does have more in common with a trajectory of pre- and post-Vatican II Catholic moral theology represented by Dominicans like Pinckaers and Cessario, and indeed Popes John Paul II and Benedict XVI, than those Sedgwick has in mind, like Fuchs, Häring, Charles Curran or Richard McCormick. (O'Donovan would have been firmly on Ramsey's side in his debate with the last, and in agreement with *Veritatis Splendor*'s criticism of proportionalism.) That first trajectory, it has been argued by another Anglican Sedgwick – Peter – inhibited ecumenical progress on moral matters: a claim with some plausibility as regards the possibility of easy ecumenical concord, but too committed to the assumption that Anglican moral

is ventriloquized again comes close to taking back what was given in O'Donovan's own belated but significant affirmations of eschatology. For historicism,

> what we took to be natural orderings-to-serve and orderings-to-flourish within the regularities of nature are in fact something quite different: they are orderings to transformation, and so break out altogether from nature's order. The natural exists only to be superseded: everything within it serves only a supernatural end, the end of history.[104]

This is a little curious because later we will note O'Donovan clarifying that the restoration of Eden is precisely restoration to its ordering-to-transformation, that the supernatural end is the created order's true *telos*, and that this eschatological ordering becomes visible at particular moments ('breaking out', for example, in the vocation of singleness). Nonetheless, the basic sketch is clear enough, and the aim of passages like those quoted is to distinguish historicist attitudes to *nature* from O'Donovan's own. For him, nature's objective value (and thus normativity) is never superseded; for them, 'natural order and natural meanings are understood only as moments in the historical process, and their value lies not in any integrity of their own but in being raw material for transformation'.[105]

Similar treatments of historicism elsewhere in O'Donovan's work can be adduced. In *Common Objects*, for instance, he identifies a historicist 'conviction that the identity of any thing lies in change', a 'rejection of fixed essences' that marks 'a society that has departed from the philosophical beliefs of its ancestors'.[106] But another place where these themes are tackled at greater length, where we find passages that display as frankly as anywhere the theological rudiments of O'Donovan's critique, is *Church in Crisis*. As *Begotten or Made?* provided a helpful case study of the major principles of 'The Natural Ethic', so *Church in Crisis* displays a number of aspects of the argument of *Resurrection and Moral Order*.

Case study: *Church in Crisis*

Here, in an excoriation of liberal theology, O'Donovan writes:

> The dialectic of creation and redemption is not merely one episode in the struggle between orthodoxy and revision. It is its central and decisive battleground. It

theology will *always* be more compatible with the second trajectory. That is falsified by O'Donovan's work and presence on ARCIC II, apart from anything else. (Peter Sedgwick, 'Anglican Moral Theology and Ecumenical Dialogue', *Religions* 8, no. 9 (2017): 63–70).

[104] O'Donovan, *Resurrection*, 58. Whether that is true of all historicisms, I am not sure; for Hegel at least, the reality may be more complex – see Frederick C. Beiser, 'Hegel's Historicism', in *The Cambridge Companion to Hegel*, ed. Frederick C. Beiser (Cambridge: Cambridge University Press, 1993), 279.
[105] O'Donovan, *Resurrection*, 59.
[106] O'Donovan, *Common Objects*, 67.

gives their shape to the creeds that differentiate Christianity from deism. What is the underlying doubt that causes them, with greater or lesser embarrassment, to shuffle uncertainly towards doctrinal revision at this decisive point? The answer is, as I take it, a simple moral mistake, centrally characteristic of liberal Christianity. The mistake is called 'historicism', and it consists in confusing the good with the future. It induces a profound loss of nerve over any claim to discern the good hand of God within the order of a good creation.[107]

The overall point is powerful. But its presentation in this quotation does not do as much as we might like, though, to avoid the risks of the typology found in 'The Natural Ethic', which threatened to conflate constructive moral-theological mention of the future with historicism, in opposition to the protological good that such an ethic prefers.[108] While I have no desire to wade here into the specific issues that the book speaks to (I think it is in many ways an acutely insightful treatment), I will offer a structural observation relevant to my theme.

Chapter 6 of *Church in Crisis* is entitled 'Creation, Redemption, and Nature', and can be read as locating something like O'Donovan's core convictions within the fundamental theological strata of the ecclesial conversation about human sexuality. In the pages that follow, he deploys them in a disagreement with Robert Merrihew Adams. And I would suggest that O'Donovan likely overreaches towards a 'creation ethic' in his argument, partly because of a basically well-founded allergy to the way in which Adams transfers 'the whole normative content of creation … to eschatology' without theological warrant.[109] Witness how it is antipathy to an unwarranted relocation of normative content that educes from O'Donovan the strongest possible enunciations of a set of core convictions. 'New creation is creation renewed, a restoration and enhancement, not an abolition. Not everything that can be thought of as future can be thought of as the kingdom of God.'[110] What is at stake is 'moral responsibility to the real', that 'love of what is', which 'is precisely what the dialectic of creation and redemption safeguarded', and without which '"the new creation" is an empty symbol'.[111]

Slightly earlier, O'Donovan has defended 'the step from a philosophy of nature to a theology of creation'.[112] This 'is not to abandon one set of interests in favour of another', contrary to the perception.[113] A theologian can make the step without trepidation or trespass, because

> the revealed purposes of God in creation will direct our attention back to *the world*, i.e. the totality of what there God has made, and teach us how to see the good he has given us within it. Any purposes God has in making the world are to be discerned in the world; they are not set apart from it somewhere else. Any

---

[107] O'Donovan, *Church in Crisis*, 88.
[108] Ibid., 97–9.
[109] Ibid., 98.
[110] Ibid., 99.
[111] Ibid.
[112] Ibid., 96.
[113] Ibid.

discernment of how the world works will, *pari passu*, be a discernment of the purposes of God.[114]

Now, I readily agree that Adams's argument seems theologically unsteady, as relayed and possibly on its own terms. O'Donovan's sharp rejoinder has, for the most part, the tradition's 'dialectic of creation and redemption' on its side. But I do not think he has to set the matter up this way in order to make it, and setting it up this way leaves something important out. A theological dialectic of creation and redemption, should it be rigorously pursued, must surely identify the normative content, not just of creation but *of redemption*, beyond refutation of some contemporaries' transfer of normativity from first things to last in an attempt to move the goalposts of ethical value.

Understanding better why O'Donovan is prone to overreach towards a purely 'creation ethics' requires clarifying his concerns about historicist moral philosophy and the faulty metaphysics he argues it conveys. Let us return from our case study in *Church in Crisis* to the examples he gives in the part of *Resurrection and Moral Order* we began exploring beforehand.

On historicist metaphysics

As historicism departs from classical Christian divinity ontologically, O'Donovan says, it also takes leave of orthodox thought on moral matters. In traditional theology, the link was tight between the two: moral thought 'proceeded from a universal order of meaning and value, an order given in creation and fulfilled in the kingdom of God, an order, therefore, which forms a framework for all action and history, to which action is summoned to conform in its making of history'.[115] In historicism, it is also tight, but to opposite effect. Denying any such order and ascription of value, historicism teaches that '[a]ction cannot be conformed to transhistorical values, for there are none, but must respond to the immanent dynamisms of that history to which it finds itself contributing'.[116] For O'Donovan, this teaching alters humankind's conduct towards nature for the worse. Given that 'the ends of natural life which human action should respect are no longer understood to be given objectively in nature itself, but to be conferred upon nature by the interpretation of a human culture', it inevitably 'promotes a strong tendency to intervene and manipulate'.[117] I will appraise a particular example of O'Donovan's concern later, but let us now consider the ethical examples he gives. In them the question of eschatology resurfaces.

---

[114] Ibid.
[115] O'Donovan, *Resurrection*, 67.
[116] Ibid.
[117] Ibid., 68. Cf. Hans Jonas's seminal account of modernity's understanding of nature as manipulable in e.g. *Philosophical Essays: From Ancient Creed to Technological Man* (Upper Saddle River: Prentice-Hall, 1974).

Against historicist ethics

The moral implications in regard to our own nature, O'Donovan proposes, can be demonstrated by taking 'as ... paradigm a natural institution of which the New Testament has a good deal to say, the institution of marriage'.[118] The account here of what 'Christians have classically believed' about marriage is as one might imagine: it touches on marriage as a teleological structure that is 'a fact of creation and therefore not negotiable', on 'the dimorphic organisation of human sexuality' and so on.[119] Marriage is a non-contingent feature of creaturely existence, perduring 'whatever happens in history'.[120] By contrast, a historicist account, narrating marriage as 'an item of cultural history', cannot but place it under a question mark: 'Historicism makes all created goods appear putatively outmoded.'[121] (Commenting elsewhere on another contemporary's revisionist sexual ethics, he worries about lack of suspicion of 'the pretensions of history to change the world'.)[122]

The treatment becomes especially relevant in its discussion of singleness, which counters the historicist conception with 'one that is, in a fuller sense, "eschatological"'.[123] Singleness points forward to the eschatological quality of community 'in which the fidelity of love which marriage makes possible will be extended beyond the limits of marriage'.[124] The early church took this vocation seriously, witnessing to the hope it declared by 'fostering the social conditions which could support a vocation to the single life'.[125] Ecclesial approval of two vocations maintained a double testimony:

> The one declared that God had vindicated the order of creation, the other pointed beyond it to its eschatological transformation. ... Neither would accommodate in itself or evoke in the other an evolutionary mutation [the historicist outcome]. Marriage that was not marriage could not witness to the goodness of the created order, singleness that was not singleness could tell us nothing of the fulfilment for which that order was destined.[126]

---

[118] O'Donovan, *Resurrection*, 69.

[119] Ibid. For a longer argument that explores the dimensions of claims like these in the Christian tradition, including contemporary theologians like O'Donovan, see Christopher C. Roberts, *Creation and Covenant: The Significance of Sexual Difference in the Moral Theology of Marriage* (New York/London: T & T Clark International, 2007).

[120] O'Donovan, *Resurrection*, 69. See O'Donovan's comment in a contemporaneous dictionary article 'Augustinian Ethics', in *A New Dictionary of Christian Ethics*, ed. James F. Childress and John Macquarrie (London: SCM/Westminster: John Knox, 1986): 'The defence of created goods is the key to Augustine's conception of marriage' (47).

[121] O'Donovan, *Resurrection*, 70.

[122] O'Donovan, 'Archbishop Rowan Williams', 8. Eugene Rogers explores both the material disagreement between and the commitment to ecclesial unity shared by Williams and O'Donovan in *Sexuality and the Christian Body: Their Way into the Triune God* (Oxford/Malden: Blackwell, 1999), 42–4.

[123] O'Donovan, *Resurrection*, 70.

[124] Ibid.

[125] Ibid.

[126] Ibid.

(Here the presentation is neatly parallel to the explanation of the resurrection's 'double aspect', with the sense of the vindication of the created order we have already explored, and the sense of eschatological transformation we will explore later in the chapter.) O'Donovan suggests that despite later confusion, marriage and singleness were not conceived of hierarchically as objects of moral choice. Rather, they were respective appropriate responses to a vocational gift.[127]

What we find is, I think, an advance on 'The Natural Ethic'; it is clearer that singleness points to eschatological transformation. But making sense of singleness in the way O'Donovan persuasively does here surely means accepting a good derived from the future. Can singleness really be a vocation derived exclusively from 'how the world works' – which seemed to be O'Donovan's proper criteria of discernment elsewhere? Rather, if O'Donovan is right here (and I think he is), then singleness in its deepest witness is governed by a criterion that is not intrinsic to the created order. It would represent a form of life that requires non-naturalistic reference to an eschatological whither (and thereby whence). Again, I am not saying that the eschaton is the only reference point for singleness, just as we should not say that marriage is only a natural good.[128] But to say, rightly, that singleness points to 'eschatological transformation' implies that the kingdom has normative content *along with* creation.[129]

---

[127] Ibid., 71. I explore *Resurrection*'s discussions of vocation, freedom and the good some in Chapter 3. See also *Resurrection*'s discussions of the distinction between a command and a counsel (170–1), and monastic renunciations (283).

[128] At the sharp end of the point that singleness, 'the harbinger of the coming rule of God', involves 'Apocalyptic Allegiance and Disinvestment', see the article of that title by John Barclay – a reading of 1 Cor. 7.25-35 (in *Paul and the Apocalyptic Imagination*, ed. Ben C. Blackwell, John K. Goodrich and Jason Maston (Minneapolis: Fortress Press, 2016)). For the appropriate synthetic, integrative move see again Bennett, *Water Is Thicker than Blood*, especially ch. 5. Of course, the term 'singleness' covers multiple states of life, not all of which correspond to what the tradition understands as vocational celibacy or virginity, but each theologically intelligible in different ways, as Augustine shows. For careful consideration of different states see Bennett's more recent *Singleness: A New Theology of the Single Life* (New York: Oxford University Press, 2017). Related, and worth adverting to here, is that Bennett's interpretation of Augustine's understanding of marriage and singleness in redemption history parts ways with Ramsey's, as seen in his 'Human Sexuality in the History of Redemption', *Journal of Religious Ethics* 16, no. 1 (1988): 56–84, and *One Flesh: A Christian View of Sex Within, Outside, and Before Marriage*, Grove Booklet E:8, ed. E. David Cook and Oliver O'Donovan (Nottingham: Grove Books, 1990).

[129] This study is not primarily intended as an adjudication of the theological basis of positions in debates concerning sexual ethics, but note that doing justice to the way scripture and tradition have understood this '*along with*' would be a condition revisionist proposals must meet if they do not want to fall foul of something like O'Donovan's critique of Adams. Of course, some are contentedly historicist. Among others, Robert Song's *Covenant and Calling: Towards a Theology of Same-Sex Relationships* (London: SCM Press, 2014) intends to meet that condition; we await his fuller proposal. Samuel Wells, *How Then Shall We Live? Christian Engagement with Contemporary Issues* (Norwich: Canterbury Press, 2016), also seeks to make his proposal in terms of what he calls 'the five-act play' of salvation history. Specifically, his intention is 'to advocate [a] view of sexuality ... based less on what we believe about Act 1 (creation) than on what we understand about Act 5 (consummation)'. He is right that sometimes 'Christianity is presented as asking, "What is the rule book that was given in Act 1 and how can we stay close enough to it to qualify for Act 5?"' and that 'living in Act 4 is more about asking the question, "What kind of life in Act 4 reflects the joyful heritage of Acts 1-3 ... and the breathtaking destiny of Act 5?"' (104). But I worry that this does not yet tell us enough about how we should understand the present heritage of Act 1 to know whether the way his prioritization of Act 5 functions is theologically defensible.

We must leave until later O'Donovan's attempt to distinguish between vocation and moral norm – a distinction made in order to tie moral norms 'back' to the goods of creation while allowing vocations to be eschatologically oriented. Yet we can see already that if marriage can also point forwards as well as backwards, and do so not as an 'evolutionary mutation' of historicism but as an estate given in creation and transfigured by redemption history, then whatever its merits, the distinction between vocational command and moral law should not allow O'Donovan or anyone else to ground the entire conspectus of Christian ethics in creation without remainder.

Besides the implications for moral theology, *Resurrection and Moral Order*'s discussions of historicism's failures that we also find arguments that come to the fore in later theo-political work: 'If historicism fails in its treatment of nature for lack of a concept of creation, its social thought fails equally for lack of a strong eschatology.'[130] That is not to say that Western political thought has deemed eschatology irrelevant:

> The opposition in Western theology between the City of God and the earthly city has enabled political thought to avoid theocratic conceptions of government, which, by claiming to express the rule of heaven on earth, must unify the earthly and heavenly into a single totalitarian claim. Western theology starts from the assertion that the kingdoms of this world are *not* the kingdom of ... God ... not, at any rate, until God intervenes to make them so at the end ... earthly politics, because they do not have to reconcile the world, may get on with their provisional task of bearing witness to God's justice.[131]

Historicism fails, by contrast, to concede the 'distance' between divine and human kingdoms – despite the prominence of the concept of the kingdom of God in its political thought.[132] Actually, according to O'Donovan, 'eschatological categories' like this are used by historicist thinkers to '*legitimise* the immanent tendencies of history rather than to *criticise* them.'[133] This is true whether historicism issues in state-totalitarianism or what he dubs 'liberal culture-totalitarianism.'[134] The latter, we are told, relies on protest (rather than administration) to propel 'history forwards on its way.'[135] And we should find reliance on protest problematic despite 'the sincere determination of many theologians to assert a Christological foundation' for it: 'Not in the immanent turbulence of social movements is hope to be found, but in the revelation of divine justice at Calvary.'[136]

O'Donovan's negative assessment of Helmut Thielicke's apparently eschatologically driven reading of Jesus' moral teaching touches on the same theme: 'It is no answer to say that "the Sermon on the Mount does not overlook the reality of the world; it

---

[130] O'Donovan, *Resurrection*, 71.
[131] Ibid., 72.
[132] Ibid., 73.
[133] Ibid.
[134] Ibid., 74. For incisive phenomenological characterization of 'culture-totalitarianism' see O'Donovan, *Common Objects* (45–72).
[135] O'Donovan, *Resurrection*, 74.
[136] Ibid., 73–4.

protests against it" for protest, in itself, is formless.'¹³⁷ This distaste for protest – shared with MacIntyre, for instance – is present throughout his work. Elsewhere, he admits that protests do bear 'unconscious witness to the principle of universality in ethics', but they become 'self-defeating when divorced from a recognition of this principle' (and he seems to count much contemporary activism as exactly that).¹³⁸ Now, it *could* very well be the case that nearly every contemporary protest movement is divorced from that perception of universality (a strange thing to say in the era of human rights, though of course O'Donovan has his reservations about the adequacy of that framework). But the note of presumption and paternalism here is unfortunate, and protest can achieve that recognition even if it does not know to aim for it in the terms of a moral philosopher. Debate about the critique of protest in O'Donovan's work resurfaces in relation to *Desire of the Nations*.¹³⁹ I will make the specific point here that O'Donovan's instinct (as MacIntyre's) seems to necessarily inhibit the critical function of eschatological hope. Why?

As a preliminary observation, could it not be the case that protest on occasion embodies the criticism of the immanent tendencies of history – criticism inspired by 'eschatological categories' – that O'Donovan laments as lacking in historicism?¹⁴⁰ The reading of Moltmann, in *Resurrection and Moral Order*, generally shrewd, risks overextending in the same way. By grounding hope in 'dissatisfaction' and 'suffering' rather than in the resurrection, we are told, Moltmann bleaches hope's Christian specificity, 'subordinating it to the more general phenomenon'.¹⁴¹ Moreover: 'If we base our hope on the resurrection of Christ, it is impossible to say that it is "founded" in dissatisfaction, for our dissatisfaction with the present is overwhelmed by the glorious vindication of creation which God has effected in Christ.'¹⁴² O'Donovan overstates his case despite a generally well-founded basic concern.¹⁴³ I agree entirely that, in John

---

¹³⁷ Ibid., 145.
¹³⁸ O'Donovan, 'What Can Ethics Know about God?' in *The Doctrine of God and Theological Ethics*, ed. Alan J. Torrance and Michael Banner (London/New York: T & T Clark, 2006), 46, n. 6. On protest as 'a distinctive moral feature of the modern age', see MacIntyre's (harsh) comments in *After Virtue: A Study in Moral Theory*, 3rd edn (London/New York: Bloomsbury, 2013), 85.
¹³⁹ See especially Tim Gorringe's review and O'Donovan's response, cited in Chapter 4.
¹⁴⁰ Cf. Stefan Skrimshire, *Politics of Fear, Practices of Hope: Depoliticisation and Resistance in a Time of Terror* (London/New York: Continuum, 2008), e.g. 141–201, though I have reservations about the book, including its earlier reading of theologians on eschatology and apocalyptic, and the way in which the contemporary philosophical evocations of cultural mood that are considered perhaps determine the normative conclusions more than they should for a theological account.
¹⁴¹ O'Donovan, *Resurrection*, 66.
¹⁴² Ibid. Interesting to compare here would be the work of Johann Baptist Metz and perhaps Edward Schillebeeckx, as well as a raft of liberation theologians. What is interesting in the case of Metz and Schillebeeckx, at least on one reading, is that each thinker's deepening attentiveness to suffering and injustice ('contrast experiences', 'the underside of history') represented a *break* with the immanentist and progressivist eschatology of historicist thought, as they assimilated the insights of the Frankfurt school and other critical theorists. See Rodenborn, *Hope in Action*.
¹⁴³ See the generally sympathetic reading of O'Donovan's critique of Moltmann in Tim Chester, *Mission and the Coming of God: Eschatology, The Trinity and Mission in the Theology of Jürgen Moltmann and Contemporary Evangelicalism* (Milton Keynes: Paternoster, 2006), 179–95. Note, though, Timothy Harvie's claim that Chester 'relies far too much on Schuurman's work', which overestimates Moltmann's stress on eschatological discontinuity and does not defend its own proposal 'of the eschaton re-instituting an Edenic state'. Harvie, *Jürgen Moltmann's Ethics of Hope: Eschatological Possibilities for Moral Action* (Farnham: Ashgate, 2009), 24 – a book with Moltmann's imprimatur,

Webster's words, 'a Christian moral theology of hope' should not be 'much disposed to take its bearings from prestigious readings of our cultural situation developed without the gospel's tutelage'.[144] Indeed, 'little is to be gained (and a good deal may be lost) by expounding Christian hope as a counterpart to some philosophical or cultural-theoretical presentation of the human condition'.[145] But it must be possible to ground decisively Christian hope in the resurrection *and with that* find grounds for dissatisfaction with all that in the present opposes itself to the goodness, justice and peace of God's future – a future reality presently determinative in some way of the moral order, if that is a cohesive order. As Richard Hays writes: 'The eschatological framework of life in Christ imparts to Christian existence its strange temporal sensibility, its odd capacity for simultaneous joy amidst suffering and impatience with things as they are.'[146]

O'Donovan is surely right to find in Moltmann's thought the seepage of historicist presuppositions into Christian theology.[147] But does the way this assessment is made prevent O'Donovan from taking the time to make sense of the properly theological commitments that might also shape Moltmann's more salient concerns? I think it does; in fact, exactly this is what we will find in O'Donovan's *Finding and Seeking*.

Against historicist theology

Moltmann's early partner in the 'theology of hope', Wolfhart Pannenberg also makes a fleeting appearance in the discussion of historicism.[148] O'Donovan's focus is Pannenberg's 'articulate attempt', in a section of *Theology and the Kingdom of God* entitled 'Appearance as the Arrival of the Future', 'to discover historical teleology in certain strains of Socratic and Aristotelian thought'.[149] Conceived there is an eschatological ontology in which 'the relation of appearance to reality' is imagined as 'essentially the relation of present to future'.[150] But, O'Donovan argues, it cannot be found in those sources: 'classical categories' such as 'Plato's "Idea of the Good"' do

---

written before Moltmann's own *Ethics of Hope* and affirmed in it (xi). Of course, it is possible to think that neither Schuurman nor Moltmann get things quite right.

[144] Webster, 'Hope', 299.
[145] Ibid.
[146] Richard B. Hays, *The Moral Vision of the New Testament: A Contemporary Introduction to New Testament Ethics* (New York: HarperCollins, 1996), 198.
[147] The critique of Moltmann, and 'Moltmannian' eschatology, in Adam, *Our Only Hope* is salient. See also Elliot, *Hope and Christian Ethics*, 47–54. In an article sharply critical of the wholesale philosophical borrowings in later twentieth-century eschatology, Nicholas Adams notes the influence of Bloch on Moltmann (as well as Heidegger on the eschatology of Rahner, and Hegel on Pannenberg). Adams, 'Sacred and Profane: The Effects of Philosophy on Theology in Pannenberg, Rahner and Moltmann', *International Journal of Systematic Theology* 2, no. 3 (2000), 283–306.
[148] For a fuller impression of O'Donovan's misgivings about Pannenberg's apparently Troeltschian historicism, see his review of Pannenberg's *Ethics*, *The Journal of Theological Studies* 35, no. 1 (1983): 358–64.
[149] O'Donovan, *Resurrection*, 59.
[150] Ibid.

not 'contain any element of futurity' and cannot be incorporated into the "historicist concept of good-as-project".[151]

O'Donovan is surely correct here, and it is important to be accurate about classical philosophies and their relation to modern ideas; informed debate about them is preferable to the bald assertion of 'theology's fall into Hellenism' found in many iterations of Protestant theology (from Luther to Harnack to Moltmann).[152] O'Donovan resists any simplistic opposition of biblical world view to classical metaphysics. He seems to hold to a sense of a patristic and scholastic (perhaps even Anglican) synthesis of biblical wisdom and Greek philosophy, given granular detail by his close reading of the Fathers, and enhanced by sensitivity to those texts' worlds owed to a background in classics. Moreover, the understanding of this synthesis expressed in O'Donovan's early work is unusually assured for its time, especially for an evangelical Protestant of his generation – present already in 'The Natural Ethic' and *Self-Love*. Equally, and crucially, it is seldom complacent: chastened, maybe, by Barth and others, and undoubtedly by O'Donovan's evangelical formation. (It is therefore often expressed in a more biblically literate, case-by-case and watchful way than contemporary exponents of the sensibility known as Radical Orthodoxy.)[153] Still, this observation does not yet tell us how O'Donovan sees this synthesis directly informing the subjects we are investigating, though we may already be able to make a decent estimation of how it might.

In the interaction with Pannenberg, O'Donovan writes that Christianity's idea of history is not that history is insignificant, but that its significance is secured precisely by its proper limitation, its dependence on a prior reality:

> When history is made the categorical matrix for all meaning and value, it cannot then be taken seriously *as history*. A story has to be a story about something; but when everything is a story there is nothing for the story to be about … . The story of what has happened in God's good providence to the good world which God made is 'history' in the fullest sense. But when the world itself is itself dissolved into history … we have no history any more … only … process.[154]

This formulation, not least the 'story' language, certainly invites comparison with recent systematicians besides Pannenberg. In a probative paper delivered at a symposium

---

[151] Ibid.
[152] The description of Paul Gavrilyuk, *The Suffering of the Impassible God: The Dialectics of Patristic Though* (Oxford: Oxford University Press, 2006).
[153] It may be that they consider O'Donovan, when they do, to 'tend to the ploddingly exegetical' – as they say of Barthians. *Radical Orthodoxy*, ed. John Milbank, Catherine Pickstock and Graham Ward (London: Routledge, 1999), 2. In the context it is unclear whether the comment refers to exegesis of Barth's texts, or of scripture. In O'Donovan's generally impressed review of Milbank's *Theology and Social Theory* (*Studies in Christian Ethics* 5, no. 1 (1992): 80–6), he wrote that 'encounters with scriptural studies in this book are rare. … There are hints that his own way of reading the Scriptures will tend to Marcionism; and occasionally we may think we glimpse a ghost of the old reactionary Catholic disdain for those who imagined that these texts can be read at all except in the liturgical performance of the Mass. … The logical next step for Milbank would be to turn from apologetics to a pure theology of society, developed more fully in responsibility to Scripture and tradition' (85).
[154] O'Donovan, *Resurrection*, 60.

on O'Donovan's reading of Scripture, Craig Bartholomew ventured a quite different formulation by Robert Jenson:

> The world God creates is not a thing, a 'cosmos', but it is rather a history. God does not create a world that thereupon has a history; he creates a history that is a world, in that it is purposive and so makes a whole. The great turnings in God's history with his creation, at the call of Abraham, the Exodus, the Crucifixion and Resurrection and the final Judgement, are not events within a creation that is as such ahistorical, they are events of the history that is created. Even the biblical account of the absolute beginning is itself a narrative; the six days if Genesis do not recount first an absolute beginning on the first day and then what happens to the creation on subsequent days; the whole story of one week tells the absolute beginning. ... The loss of this insight is the great historical calamity of the doctrine of creation. ... Perhaps the key diagnostic question is whether redemption is understood to fulfil creation or merely to restore it; theology has too much tended to the latter.[155]

O'Donovan responded, affirming that creation 'cannot be thought of existing apart from history; it exists *with* history and *under* history, in a dialectic that allows neither order nor event to disappear into the other', but criticizing Jenson's expression severely: 'I do not see how that can be excused from conflating moral and historical teleology, "the good" and "the future", precisely as ... I complained that ... Pannenberg did'.[156] Among a number of finely wrought ensuing statements, O'Donovan provides us with something like his definitive articulation of the relation of creation and history: 'In viewing creation we see what underlies the history through which we move; in viewing God as seated in creation's throne we see the implications for creation of what has been shown us of God's rule in history.'[157]

Indeed, in *Resurrection and Moral Order*, a similar point was made as a rejoinder to Pannenberg, against what O'Donovan sees as the replacement of history with 'process': creation is complete, and can be defined as 'the given totality of order which forms the presupposition of historical existence'.[158] Created order, then, is 'that which is not

---

[155] Robert W. Jenson, *Systematic Theology*, vol. 2, *The Works of God* (Oxford/New York: Oxford University Press, 1999), 14–15. Cited in Craig Bartholomew, 'A Time for War and a Time for Peace: Old Testament Wisdom, Creation, and O'Donovan's Theological Ethics', in *A Royal Priesthood? The Use of the Bible Ethically and Politically: A Dialogue with Oliver O'Donovan*, ed. Craig G. Bartholomew, Robert Song, Jonathan Chaplin and Al Wolters (Carlisle: Paternoster Press, 2002), 109. Compare Robert W. Jenson, 'The Great Transformation', in *The Last Things: Biblical and Theological Perspectives on Eschatology*, ed. Carl E. Braaten and Robert W. Jenson (Grand Rapids/Cambridge: Eerdmans, 2002), 33. It might be a rare distinction that a moral theologian is taken with such seriousness by Old Testament scholars – admittedly, largely evangelicals, including Christopher J. H. Wright, who also draws on O'Donovan at numerous points in *Old Testament Ethics for the People of God* (Downers Grove: IVP, 2004). But not exclusively: witness O'Donovan's sometime Oxford colleague John Barton's acknowledgement of indebtedness in 'Virtue in the Bible', *Studies in Christian Ethics* 12, no. 1 (1999), 12–22, 22.

[156] O'Donovan, 'Response to Craig Bartholomew', in *A Royal Priesthood?*, 114. O'Donovan continues, parenthetically: 'The older Pannenberg of *Grundlagen der Ethik* makes full amends'.

[157] Ibid., 115.

[158] O'Donovan, *Resurrection*, 61.

negotiable within the course of history, that which neither the terrors of chance nor the ingenuity of art can overthrow'.[159] This description resonates with the traditional idea, following Aristotle and taken up as axiomatic by classical Christian theology, that 'art imitates nature' – a reversal of understanding about which arguably precipitated both epoch-making technological advance and scientific progress and incalculable damage to creaturely life and humility.[160] In a similar sense, McKenny notes that for O'Donovan:

> The sharp distinction between creation as an order that demands respect and as raw material available to the human will-to-form corresponds to a broadly Aristotelian distinction between two kinds of human action: acting properly understood, which recognises generic and teleological orders as created by God and respects them as such, and making, which treats created things as unformed matter available for human fashioning.[161]

We can see that this definition underlies the commanding critique of technological modernity in *Begotten or Made?* and elsewhere. Nevertheless, phrased thus might O'Donovan not be a little too optimistic about the natural order's ability, in all its material minutiae, to resist the 'ingenuity of art'? I will return to this point later in the chapter.

As alluded to earlier, a conviction about creation's immovability that O'Donovan finds in the Psalms bolsters this understanding. He invokes it in *Resurrection and Moral Order* when he goes on to say that created order 'defines the scope of our freedom and the limits of our fears':

> The affirmation of the psalm, sung on the Sabbath which celebrates the completion of creation, affords a ground for human activity and human hope: 'the world is established, it shall never be moved'. Within such a world, in which 'the Lord reigns', we are free to act and can have confidence that God will act. Because created order is given, because it is secure, we dare to be certain that God will vindicate it in history.[162]

---

[159] Ibid.
[160] The kind of point made by Robert Spaemann. See e.g. 'What Does It Mean to Say that "Art Imitates Nature"?' in *A Robert Spaemann Reader: Philosophical Essays on Nature, God, and the Human Person*, ed. D. C. Schindler and Jeanne Heffernan Schindler (Oxford: Oxford University Press, 2015). Spaemann is an important (acknowledged) influence upon O'Donovan, who translated Spaemann's *Persons: The Difference Between Someone and Something* (Oxford: Oxford University Press, 2006), and whose students Guido de Graaff and James Mumford translated and edited Spaemann's *Essays in Anthropology: Variations on a Theme* (Eugene: Cascade, 2010).
[161] McKenny, 'Evolution, Biotechnology, and the Normative Significance of Created Order', *Toronto Journal of Theology* 31, no. 1 (2015): 15–26, 18. The evaluation of *Resurrection* here is similar to part of chapter 2 of McKenny, *Biotechnology, Human Nature, and Christian Ethics* (Cambridge: Cambridge University Press, 2018). I draw on that book below, and engage a critical response to McKenny's article (from John Berkman and Michael Buttrey).
[162] O'Donovan, *Resurrection*, 61.

For the tradition, divine sovereignty 'in and through the perilous contingencies of history was assured by the order which was God's primary gift in creation'.[163] But contemporary theology and piety is muddled about creation and providence: '[M]odern faith in "continuous creation" is merely the latest form in which forgetfulness of this dialectic between order and contingency betrays itself'.[164] Remembering the biblical trope of Sabbath rest would have kept historicism at bay: 'The sign which celebrates the completeness of creation looks forward also the fulfilment of history. Does the eschatological meaning replace, or annul, the reference to creation?'[165] Of course the answer is No. 'Historical fulfilment means our entry into a completeness which is already present in the universe.'[166]

O'Donovan does, however, allow for a hint of incompleteness. If the divine work of creation can rightly be said to be complete, the divine works of 'providential government and redemption of history' cannot.[167] Nonetheless, as so often in his writing, the argument loops back around from this counter-subject to the principal theme – this awaited completion is nothing other than the 'vindication of creation from death, the manifestation of its wholeness'.[168] As before, we are enjoined to renounce historicism's idea of history as progress, which 'replaces the categories of good and evil with those of past and future'; a misstep closely related to 'gnostic' dualism's denial of creation's goodness and 'idealism's' denial of evil's reality.[169] 'Progress', O'Donovan says, is opposed to 'the Christian threefold metaphysic of a good creation, an evil fall and an end of history which negates the evil and transcends the created good'.[170]

Historicism's hubristic claim to know the direction of history is at odds with theological modesty, too, even if it was encouraged by an element of ancient (including Christian) thought that explained history with similes of growth. All historicisms, whether optimistic, pessimistic, revolutionary or conservative, 'have in common … the confidence that history will declare its own meaning'.[171] What this loses sight of is 'the mystery of God's dealings, the inscrutability of historical events which reduced the prophet to tears', and the decisive role of revelation, since 'the fulfilment of history is not generated immanently from within history … to speak of "grace alone" … is to speak of a work "from outside"'.[172] Here O'Donovan makes space for consideration of the novelty inherent in God's eschatological work, in a passage worth quoting in full:

> In transforming the world that he has made, God is not merely responding to necessities intrinsic to it, but is doing something new. The transformation is in keeping with creation, but in no way dictated by it. This is what is meant by

---

[163] Ibid. Surely God's *primary* gift in creation is the gift of existence itself.
[164] Ibid.
[165] Ibid.
[166] Ibid., 62.
[167] Ibid.
[168] Ibid.
[169] Ibid., 63. Cf. O'Donovan, *Small Boats*, 48. For more positive invocations of progress, see *Ways*, 134, 179.
[170] O'Donovan, *Resurrection*, 63.
[171] Ibid., 64.
[172] Ibid.

describing the Christian view of history as 'eschatological' and not merely as 'teleological'. The destined end is not immanently present in the beginning or in the course of movement through time, but is a 'higher grace' which, though it comes from the same God as the first and makes a true whole with the first as its fulfilment, nevertheless has its own integrity and distinctness as an act of divine freedom.[173]

In warding off progressivist assumptions of transformation propelled by forces immanent to history, then, O'Donovan makes one of his strongest cases for the novelty of divine action. Having to specify his dispute with historicism, he now produces greater clarity about nature, too. If we make the mistake of suggesting the world's destiny is 'immanently present within its natural orderings' he writes, 'it must be present universally'.[174] This cannot but reduce Christ to a mere instance of disclosure of 'tendencies that are already present in world history as a whole'.[175] There were eighteenth- and nineteenth-century Christologies that realized exactly such a reduction. In *Thirty-Nine Articles*, O'Donovan commends the Reformers (and Kierkegaard as their heir) for seeing, unlike these Christologies, the implications for a theology of history of the once-for-all, eschatological character of Christ's advent and atoning sacrifice.[176] In *Resurrection and Moral Order*, O'Donovan goes on to warn, nonetheless, that the appropriate 'distinctness' is not maintained by portraying '"saving history" so zealously that the kingdom of God ceases to be the destiny and purpose of *all* history and appears relevant only to a narrow band of special activity within it'.[177] Yet neither should that 'universalism' make 'every act of providence by definition an act of salvation' as historicism is wont to do.[178] This question of historical and eschatological novelty is addressed earlier in the book, too, in a discussion of voluntarism that can be engaged profitably at this point, in the final brief section before we turn to three challenges to O'Donovan's thought.[179]

Voluntarism

Voluntarism, which O'Donovan defines here as 'the attack upon kinds', can be understood sympathetically as an attempt to recognize divine freedom.[180] When pursued within Protestant theology, this attempt is usually galvanized by the judgement that such recognition was not adequately preserved in pre-Reformational moral systems. That may be true, but disastrously, voluntarism eventuates in 'theological reservations

---

[173] Ibid.
[174] Ibid., 65.
[175] Ibid.
[176] O'Donovan, *Thirty-Nine Articles*, 33, 124.
[177] O'Donovan, *Resurrection*, 65–6.
[178] Ibid., 66.
[179] It features in a slightly different way in the later discussion of the 'moral field', passages which I consider in Chapter 3.
[180] O'Donovan, *Resurrection*, 38.

... about the linking of moral obligation to the natural generic-teleological order'.[181] These reservations accompany suspicion that a universal ethics 'ties God's will down to an eternal and necessary structure over which he has no more power to command'.[182] According to the voluntarist:

> We cannot be content to say that God has made his dispositions once and for all, so far as this world is concerned, in the creation of an order of kinds and ends, that he made these dispositions freely, and that he is at liberty to make any other world than this whenever he chooses. We must also insist on his freedom within this world to do more than merely reiterate the changeless summons of the generic order once given. And so the theological objector goes on to argue that morality must respond to the agency of God in history, and not rest solely upon the uniform structures which stand apart from history. But as soon as he says this, he appears to be committed to denying the generic character of morality; for any command or principle that changes in history thereby becomes a particular, a mere item in the history of ideas. The demand that morality must change with God's acts in history therefore puts the axe to the root of the doctrine that morality is generic.[183]

Needless to say, O'Donovan rejects voluntarism. But he does identify 'elements in this position which no theology can ignore without forfeiting its claim to be Christian'.[184]

One is the maintenance of 'God's right to command particularly, to address individuals in a way not susceptible of universalisation', for instance in election, grace and conversion, or in 'a special exercise of such divine freedom in individual vocation'.[185] Another reason to countenance voluntarism's good intentions, if not its proffered resolution, is that 'Christianity is committed to the meaningfulness of history as the stage on which mankind's salvation has been wrought':

> 'Salvation-history' means change and innovation; it means that God can do a 'new thing'. Consequently we must not proceed on the assumption of a uniform pattern of divine activity in all ages, for it is central to Christian belief that there is a difference between God's self-manifestation before and after the coming of Christ.[186]

Having acknowledged all this, however, O'Donovan settles the matter in terms that anticipate his definition of the relation of creation and history that we have already seen:

---

[181] Ibid., 39.
[182] Ibid.
[183] Ibid., 41.
[184] Ibid., 42.
[185] Ibid. We have already touched on it, but vocation is a reoccurring theme in O'Donovan's writing, often in conversation with the figure and works of Kierkegaard. I return to it later. Cf. O'Donovan, *Ways*, 75, 82.
[186] O'Donovan, *Resurrection*, 42–3.

> There is ... an irreducible duality between the freedom of God to act particularly in history and the generic ordering of the world which is reflected in morality. For history to be meaningful history, and for God's freedom to be gracious freedom, there must also be order which is not subject to historical change. Otherwise history could only be uninterpretable movement, the denial of what has been in favour of what is to be. The fact that temporal movement is comprehensible as 'history' points to the prior fact that temporal movement is not the sole manifestation of God's work. He who is unchanging ... is the author, not only of change itself, but of the order which makes that change good.[187]

We need to preserve a sense of divine freedom in history, then, to safeguard particular divine commands, vocation and salvation history itself. But to safeguard *ethics*, we will need to presume an unchanging order: 'Morality is that to which one is summoned, not particularly ... but by virtue of being mankind in God's world.'[188] There is much to appreciate within this settlement, but there are still questions to be asked, as Errington writes: 'The fundamental issue raised by this section is whether this account of God's action in history does justice to his act of redemption in Christ.'[189]

At this point, having rehearsed and at points introduced queries about some of the major claims O'Donovan makes in *Resurrection and Moral Order*, we can proceed to a more synoptic evaluation of the book's agenda, asking the question with which 'The Natural Ethic' concluded.

What, then, can we do with creation and kingdom?

All of the foregoing summary and interpretation suggests that in *Resurrection and Moral Order* we may take O'Donovan as offering an answer to that question: 'If we cannot *balance* creation ethics and kingdom ethics, what *can* we do with them?' The book's aim is to embrace the 'double-aspect' within the integrated whole of a 'Christian metaphysic', and therein to transcend balance. As he writes in the preface to the second edition:

> I was concerned to overcome the confrontation between advocates of 'creation ethics' and of 'kingdom ethics', and I claimed that, in the resurrection of Christ, where creation is restored and fulfilment promised, ethics had a foundation which embraced the partial truths of both these points of view.[190]

---

[187] Ibid., 45.
[188] Ibid., 43.
[189] Errington, *Every Good Path*, 151.
[190] O'Donovan, *Resurrection*, xvi. See Parry, 'Evangelicalism and Ethics' (173, 187) and Barclay, 'Creation and Providence' (6) for the suggestion that O'Donovan succeeded in this task. Yet mark the evident asymmetry each simultaneously evinces. Thus Parry: 'Evangelical *creation ethics* will look to this magnificent work as a primary source for some years to come' (173; italics added), and Barclay (4):

In this subsection, I offer my first extended analysis of the book's answer.

We have already seen enough to realize that O'Donovan's argument for the 'double-aspect' is often pursued through exegetical means and now assessing it fully involves investigation of some passages not yet treated, among which are two pieces of biblical commentary. While we cannot bring in for discussion all the many passages of moral-theological commentary that O'Donovan presents as corroborating his case, we can appreciate that the hermeneutic is canonical and integrative.[191] Differences of emphasis among biblical texts are recognized, but his aspiration is a coherent constructive reading of Scripture. I mark this because it bears on the first passage I have in mind, at the beginning of which O'Donovan carefully notes the gospels' distinctive presentations of the resurrection's 'backwards looking' and 'forwards looking' implications. But he continues:

> The important thing is not which of these two aspects of the resurrection we emphasise at any moment, but that it does properly have both aspects; origin and end are inseparably united in it. The humanity of Adam is carried forward to its 'supernatural' destiny precisely as it is rescued from its 'sub-natural' condition of enslavement to sin and death. The vindication of that humanity in Christ's resurrection includes both its redemption and its transformation.[192]

In the following lines, he mentions the same pair of partial positions identified in 'The Natural Ethic' as 'creation' and 'kingdom' ethics, writing again that some are forced into a decision for 'kingdom' over 'creation' because of its 'radical' rather than 'conservative' appearance.

What is newly stipulated here is the need to make the resurrection central to Christian ethics, which overcomes that confected dichotomy. 'This way of posing the alternatives is not acceptable, for the very act of God which ushers in his kingdom is the resurrection of Christ from the dead, the reaffirmation of his creation.'[193] Standalone kingdom ethics 'set up in opposition to creation could not possibly be interested in the same eschatological kingdom as … the New Testament …. At its root there would have to be a hidden dualism which interpreted the progress of history to its completion not as a fulfilment, but as a denial of its beginnings.'[194] Yet a standalone ethics of creation, 'set up in opposition to the kingdom, could not possibly be evangelical ethics, since it would fail to take note of the good news that God had acted to bring all that he had

---

> I maintain that we shall not understand or apply correctly many features of biblical ethics unless we recognize that they are essentially based on creation. They reflect the nature of God, creator, providential ruler and redeemer of his creation. That will encompass the ethical features of the valid but ethically more limited concept of the Kingdom of God. To use Oliver O'Donovan's phrase, Christian ethics are 'a reaffirmation of creation'. They are the Creator's instructions arising from his love for the world which he alone understands and brings to restoration and fulfilment.

[191] Cf. O'Donovan, 'Scripture and Christian Ethics', *Anvil* 24, no. 1 (2007): 21–9, and 'The Moral Authority of Scripture', in *Scripture's Doctrine and Theology's Bible: How the New Testament Shapes Christian Dogmatics*, ed. Markus Bockmuehl and Alan J. Torrance (Grand Rapids: Baker, 2008).
[192] O'Donovan, *Resurrection*, 57.
[193] Ibid., 15.
[194] Ibid.

made to fulfilment'.¹⁹⁵ (This point, incidentally, is one that many sympathetic Protestant natural lawyers, nor Jean Porter, seem to have heeded as much as they might.)¹⁹⁶ The restatement of O'Donovan's own position over against these options is familiar: 'In the resurrection of Christ creation is restored and the kingdom of God dawns.'¹⁹⁷ But it is followed by a revealing comment about the variegated way that the two aspects can be drawn upon: 'Ethics which starts from this point may sometimes emphasise the newness, sometimes the primitiveness of the order that is there affirmed. But it will not be tempted to overthrow or deny either in the name of the other.'¹⁹⁸

Yet O'Donovan seems again to expend more energy on the dangers of kingdom ethics than on creation ethics. Note the sentences that immediately follow the book's earliest affirmation of a 'world-transcending aspect, in which we are to seek the things that are above'.¹⁹⁹ First they detail, cursorily, moral impulses thought to derive from it: eschatological 'aspects, of abnegation and transcendence in personal ethics, of criticism and revolution in social ethics'.²⁰⁰ They are then firmly regulated by prioritizing the objective first aspect: they 'are prevented from becoming negative and destructive by the fact that they are interpreted from the centre, the confirmation of the world-order which God has made'.²⁰¹ Given this habit of introducing eschatological themes and their ethical corollaries with caveats hedged all around, a reader expecting to find balance between the aspects would again be disappointed.

O'Donovan does indisputably intend that balance, however. A few pages later, we are returned to the central theses of 'The Natural Ethic', now with the resurrection well defined as their fulcrum:

> Creation and redemption each has its ontological and its epistemological aspect. There is the created order and there is natural knowledge; there is the new creation and there is revelation in Christ. This has encouraged a confusion of the ontological and the epistemological in much modern theology, so that we are constantly presented with the unacceptably polarised choice between an ethic that is revealed and has no ontological grounding and an ethic that is based on creation and so is naturally known. This polarisation deprives redemption and revelation of their proper theological meaning as the divine reaffirmation of created order. If, on the other hand, it is the gospel of the resurrection that assures us of the stability

---

¹⁹⁵ Ibid.
¹⁹⁶ Hauerwas's assessment of Porter's use of O'Donovan to the end of developing 'an account of God from creation' seems implicitly, I think, to draw this distinction between them – but it is not quite clear. See Hauerwas, 'The End Is in the Beginning: Creation and Apocalyptic', in *Approaching the End: Eschatology Reflections on Church, Politics, and Life* (Grand Rapids: Eerdmans, 2013), 14, n. 33.
¹⁹⁷ O'Donovan, *Resurrection*, 15.
¹⁹⁸ Ibid.
¹⁹⁹ Ibid., 14.
²⁰⁰ Ibid.
²⁰¹ Ibid. These 'eschatological aspects' are prominent in Moltmann, and Reformed theologian Douglas J. Schuurman – an appreciative reader of *Resurrection* – offers a critique of Moltmann that turns on the same point O'Donovan makes here. Schuurman also expands upon his teacher Gustafson's worries about Moltmann in terms of the subordination of creation to eschatology, the lack of distinction between creation and sin, and the lack of practicable ethical direction. See Schuurman, *Creation, Eschaton, and Ethics: The Creation-Eschaton Relation in the Thought of Emil Brunner and Jürgen Moltmann* (New York: Peter Lang, 1991).

and permanence of the world which God has made, then neither of the polarised options is right.[202]

What is at first sight a neat passage without loose ends becomes slightly puzzling on reflection. The first sentence's parallel and complementary logic places creation's ontological and epistemological aspects alongside redemption's. But it seems to break down. Based on the language and logic within these few sentences alone, 'an ethic that is revealed' would seem to require as its ontological grounding a notion of 'new creation', just as 'an ethic that is based on creation' would seem have its ontological grounding in 'the created order'. Yet when two polarized options are ranged against one another, we find 'an ethic that is based on creation and so is naturally known', versus 'an ethic that is revealed *and has no ontological grounding*'. Somehow, redemption's ontological aspect, described in the second sentence as 'new creation', has gone missing. Or at least – and I suggest this is the case – has transmuted into something else by the time O'Donovan comes to give his own presentation in the final sentence.

It might be that O'Donovan cannot in fact conceive of 'new creation' as denoting any ontological weight, so discounts it, despite the place he finds for it in the formal parallels of the first sentence. He evidently sees nothing substantial, ontologically, in the moral vision of those who promote 'an ethic that is revealed'. More likely is that 'new creation', the ontological aspect of redemption that corresponds to revelation as its epistemological aspect, is, by the final sentence, the self-same reality as the ontological aspect of creation, that is, created order. To draw the equation more straightforwardly: the revelation and reality of new creation *is* 'the reaffirmation of created order'; new creation *is* created order. The double-aspect appears a lot like a single principle at this point. To a critical eye, that may in the end amount to not being able to imagine the reality-claims involved in eschatological affirmations. O'Donovan's intention to outline a unified ethic is seen here in its conflationary force rather than in its promise. Of course he would reply that there *could be* no other reality than this one; a Christian metaphysic does not admit two planes of reality existing together. However significant it is for O'Donovan, an 'inaugurated' eschatology does not mean so much a sense of the even-now co-existing realities of two aeons, say, so much as the 'the whole order of things created', *already* 'restored', *to be* 'transformed'.

I entirely agree that the danger of polarized ethics is real and the outcome irrefutably damaging. Yet the cost O'Donovan incurs in taking precaution against it is too high. It may not be enough to describe revelation and redemption's 'proper theological meaning' as the divine reaffirmation of created order'. One would not want to say less than that, perhaps, but Christian eschatology is improperly bounded by the reductionism involved in such a claim. Perhaps – if heavily invested in a natural ethic – one could say more

---

[202] O'Donovan, *Resurrection*, 19. Craig Bartholomew quotes this passage in order to provide contemporary support for Herman Bavinck's view of grace's restoration of nature, which he notes is more eschatological than Abraham Kuyper's. See Bartholomew, *Contours of the Kuyperian Tradition: A Systematic Introduction* (Downers Grove: IVP, 2017), 68. Still, given what looks to be Bartholomew's reliance on Albert Wolters' account of nature and grace, I have my doubts these worries about O'Donovan's presentation would be alleviated there. Compare Albert M. Wolters, *Creation Regained: Biblical Basics for a Reformational Worldview*, 2nd edn (Grand Rapids: Eerdmans, 2005 [1985]).

exactly that the core of redemption and revelation's proper *moral* meaning is 'the divine reaffirmation of created order'. But the moral entailments of the gospel's depiction of the resurrection still seem restrained if its role is essentially assurance 'of the stability and permanence of the world which God has made'. That may be a plausible, even attractive, moral-theological inference based on a perceived need to make sense of the structures of the world around us as authoritative for our conduct – quite literally, perhaps, to make a virtue of necessity. And I have no intention to disparage the effort to craft a Christian ethics imagined as in good part faithful responsiveness to the contours of creaturely life. Yet to put it rather technically: unless this moral-theological instinct for stability and permanence – found in this kind of natural law–like natural ethic – is also shared as unalloyed by apostolic teaching concerning the structures of the world, then the ethicist's designs upon a solid, unchanging and objective created order seems unlikely to prove adequate presupposition for veracious reception of the full scope of scriptural moral ontology.[203]

Both the plausibility of O'Donovan's interpretation of the double aspect and its potential tendencies to limitation can be seen in two set-piece interpretations of the First Epistle of Peter.[204] Here is the first:

> We are driven to concentrate on the resurrection as our starting point because it tells us of God's vindication of his creation, and so of our created life. Just so does 1 Peter, the most consistently theological New Testament treatise on ethics, begin by proclaiming the reality of the new life upon which the very possibility of ethics depends: 'By his great mercy we have been born anew to a living hope through the resurrection of Jesus Christ from the dead.' (1.3)[205]

If my anxieties about the adequacy of O'Donovan's treatment of eschatology so far have been at all comprehensible, I hope it will strike the reader that these sentences' gloss draws out one aspect more than the other, based on a generous amount of canonical inference about creation's vindication. At the same time, I do not think the inference is illegitimate. (And the problem is not as such that O'Donovan is engaging in avowedly theological interpretation – *contra* Richard Burridge, who criticizes O'Donovan in a crass way on this score.)[206] But O'Donovan's interest in created order does dictate the manner in which it is made, marginalizing other possible elucidations of 'the reality

---

[203] I realize putting it like this leaves my point entirely open to counter proposals from scriptural interpretation – so much the better, in the long run! As I was completing this project, it came to my attention that Markus Bockmuehl's *Jewish Law and Gentile Churches: Halakhah and the Beginning of Christian Public Ethics* (Grand Rapids: Baker, 2003), might represent a particular challenge in this respect. If so, more and subsequent work will have to be done to see how that moral vision may knit with those drawn from St Paul by, for example, Richard Hays or John Barclay, and those received into dogmatic theology by, for example, Philip Ziegler (see references to each elsewhere in this book).

[204] As we will see, a third instance of exegetical comment on these verses occurs in *Desire*.

[205] O'Donovan, *Resurrection*, 13.

[206] Burridge sweepingly dismisses what he calls the 'overall worldview approach' of O'Donovan and Michael Banner. It is, apparently, necessarily 'a long way from the actual text of the Bible and is in danger of imposing a doctrinal or theological framework on the text … the text could just be a convenient peg from which to hang the argument, which is really driven by dogmatics and

of the new life'. O'Donovan would no doubt say that 'new life' must in a real sense be 'created life' – what else could life be? – and, similarly, that the 'new world of his resurrection' must in a real sense be the vindicated order of creation. I do not doubt that the steps by which he gets from 'born anew ... through the resurrection of Jesus Christ' to 'God's vindication of his creation, and so of our created life' have been thought through. Yet here the terminus of that process of anti-'gnostic' reasoning is presented as self-evident interpretation of the text, which does not seem to bear a plain sense meaning of creation's vindication. The sense that we must be '*born anew* to a living hope' appears to recede.

Let us consider a second treatment of the Epistle:

> So it is that Christian ethics, too, looks both backwards and forwards, to the origin and to the end of the created order. It respects the natural structures of life in the world, while looking forward to their transformation. This can be seen, for example, in the First Epistle of Peter, which starts with a general characterisation of the Christian life in terms of 'hope', which is set 'fully upon the grace that is coming to you at the revelation of Jesus Christ', and then elaborates a special ethics in terms of respectful submission 'for the Lord's sake' to every institution of human life, especially the institutions of government, labour and marriage (1 Pet. 1.13; 2.13ff). There is no conflict here between what might be thought of as the 'radical' character of the general outlook and the 'conservatism' of the specific counsel. A hope which envisages the transformation of existing natural structures cannot consistently attack or repudiate those structures. Yet the 'conservatism' (if it is proper to use the word) includes a sense of distance, which springs from a sharp awareness of how much the institutions need redemption and how transitory is their present form.[207]

If one wants to offer some riposte to the line of analysis I have pursued, this is the place to turn. Because less compressed it allows fuller expression of the range of that particular epistle's theological vision than the concertinaed earlier instance. It also shows how that fuller expression is still in service of a thoroughly unified moral outlook. The unifying sensibility is worthwhile, but it is also exactly what may have pressed in too soon in the first example. It is hard not to think that it sometimes issues in such pre-emptive strikes upon *schwärmerisch* antinomian ethical invocations of the kingdom that eschatology's import itself takes the hit. Where in O'Donovan's ethics do we find an exposition of that 'sense of distance' from 'present form' that is as thorough as his steady exposition of 'existing natural structures'?

I stress *ethics* because it is intriguing at first blush to read, in *Small Boats*, this homiletic comment referring to the same verse:

---

systematic theology'. Richard Burridge, *Imitating Jesus: An Inclusive Approach to New Testament Ethics* (Grand Rapids: Eerdmans, 2007), 383–4.

[207] O'Donovan, *Resurrection*, 58.

The presence of the risen Lord and the new world of his resurrection catch us out, surprise us, find us unready, looking the other way. ... Why is the resurrection difficult to see? Because it is more than the world to which our perceptions are fashioned, within which we have learned to live and to observe.[208]

If I understand the gist of O'Donovan's thought, 'the world to which our perceptions are fashioned, within which we have learned to live and to observe' is the socio-cultural overlay of assumptions about the way things are that figures our lived experience – simulacra that prevent our apprehension of 'the world' in its truer, objective sense. In the terms of *Resurrection and Moral Order*, it is the 'present form' from which we need to achieve 'a sense of distance'.[209] I will return to this distinction of worlds a few times. But if the inferences are, in the end, substantially similar, it does seem to me that these sermons afford the opportunity to see O'Donovan meditating upon passages with unavoidably eschatological themes less guardedly than he might in his ethics. Still, that does not affect our question: Where in O'Donovan's ethics do we find exposition of that 'sense of distance' – that stance against the world that is the prerequisite of a life lived truly for it? Indeed, that is one of the questions that motivates the analysis in our remaining chapters, and is an appropriate sentiment with which to conclude these first incursions into *Resurrection and Moral Order* and to move on to reflection on three further challenges to the book.

Creation and covenant

We may take as an example of this challenge Christopher Holmes, who wondered 'whether creation at times usurps the place of Christology in O'Donovan's text', since 'the language of covenant and its necessary correlate election seem to be displaced'.[210] Is that true? In a basic sense, creation is clearly prominent as a category in a way that covenant and election are not. And besides the question of the proportions of a theological treatise with regard to creation and covenant, there is again a significant question of *taxis*. Though we can sometimes forget – especially, perhaps, when we are reading works of moral theology in which natural law is prominent – we do need to be reminded that it is customary for theology to speak of the vindication of God's covenant before its implications for the natural order.

---

[208] O'Donovan, *Small Boats*, 35.
[209] The same 'world', then, the true self-understanding of which is in a sense contingent on the witness of the church – Hauerwas's well-known point. Bernd Wannenwetsch's development of Hauerwas's claim is worth considering. He writes, for example, of the way worship gives birth to 'the world': 'First, the world becomes the totality of created beings and their activity which do not praise the Creator. But this first becoming of the world, which is really negative, is the pre-condition for a second, salutary, and in the real sense political becoming'. That is, when the world learns to see itself as *saeculum*. Wannenwetsch, *Political Worship*, trans. Margaret Kohl (New York: Oxford University Press, 2004), 249.
[210] Christopher Holmes, *Ethics in the Presence of Christ* (London/New York: T & T Clark International, 2012), 95, n. 86.

To speak of covenant first is not to make a 'historicist' move, of course. It simply reflects a responsive undertaking of theological reason, in seeking to find divine self-disclosure where the God of Abraham, Isaac and Jacob – God the Father of Jesus Christ – has promised most clearly to be found; an undertaking of *moral*-theological reason to discover where God's character and will is displayed most directly in its elicitation of faithful creaturely conduct and judgement of creaturely conduct gone astray. Indeed, in *Thirty-Nine Articles*, O'Donovan himself writes that 'the biblical God ... makes himself known by acts in history, whose self-revelation, therefore, must take the form of history. This is not to embrace modern historicism, with its denial of eternal truths and its opposition to metaphysics'.[211]

What O'Donovan understands to have been made known in those acts, however, is not least the restoration of creation in Christ, and this understanding would likely form the basis of his reply to Holmes' objection. Covenant and creation, O'Donovan might say, are mutually informing concepts, however we relate them. The moral theologian can approach them primarily from the angle of creation, just as the systematic theologian can primarily from the angle of covenant. And we can see how O'Donovan's claims might unfold unobjectionably: the vindication of Christ's humanity is the vindication of creatureliness, and in Christ – the Logos – God redeems the creation made through him, restoring its rationally intelligible form. There is still the valid question of *why* the moral theologian should approach from a different angle than the systematician. (This is a particularly interesting question to investigate in relation to O'Donovan's thought, and in Chapter 5, we will examine his segregation of theological sub-disciplines.) I have already indicated that O'Donovan's conception that the ethicist deals with the possibilities and responsibilities of free human *action in the world* determines his starting point: the resurrection's restoration of creation. To that I will add another, related, suggestion.

One of the tasks that O'Donovan seems intent on performing as an ethicist is a meta-ethical movement of translation: from a discursive idiom informed by the careful tracing of Scripture's material narratives, into one equipped for conversation with moral philosophical concepts. Under the steam of this movement, it may very well be licit to progress from the idea of the vindication of the covenant, or the vindication of Christ's humanity and so humanity in him, to the idea of the moral normativity of the natural order. Yet my impression is that it is not just O'Donovan's disciplinary methodology as a moralist that puts the language of creation before the language of covenant (or election), and that seems accordingly to risk dislodging Christology from some of its canonical footing in those themes. O'Donovan's doctrinal convictions tend to that concentration, too – if not an outright usurpation, if that is what Holmes implies. *Thirty-Nine Articles*, where we see those convictions more plainly, speaks of Christ's resurrection as 'the vindication of his humanity', 'on behalf of all men', as well as a 'moment of recovery' in relation to creation.[212] But it still does not say much about covenant.

---

[211] O'Donovan, *Thirty-Nine Articles*, 60. The first sentence's sentiment might not be unfamiliar to readers of Pannenberg or N. T. Wright.
[212] Ibid., 29.

O'Donovan's terminology of the resurrection's 'restoration' of creation may derive from patristic sources.[213] It may also come from Calvin – consider, for instance, Calvin's comment on Col. 1.18: '[I]n the resurrection there is a restoration of all things, and in this manner the commencement of the second and new creation, for the former had fallen to pieces in the ruin of the first man'.[214] Yet in neglecting this emphasis, he may part ways a little with the Reformer, for whom the language of creation cleaves more closely to that of covenant. (Where that linkage appears in Calvin, it also seems to reckon more soberly with sin's effects.) And it also signifies a parting of the ways with Karl Barth, in whose work this linkage appears in a radicalized way.[215] But not just Calvin and Barth, among O'Donovan's teachers, because it was Barth's formulations of creation and covenant that pointed Paul Ramsey towards resolution in his struggle to form 'an ethic of faithfulness … that would honour the unity and wholeness of God's activity as Creator, Preserver, and Redeemer' (a struggle that sounds otherwise similar to O'Donovan's).[216]

Holmes' argument may have about it something of the pedantic fretfulness of the (Barthian) systematic theologian when faced with an ethicist's pragmatic application of Christian teaching, pressing the questions of proportion and *taxis* on their own terms. Yet we can extend his insight to argue that the vindication of the covenant is an essential affirmation often overshadowed in O'Donovan's theology by a claim of vindication oriented primarily to a natural ethic. The moral-theological disquiet, signalled by the dogmatician's, will be about how the meta-ethical translation from the vindication of the covenant to the vindication of creation other is executed. Thus, whether and how the universal moral implications can so easily be abstracted from the unsubstitutable particularity of God's ways with God's people. The critical question is this: Does the ease of transposition permit a notion of vindicated created order not sufficiently formed by those narratives? This might seem a strange thing to worry about given O'Donovan's evidently deep familiarity with Scripture and intention to

---

[213] I touch on this in contemplating the next challenge to O'Donovan's thought.
[214] Quoted in T. F. Torrance, *Kingdom and Church: A Study in the Theology of the Reformation* (Eugene: Wipf and Stock, 1996), 153). Notice also Calvin's comment on Jn 13.31, where he uses similar terms speaking not as such about resurrection but about the *cross*, 'in which there is a wonderful change of things – the condemnation of men was manifested, sin blotted out, salvation restored to men; in short, the whole world was renewed and all things restored to order' (quoted in Randall C. Zachman, 'The Christology of John Calvin', in *The Oxford Handbook to Christology*, ed. Francesca Aran Murphy (Oxford/New York: Oxford University Press, 2015), 295). Compare also Herman Bavinck's slightly different ascription of salvific effects to moments of the divine economy: 'The essence of the Christian religion consists in the reality that the creation of the Father, ruined by sin, is restored in the death of the Son of God and recreated by the grace of the Holy Spirit into a kingdom of God'. Bavinck, *Reformed Dogmatics I: Prolegomena*, ed. John Bolt, trans. John Vriend (Grand Rapids: Baker Academic, 2003), 112.
[215] See e.g. Karl Barth, *Church Dogmatics*, vol. III/2, trans. Harold Knight et al. (Edinburgh: T & T Clark, 1960), 204.
[216] William Werpehowski, *American Protestant Ethics and the Legacy of H. Richard Niebuhr* (Washington: Georgetown University Press, 2003), 34; 40–4. See Werpehowski's warranted judgement that the conceptuality of covenant was critically absent from Ramsey's *political* theology (51–4). Adam Edward Hollowell, *Power and Purpose: Paul Ramsey and Contemporary Christian Political Theology* (Grand Rapids: Eerdmans, 2015) – originating in an Edinburgh PhD supervised by O'Donovan – exposits it nicely (15–38), but I think offers an unconvincingly high estimate of Ramsey as political theologian.

discipline concepts according to it (seen pre-eminently in *Desire of the Nations*, though commentators worried about covenant's minor role there, too).[217] But there is a nagging sense that it is sometimes made to yield universal principles too quickly, or that analogous relationships between particular biblical realities and other entities (in *Desire of the Nations* between Israel and other nations, in *Resurrection and Moral Order* between the biblical concept of creation and a philosophical notion of moral order) are drawn a little too closely, becoming bridges across which assertions can move too freely. So we must keep that question in mind.

The book's first direct foray into the theme of eschatology – its third chapter, 'Eschatology and History' – suggests that O'Donovan does consider his case scripturally responsible in these respects. An exegetical passage provides the chapter's point of departure, and while it enlarges the overall argument, nothing found there diverges from the earlier assertions. The initial signs are that it might, however. When the author to the Hebrews writes that 'as it is, we do not yet see everything in subjection to [Christ]', we read, it seems as though the vision of created order in Psalm 8 is dismissed.[218] 'The order which the psalmist believed that he beheld in the world around him the author to the Hebrews declares to belong to "the world to come". It is not realised – yet. It is not something that we can already count on. "But", the author goes on, "we see Jesus".'[219] At pains to mitigate against a misreading of this, O'Donovan continues:

> The writer is not guilty of ignoring [Psalm 8's] obvious sense as cosmology. He is not attempting to *replace* the psalmist's doctrine of creation with an eschatology which will better suit his own Christological interests. Rather, he sees in Christ, and in the order of the world to come, the vindication and perfect manifestation of the created order which was always there but never fully expressed. The elusiveness of that order in our experience did not mean that it had no kind of existence ...
>
> The triumph of the Son of man prepares the way for the future triumph of his 'brethren', mankind as a whole. But this eschatological triumph of mankind is not an innovative order that has nothing to do with the primal ordering of man as creature to his Creator. It fulfils and vindicates the primal order in a way that was always implied, but which could not be realised in the fallen state of man and the universe.[220]

The canonical conclusion, then, reinforces the metaphysic for morals that O'Donovan derives from his interpretation of the resurrection.

Nevertheless, here following more closely Scripture's telling of 'eschatological triumph', O'Donovan does say more about that eschatological fulfilment 'that was

---

[217] E.g. Victor P. Furnish, 'How Firm a Foundation? Some Questions About Scripture in *The Desire of the Nations*', *Studies in Christian Ethics* 11, no. 2 (1998): 18–23, 21; Stanley Hauerwas and Jim Fodor, 'Remaining in Babylon: Oliver O'Donovan's Defense of Christendom', 30–55 of the same edition (38).

[218] O'Donovan, *Resurrection*, 53.

[219] Ibid.

[220] Ibid., 53, 54.

always implied', and not just about the vindication of created order. He clarifies that it is mistaken to understand redemption as purely repristination:

> We must go beyond thinking of redemption as a *mere* restoration, the return of a *status quo ante*. The redemption of the world, and of mankind, does not serve only to put us back in the Garden of Eden where we began. It leads us on to that further destiny to which, even in the Garden of Eden, we were already directed.[221]

In *Thirty-Nine Articles*, a very similar clarification is issued, though he is a little clearer a little earlier. There, too, 'the meaning of Christ's resurrection is that the renewal of all creation has begun', and this renewal has 'two aspects ... which have to be kept in proper balance'.[222] The first aspect, as in *Resurrection and Moral Order*, means that 'we must not understand the newness of the new creation as though it implied a repudiation of the old', which is 'brought back into a condition of newness ... its integrity and splendour', but 'restoration is not an end in itself' and besides it there is 'advance' – 'Adam's "perfect" humanity was made for a goal beyond the mere task of being human ... intimacy of communion with God'.[223] O'Donovan does recognize, then, that creaturely life was – as, for instance, Irenaeus taught – 'already set in an arc leading to something greater'.[224]

Certainly, O'Donovan shares what he describes in *Self-Love* as Augustine's sense of 'the one dominant cosmic movement, the return of the created being to its source and supreme good'.[225] But it is clear that O'Donovan's sense of the economy of salvation, like

---

[221] Ibid., 55.
[222] O'Donovan, *Thirty-Nine Articles*, 28.
[223] Ibid. The idea of restoration of an ordering-to an eschatological end is there in Calvin (See *Institutes* 2.1.3.). Though they are largely beyond my ken, it figures in some neo-Reformed theologies, too, especially Bavinck's, whose understanding of nature and grace is seen as exemplary by many in that school. Debate seems to persist, though, over whether 'restoration' adequately captures Bavinck's position, as well as about its compatibility with 'glorification' in his thought. See Jon Stanley, 'Restoration and Renewal: The Nature of Grace in the Theology of Herman Bavinck', in *The Kuyper Center Review, Vol. 2: Revelation and Common Grace*, ed. John Bowlin (Grand Rapids: Eerdmans, 2011); Brian G. Mattson, *Restored to Our Destiny: Eschatology and the Image of God in Herman Bavinck's Reformed Dogmatics* (Leiden/Boston: Brill, 2012); and Michael Allen, *Sanctification* (Grand Rapids: Zondervan, 2017). Popular presentations of neo-Calvinism, like Albert Wolters' *Creation Regained*, seem to have few qualms about absolutizing 'restoration'. Yet that would appear to contrast markedly with the sentiments of prominent others in their tradition – e.g. Geerhardus Vos, who wrote: 'Eschatology aims at consummation rather than restoration' (*The Eschatology of the Old Testament* (Phillipsburg: P&R, 2001), 73–6. It is also a bit of a puzzle to establish what goes on when this tradition maps its categories onto debates within Catholic theology over nature and grace – Jon Stanley, for instance, finds de Lubac's vision of nature and grace (and thence Radical Orthodoxy's) an 'ally' for the neo-Reformed tradition (Stanley, 'Restoration and Renewal', 100), but Allen (Allen, *Sanctification*, 138, 214–15) thinks that this tradition coheres more with recent neo-Thomist critical responses *to* the de Lubac/RO approach (i.e. with the defence of 'pure nature' issued by Lawrence Feingold, Steven A. Long, Thomas Joseph White, and Reinhard Hütter).
[224] John Behr, *Irenaeus: Identifying Christianity* (Oxford: Oxford University Press, 2013), 148.
[225] O'Donovan, *Self-Love*, 36, 23. Like Augustine, O'Donovan articulates that movement in terms informed by 'the Christian doctrine of creation-from-nothing', not simply 'the Neoplatonic conceptions of Plotinus'. Among other commitments, this doctrine determined the reshaping of Aristotelian, Platonic and neo-Platonic philosophies in Christian theological reception. Recent philosophical theology (e.g., Robert Sokolowski, Janet Martin Soskice, David Burrell, David Bentley Hart and Simon Oliver) has reflected with great insight upon 'the great discovery' (Hart) of

Augustine's, is ultimately linear rather than cyclical – and that casting redemption as recovery besides advance does not controvert this linearity. As we read in *Resurrection and Moral Order*:

> For the creation was given to us with its own goal and purpose, so that the outcome of the world's story cannot be a cyclical return to the beginnings, but must fulfil that purpose in the freeing of creation from its 'futility'. This fulfilment is what is implied when we speak of the 'transformation' of the created order. Thus there is an important place in Christian thought for the idea of 'history'. ... The Christian understanding of this idea is, of course, only to be reached through a Christian understanding of the end towards which events are directed, that is, through eschatology.[226]

O'Donovan's own *exitus-reditus* scheme does seek to mould itself to the canonical story, even as it sees innate (if imperfect) compatibility with other teleological visions of nature and its destiny, and with other visions of nature's ordered givenness.

Yet satisfying ourselves that O'Donovan sees 'the world's story' as definitively directional rather than cyclical does not mean there is not debate to be had. Once we have allowed his acknowledgement of transformation as well as vindication, the debate to stage will be an intramural theological quarrel: about this scheme's internal coherence, contesting its topography. There could also be a quarrel to be had about any strongly linear scheme's fittingness as a way of understanding the gospel's relation to history. Some thinkers do advocate for a non-linear understanding of eschatology, seeing in that a better basis for ethics. I am unconvinced about that, when adopted to the exclusion of other tellings of the world's story, though there are some things to learn for the Christian moral life from some proponents of non-linearity. Elsewhere, we will also be able to compare other theologians' linear topographies and their implications for ethics; interest in those comparisons, I hope, has been piqued by close examination of O'Donovan's scheme in this chapter.

Restoration and transformation

I have drawn attention to the past tense employed in some of O'Donovan's statements about the resurrection's vindication of created order. But we have seen quite clearly that the argument in *Resurrection and Moral Order* does not just comprise an 'already' of past restoration and fulfilment – what O'Donovan calls the resurrection's backward-looking aspect. It also includes a pair of articulations that look to the future. One is more closely tied to the 'already': 'The sign that God has stood by his created order implies

---

the 'Christian distinction' (Sokolowski), that is, the difference between God and creatures, in light of this doctrine of *creatio ex nihilo*. O'Donovan seems to have espoused a traditional understanding throughout, untroubled by earlier departures from traditional understandings now recuperated for mainstream academic theology (at least).

[226] O'Donovan, *Resurrection*, 55. Cf. 62.

that this order, with mankind in its proper place within it, is to be totally restored at the last.'[227] The other would appear to be less so: as a 'new affirmation of God's first decision that Adam should live, the resurrection of Christ is also an affirmation that *goes beyond and transforms the initial gift of life*'.[228]

We can see the fittingness of each of these claims. We may also wish to ask what relationship obtains between the 'transformation' or 'going-beyond' mentioned in this last quotation, and the 'total restoration' of creation featured in the first. On the one hand, if we want to maintain that God has in the resurrection stood by his created order in such a way as to suggest it will be 'totally restored at the last', then transformation might seem too discontinuous a term for what eschatological consummation will involve. Conversely, if transformation is what we await, then total restoration might not seem quite the right way to express our understanding of eschatological continuity. These are difficult matters, then, and thinking with O'Donovan on this question of eschatological restoration, transformation, and their ethical implications will take us a good distance into some questions that are important for this study (and, I hope, for the practice of Christian ethics and the Christian life).

Restoration

Let us consider first the idea of eschatological restoration and its attractiveness for moral theology before we think about how it might sit alongside the idea of eschatological transformation. It is a refrain echoing throughout O'Donovan's writing that the resurrection of the creature Jesus Christ disallows 'gnostic' yearning for rescue from the created realm. To hope for redemption from the world rather than the redemption of it, it follows, is to contradict the world-affirming implication of Christian teaching.[229] From a contemporary standpoint (like mine) that sees ecological responsibility as a priority for Christian ethics, the wide horizons of O'Donovan's view of salvation are agreeable. Though he does not typically prioritize ecological concerns, they do feature in his thought and are rendered intelligible by his natural ethic; in this we should readily credit his prescience.[230] Moreover, O'Donovan accentuates scriptural

---

[227] Ibid., 15. Douglas Schuurman espouses his own similar position – he calls it 'restorationist' – in fierce criticism (unsurprisingly) of Moltmann, and (more surprisingly) Emil Brunner. See again Schuurman, *Creation, Eschaton, and Ethics*. For debate between Schuurman and Miroslav Volf, see Volf, 'Eschaton, Creation, and Social Ethics', *Calvin Theological Journal* 30, no. 1 (1995): 191–6, and Schuurman, 'Creation, Eschaton, and Social Ethics: A Response to Volf', 144–58 of the same edition.

[228] O'Donovan, *Resurrection*, 13.

[229] Ibid., 14. Opposing the Christian theology of creation and redemption to 'gnosticism' is commonplace in Christian moral reasoning about all kinds of things. See, among multitudes, O'Donovan's student Robert Song's *Human Genetics: Fabricating the Future* (London: Darton, Longman, and Todd, 2002), 67–8. Song also draws on *Begotten or Made?* and *Resurrection* in 'Knowing There Is No God, Still We Should Not Play God? Habermas on the Future of Human Nature', *Ecotheology* 11, no. 2 (2006): 191–211, 206–10.

[230] For all-too-brief indication of how O'Donovan relates the fundamental insights of his work to the ecological crisis, for instance the genealogy of voluntarism, nominalism and historicism, see the article 'Where were you …?'.

themes of creation's renewal and redemption, an emphasis that is now routine in plenty of Christian thought.[231] Relatedly, he praises the Orthodox tradition for its refreshingly cosmic vision; this too is now commonplace.[232] And in an important way, O'Donovan's account is not just congruent with but also lies immediately behind pioneering work in environmental theology and ethics by Michael Northcott and others.[233]

Moreover – and here I draw on Willis Jenkins' portrayal of the pluralism of Christian environmental ethics – O'Donovan's thought is exemplary in affirming (and refining) two principles that can animate theological concern for ecology but that are usually held in isolation, one to the exclusion of the other. First is the notion of 'stewardship'; second, the 'created orders' approach often associated with 'ecojustice'.[234] O'Donovan senses that the 'management ethos' of stewardship 'may dull the gracious awe by which nature humbles humans before God', and that 'without an account of nature's relation to God', the notion of stewardship 'remains unaccountable to the manifold flourishing of earth's creatures and vulnerable to bad anthropocentrisms'.[235] But, having established this important sense of nature's relation to God outwith our possession and construction, O'Donovan also sees that it is in the redemption of humanity that God redeems creation: 'On this', for O'Donovan, 'hangs the project of any fully Christian environmental ethic'.[236]

I would suggest that O'Donovan's unusual ability to make this double affirmation is connected to his ability to sustain an argument we have noticed already, which maintains that redemption 'presupposes the created order':

> 'Redemption' suggests the recovery of something given and lost ... not just 'mankind', but mankind in his context as the ruler of the ordered creation that God has made; for the created order, too, cannot be itself while it lacks the authoritative and beneficent rule that man was to give to it. ... We cannot speculate on what

---

[231] Perhaps my confidence that the churches have embraced the full biblical scope of salvation is the product of short memory. In her survey of sermons on Romans 8.18-25 fifteen or so years ago, Marguerite Shuster found a real lack of concern for the holistic and the cosmic. See 'The Redemption of the Created Order: Sermons on Romans 8:18-25', in Steven T. Davis, Daniel Kendall, Gerald O'Collins, eds, *The Redemption: An Interdisciplinary Symposium on Christ as Redeemer* (Oxford: Oxford University Press, 2004).

[232] O'Donovan, *Resurrection*, xv, 55, 243. Also O'Donovan, 'The Natural Ethic', 25. O'Donovan participated in Anglican-Orthodox discussions during the 1980s.

[233] The work of Northcott (later O'Donovan's Edinburgh colleague) is self-consciously indebted to *Resurrection and Moral Order*. The book's basic contentions undergird in particular the argument in Northcott's groundbreaking *The Environment and Christian Ethics* (Cambridge: Cambridge University Press, 1996), esp. chapter 5, 'The Order of Creation', and 6, 'Creation, Redemption, and Natural Law Ethics'. O'Donovan's book supplied evangelical scholarship on ecological issues with a framework, too. See e.g. Raymond C. Van Leeuwen, 'Christ's Resurrection and the Creation's Vindication', in *The Environment and the Christian: What Does the New Testament Say about the Environment*, ed. Calvin B. DeWitt (Grand Rapids: Baker Book House, 1991); Douglas J. Moo, 'Nature in the New Creation: New Testament Eschatology and the Environment', *Journal of the Evangelical Theological Society* 49, no. 3 (2006): 449-88, 486.

[234] Willis Jenkins, *Ecologies of Grace: Environmental Ethics and Christian Theology* (Oxford/New York: Oxford University Press, 2008). See Jenkins' similar later comments (235) indicating how Reformed 'covenant theologies' can balance the two.

[235] Jenkins, *Ecologies of Grace*, 90-1.

[236] Ibid., 91.

'redemption' will imply for the non-human creation. And yet Scripture speaks of such a redemption. For redemption is what God has done for the whole, and not just for a part of that which he has made.[237]

Incidentally, it is intriguing that in this example O'Donovan waxes apophatic about non-human creation for a moment. Patristic authors speculated quite freely about this wider scope of redemption. Contemporary theology also sees bold attempts to speculate in this area – notably from Paul Griffiths, and more particularly with regard to non-human animals, from David Clough.[238] (By saying 'speculation', I do not intend disapprobation, but it is surely necessary, especially when building a moral argument, to distinguish between speculation and core teaching.) More to the point, we might argue that O'Donovan himself speculates about aspects of the redemption of non-human creation, in the sense that his case for nature's moral normativity appears to be buttressed by the assertion of nature's vindication in the resurrection and thereafter its strong eschatological continuity.

A construal of redemption as the total restoration of the created order does appear especially appealing as a doctrinal premise for moral theology's interest in realities beyond the human creature, and its commendation of an ethos of attentiveness to ecological crisis. There is an undeniable, persuasive simplicity to the line of argument that runs that because God will totally restore the whole world – *this* world – we should take better care of it. And I do not think the inference is mistaken: it is right to say that Jesus in his victory 'inaugurated a complete restoration' (St Maximus the Confessor),[239] which will be consummated in the eschaton, and it is right to imagine that this signifies God's concern for creaturely life in this world here and now. Further, the broadening ethical engagement in some parts of the church does seem to run together with a welcome and ever-growing doctrinal confidence in redemption's range beyond the *anthropos*. And at the most basic level, I want to affirm that accounts such as O'Donovan's are absolutely right in thinking that future-oriented Christian eschatological hope should not be imagined as inimical to ecological concern but rather as compatible with it.[240]

Let us turn now to see what might happen if we introduce the notion of transformation alongside that of restoration. I will sketch two different considerations, each of which entails within eschatological renovation a significant degree of transformation. In both cases, however, what we will find is that we must reckon with eschatological *discontinuity* as well as *continuity* – a consideration that the term restoration on its own does not necessarily intimate.

---

[237] O'Donovan, *Resurrection*, 54.
[238] Paul Griffiths, *Decreation: The Last Things of All Creatures* (Waco: Baylor University Press, 2014), especially Part VI; David Clough, *On Animals, vol. 1, Systematic Theology* (London: Bloomsbury T & T Clark, 2013), especially Part 3 'Redemption'.
[239] Paul M. Blowers and Robert Louis Wilken, *On the Cosmic Mystery of Christ: Selected Writings from St Maximus the Confessor* (Crestwood: St. Vladimir's Seminary Press, 2003), 11.
[240] Unfortunately some do think it intrinsically inimical, among whom see e.g. Catherine Keller, 'Women against Wasting the World: Notes on Eschatology and Ecology', in *Feminist Theological Ethics: A Reader*, ed. Lois K. Daly (Louisville: Westminster John Knox, 1994).

Positive discontinuity

First, there is a view of discontinuity that we might call simply a 'positive' view. For instance, it would not entail contradiction to believe that God created, sustains and will perfect everything that is (and to embrace these truths as morally significant), and to also hold that such perfection will involve a transformation of the material order far beyond our expectations. On that view, despite the real continuity in eschatological transformation – the genuine identity (personal, social and cosmic) of the realities made new – there will be a significant discontinuity, too. The new creation will exhibit unutterable difference from the current order, a difference illustrated by the shifting images of Scripture's eschatological imaginary.[241] Besides, it might be said, what will be continuous in God's gift of new creation could surprise even the saintliest.

In other words, conceivable within Scripture and tradition is a certain kind of apophatic hope as regards the persistence of this world as presently constituted. That apophasis does not denote any lack of trust that God will restore the fortunes of God's vindicated people (a conspicuous prophetic theme) or that the Lord Jesus will return, inaugurating a 'time of universal restoration that God announced long ago through his holy prophets' (Acts 3.21). Nor is it at all incommensurable with belief in the resurrection of a 'spiritual body' (1 Cor. 15.44), or in the 'new heavens and the new earth' (Rev. 21.1). It simply recognizes that 'what we will be has not yet been revealed' (1 Jn 3.2).

Fuller cases for the positive sense of transformative discontinuity just outlined have recently been made by, for example, Matthew Levering and Margaret Adam – the latter with particular sensitivity to ethics. They show, in the company of large swathes of Christian tradition, that belief in the resurrection of the body is compatible with hope in the beatific vision, and that imagining eschatological discontinuity does need not to be ethically enfeebling, despite caricatures.[242] Since we are enquiring into the compatibility of transformation and restoration, it is worth underlining that Levering makes his case while being a theologian who can hold to salvation's restoration of creation; he is quite happy to quote *Resurrection and Moral Order*, saying that in the resurrection, 'the moral order was publicly and cosmically vindicated'.[243] However, both works engage N. T. Wright's *Surprised by Hope* critically – a book that, I suggest, contains by contrast a strongly continualist element of eschatology somewhat redolent of *Resurrection and Moral Order*, though perhaps sometimes lacking the sense of

---

[241] On this see, for instance, Richard Bauckham and Trevor Hart, *Hope against Hope: Christian Eschatology in Contemporary Context* (London: Darton, Longman, and Todd, 1999), 77–80.

[242] Margaret Adam, *Our Only Hope: More than We Can Ask or Imagine* (Cambridge: James Clarke & Co., 2014); Matthew Levering, *Jesus and the Demise of Death: Resurrection, Afterlife, and the Fate of the Christian* (Waco: Baylor University Press, 2012), especially ch. 7, 'Bodily Resurrection and Beatific Vision', 109–26. For an account of what the redemption of bodies might mean see the final chapter of Beth Felker Jones, *Marks of His Wounds: Gender Politics and Bodily Resurrection* (New York: Oxford University Press, 2007).

[243] Levering, *Jesus and the Demise of Death*, 150, n. 37. Cf. *Engaging the Doctrine of Creation: Cosmos, Creatures, and the Wise and Good Creator* (Grand Rapids: Baker Academic, 2017), esp. ch. 7 on atonement and creation. Indeed, Levering is much more interested than I am in constructing an account of natural law. See Levering, *Biblical Natural Law: A Theocentric and Teleological Approach* (Oxford/New York: Oxford University Press, 2008).

transformation 'going beyond' the this-worldly that is there from time to time in O'Donovan's book. (*Resurrection and Moral Order* is a moral-theological treatise to which, more broadly, the writings of O'Donovan's old friend Wright might be thought in some ways the biblical-theological counterparts.)[244]

Negative discontinuity

If that is the positive case for eschatological discontinuity, then, second, a negative case is also theologically possible. We might ask ourselves the sober question of whether we think God would allow humankind to so destroy this good home that any eschatological continuity will necessarily presuppose a high degree of transformative discontinuity, materially speaking: of *re*-creation in a strong sense. If we answer that in mysterious divine wisdom there may be such a possibility, then real destruction is not unthinkable. To be clear, by answering like this we would not need to imply that human beings have the power to hasten 'the Day of the Lord' by their sin. Neither would we have to imply diminished regard for our bodies or dismiss efforts to preserve the natural world as futile.[245] Nor again would we infer that new creation's form will make any concession to creaturely sin; disorder's only mark there may be the wounds of Christ, and he bears them having triumphed over it. We could still hold that consummation will overcome the effects of sin, truly and totally restoring creation. While new creation 'is given and comes to us from beyond any immanent possibilities ... new creation is not *ex nihilo*. It is *ex vetere*, a remaking of the old' (David Fergusson).[246] The thought, rather, that we would be entertaining is that in the meantime human beings have the power to gravely damage this world.

Now it seems to me that if there is some possibility of O'Donovan's notion of total restoration being compatible with a more expansive positive notion of eschatological transformation, then he would not so comfortably countenance this second account of eschatological discontinuity that is avowedly pessimistic. This is because O'Donovan's account of providence and redemption seems to contain as a supposition the thought that within the patience of the divine economy, God would not allow creatures to mar the form of creation in any thoroughgoing way – it is given, it is vindicated, and its

---

[244] Tom Wright, *Surprised by Hope* (London: SPCK, 2007). I expect New Testament scholars grappling with Wright might find many basic instincts underlying his project in O'Donovan's book. If the connection between O'Donovan – and in particular *Resurrection and Moral Order* – and Wright seems tenuous, see from the latter *Virtue Reborn* (London: SPCK, 2010), 247, and *The Resurrection of the Son of God* (London: SPCK, 2003), xxi, 737; and from the former the acknowledgments in *Desire* (xii), and *Entering into Rest* (ix). Certainly, Wright's own moral-theological and theo-political writing takes some different tacks than O'Donovan's. The elements of O'Donovan's thought which cohere well with Wright's may issue from a similar experience in and shared judgement about a particular ecclesial context; those which wouldn't probably owe to O'Donovan's reading of historical and dogmatic theology, and his relative caution over articulating practical programmes.
[245] See Margaret Adam's response to Ellen Ott Marshall in *Our Only Hope*.
[246] David Fergusson, 'Introduction', in *The Future as God's Gift: Explorations in Christian Eschatology*, ed. Fergusson and Marcel Sarot (Edinburgh: T & T Clark, 2000), 3.

form will be restored. For O'Donovan, remember, 'it is the gospel of the resurrection that assures us of the stability and permanence of the world which God has made'.[247]

We can, though, agree when he writes the following: 'Eschatological transformation rules out all the other conceivable eventualities which might have befallen creation, all those ends to which God did not destine it ... it rules out that threatened end of all things which is implied by the Fall: corruption and disintegration.'[248] It is just that this confident hope in the promise of a new creation already begun does not in itself tell us how dark things can get – and have got – in the night before the dawn. (Scripture gives us that ultimate promise, but it also sets forward images that suggest that the prophets and apostles could imagine dark episodes to be endured en route.)

For those less sanguine than O'Donovan about nature's resilience against the damage humankind can do, this would not mean projecting some kind of process-theological vulnerability of divine plan to human caprice. Rather, it could follow from a commitment to divine sovereignty that, following a possibility apparently allowed for by the scriptural witness, could envisage God giving us over to our sin and its consequences to an extent more impactful upon creation's form (including ourselves) than what we have yet seen. And seen from a certain viewpoint, this possibility may not be hypothetical but all too actual, in view of the destruction of God's good creatures already wrought in countless far-reaching horrors world history has known. This sense of negative discontinuity might equally issue from realization of the great 'Devastation'[249] of this order already effected in ecological degradation and damage to fellow creatures. Or most mundanely and modestly of all – and conceived not so much in a pessimistic as an apophatic sense – from pondering how the 'sum total' of 'zoological and botanical' nature of many millennia could be said to perdure together in continualist total restoration, without necessarily strong discontinuity.[250] Something like these points are perhaps the strongest 'negative' cases for discontinualist reserve.

Interestingly, Stephen N. Williams expressed reservations about O'Donovan's cheerfully continualist eschatology in his review of *Resurrection and Moral Order*, though from a perspective of analytic rigour intending to preserve the possibility of belief in the world's eschatological destruction (with regard to 2 Pet. 3.10).[251] We should not airbrush away that text, which may or may not be plausibly annexed by an overall understanding of continuity. But my intention is first to preserve space for positive discontinuity – eschatological transformation – as a legitimate doctrinal reception of the various eschatological scriptural texts and a true and valid object of Christian hope.[252] And thereby to ask what it looks like to place a notion of restoration next to one of transformation within a Christian eschatology.

---

[247] O'Donovan, *Resurrection*, 19.
[248] Ibid., 55.
[249] Paul Griffiths' term, in *Decreation*.
[250] Stephen N. Williams, 'Outline for Ethics: A Response to Oliver O'Donovan', *Themelios* 13, no. 3 (1988): 86–91, 88–9.
[251] Williams, 'Outline for Ethics'.
[252] See Hans Boersma, *Seeing God: The Beatific Vision in Christian Tradition* (Grand Rapids: Eerdmans, 2018), and R. Michael Allen, 'The Visibility of the Invisible God', *Journal of Reformed Theology* 9, no. 3 (2015): 249–69 – part of his longer study *Grounded in Heaven: Recentering Christian Hope and Life on God* (Grand Rapids: Eerdmans, 2018).

Implications

Where does this lengthy detour leave us, as regards O'Donovan's theological ethics? It shows us that 'total restoration' and 'transformation' are in principle compatible, as O'Donovan maintains. It also underlines his acknowledgement that we must not be dealing with 'mere restoration, the return of a *status quo ante*'; as he says later in the passage, the 'eschatological transformation of the world is neither the mere repetition of the created world nor its negation. It is its fulfillment, its *telos* or end'.[253] On the following page, contemplating John the Seer's great vision of a new heaven and new earth, O'Donovan writes: 'A redemption that is *merely* restoration cannot observe that transformation.'[254] We can see that this is exactly right. And he holds together the different strands of eschatological affirmation when he discusses the patristic idea of redemption as 'divinization':

> Certainly this idea has to be understood properly, without any suggestion that it involves the 'de-hominization' of man or the 'uncreation' of the created world' but does succeed in conveying the truth that man is summoned to a destiny that is not given immediately in his creation, a 'higher grace', as Athanasius puts it, 'to reign eternally with Christ in his heaven'.[255]

To this extent, nothing we have reviewed that describes 'positive' eschatological transformation necessarily challenges O'Donovan's account.

However, if we ought to acknowledge the possibilities (and hopes) of discontinuous transformation as well as continuity, then the two concepts will not fit together coherently *if* 'total restoration' is applied to a very fixed conception of created order. If that is meant, then restoration would not seem to have the conceptual elasticity to encompass a meaningful notion of transformation. It follows from this – and here we are coming closer to the implications for O'Donovan's basic contentions – that if we want to take up O'Donovan's thought constructively, we probably ought not interpret or apply a 'maximalist' idea of eschatological continuity in which created order stays much the same in its renovation. And, going further, we ought not employ a maximalist idea of eschatological continuity to reinforce an untroubled idea of the stability of the present natural order, as though its features are materially consistent through creation-fall-salvation-eschaton, and thereby that its present features are straightforwardly morally normative. Yet that, I think, is what O'Donovan sometimes seems to do, when we consider how he uses the past tense of 'vindication' and 'restoration' alongside this future 'total restoration', so as to present the created order as that perduring reality to which our action ought to conform, without adequate acknowledgement of the morally relevant double impingement of sin and salvation, besides eschatological transformation.

---

[253] O'Donovan, *Resurrection*, 55.
[254] Ibid., 56.
[255] Ibid.

My argument is that a doctrinally precise response to this combination of claims – and the doctrine must lead the ethics, as a claim about the reality in response to which we act – must acknowledge that hope in the eschatological restoration of creation does not necessarily imply O'Donovan's particular stance on the moral status or knowability of creation's form in the present. Disentangling the elements is admittedly a delicate undertaking. Let us be clear that the problem is surely not with the language of restoration *simpliciter* – or any *re-* language as such. 'Restoration' has been an important motif of Christian soteriology from the earliest centuries, applied to a range of aspects of created reality (perhaps principally to the image of God).[256] But I suspect that 'restoration' loses some of its wide patristic valence if applied to a somewhat static notion of created order to be restored in the eschaton. That application is not the only biblically responsible and doctrinally coherent interpretation of new creation.

We can still affirm the notion of restoration. Moreover, we can still by faith confidently affirm a set of further wonderful truths about the fulfilment and perfection that consummation will hold: the Father's steadfast, loving purposes for the blessing of creation are unshakably secured in the Son's mission to reconcile creatures who have brought ruin upon themselves, and will be moved to completion in the Spirit's mission to perfect those reconciled creatures. It is true that, as Pope Francis says, 'all the good which exists here will be taken up into the heavenly feast', for God 'has united himself definitively to our earth'.[257]

So too we can secure theologically motivated concern for the body and for nature without holding to a particular strongly continualist construal of new creation where 'restoration' is meant univocally and 'transformation' equivocally. If at first blush this maximalist position may have seemed imperative, we can now see that it is not. Though O'Donovan may at times appear to, we do not need to fuse two claims that can be deemed separable without lapse into any kind of 'gnostic' *contemptus mundi*. In fact, it may be important to conceptually uncouple these broader ethical concerns from that particular eschatological conception, because Christians of all eschatological stripes have reasons within their faith to care for creation as it now is.

Neither of the important affirmations that Jenkins showed that O'Donovan is able to make – of the responsibilities of stewardship, and of the divine care for nature outwith that stewardship – requires a strong sense of eschatological continuity, which illustrates that it is not a necessary prerequisite for the possibility of renewed faithfulness in respect to non-human creation. To take one issue: I do not wish to dispute – quite the opposite – that moral theology must take the present givenness and particularity of other creatures seriously, recognizing their dignity in light of the doctrine of creation. Non-human animals are fellow creatures of God, and were this facet of their theological intelligibility readily recognized so as to determine the formation of Christians' affections, that would be enough for sincere repentance and for patterns of consumption to alter drastically. Of course, eschatological visions of

---

[256] Consider those gathered in the section on 'Restoration' in Norman Russell, 'The Work of Christ in Patristic Theology', in *The Oxford Handbook of Christology*, ed. Francesca A. Murphy (New York/Oxford: Oxford University Press, 2015), 157–60. Or see again Acts 3.21, from the interpretation of which 'restoration' (*apokatástasis*) came all manner of controversy with regard to Origen.

[257] Pope Francis, *Laudato Si* (2015), 244, 245.

the mutual flourishing of different kinds of creatures are a wonderful reminder of that status, and they can also incite ethical sensitivity (so too, perhaps, could the warning of judgement against those who have not well treated 'the least of these').

In terms of my effort to uncouple a certain understanding of the created order's perdurance and restoration from a concern for creation in the present, I find great promise in Jenkins' claim (though he is not leveraging it to make the same point) that Anabaptist theology 'keenly appreciates worldly evil and intensely anticipates a new creation', but expresses its commitments in 'Christian communal practices' that show how 'nature ... shapes the faithful living of a particular people in a particular place'.[258] This legacy, Jenkins continues, 'suggests that redemptionist soteriology, even accompanied by strong senses of worldly evil, need not dislocate humanity from nature'.[259]

Finally, as I have sought to stress, qualifications of O'Donovan's metaphysic for morals should not be thought to invalidate his understanding as a whole. Though O'Donovan's expressions of eschatological continuity redouble his creation-based 'natural ethic' rhetorically and insulate it from the pressure of other doctrinal *loci* – namely, sin and the kingdom of God – those expressions could also be seen as something like an auxiliary hypothesis with regard to most of his claims. Readers may judge how they relate to particular ethical issues, but if they are a flying buttress that might be taken away leaving the main edifice largely intact – that is, an ethic of redeemed creatureliness – then, for example, the goods of ecological commitment and commitment to the dignity of human being's embodied nature already stand on the basis of more modest claims. And if *that* is the case, then it seems as though some of those aspects of Christian moral teaching already established can be unproblematically placed alongside more extended moral reflection oriented towards the transformative aspects of eschatology – reflection that O'Donovan sometimes seems to think would gainsay those aspects of Christian commitment to creaturely life, exchanging them for gnostic flight. Let us turn now to another possible challenge to O'Donovan's position.

Creation, redemption and 'the ingenuity of art'

At this point, I want to return to the question of nature's susceptibility to the ingenuity of art, and to its implications for O'Donovan's understanding of creation and redemption. What follows offers another example of the way his basic view of created order and dismissal of historicism play out. It also lays out a useful, if complicated, indication of the way the arrangement of doctrines figures moral stances, and of the challenges to doctrinal coherence that seem to derive from an ethical issue.

Recall that O'Donovan describes created order as 'that which is not negotiable within the course of history, that which neither the terrors of chance nor the ingenuity of art can overthrow'.[260] In the face of the prospect of radical *technique*, capable of

---

[258] Jenkins, *Ecologies of Grace*, 91–2.
[259] Ibid., 92.
[260] Ibid., 61.

altering human and non-human creatures in more than trivial ways, this description will be subject to scrutiny. And if morally normative features of our world are equated with its non-negotiable features, then either the sanitary cordon around that which is morally normative will grow tighter as more and more features of our world turn out to be humanly manipulable, or the non-negotiable, morally normative features must be in fact a different kind of 'given' than strictly (biologically, say) non-negotiable features. But this first outcome is surely not what O'Donovan intends, and the second does not, at first glance, seem to be the claim he is making.

As McKenny says, O'Donovan does seem to suggest that 'the immunity of human nature to determination by biotechnology' follows 'in a straightforward way from the goodness and completion of human nature as God's creation':

> If creation is both good and finished, and if its eschatological transformation occurs at the end of history and not in it, then respect for creation appears to require us to leave human nature as it is, intervening only to prevent or restore threats to it in the form of disease and injury. With regard to eschatology, this position astutely recognises that it is far from obvious that the transformation of creation for which Christians hope is continuous (or even compatible) with the transformations of human nature which biotechnology is poised to bring about. But with regard to creation, this position also seems to court the problems that attend conceptions of human nature as separable from our constructions of it and to ignore the changes human nature has undergone at the hands of unintentional human activity.[261]

On my reading of O'Donovan's eschatology, this impression would be exacerbated: if the transformation hoped for is more-often-than-not understood as *continuous* with the given, non-negotiable form of created order, any significant alteration to that order (whether or not we oppose it) would seem to place strong material continuity under a question mark. It would mean eschatological restoration either against the grain of altered nature, and therefore discontinuity with creaturely reality in order to 'reset' to prior creaturely reality, *or* restoration with the grain of altered nature, and therefore discontinuity with prior creaturely reality (its past tense 'created' form, say). Whether or not my amendment is accurate, the main point to realize is that O'Donovan's concept of created order, taken at face value, seems to fall foul of powerful criticisms of such concepts.

One salient objection is that seeing nature, as *Begotten or Made?* put it, as 'a world which we have not made or imagined', that 'simply confronts us', is naïve, because it is now clear that access to nature is culturally mediated. Another more immediately moral objection – also salient – is that ideals of 'pure' biological nature as preceding culture, and in particular human nature, will always be inscribed societally in 'morally repugnant ways'.[262] We have seen, in 'The Natural Ethic', that O'Donovan is not unapprised of these dangers. But his strong sense of creation's completion, not just in

---

[261] McKenny, *Biotechnology, Human Nature, and Christian Ethics*, 66.
[262] Ibid., 30.

the fitting theological sense associated with a full-orbed doctrine of creation ex nihilo but in an additional moral-theological gloss that suggests imperviousness to human activity, does seem untenably innocent of historical change.

Yet McKenny also supplies an alternative interpretation, showing that while O'Donovan unquestionably subscribes to an understanding of creation in which creation is exempt 'from temporal becoming and creaturely activity', he should be taken to posit not so much the view that 'created things themselves ... are static', but rather that 'their changes and activities are intelligible only in terms of a created *order* that is itself finished and unchanging'.[263] Intelligible, in other words, in terms of that 'given totality of order' we saw postulated in *Resurrection and Moral Order*, 'which forms the presupposition of historical existence'.[264]

The distinction McKenny makes may seem elusively fine, but he illustrates its significance for a plausible formulation of the normativity of nature. If read in this second way, we find that 'the assumption that human nature is given once for all in an initial creative act is avoided while anthropogenic changes to human nature can be accommodated', but that a rationale for opposing wilful alteration can still be maintained:

> Intentional determination of human biological characteristics cannot be opposed on the grounds that it violates creation as a finished work of God. It can, however, be opposed on two other grounds, namely, that it disrespects created order by virtue of the kind of action it is (which treats nature as inherently unordered and susceptible of imposition of order by human action), or that it directly violates created order by disregarding the generic and teleological relations in which things exist. It is significant that on these last two grounds normative status attaches to human nature not in itself but in relation to the created order in which it exists. On the last of the two grounds, the determination of someone's biological characteristics is morally suspect insofar as it violates the generic equality of the person whose nature is determined with the one who determines it. Normative status properly attaches to the created order as such, and within this order it attaches to human persons with respect to their generic equality and to their biological nature as constituents of their personhood. If human nature should be kept off-limits to biotechnology, it is because intentional determination of it violates the generic equality of the one whose nature is determined and not because it possesses normative status in itself.[265]

The definition of nature offered in *Begotten or Made?*, accordingly, can be refined to state that nature (in this case human nature) is 'a world which we have not *intentionally* made, but which simply confronts *our willful activity*'.[266] This captures the heart of O'Donovan's contention, resolving his objections – in that book to the determination

---

[263] Ibid., 35. Italics mine.
[264] O'Donovan, *Resurrection*, 61.
[265] McKenny, *Biotechnology, Human Nature, and Christian Ethics*, 36, 67.
[266] Ibid., 37.

of children's biological characteristics – into a single 'indispensable' concern that the reformulation preserves. Namely, 'the principle that the biological nature of others is not at our disposal', because it would involve 'a morally problematic comportment toward them', what O'Donovan calls 'making'.[267]

I have focused attention, with the assistance of McKenny's percipient commentary, upon some ethical ramifications of O'Donovan's theological commitments. Much more could be said, but I limit myself to one further comment, intended as suggestive rather than definitive. Comparing the chapter in Bonhoeffer's *Ethics* entitled 'Natural Life' with statements in *Resurrection and Moral Order* that speak of the 'failure to reckon with creation' might help us see further what is at issue between O'Donovan and McKenny (and others).[268] Perhaps the best way to read Bonhoeffer's chapter – whether or not it is found inharmonious with the rest of *Ethics* – is to see it as a particular deployment of part of the theological tradition in response to extreme circumstances of degradation and exploitation.[269] After all, the confusion of morality with what is perceived to be natural is usually the very target of Bonhoeffer's Christocentric culture-criticism. Yet here Bonhoeffer articulates a number of convictions that O'Donovan shares. A statement early in O'Donovan's book could easily be mistaken for Bonhoeffer's 'Natural Life':

> True, man has rejected, despised and flouted this order. Human nature, as Christians believe, is flawed not only in its instances but also in its mould, so that to be human itself means that we find this order of things a problem and are rebelliously disposed towards it. And yet this order still stands over against us and makes its claims upon us. When man is least on guard against God he finds his natural ordering reasserting itself and carrying him in directions against which his self-will revolts.[270]

If Bonhoeffer's theological appeal to the natural is primarily driven by discernment of the times, then so, it seems, is O'Donovan's. The element of rhetorical overstatement that McKenny picks up in O'Donovan's writing (and that we have also seen) does suggest something of contextually occasioned hyperbole – but who bears the burden of proof that O'Donovan has been writing moral theology in similarly extreme circumstances of nature's debasement? Technological high-modernity and its precipitation of ecological crises could be thought just that (that may be the force of Michael Northcott's employment of *Resurrection and Moral Order*). And it is possible to trace distressingly direct genealogical lines from overt eugenics to subtler post-Second World War bioethical legitimation of the kind O'Donovan has written about.[271]

---

[267] Ibid., 69, 68. Cf. 186.
[268] O'Donovan, *Resurrection*, 16.
[269] For a recent reading of the essay, see Hans G. Ulrich, 'Understanding the *Conditio Humana*', in *Bonhoeffer and the Biosciences: An Initial Exploration*, ed. Ralf K. Wüstenberg, Stefan Heuser and Esther Hornung (Frankfurt: Peter Lang, 2010), 155–8.
[270] O'Donovan, *Resurrection*, 16.
[271] Tracing such lines and churches' complicity in that legitimation is one achievement of Amy Laura Hall's arresting *Conceiving Parenthood: American Protestantism and the Spirit of Reproduction* (Grand Rapids: Eerdmans, 2008).

Of course, we can make equally stringent contemporary judgements and not think we need to appeal remedially to a transhistorical and transcultural natural order in the same way. We could hold to what McKenny shows can be O'Donovan's more understated and defensible position. Or, like McKenny himself, having formulated a defensible version of O'Donovan's concern, we could also look elsewhere for other theological accounts of nature's normative status.[272]

Ultimately, these reflections underline the essential power and enduring value of O'Donovan's position regarding the 'objective reality' of ethics, but only after whittling away at the exaggerated claims involved in his account of nature's normativity and factoring in more robust acknowledgements of historical alteration – acknowledgements that in *Resurrection and Moral Order* are fewer and feebler than they ought to be. From my perspective, however, it is not just that O'Donovan's position presented nature, and human nature in particular, as 'something which lies behind the complexity and variety of human histories ... an artifact, assigned a fixed place in a taken-for-granted scheme of things' (as John Webster described some mistaken 'ways of thinking – which, it has to be conceded, have certainly found their way into some theological anthropology').[273] It is also the more directly theological point that O'Donovan's position thereby also seems, as Webster worried about those mistaken ways of thinking, to 'extricate human nature from the temporal processes of the divine economy, isolating human being from the unfolding drama of fellowship with God in which humankind acquires its identity'.[274] But there is more to O'Donovan's book than an apologia for an objective and fixed reality, some of which 'more' we can now consider.

---

[272] For a summary of why McKenny does not settle for the approach represented by O'Donovan, see *Biotechnology, Human Nature, and Christian Ethics*, 186–7.
[273] John Webster, 'The Human Person', in *The Cambridge Companion to Postmodern Theology*, ed. Kevin Vanhoozer (Cambridge: Cambridge University Press, 2003), 226.
[274] Ibid.

3

Contour

Resurrection and Moral Order – 'The Subjective Reality' and 'The Form of the Moral Life'

Introduction

In Chapter 2, I examined in detail the foundations of *Resurrection and Moral Order*. This chapter ranges more freely and a little less forensically, exploring eschatology's part in a number of themes key to the book's unfolding argument. I address elements of what Part Two of O'Donovan's book calls 'the subjective reality' of ethics – freedom, love, authority, knowledge and sin – and elements of what Part Three calls 'the form of the moral life' – conversion and character, and the form of obedience in light of cross and resurrection. Nonetheless, these themes are previewed in the first chapter of *Resurrection and Moral Order*, 'The Gospel and Christian Ethics', which I draw on here, and which are woven throughout the book, so I draw on material from Part One, too. Furthermore, it would be a mistake to think that these topics take us much away from the 'objective reality' of the first part. In fact, O'Donovan's elucidation of each theme is determined by the particular interplay between objectivity and subjectivity. The same interplay is further apparent in discussions of the relation between the order of creation and the divine command, between natural stability and historical novelty, and between Christology and pneumatology.

O'Donovan offers a wealth of insights about each of the themes just mentioned, and I seek to present a number here, often seeking to situate them by comparison with the contributions of other theologians. However, as before, I also entertain challenges to various elements of O'Donovan's argument: Is his acknowledgement of sin's impingement upon knowledge robust enough? And, relatedly, is his account of the authority of worldly order less qualified than it should be? Might we suspect a certain devaluation of the cross's moral import? Or an inability to reckon fully with eschatological newness? Or, finally, an undue restraint in pneumatology? *Resurrection and Moral Order* has an answer to each of these challenges, but I will discover some merit in each criticism. The Spirit and the kingdom, though, do find ampler witness – without any detriment to Christology or creation – in the book's doctrine of the church. I explore that here as well, and I also relay the insights of the book's final two chapters, on the moral life's 'double aspect' and its 'end'; these approach eschatology most directly. Yet there too I find the account inhibited by familiar reticence, seen most clearly in O'Donovan's faltering mentions of hope. Before we get to that point, though, there is much material to cover, and having summarized where this chapter will go, we can now dive into its first themes.

Freedom, love and authority

I have shown how O'Donovan's basic moves grounded his ethic in an account of created order and its moral normativity. Salvation and eschatology were not absent as such, but they first and foremost signified that order's decisive vindication. Moreover, the important mentions of renewal or transformation beyond this vindication might have seemed, left as they were, generally irrelevant for morality. Indeed, part of the case I am making is that in the final instance O'Donovan does present an approach to moral reasoning in which these eschatological aspects of soteriology can appear worrisomely immaterial. But there are segments of his argument that they do begin to inform materially. Freedom is one. Let us turn first to what he writes in the book's opening chapter.

O'Donovan is aware that the resurrection, 'viewed in isolation, might appear to be two removes away from ethics'.[1] After all, he continues – in a line we have noticed before – 'it is the promise, but not the fulfilment, of a world-redemption yet to be completed; the order there renewed and vindicated in principle still awaits its universal manifestation'.[2] That vindication can seem to be of 'a renewed order of things apart from myself'.[3] Not so, however. 'There is a transition from the objective to the subjective mode. In that transition, marked by mention of the believer's "freedom", the eschatologically awaited world-redemption has an anticipated reality already present.'[4] Here, significantly, we learn that an answer to the question of eschatology and ethics must be thoroughly pneumatological. As O'Donovan writes, in a subsection on 'The Spirit and Christian freedom':

> The evangelical character of Christian morality appears in its relation to the resurrection of Christ from the dead. But even so it does not appear fully until we add a word which, had we been following Saint Paul directly, we should have placed first. From the resurrection we look not only back to the created order which is vindicated, but forwards to our eschatological participation in that order. Of that final enjoyment we have a present anticipation through the Pentecostal gift of the Holy Spirit.[5]

---

[1] O'Donovan, *Resurrection*, 22.
[2] Ibid.
[3] Ibid., 23. In the terms of Reformed divinity, I suppose, something like an *historia salutis* unconnected from an *ordo salutis*.
[4] Ibid., 23.
[5] Ibid., 22.

As our present anticipation, this gift 'means that the renewal of the universe touches me at the point where I am a moral agent'.[6] Following the Reformers, this means liberation from 'the bondage of the will': 'the removal of psychological barriers which prevent us from responding to the challenge of God's will'.[7]

If we are tempted to think that this transition of modes means that the prior commitments fade into the background, the reminder is swift that they do not. It is never enough to have 'an ethic of the Spirit alone': many 'revival' movements became terribly legalistic because they emphasized 'the inward moral power of the Holy Spirit unchristologically'.[8] A bit drastically – though it is not irrelevant – O'Donovan mentions Montanism here, a favourite historical illustration of doctrinal distortion and moral decay that features repeatedly in more polemical passages.[9] With Joachimism, Montanism is invoked to similar effect in *Thirty-Nine Articles* and *Church in Crisis*.[10] I will return to the second example later, reflecting on the contextual discernments animating O'Donovan approach to pneumatology. But O'Donovan's consistent argument is that any discussion of liberty needs a Christological determination; specifically, 'we must characterise Christian freedom as participation in Christ's authority within the created order'.[11] That order was not 'ever anything other than what God made it', and, because of that, 'in the redemption of the world I, and every other "I", yield myself to God's order and freely take my place within it'.[12] In freely taking our place within that order, there really is 'by the Holy Spirit … the possibility of creative discernment, "the mind of Christ" (1 Cor. 2.16), since the second Adam has restored the first's 'lordship'.[13] We ourselves assume a recovered authority, then, 'yet this characterisation of freedom, too, is inadequate':

> Indeed, it is perilously misleading – if it is left to stand on its own. For it may be taken to mean that the Holy Spirit, in conferring such authority upon man, has, as it were, withdrawn authority from the rest of the natural order which confronts man, and has left him to make what he will of it. … But creative freedom conceived in this way can only break down into mere improvisation, dominion become domination. … How can creativity function with its eyes closed upon the universe?[14]

So how can we speak properly of freedom as clear-eyed and thoroughly this-worldly?

---

[6] Ibid., 23.
[7] Ibid.
[8] Ibid., 24.
[9] Gnosticism, as we have seen, and Manichaeism, are other well-played tunes in the repertory of cautionary tales. Compare the equally drastic and perhaps related suggestion of H. Richard Niebuhr that these are always developing at the edge of the radicalism represented in any 'Christ against culture' mentality, which cuts itself off from nature. See *Christ and Culture* (New York: HarperCollins, 1996), 79–81.
[10] O'Donovan, *Thirty-Nine Articles*, 45, 124.
[11] O'Donovan, *Resurrection*, 24.
[12] Ibid., 25, 23.
[13] Ibid.
[14] Ibid.

O'Donovan's compelling proposal is that it is love that delivers the integration of subjective and objective in an account of evangelical freedom; 'the form of the human participation in created order', it is thereby 'the overall shape of Christian ethics'.[15] Love is the Spirit's work, shaping *'the appropriate pattern of free response to objective reality'*, a creativity achieved 'by being perceptive' – much like Adam's task of naming – rather than by manipulation.[16] Following 'classical Christian descriptions', love can be further expounded by two terms: wisdom, 'which is the intellectual apprehension of the order of things which discloses how each being stands in relation to each other', and delight, 'which is affective attention to something simply for *what* it is and for the fact *that* it is'.[17] These specific terms of wisdom and delight in relation to the given order resonate strongly with David Kelsey's treatment of fitting creaturely disposition and action in response to God's creative work – a comparison I will return to. More important to observe here is that the understanding of love that *Resurrection and Moral Order* promotes has its roots in O'Donovan's interpretation of St Augustine, and the fruits of what he describes in *Self-Love* as Augustine's 'search for an "ordered" love in which the subject was neither victim nor master'.[18]

Central to that inquiry is O'Donovan's creation-oriented reading of the notion of an *ordo amoris*, in which love's order 'is given by its comprehending conformity to the order of reality. … Love accepts and does not impose its ordering'.[19] As he writes in *Resurrection and Moral Order*: 'The real world authorises man's agency'.[20] On this understanding, we might say moral responsibility is not inaugurated in the spontaneity of the first person (Kant), nor in the communal answerability of the third person (Aristotle), but rather established in the authoritative alterity of something like the second person – not, though, primarily the interpersonal other of a Levinasian ethic, but the claims of the natural order.[21] Just so, a core claim across much of O'Donovan's work is that 'authority is the objective correlate of freedom'.[22] O'Donovan's aim, then, is not exactly to find 'a middle ground between authority and liberty' – a description, we read, of Anglican moral theology's particular *via media* (Paul Elmen).[23] Nor even is it quite to specify the 'essential complementarity' of their demands – another description

---

[15] Ibid.
[16] Ibid., 25, 26.
[17] Ibid., 26. Cf. O'Donovan, 'The Foundations of Ethics'.
[18] O'Donovan, *Self-Love*, 18.
[19] Ibid., 31. Cf. 64; O'Donovan, 'Augustinian Ethics', 47; O'Donovan, *Common Objects*, especially chapter 1.
[20] O'Donovan, *Resurrection*, 120.
[21] Applying and extending, here, the terms of analysis used in Gerald P. McKenny, 'Responsibility', in *The Oxford Handbook of Theological Ethics*.
[22] O'Donovan, *Resurrection*, 122. Cf. O'Donovan, *Thirty-Nine Articles*, 98, *Ways*, 68, 'What Can Ethics Know about God?' 33, 40. For perceptive reconstruction of these themes see Victor Lee Austin, *Up With Authority: Why We Need Authority to Flourish as Human Beings* (London/New York: T & T Clark International, 2010), 74–91. O'Donovan's understanding of authority develops, as is well noted by Austin, as by Andrew Errington, in 'Authority and Reality in the Work of Oliver O'Donovan', *Studies in Christian Ethics* 29, no. 4 (2016): 371–85.
[23] Paul Elmen, 'Anglican Morality', in *The Study of Anglicanism*, ed. Stephen Sykes, John Booty and Jonathan Knight (London: SPCK/Minneapolis: Fortress Press, 1988), 364.

of the Anglican attempt (A. J. Joyce).[24] Rather, O'Donovan intends to assert their inner connection.[25]

Yet O'Donovan's definition of authority's relation to reality as currently configured is not wholly undialectical. It has two facets: one critical, in which unreality is exposed and judged, and one constructive, in which 'a new and truer structure for existence' is called into being.[26] Though this is, crucially, a single work of the Spirit, the double effect can be said (ambitiously) to correspond to a range of contrasting pairs within 'Christian moral thought: reflexive and ... directive conscience ... deontic and teleological ethics ... reason and will ... repentance and moral learning ... justification and sanctification ... conversion and instruction.'[27] It also corresponds to Christ's death and resurrection, showing something of the opposition of the two, which should not be 'collapsed': 'A moral authority which does not both judge and recreate is not the authority of Christ, but a purely natural authority, to follow which is to be conformed to the world.'[28]

To understand O'Donovan correctly, it is again important to see that what he means here by 'conformity to the world' is conformity to the 'apparent structure of order which is presented within the world': the kind of naturalism he earlier distinguished from his own natural ethic.[29] After all, his own ethic does very much recommend conformity to the authority of the world, the 'real' world behind that which is judged. If this real world is 'recreated', then he intends by that primarily that it is vindicated:

> God's authority, located as it is in a man's life and in his victory over death, may oppose the natural authorities in their rebellion and disorderliness, but is not opposed to the created order as such. It does not override our obligation to the truth in a 'teleological suspension of the ethical' such as Kierkegaard described, though it may criticise our perceptions of it. It promises to vindicate the authority of creation.[30]

What this means for eschatology's import is that the kingdom is not 'purely transcendent'; rather, it imposes 'true order upon our worldly obligations'.[31] Under it

---

[24] A. J. Joyce, *Richard Hooker and Anglican Moral Theology* (Oxford: Oxford University Press, 2012), 6, paraphrasing the view of Henry McAdoo. Cf. David H. Smith, 'Kenneth Kirk's *The Vision of God*', in *The Oxford Handbook of Theological Ethics*, 450.

[25] Among contemporary Christian ethicists, O'Donovan's basic instinct here is perhaps closest to one shared by that strand of Catholic moral theologians I mentioned earlier. Compare Pinckaers, *The Sources of Christian Ethics*, 354–78; Livio Melina, *Sharing in Christ's Virtues: For a Renewal of Moral Theology in Light of Veritatis Splendor*, trans. William E. May (Washington: Catholic University of America Press, 2001), 61–5.

[26] O'Donovan, *Resurrection*, 104.

[27] Ibid.

[28] Ibid., 105.

[29] Ibid., 104.

[30] Ibid., 142. Though beyond this study's remit, closer examination of O'Donovan's reading of Kierkegaard would get to the heart of some contemporary discussions in more theologically-conversant moral philosophy. I suspect O'Donovan is not always quite fair to the Dane. See C. Stephen Evans, *Kierkegaard's Ethic of Love: Divine Commands and Moral Obligations* (Oxford/New York: Oxford University Press, 2004), for a compelling reading – though, to be clear, one which does not base its case on *Fear and Trembling*, the work O'Donovan alludes to here.

[31] O'Donovan, *Resurrection*, 142.

'we can discover a positive ethic for life in the world', he writes, returning to a familiar refrain:

> We should not ... be tempted to set Jesus' 'radical' ethic of the kingdom against the practical this-worldliness of the apostolic churches, as we see it, for example, in the so-called Household Codes of the epistles. ... The moment of divine irruption is more than an irruption: it is the foundation of a renewed order.[32]

Though the book typically leans on the resurrection to make these claims, O'Donovan's conviction about divine authority's this-worldliness is also inferred from the incarnation. Of course, the resurrection presupposes the incarnation, and we should probably assume that a strong claim about the moral implications of the incarnation is made whenever we read one about the resurrection. (The best indication of the centrality of the incarnation to O'Donovan's argument may actually be seen outside his work, in the theological ethics of Brent Waters, who over an entire career has deployed the theology and ethics of *Resurrection and Moral Order* largely by foregrounding the incarnation.)[33] But in defending the place of this sense of worldly obligation in the moral life, O'Donovan will at times write directly of 'the foundation of Christian ethics in the incarnation':

> Since the Word became flesh and dwelt among us, transcendent divine authority has presented itself as worldly moral authority. It comes to us not as a *mysterium tremendum* which simply destroys all worldly order, but as creation restored and renewed, to which God is immediately present in the person of the Son of man. The teaching and life of Jesus must be *morally* authoritative if we are not to be thrown back upon the gnostic gospel of a visitor from heaven who summons us out of the world. We cannot regard the divine command, in Helmut Thielicke's distressing phrase, as 'extraplanetary material'. For though the redemption of the world had to be wrought from outside it by God's gracious intervention, it had still to be the redemption of the world. The meaning of Jesus' life and teaching must be a worldly meaning, a reality of human existence which can command our lives in the world and reorder them in the restored creation.[34]

---

[32] Ibid., 142, 143.
[33] For Waters's direct appeal to the book, see a long list besides *The Family*, where summary of *Resurrection*'s argument is the book's principal 'Theological Theme': 'The Incarnation and the Christian Moral Life', in *Christology and Ethics*, ed. Brent Waters and F. LeRon Shults (Grand Rapids: Eerdmans, 2010); *Reproductive Technology*, 34–7; 'What Is Christian about Christian Bioethics', *Christian Bioethics* 11, no. 3 (2005): 281–95, 289–91; *From Human to Posthuman: Christian Theology and Technology in a Postmodern World* (Aldershot: Ashgate, 2006), part 5 'An Alternative Theological Framework'; *This Mortal Flesh: Incarnation and Bioethics* (Grand Rapids: Brazos, 2009), 124–30, 160; 'Christian Ethics and Human Germ Line Genetic Modification', *Christian Bioethics* 18, no. 2 (2012): 171–86, 174–5; and *Christian Moral Theology in the Emerging Technoculture: From Posthuman Back to Human* (Farnham: Ashgate, 2014). The construct 'vindication' is central to each of these, too.
[34] O'Donovan, *Resurrection*, 142, 143.

O'Donovan's account of Christ's authority, then, centres on his identity as the One in whom 'we meet the moral order itself revealed as incarnate'.[35]

The engagement with Helmut Thielicke sheds further light. To O'Donovan's ears, Thielicke seems to be propounding an incipiently gnostic theology, 'troublingly like a gospel of deliverance from the world rather than of it'.[36] (A similar judgement on much twentieth-century Lutheranism is found in the work of theologians like David S. Yeago and Reinhard Hütter.)[37] Nonetheless, O'Donovan recognizes that Thielicke gives 'eschatological categories ... impressive existential immediacy', and alleviates the 'gnostic leaning' by maintaining that 'the new aeon, too, is "the world" in its renewed state'.[38] Ultimately, however, Thielicke's law-and-gospel schema fails to deliver: '[S]ince the new aeon can assume no form in this aeon except the formless form of protest, we are left, in effect, to be guided by the emergency orders.'[39] In other words, our form of life is not governed by the gospel, but by making do with law. This cannot satisfy O'Donovan, who wants a genuinely 'evangelical' worldliness, in which the gospel's normative force is felt. It is not 'that life in Christ can break out of its ambiguities and incompleteness before the parousia, but that life in Christ must not be denied its own ... (but with safeguards) law'.[40]

Wherever it appears, O'Donovan's dissatisfaction with Lutheran ethics ramifies from disagreement over this question.[41] In a way, I think O'Donovan sees in law-and-gospel the worst of what he sees in 'creation ethics' *and* 'kingdom ethics'. Law-and-gospel approaches cannot make sense of any ordered moral demand as positive, he says, because they envisage 'the liberating activity of God' simply as transcendent.[42] Normative Christian ethics is returned to 'something unevangelical', concerned with the 'purely provisional and transitory significance' of order, 'even the order of creation'.[43] In line with our aims in this study, O'Donovan response to these Lutherans is exactly about finding a positive moral role for eschatology in the current order:

> Jesus' moral authority is evangelical in the fullest sense, since the moral order which he proclaims is the kingdom of God, the theme of his message of salvation. It is a moral order in which the arbitrariness of sinful man's relation to God's purposes has been overcome and done away with. When Saint Matthew introduces Jesus' teaching with the programmatic summary, 'Repent, for the kingdom of heaven is

---

[35] Ibid., 147.
[36] Ibid., 145.
[37] See e.g. David S. Yeago, 'Gnosticism, Antinomianism, and Reformation Theology', *Pro Ecclesia* 2, no. 1 (1993): 37–49; Reinhard Hütter, *Bound to Be Free: Evangelical Catholic Engagements in Ecclesiology, Ethics, and Ecumenism* (Grand Rapids: Eerdmans, 2004), esp. part II. Hütter, with others like Bruce D. Marshall, is numbered among a number of high-profile ex-Lutherans, now Roman Catholic.
[38] O'Donovan, *Resurrection*, 145.
[39] Ibid.
[40] Ibid.
[41] Reiterated in the interaction with Martin Honecker in *Resurrection*'s preface.
[42] Ibid., 153.
[43] Ibid., 153–4. This extends to the realm of political theology and ethics. See Chapter 4.

at hand' (Mt. 4.17), he shows quite clearly how the moral challenge belongs with the eschatological message.[44]

Though I have already expressed misgivings about some aspects of the endeavour, *Resurrection and Moral Order* does attempt to weave the starkly eschatological biblical depiction of Jesus' proclamation and identity into the warp and weft of a philosophically realist ethic based on a – *the* – moral order. Unlike some Catholic and (historically) Anglican natural lawyers, or some law-and-gospel Lutherans, O'Donovan does not mean to consign the kingdom to an interior spiritual realm if by that it is meant any not-yet-ethical sphere.[45]

At his clearest, O'Donovan rightly shows that any reality we are given to know by Christian teaching (be that God's works of creation and redemption, or God's kingdom) must be taken to constitute the order of things that is morally normative. Or, to put it more precisely, as the claim seems sometimes to operate within O'Donovan's thought: in the case of creation it must be understood to *constitute* that order, and in the case of redemption and the kingdom of God it must be understood to be articulated in reference to such an order. If O'Donovan's construal of gospel and law – to which Barthians can assent[46] – is surely correct, then the way it interlocks with creation and eschatology in *Resurrection and Moral Order* may make us wonder what 'the kingdom of God' signifies in terms of reality.[47] Here, it is 'the moral order' that 'Jesus … proclaims'. And we know that O'Donovan portrays one, unified moral order, heretofore and hereafter understood as that which is created and restored in the resurrection. How exactly, then, does the kingdom of God form that order? Does it contribute anything distinctive? Perhaps the 'kingdom of God' and its 'eschatological message' mentioned here are coterminous with the vindication of creation and the proclamation of that vindication, respectively. If that is so, then O'Donovan's stated understanding of the way divine authority 'both judges and recreates' therefore seems less dialectical than it seemed.

In sum, it seems that in response to positions like Thielicke's, O'Donovan's attempt to work through both 'the subjective and the objective aspects of salvation' in terms of morality intentionally and reparatively amplifies the objective aspect when talking of

---

[44] Ibid., 155.

[45] Cf. earlier comments on Joachim Jeremias, whose 'anti-prescriptivist stance' to the commands of Jesus is dictated by convictions about '"Gospel and Law"'. O'Donovan, 'Towards an Interpretation of Biblical Ethics', *Tyndale Bulletin* 27 (1976): 54–78, 70. In 'How Can Theology Be Moral?', we find similar criticism of Luther, besides comments on the Reformed tradition, which 'tried to speak … more positively … about the ethical content of the Christian life', pioneering 'the work of Protestant moral theology', but itself did not relate 'this concern to soteriology' satisfactorily. Calvin's third use of the law 'still justified Christian ethics in terms of Paul's law-Gospel dichotomy, as a burden and a discipline' (90–1). That may sometimes be so, but would *not* be the case with the account of the *usus didacticus* as 'the law of the Spirit of life in Christ Jesus' (Rom. 8.2) which Calvin and the Reformed tradition can also expound. See e.g. Paul T. Nimmo, 'The Law of God and Christian Ethics', in *Christian Dogmatics: Reformed Theology for the Church Catholic*, ed. Michael Allen and Scott R. Swain (Grand Rapids: Baker Academic, 2016). And consider Aquinas's antecedent treatment of 'the New Law', 'the Law of the Gospel' (*Summa Theologiae*, Ia IIae, q. 106–8). Cf. Pamela M. Hall, 'The Old Law and the New Law', in *The Ethics of Aquinas*.

[46] Note O'Donovan, *Resurrection*, 154.

[47] Ibid., 154–5.

the subjective. Topics O'Donovan understands to belong to the subjective mode are never without reference to an objective baseline, which can itself be outlined with more abstraction from the subjective themes.[48] While he is able to expatiate upon themes like freedom and love with real insight, the anxieties over antinomianism (the other side of the law-and-gospel coin from legalism) and subjectivism sometimes impede the account's ability to reflect as well as it might on a number of dogmatic *loci* and related moral-theological implications. In the next section, I identify one as the doctrine of the Holy Spirit, and demonstrate the impact this has on O'Donovan's understanding of the moral significance of eschatology.

Pneumatology and Christology

If we have steadily observed the particular Christological determination of O'Donovan's thought, then we should also realize that his moral vision is richly pneumatological.[49] We saw in the discussions of freedom, love and authority how the doctrine of the Holy Spirit begins to figure. But my occasional concern about the book's handling of pneumatology arises, among other places, exactly in its account of Christ's authority, which seems sometimes to constrain recognition of the Spirit's role.

We read that God the Father, 'not the Holy Spirit', conferred authority upon Christ 'when God raised Jesus from the dead'.[50] I agree that the vindication of Jesus' authority is accomplished in the resurrection – and perhaps in some sense we have carefully to specify, the conferral of authority too (Rom. 1.4). But to state baldly that it is achieved without the Spirit's work is mistaken (compare again, perhaps, Rom. 1.4). It is also to skip over or elide significant moments earlier: think of the Father's spoken conferral in Jesus's baptism, in which the Spirit does not simply effect the viewer's faith but the conferral itself, or Jesus's own self-recognition of vocation in the synagogue ('the Spirit of the Lord is upon me ...').[51] There are paradigmatic examples of the recognition of Christ's authority given by the Spirit before the resurrection, too.[52] And to state that the resurrection confers authority upon Christ without the agency of the Spirit is to appropriate the indivisible external works of the undivided Trinity to persons in a way that divides rather than distinguishes. A divine work *ad extra* can be attributed to the

---

[48] Ibid.
[49] Perhaps unusually so – if any group of theologian were incorrigible semi-Pelagians, surely it would be moralists, capable of Spirit-quenching concern for the importance of self-starting human action.
[50] O'Donovan, *Resurrection*, 140.
[51] On Christ's baptism, see Mt. 3.13-17, Mk 1.9-11, Lk. 3.21-23. On Christ's self-recognition, Lk. 4.18. We should not forget the transfiguration, either (Mt. 17.1-9, Mk 9.2-8, Lk. 9.28-36 (cf. O'Donovan, *Resurrection*, 150), 2 Pet. 1.16-18).
[52] Consider the synoptics' accounts of the people's amazement at one who taught 'with real authority' (Mt. 7.29; Mk 1.22; Lk. 4.32), and, in the Johannine account of the wedding at Cana (Jn 2), Mary's bold recognition of Jesus' authority (which, if we were so inclined, could also represent her participation in authority's conferral).

Father (or the Son or Spirit) eminently, but not exclusively; not so that we can say 'not' about the other persons' involvement.[53]

This misstep, like some others we will consider later, seems a little strange given that O'Donovan absolutely does seek a constructive understanding of the work of the Spirit in the divine economy, and of pneumatology's ethical entailments. And O'Donovan aims to do so specifically in regard to authority. Before Easter, he observes, there may have been doubt that the created order was good; now he observes that before Pentecost (and personal sharing in the life of the Spirit) there may still be doubt that the restoration of that order in Christ is good news *for us*. 'Even a realist understanding of the redeemed world-order can be arbitrary if it is not related to the existential situation of the agent.'[54] Apostolic proclamation of the Spirit does just this, speaking 'of God at work within us, applying and confirming God's act in Christ for us', showing that 'the redeemed creation does not merely confront us moral agents, but includes us and enables us to participate in it'.[55]

Intriguingly, the strict theo-logic governing O'Donovan's use of 'the words "objective" and "subjective" turns out to be the distinction between the act of God in Christ for us and the work of God in the Spirit within us.[56] I am particularly interested in this because the distinction shapes a number of passages in Part Two that portray the Spirit's work in terms of ethics, and in so doing, often start to entertain eschatology's import. For example:

> When we say that the Spirit makes the reality of what God has done in Jesus 'authoritative to us', we are speaking not of how the authority of Christ comes to *be*, but of how, originating apart from us, it comes to *claim* us, of how we 'enter' the kingdom of heaven. The work of the Spirit, who does not speak 'from himself', is to bear witness to the kingdom, making its reality present to us as he elicits our faith, and making its authority bear upon us as he elicits our free obedience.[57]

O'Donovan elucidations of the Spirit's work in creaturely life, then, anchor it in Christology, countermanding any drift towards understanding that work in abstraction from Christ's. The lines that follow those just quoted are a small-print excursus on the Holy Spirit's ministry that detail this theo-logic very tightly:

> In Jesus all truth, the truth of world-order and the truth of world-history, is summed up. The Spirit is not given to create the new reality, since in the exaltation of the Christ the new reality has been given its decisive form; but he is given to bring that new reality to bear upon the old, to 'speak what he hears' (i.e. the Father's

---

[53] 'We believe and confess that in every deed and thought, either of this world or beyond this world, either in time or eternity, the Holy Spirit is to be understood as joined with the Father and Son'. Gregory of Nyssa, *On the Holy Spirit: Against the Followers of Macedonius*, 14, quoted in John Anthony McGuckin, *The Orthodox Church: An Introduction to Its History, Doctrine, and Spiritual Culture* (Oxford: Wiley-Blackwell, 2008), 137.
[54] O'Donovan, *Resurrection*, 151.
[55] Ibid., 101.
[56] Ibid.
[57] Ibid., 140.

decree concerning the Son) and to 'declare what is to come' (i.e. the universal manifestation of the kingdom of God at the fulfilment of history). Thus he is to 'glorify' Jesus, which is not to usurp the Father's prerogative in exalting him, but to give what the Father has done a universal resonance in the praise offered by a redeemed and obedient creation. ... To speak of a divine authority after the resurrection of Christ is to speak of the authority of the exalted Christ. There is nothing left to say, no codicil or postscript in which the Spirit might address us with a divine claim that did not refer us to Christ's rule.[58]

More doctrinal passages of *Thirty-Nine Articles* convey much the same understanding: 'What God does for the individual believer ... is not a new and different work, a further "making righteous", but an application of the one complete work, a "counting" of this believer into the righteous Kingdom already established.'[59] Most pithily: 'Pentecost is not *added* to the sequence, Christmas, Easter, Ascension, as a further and additional moment of divine revelation, but rather stands apart from them, casting light back on them and interpreting them.'[60] A Pentecost sermon O'Donovan preached around the same time strikes a similar note: 'The Spirit, as Christ's Spirit, initiates us into the whole of Christ's life, and especially into his death and resurrection': 'The gift of the Spirit is, first and foremost, the gift of recapitulating Christ's way. ... The Spirit is the Recapitulator, who makes the achieved work of Christ present in every age. In recapitulation is our newness.'[61]

On my reading, many of these theological statements are sound enough. But there is perhaps a pattern worth noticing, in which O'Donovan more frequently reminds us to connect talk of the Spirit in ethics to talk of Christ than vice versa. Christological aspects, like aspects of creation, are dilated upon freely – though each of these as 'objective' is, in theory, not to be left unsupplemented, and though together, as the structure of the book suggests, they are without subjective counterparts incomplete as an account of the moral life. Yet pneumatological themes, like themes of the kingdom and subjectivity, are often allowed no such unhurried treatment before we are returned to the main subjects.[62] Why is that the case – and is there anything objectionable in it?

---

[58] Ibid. One might think, uncharitably, of Eugene Rogers' somewhat irreverent question, 'is there anything the Spirit can do that Jesus cannot do better? And if Jesus can do everything better than the Spirit, what is the Spirit for?' (Rogers, 'Holy Spirit', in *The Cambridge Dictionary of Christian Theology*, ed. Ian A. McFarland, David A. S. Fergusson, Karen Kilby and Iain R. Torrance (Cambridge: Cambridge University Press, 2011), 221). However, we must not merely assume that the right way to testify to the Spirit's divine dignity and distinct mode of operation is, as it were, for theology to give the Spirit something else to do off in his own; rather, the point here is probably for theology to indicate what it discovers of the distinct way in which the Spirit participates fully within all of the divine works *ad extra*. And O'Donovan is, here, seeking to show the mutual co-inherence of the distinct missions of Son and Spirit.
[59] O'Donovan, *Thirty-Nine Articles*, 79.
[60] Ibid., 45.
[61] O'Donovan, *Small Boats*, 48 (Sermon from 1988).
[62] By saying this, I am not saying that we *should* think kingdom a more subjective or a more pneumatological concept than it is an objective or Christological one: it is just that O'Donovan's categories seem sometimes to line them up this way.

O'Donovan's relative pneumatological restraint has a theological commitment behind it, which I think is likely reinforced by judgements of circumstance. Let us examine first the contextual factor, and then the theological dimension. When O'Donovan writes about pneumatological themes, his awareness of the dangers associated with enthusiasm seems to crowd in quickly, perhaps determining the account of freedom to a greater extent than any worries about naturalism, for example, determined the account of created order. There seem to be two kinds of enthusiasm in view. On one front, reasonable conjecture would be that O'Donovan has conversations occasioned by the charismatic renewal movement in mind. When he speaks, for instance, of the need to bring a 'Christological principle of criticism to the manifestation of spirits, present or past, within the church ... avoiding excessive admiration of spontaneity ... and ... excessive reverence for tradition', it might be read that way.[63]

On another front are ongoing disputes with liberal Protestantism, most sharply delineated in *Church in Crisis*. Commenting there on the 'fall into incoherence' that imperils 'the liberal hermeneutic', O'Donovan writes that avoiding it means facing 'a simple alternative':

> Either it posits some further climax of salvation history over and beyond Christ, some 'age of the Spirit' such as Montanus or Joachim conceived of, or a Hegelian dialectical history with an Absolute Future, something, at any rate, that will allow a 'deepened moral sensitivity' to which the revelation of the incarnation looks immature and outgrown. Or else it makes a distinction between the normative position of Jesus himself and the subnormative position of the apostolic authors, refusing to claim on their behalf the kind of finality it claims for him.[64]

Thus O'Donovan's pneumatological restraint might be a point of deliberate differentiation from much contemporary Christianity on both 'left' and 'right'. Perhaps, then, if the pneumatology of *Resurrection and Moral Order* may seem at times a little thin, then that leanness represents an overreaction to 'pneumatological hypertrophy' in contemporary church life and thought.[65] The theological tendency O'Donovan is reacting against, I think, is what Ephraim Radner has in an outspoken essay called 'pneumatological expansionism', and characterized fiercely as 'a bane of modern theology'.[66] Yet I do not think O'Donovan imagined his project as essentially cautious in terms of speech about the Spirit, so much as, in fact, remedially pneumatological. In

---

[63] O'Donovan, *Resurrection*, 141. O'Donovan's account of tradition involves confident affirmations and Protestant qualifications. See 'Scripture and Christian Ethics', 23.

[64] O'Donovan, *Church in Crisis*, 62. Again, there is more of interest in the link to Joachim of Fiore than I am able to do justice to. For brief introduction, see Yves Congar, *I Believe in the Holy Spirit*, 1.126-37. Cf. Löwith, *Meaning in History*, ch. 8, and Bernard McGinn, *The Calabrian Abbot: Joachim of Fiore in the History of Western Thought* (New York: MacMillan, 1985).

[65] Geoffrey Wainwright, 'The Holy Spirit', in *The Cambridge Companion to Christian Doctrine*, ed. Colin Gunton (Cambridge: Cambridge University Press, 1997), 289.

[66] See Ephraim Radner, 'The Holy Spirit and Unity: Getting Out of the Way of Christ', *International Journal of Systematic Theology* 16, no. 2 (2014): 207–20, 207. And now, a book: Ephraim Radner, *A Profound Ignorance: Modern Pneumatology and Its Anti-modern Redemption* (Waco: Baylor University Press, 2019).

Thirty-Nine Articles, he expresses as much worry about an eclipse of proper reflection on the Spirit's work – criticizing its status as an 'afterthought' in that document and much theology – as about the excesses of a Christologically untethered pneumatology.[67] It is the latter concern, though, which seems to motivate some passages in *Resurrection and Moral Order* and elsewhere.

Nevertheless, it is first and foremost for theological reasons, I think, that O'Donovan firmly situates pneumatology's bearing on the moral life as an irreversibly second thought, consecutive upon Christology. And let us be absolutely clear, before saying anything else, that there is nothing unfitting about a Christological focus in an account of divine economy – such is the focus of biblical and traditional descriptions. (And Christ is the measure of an account of moral action, too.) This fitting Christocentrism does not at all have to mean derogation of the Spirit's work, and O'Donovan for the most part shows that well. I do not consider his strict reminders of the Christological anchoring and directionality of pneumatological speech unnecessary; absent recognition of the Christological origin and Christoform goal of the perfection wrought by the Holy Spirit, pneumatology will lose its footing in the gospel proclamation of the economy of salvation, and just so its right trinitarian definition.

It is true that we should not allow due cognisance of these considerations, which as regards status entail simply a 'distinction of order' or 'mere sequence' between the Son and the Spirit (Gregory of Nyssa),[68] to shade into an apparent distinction of dignity, relegating the Spirit to a lesser place in an apparent baton-exchange of divine missions.[69] Yet in O'Donovan's sketches of salvation's narrative, we have also seen the ability to illustrate the distinct dignity of the Spirit's work 'after' the Son's. We may compare, for example, this fine depiction of sanctification rendered by Ivor Davidson, and notice its consonance with the general shape of O'Donovan's:

> As Spirit, God brings this work to actuality, perfecting creatures in their personal histories by uniting them to Christ, working in them what has been wrought for them by the Son in fulfilment of the Father's purpose. The Spirit does this in our individual histories, making a saint of this, and this, and the next sinner, awakening, calling and enabling him or her, as a personal subject, to realise the freedom, obedience, love and fulfilment of a status objectively appointed and objectively secured.[70]

Still, at times, including in some of those passages quoted earlier, O'Donovan's allergy to pneumatological projection does seem to produce too severe a hermeneutic of suspicion about ethical invocations of the Spirit – suspicion aroused especially when

---

[67] This is the title of the third chapter of *On the Thirty-Nine Articles*.
[68] Gregory of Nyssa, *On the Holy Spirit*, 14, quoted in McGuckin, *The Orthodox Church*, 137.
[69] Rogers' memorable critical characterization of a (near-modalistic?) 'linear' conception of the divine economy (Rogers, 'Holy Spirit', 221; though to my mind it is not clear that Rogers' alternative proposal always escapes charges justly made against 'social trinitarianism' by Karen Kilby and others).
[70] Ivor J. Davidson, 'Gospel Holiness: Some Dogmatic Reflections', in *Sanctification: Explorations in Theology and Practice*, ed. Kelly Kapic (Downers Grove: IVP, 2014), 204.

such invocations carry the impression that the eschatological (perhaps immanently historical) future will 'leave behind' the definite form of creation and its vindication in Christ. That is not to say there is nothing to be suspicious about. A Joachimite tendency in modern theology has been powerfully criticized in all its many iterations – including Moltmann's – by Henri de Lubac and Hans Urs von Balthasar.[71] And, relatedly, the 'Hegelian (and subsequent idealist) influence' within recent theology is 'diverse and widespread', perhaps especially within Protestant systematic theology and theological ethics of the kind written during O'Donovan's career.[72] (O'Donovan's thumbnail sketches of that influence now find a massively ramified counterpart in Cyril O'Regan's efforts to detail the Hegelian tradition as the resurgence of a Gnosticism.)[73]

O'Donovan does not overreact to pneumatological projection to the same extent as, for instance, Radner, who can write incautiously that 'pneumatological categories are, by their very nature, voracious of temporal concretization, and seem always to end by subverting the acute focus of christological form, ethically'.[74] That unfortunate phrasing, more so than anything O'Donovan says, is wont to imply that pneumatology – perhaps even the Spirit – is the problem, rather than a Christologically underdetermined expression of the Spirit's work.[75] Perhaps O'Donovan's early work – we shall see a shift in more recent writing – does not always steer entirely clear of that implication. At its best, however, *Resurrection and Moral Order* supports the contention that there is no reason why a careful exposition, attentive to the order of teaching and to the way salvation plays out, should curtail pneumatological elaboration of the moral life.

Finally, and to integrate these reflections directly with the particular question of eschatology, we may observe that pneumatological elaboration of the moral life should be one of the ways in which moral theology sets out eschatology's import for ethics.

---

[71] See Jürgen Moltmann, *Theology of Hope: On the Ground and Implications of a Christian Eschatology*, trans. J. W. Leitch (London: SCM Press, 1967); *The Trinity and the Kingdom*, trans. Margaret Kohl (London: SCM Press, 1981); *The Coming of God: Christian Eschatology*, trans. Margaret Kohl (Minneapolis: Fortress, 1996). Neither Flipper's already-referenced book nor Nicholas J. Healy, *The Eschatology of Hans Urs von Balthasar: Being as Communion* (Oxford/New York: Oxford University Press, 2005), touched on this engagement, which is a shame because it seems to me a neglected divergence in twentieth-century theology. But see Kenneth Oakes, 'Henri de Lubac and Protestantism', in *T & T Clark Companion to Henri de Lubac*, 388–90, and especially Cyril O'Regan, *Theology and the Spaces of Apocalyptic* (Milwaukee, Marquette University Press, 2009), 48–50, 104–7, 122–3.

[72] Quoting here Lewis Ayres, in the provocative final chapter, 'In Spite of Hegel, Fire, and Sword', of *Nicaea and Its Legacy: An Approach to Fourth-Century Theology* (Oxford: Oxford University Press, 2004), 406. Here Ayres indicates Pannenberg, Moltmann, and Jüngel, besides their influence on English-speaking theology, exemplified by Jenson.

[73] Cyril O'Regan, *The Heterodox Hegel* (Albany: SUNY Press, 1994), and many subsequent volumes.

[74] Radner, 'The Holy Spirit', 219. With more specific relevance for my question of eschatology and ethics, Radner writes elsewhere, in a similarly provocative article, of an 'uncertain pneumatic dynamism' in eschatological transformation, which needs 'a concrete form … the human body assumed by Jesus', to 'stabilise' it ('The Mystery of Christian Anthropology', in *Anthropology and New Testament Theology*, ed. Jason Maston and Benjamin E. Reynolds (London/New York: Bloomsbury T & T Clark, 2018), 260). Yves Congar, one of the most wonderful pneumatologists of recent times, is unfailing in the Christological anchoring of his doctrine of the Spirit, but within these proper bounds does not misspeak like this and finds plenty more to say.

[75] To speak of 'pneumatological hypertrophy' runs the same risk: we mean a set of mistaken extensions of 'pneumatological' categories, and pneumatology insufficiently integrated with the rest of Christian teaching. The problem is not 'too much of the Spirit'!

Consider in this vein a last quotation on the work of the Holy Spirit from *Resurrection and Moral Order*, in which O'Donovan explains the way in which 'the Spirit makes the reality of redemption, distant from us in time, both present and authoritative ... evokes our free response to this reality'.[76]

> The restoration of created order is an event which lies in the past; its universal manifestation belongs to the future. Yet on these two points, the resurrection of Jesus Christ from the dead and his Parousia, the whole of our life is made to depend even now, as each moment of it successively forms our present. ... We speak of the Spirit when we make the transition from 'then' to 'now', when the remembered past and the unthinkable future become realities which shape our present. The work of the Holy Spirit defines an age – the age in which all times are immediately present to that time, the time of Christ ... the Spirit makes the reality of redemption *authoritative* to us; for authority is the mode in which this past and future reality is also present. There are other ways, immanent and non-authoritative, by which past and future events enter into the present and affect it. Events have consequences which endure, sometimes in the form of lasting institutions or pervasive habits of thought. Events can be anticipated, and excite us to action in expectancy and hope. But the redemptive moment, or moments, of Christ's passion and triumph act upon our present in quite another way. They are God's final deed, the *eschaton* in which history is given its meaning; and as such they stand equidistant from all moments of time and determine what the reality of each moment is. 'Authority' and 'reality' are inseparable aspects of the presence of God.[77]

Granted, we may again stumble over the past tense 'restoration of created order' and wonder about its relation to the 'universal manifestation' that 'belongs to the future'. And there are other details we may pause over, for instance, the way hope is used as a forwards-looking example of how future events immanently and non-authoritatively enter into the present and affect it. Though this is presumably meant in relation to anticipation of events other than the Christ event, the argument may run parallel to the way even Christian hope appears as non-authoritative, morally at least, in other places within O'Donovan's earlier thought. Equally we may be wary of the way lasting institutions or pervasive habits of thought are used as the backwards-looking example of this immanent and non-authoritative influence; again, one presumes this is meant in relation to institutions other than the church and its patterns of belief, so there is likely nothing to worry about. At any rate, there is much to appreciate in this passage, and perhaps especially its pneumatological articulation of the moral implications of the saving work of Christ – once for all, yet still to be fully unveiled.

Now we may turn to consideration of another of the themes in *Resurrection and Moral Order* in which the interplay of objective and subjective plays out, and regarding which we must again entertain a critical question about the reduction of the subjective aspect.

---

[76] O'Donovan, *Resurrection*, 102.
[77] Ibid., 102–3. Cf. O'Donovan, *Thirty-Nine Articles*, 38, 41–4, 123.

The divine command and the order of creation

Among those questions raised and answered in Part Two of his book is one O'Donovan thinks is 'basic to all theological ethics … the relation of the divine command to the order of creation. How does God's word engage our obedience when it would seem that our obedience is totally committed to the authority of created order as it is present to our reason?'[78] In what follows, I evaluate O'Donovan's answer on its own terms, concentrating both on its significance and its tendency to flatten the angularity of divine command wholesale into the consistencies predicated of created order. I also show how this answer – indeed the book's ethical approach as a whole – places us within the ambit of contemporary meta-ethical debates in Christian ethics, and how, despite that limitation, it contributes to them.

Two traditions, says O'Donovan, present different answers to this question of the relation of divine command to the order of creation. Theological rationalism gives one that is 'continualist': 'God speaks *through* the order which reason perceives.'[79] It seeks 'to trace an ontological continuity between the secondary authorities of creation and the primary authority of God'[80] This attempt can avoid pantheism if executed with the care of Thomas Aquinas, but particular formulations – even Thomas's – engender overweening confidence in human rationality, bereft of 'self-critical responsibility to objective truth.'[81] By contrast, theological voluntarism gives a 'discontinualist' answer: 'God's command *cuts across* our rational perceptions and relativises them.'[82] It is 'concerned to make a sharp distinction between the authority of the divine command and any authority that man might discern within the order of creation'.[83]

Both traditions can claim biblical warrant; yet each taken in isolation 'has shown a tendency to degenerate into humanism' (by this I think O'Donovan means an inappropriately anthropocentric conception of the moral life).[84] We therefore need to 'include true perceptions from both sides, just as the corresponding statements about created order and history … needed to accommodate both the inherent teleology of creation and its historical destining to transformation'.[85] Rationalism, for its part, 'was not wrong to promise an ultimate scrutability in the divine purpose; it was wrong only as it attempted to empty that promise of its eschatological character and hurry forward to a premature fulfilment by the route of a reductive immanentism'.[86] Voluntarism, too, witnessed to a particular theological truth. For late medieval theological voluntarists did not imagine creation without divine ordering, but held to their position because they sought to maintain 'the immediate contingency of morality upon the declared will of God … not derived from God *through* the created order':

---

[78] O'Donovan, *Resurrection*, 132.
[79] Ibid.
[80] Ibid., 133.
[81] Ibid.
[82] Ibid., 134.
[83] Ibid.
[84] Ibid., 132.
[85] Ibid.
[86] Ibid., 136.

The voluntarist was also right to stress that God's freedom to innovate was not adequately described in terms of a *lex aeterna*, a blueprint which could not be changed but could only be successively realised. God's action can encompass novelty, that which is itself unpredictable except in terms of God's own declaration of his intent: 'Behold, I am doing a new thing'. (Is. 43.19)[87]

If God's action can encompass novelty, though, then 'God's freedom also implies his self-posited faithfulness':

> When we say that God 'bound himself' in the covenant of creation, we use a paradoxical metaphor, certainly, but what we say is not meaningless. … God's freedom is exercised in congruence with itself. It is not randomness, turning idly back upon itself and cancelling out its own creative deed, but redemptive transformation, which respects and exalts that which has gone before. Rationalism was correct to predicate coherence of God's deeds. 'He cannot deny himself', says the apostle (2 Tim. 2.13) not thereby setting a limit on God's power, but declaring that God's unlimited power includes also the power to be consistent with itself.[88]

Altogether, O'Donovan perhaps takes a more nuanced line there than we might have expected, then, given 'The Natural Ethic'. Nonetheless it would still be safe to say that what he considers indispensable in the voluntarist contention is preserved so as to accommodate it into a broadly rationalist proposal.

Resurrection and Moral Order repeatedly emphasizes the essential unity and constancy of God's action – and sees divine action expressed normatively in the forms of natural life – even as it acknowledges that moral discernment of it in time is diverse. Love, once more, is the key, 'the unitary orientation that lies behind all the uniquely varied responses to the generic variety of the created order'.[89] As before, O'Donovan connects this point with vocation, again sublating it into an account of the unified ground, form and *telos* of action:

> The particularity of vocation must serve as a window through which the universal character may appear. Just as the variety of voices within the church are unified in a common confession, 'Jesus is Lord' so the variety of forms of life are unified within a common form of life according to God's order, the life of love.[90]

Church in Crisis puts it more strongly still: '[V]ocation cannot provide a comprehensible idea of the good on its own. To appreciate its contribution, we have to tie it back into

---

[87] Ibid.
[88] Ibid.
[89] Ibid., 224.
[90] Ibid., 222. Thomist moral theologians are also concerned with this relationship. So Melina: 'The singularity of the person and the universality of human nature are the undeniable poles for exercising Christian prudence, which, perfected by the gifts of the Spirit, guides one to fulfilment of one's own personal vocation in Christ'. Melina, *Sharing in Christ's Virtues*, 8.

the goods of creation'.[91] The reason for this, as *Resurrection and Moral Order* argues, is that 'a metaphysic of ethics must be unitary. If an act is obligatory, it is so by virtue of its relation, whether direct or indirect, to the good; and by virtue of that same relation the performance of it is free'.[92] This means something quite concrete:

> The disciple who obeys the divine word in defiance of his own limited perceptions of right is genuinely trustful only if he believes that the paradox is not an ultimate contradiction in reality. He must hope to see the moment of critical confrontation finally resolved by the elevation of his reason to grasp God's action as a coherent whole.[93]

Such an elevation, however, is truly eschatological, given 'in moments of grace'.[94]

Rowing back for the time being from what are noteworthy practical and pastoral implications, we should notice that O'Donovan intends the relation posited here to, at the same time, outline, metaethically, the right connection between the divergent considerations that lie behind the 'antithesis of voluntarist and rationalist understandings of morality'.[95] And inasmuch as O'Donovan seeks like this to integrate voluntarist and rationalist commitments, his moral anthropology seeks to comprehend and integrate the powers of will and of reason. It may be that O'Donovan was quite ahead of his time within Protestant moral theology in attempting this.[96] Moreover, by offering a theological case for that integration, rather than an Aristotelian-Thomist argument about the structure of practical reason, he represents an advance on otherwise similar positions.[97]

---

[91] O'Donovan, *Church in Crisis*, 99. Cf. the partly autobiographical preface to *Self, World and Time*: 'stern activism is more attractive as a charism than as a universal prescription' (ix), and the distinction between vocation and personal choice on the one hand, and moral stance on the other, already made in 'The Natural Ethic' (20). I find it helpful to imagine O'Donovan's sense of his vocation as similar to the way Marcia Colish describes that of St Ambrose: 'a teacher of moderation for the many, and not merely ... a teacher of asceticism for the few'. Colish, *Ambrose's Patriarchs: Ethics for the Common Man* (Notre Dame: University of Notre Dame Press, 2005), 158.

[92] O'Donovan, *Resurrection*, 170. O'Donovan's claims here can again be compared with those of C. Stephen Evans, and with a number of thinkers also cited later in this chapter, like R.M. Adams, who O'Donovan takes as an interlocutor throughout his career. I can only suggest this comparison here, prioritizing other questions.

[93] Ibid., 136.

[94] Ibid., 139.

[95] Ibid., 137–9.

[96] Renewed study of the distinct characteristics of will and reason and their place in moral reasoning within Catholic moral theology has been fuelled by new studies of Aquinas, for example, Michael Sherwin, *By Knowledge and By Love: Charity and Knowledge in the Moral Theology of St. Thomas Aquinas* (Washington: Catholic University of America Press, 2005). As yet, this Thomistic focus seems to mean that they do not range as freely across the Christian tradition as O'Donovan.

[97] I am thinking above all of the highly impressive proposals made by the late Daniel Westberg, which nonetheless may set too great store by this structure, without correspondingly serious theological defence. See, technically, Westberg's first book *Right Practical Reason: Aristotle, Action, and Prudence in Aquinas* (Oxford: Oxford University Press, 1994), which originated in a DPhil thesis supervised by O'Donovan and Herbert McCabe. Later, in *Renewing Moral Theology*, Westberg writes: 'The harmony and unity of intellect and will are properly restored by our four-stage model' (52). This is, no doubt, a sophisticated reproduction of practical reason's operations. Yet putting it like this raises questions for those of us whose worries about sin's noetic effects suggest themselves

Relatedly, when I say that O'Donovan's approach is on its own terms broadly rationalist, I do so not just because it seeks to incorporate insights from voluntarism, but because he adopts rationalism's concern for moral order in the world, rather than what he sees as its inappropriately anthropocentric concern for moral order in the human mind. O'Donovan's comments elsewhere, on the encyclical *Veritatis Splendor*, highlight the distinction. Though impressed by John Paul II's criticism of much twentieth-century ethics, he worries that the pope speaks 'out of a species of Christian idealism', offering 'some startling hostages to the claims of unaided natural reason': 'What is lacking in contemporary trends in moral thought is a sense of moral order in the world. Can he repair this with a stress on moral order in the mind? I am not sure.'[98] I agree that the encyclical offers such hostages. But we can imagine that a defender of *Veritatis Splendor* could reply to O'Donovan that O'Donovan's need always to show, by a *second* move, how the restored order of creation is directly relevant for human action, could have been avoided by what Livio Melina terms the encyclical's 'personalistic interpretation of the classical doctrine of the natural law'.[99] Still, the general thrust of O'Donovan's integration is in the same direction as the Catholic trend towards personalistic and increasingly theological interpretation of natural law.[100]

In any event, for O'Donovan, we must principally attribute moral order to the world, and this is imperative if we are to understand divine commands correctly. As he writes in an article on 'Scripture and Christian Ethics': '[C]ommands are events that occur within a relationship. A bare order barked out parade-ground fashion means nothing unless there is some parade-ground that will constitute a relation between the barker and the barked at.'[101] That constitutive relation, I presume, is the created order. The emphasis, again, is partially 'rationalist' but not, perhaps, rationalistic. A helpful comparison can be made with the thought of Nigel Biggar, who conjures a similar image in more pronounced fashion when writing, *contra* Barth, that 'command should be legislative before it is military', because 'conceiving God's commands in military rather than legislative terms … implies that receiving or hearing a command of God

---

sooner than they seem to for Aristotelian-Thomists – especially when reading an introduction to Christian ethics the first four chapters of which detail a not-necessarily theological approach to moral reason. Even if a model of practical reason can purport to restore the harmony of unity and will, we want to know how sin has fractured the moral reason of actual moral actors, not just of incomplete theories of moral action, and how grace reveals that fracture and begins to transform it. Thankfully, later chapters (see 76, 98–9) return to the theme, culling vital Augustinian insights (think of Augustine's developing interpretation of Rom. 7). The book's order of presentation is not illogical: human reason is created before fallen. And general human reason is the subject of 'ethics' before Christian moral reason is, on Westberg's understanding. But should Christian ethics have to piece together *ex post facto* from 'natural' accounts, the actuality of the way reason and will present themselves in the moral life of those who, we know all too well, are not just creaturely but sinful?

[98] O'Donovan, 'A Summons to Reality', 44.
[99] Melina, *Sharing Christ's Virtues*, 72.
[100] In the latter respect, see e.g. Russell Hittinger, 'Natural Law and Catholic Moral Theology', in *A Preserving Grace: Protestants, Catholics, and Natural Law*, ed. Michael Cromartie (Grand Rapids: Eerdmans, 1997). While welcoming these developments, we may continue to urge more developed explication of natural law's underpinnings in doctrines of creation and providence, and less isolation from Christology, soteriology and eschatology (not to mention the doctrine of sin).
[101] O'Donovan, 'Scripture and Christian Ethics', 25.

takes the place of reflecting and reasoning – that it is a substitute for ethics'.[102] Clearly their views are substantially similar. Prudential deliberation is prominent for both, and there is a shared and deep-seated resistance to any perceived moral irrationalism. But O'Donovan typically seems to strive a bit harder to acknowledge divine freedom, and his worry about 'bare' commands is more immediately determined by their apparent contentlessness and separation from an always-already provided order, than their threat to moral reasoning as such.

I still think, though, that O'Donovan subsumes divine commands too quickly under 'the authority of created order as it is present to our reason'. Why does he do so? For one thing, it is no doubt the case that any apparent absence of 'horizontal' mediations of the divine will would undermine the moral universalism inherent in some of his foundational claims. There is, as we have seen, a Christocentric particularism inherent in O'Donovan's notion of the *revelation* of this order's origin, coherence and *telos*. But his claims about that order's intelligibility and normativity as such are certainly based on the integrity of natural order in its imprint of divine purpose. Yet if God's ethically determinative address, and not just in the special calling of vocation, may bypass moral reason's generic valuations of earthly goods – or even simply disrupts those valuations in disjunctive transformation – then it would not be possible to maintain as confidently that 'the *exclusive* object of ethical reflection is the same created order shared by all persons across time and culture'.[103]

Second, and relatedly, this kind of rationalist construal perhaps seems more readily available to O'Donovan than it should because of a tendency to marginalize considerations that theology would press upon ethics besides the doctrine of creation, namely sin and redemption. More precisely as regards redemption, we might say that O'Donovan may neglect to imagine it as a reality to which divine commands can correspond, beyond creation's restoration. This disinclination is seen most clearly in comments in 'the Foundations of Ethics':

> The point of the commands is that they give a moral exposition of the response elicited by God's acts of salvation. They draw their authority *from* the acts; they do not supply an authority which the acts have somehow failed to supply. Reality is authoritative and action-evoking, and nothing else is. In his acts God has determined the reality that now conditions us; in his commands he has explained what this reality requires of us.[104]

---

[102] Nigel Biggar, 'Karl Barth's Ethics Revisited', in *Commanding Grace: Studies in Karl Barth's Ethics*, ed. Daniel L. Migliore (Grand Rapids: Eerdmans, 2010), 29–30. It is important to say that contemporary readings of Barth on these topics diverge. Compare, for instance, Paul Nimmo, *Being in Action: The Theological Shape of Barth's Ethical Vision* (London/New York: T & T Clark, 2007), and Matthew Rose, *Ethics with Barth: God, Metaphysics and Morals* (Farnham/Burlington: Ashgate, 2010). The direction in which Rose would take Barth's ethics seems much closer to O'Donovan than that presented by Nimmo.

[103] The quotation borrows a description of the universal aspect of Balthasar's moral vision which fits the same aspect of O'Donovan's ethics well. See Christopher Steck, *The Ethical Thought of Hans Urs von Balthasar* (New York: Herder & Herder, 2001), 94, who tends to call this aspect 'Catholic'. Italics added.

[104] O'Donovan, 'The Foundations of Ethics', 100–1. Cf. O'Donovan, 'How Can Theology Be Moral?' 88.

It is right to say God's acts of salvation determine *the* morally determinative reality. But, as that article goes on to demonstrate in an even more unmistakeable manner than the book, O'Donovan seems to consider those acts to be exhausted in 'the recovery of creation', and therefore the reality that now conditions us to be simply the restored created order.[105] Because of this, it is not clear to me that O'Donovan escapes the error he alleges rationalism of making, in which it 'attempted to empty the divine purpose of its eschatological character, hurrying forwarded to a premature fulfilment by the route of a reductive immanentism'.

At worst, the less qualified rationalist claims O'Donovan makes court a mislocation of moral authority. And the mistake a purely rationalist moralist would make is not trivial: '[T]o speak of a course of ethical action on the basis of a flawed perception of the cosmos … is to court disaster.'[106] Yet what we may more precisely worry about with O'Donovan is his claims fail to effect the integration of 'divine command' and 'the order of creation' in a manner that shows as much attention to the second and third articles of the creed as the first. That is, they fail to conceive the natural order in its actual history within the drama of salvation. What this means for a model of moral discernment is that O'Donovan does not emphasize as much as he might the way in which the sovereign address of God directs our evaluation of the manifold moral claims of creaturely life. More could surely be said about how the radically personal and historical events of God's call upon each of us refashion moral reason's weighing of intra-mundane goods that are themselves not always quite so simply 'given'.[107] Further, bearing in mind the common critique of 'divine command theory', we need not imagine God's address therein as arbitrary, punctiliar or occasionalistic; to imagine that the summons to free obedience issues from some kind of naked divine will sundered from divine wisdom and the display of that wisdom across the manifold works of grace is to project an abstraction forgetful of all that we have been given to know of God's self-revelation in the Lord Jesus Christ.[108] Nor does the refashioning of moral

---

[105] O'Donovan, 'The Foundations of Ethics', 97.

[106] So J. Louis Martyn, 'De-apocalyptising Paul: An Essay Focused on *Paul and the Stoics* by Troels Engberg-Pedersen', *Journal for the Study of the New Testament* 24, no. 4 (2002): 61–102, 102, quoted in Philip G. Ziegler, *Militant Grace: The Apocalyptic Turn and the Future of Christian Theology* (Grand Rapids: Baker Academic, 2018), 138. I am afraid that I have come to think that Martyn courts other kinds of error, which any pursuit of 'apocalyptic' theology should not gloss over. My sensibility here is coherent with the one well expressed in Grant Macaskill, 'History, Providence, and the Apocalyptic Paul', *Scottish Journal of Theology* 70, no. 4 (2017): 409–26.

[107] Steck's book could be a good beginning in this direction, especially chapters 3 and 4, because he works hard to articulate how the more particularist aspect of Balthasar's moral vision (the aspect owed partly to Barth) can be combined with the other. The comparison is especially apt because O'Donovan's own doctrinal particularism may to an extent be tutored by Barth, but at the same time on O'Donovan's view 'a moralist can never follow Barth in his approach to ethics' (Shortt, *God's Advocates*, 267).

[108] As D. Stephen Long points out, to base morality on an abstracted 'pure' nature seems to be a parallel modern mistake: neither natural law nor divine command approaches as purely philosophical stances can register adequately the shape of the divine economy (*Saving Karl Barth: Hans Urs von Balthasar's Preoccupation* (Minneapolis: Fortress Press, 2014), 189). I cannot adjudge, nonetheless, whether Long does justice to the Catholic scholasticism and Reformed orthodoxy he has in mind. The charge does not map especially well onto the paired contemporary theological sensibilities at which his broader argument aims – neo-Thomists and 'McCormackian' Barthians. Neither neo-Thomist moral theologians nor 'actualistic' Barthians are straightforwardly susceptible to these charges. Consider, for example, Romanus Cessario, Reinhard Hütter and Livio Melina on the one

reason that salvation effects need to be seen as opposed to our fulfilment in the earthly enjoyment of those earthly goods. Yet we must try to conceive of that refashioning so as to recognize the sense in which God's adventitious address initially and continually overturns our habits of navigating the concrete situations of 'this present age'. And that would mean construing the ongoing conversion of moral reasoning as entailing a more revolutionary unsettling of our perceptions of the world and its normative texture than O'Donovan seems sometimes to suggest.

Leaving behind these proposals for now, appreciation of what O'Donovan tries to do in these discussions – and in the integrative effort more widely – is of course enhanced when seen against ethical approaches that champion one or other variety of what is rather inelegantly christened 'principal monism' or 'metaethical monism'.[109]

Meta-ethical integration

But its accomplishment is also obvious when viewed alongside nascent attempts (especially Protestant) at meta-ethical integration.[110] If these attempts are a way

hand, and David Clough and Paul Nimmo on the other: both schools are Christocentric, though certainly neither integrates nature and grace in the manner Long prefers.

[109] See Charles Pinches, 'Principle Monism and Action Descriptions: Situationism and Its Critics Revisited', *Modern Theology* 7, no. 3 (1991): 249–68. For O'Donovan's recent comments on the need to avoid these monisms, see O'Donovan, *Entering into Rest*, viii.

[110] See Jesse Couenhoven, 'Against Metaethical Imperialism: Several Arguments for Equal Partnerships between the Deontic and the Aretaic', *Journal of Religious Ethics* 38, no. 3 (2010): 521–44. On integration of natural law and divine command, see Neil Arner, 'Precedents and Prospects for Incorporating Natural Law in Protestant Ethics', *Scottish Journal of Theology* 69, no. 4 (2016): 375–88. For a sense of the gains seen as possible by such incorporation, see Neil Arner, 'Ecumenical Ethics: Challenges to and Sources for a Common Moral Witness', *Journal of the Society of Christian Ethics* 36, no. 2 (2016): 101–19. In the first article, Arner catalogues elements of the rehabilitation of natural law in Protestant thought, counting O'Donovan among a set of thinkers contributing to this recovery. I summarize his survey, relevant to my study, as follows. First, historical research uncovered the irrefragable place of natural law in earlier Protestant thought. Second – here's where O'Donovan comes in – Protestant ethics has often been thought to focus on divine command. However, in recent, philosophical theology and ethics divine command approaches have come in for severe criticism. Common accusations focus upon a few features: the arbitrariness it seems to locate at the centre of morality; the picture of God as a capricious tyrant; the prioritizing of the *right* over the *good*; the voluntaristic prioritizing of God's will over God's reason and human will over human reason; and the seeming lack of concern for the flourishing of humankind, which other ethical systems (broadly *eudaimonistic*) foreground. In fact, human flourishing (a further element of this rehabilitation) has increasingly become a topic of Protestant theologizing, rather than the object of its suspicion. Among philosophical theologians Evans, Adams, Richard J. Mouw, Nicholas Wolterstorff and John Hare have all sought in some way to register these concerns, offering modified accounts that relate notions of moral obligation derived from divine command to those that ground morality in human nature and the fulfilment of its goods. But if they want to say that morality is *fitting* in terms of human nature, they do not say that moral duties can be *deduced* simply from knowledge of it. Arner lists O'Donovan alongside them, noting that those who share this recognition nevertheless tend to eschew nomenclature of natural law. To a greater or lesser extent, these thinkers are mindful of the Barthian disavowal of natural law (a disavowal Arner, following the wider literature, contrasts with Calvin's qualified affirmation), but attempt to move beyond it. I would add that, at best, the theologians especially among them are alert to the potential a-theological abstraction of the term 'natural law' and have sought to make much of the doctrine of creation when talking about natural moral goods. O'Donovan is clearly a case in point here,

forward – I have some doubts about their level of abstraction, as will become clear – they could probably do worse than to take O'Donovan as a guide. I offer the following minor suggestions as to how we might locate his thought within these conversations.

First, O'Donovan's historical work often tries to recognize in modern modes of moral – philosophical argumentation patterns of thought native to classical philosophical and theological morality. His excavations help reveal contemporary meta-ethical approaches as forgetful heirs – their theories the misrememberings of theological traditions in sometimes more wilful and sometimes more accidental ways. I would suggest that O'Donovan's etiological efforts are often less compelling when they attempt to trace contemporary disarray to moments when philosophical errors like nominalism arose than they are when they show in particular how the fragmentation of the Christian moral tradition came about and was confirmed through partitive biblical exegesis and theological reasoning. In the latter respect, his modernity critique surpasses much contemporary theology of otherwise similar instincts, which sometimes offers over-hasty generalization in terms of the former, and which unlike O'Donovan shows general lack of patient sensitivity to Reformational thought.

Second, O'Donovan's constructive approach to ethics exhibits commitments familiar to Kantian ethicists of obligation, besides features that Aristotelian philosophers of the natural law could heartily endorse, and still other qualities shared by aretaic ethics. It is no surprise, then, that moral theologians from a range of traditions have found his work engaging. A number of Catholic theologians have found his work congenial,[111] and if contemporary Protestant theologians schooled in an ethics of obligation – perhaps Kierkegaardian or Barthian 'divine command' ethics rather than strictly Kantian deontology – find fellow-feeling strained at some points of O'Donovan's work, any contestation is intramural. A host of meta-ethical approaches find themselves involved, then, and at his work's best the conceptual apparatus of these stances is appropriated only as it is made intelligible by the commitments of Christian orthodoxy, and shown in its relevance for the practice of the Christian life. Proposing that contemporary attempts to re-integrate moral approaches might take guidance from O'Donovan – or Hauerwas for that matter – is therefore not unrelatedly to urge that Christian ethicists continue these two figures' theological and pastoral intent.[112]

---

and also – like Hauerwas – more alert than others of potential a-theological abstraction in 'divine command theory'.

[111] Besides those already named, see, for example, the reviews by David Cloutier and Nicholas M. Healy cited in Chapter 5.

[112] The details of Hauerwas's theological commitments have been up for debate, but I hope it is indisputable that he has both embodied and made possible a search for Christian moral wisdom of both philosophical clarity and pastoral coherence. Whether or not he has been right to jettison natural law in his retrieval of major Thomist moral-theological themes (I think he makes a serious case: see references later in this note), and whether or not he has always given more theological divine-command-based conceptions a fair hearing (I am not sure he has), his retrieval of virtue and character, in addition to promotion of the post-liberal themes of narrative and community, has allowed for a generation of Christian ethicists who display more facility with the texts of the moral tradition, and more theological confidence. Incidentally, Arner notes that Hauerwas was recently happy to accept a 'Protestant Thomist' account of natural law such as the one proposed by John Bowlin (Arner, 'Precedents and Prospects', 377, n. 9). It would be interesting to know what this means for Hauerwas's earlier suggestion of natural law reasoning's innate violence. See *The Peaceable Kingdom: A Primer in Christian Ethics* (London: SCM Press, 1984), 59–61. Notably,

The treatment of vocation is a good example of O'Donovan's ambition (if not because always perfectly convincing in its details), because its theoretical account of moral reasoning's philosophical components is exegetically constructed, and it both derives concerns from pastoral practice and directs conclusions towards it.[113]

All that said, however, seeing that O'Donovan's work comprises an unusually brilliant attempt to overcome modern ethics' fragmentation should not preclude attempts to reach tentatively beyond it. Here, this means that appreciating the effort to supply an integrated approach to divine command and created order does mean accepting the book's settlement. We can learn from O'Donovan's struggle to register various pressures in a coherent moral theology, by seeing where integration seems to succeed, but also by locating those areas of tension – like eschatology. Both integration and tension are especially palpable in the book's discussions of novelty, which we turn to now.

The new

Though he clearly suggests that there is a unified moral order, O'Donovan recognizes that the moral field does not appear to us as a stable, consistent, reality. Moral questions arise that seem to be new, and their novelty induces anxiety in the moral subject. In fact some genuinely are new, and this really does pose a problem that the language of 'quandaries' apprehends, though imagining all ethics as 'quandary ethics' is not adequate.[114] Indeed, a major contribution of *Resurrection and Moral Order* is its attempt to maintain the particularity of moral situations in what is technically a deontological framework that posits an ethical universalism. For O'Donovan, wisdom in moral reasoning means alertness to apparently exceptional cases as opportunities to learn more about the underlying consistent features of generic morality: the moral law. Knowledge of particular situations and of the generic moral order are reciprocally informing. And by grounding moral law in 'objective world-order', O'Donovan self-consciously takes a step beyond Paul Ramsey in the development of Protestant theological ethics.[115] He writes: 'The moral agent approaches every new situation ... equipped with the "moral law" ... that wisdom which contains insight into the created order when it is formulated explicitly to direct decisions, i.e. deontically.'[116] But what demands our attention within this is the more focused question of novelty.

Two modern approaches, we learn, orient themselves differently to novelty. First, conservatism (understood philosophically rather than politically) seeks to 'establish

the suggestion is contested from within Anabaptist theological ethics by Paul Martens: 'With the Natural Grain of the Universe: Reexamining the Alleged Pacifist Rejection of Natural Law', *Journal of the Society of Christian Ethics* 32, no. 2 (2012): 113–31.

[113] See 'Towards an Interpretation of Biblical Ethics' for mention of O'Donovan's education in the 'disciplined attention' and 'distinctions' of moral philosophy, his sense of its neglect by biblical scholars, and a conception of his own reparative undertaking.

[114] Cf. O'Donovan's comments on ethics' 'problematical' quality in 'How Can Theology Be Moral?' 82–3. Errington's *Every Good Path* is especially excellent on this, and gives more attention to these aspects of O'Donovan's thought.

[115] O'Donovan, *Resurrection*, 188.

[116] Ibid., 190.

sufficient continuity to tame the apocalyptic strength of novelty to the point where it can be managed by a comfortable process of adaptation'.[117] It does so by calling upon past experience, but this is in fact just historicism in conservative garb, and its cords are not up to the task of binding the new. Second, consequentialism 'proposes to overcome the perils of novelty by *anticipation*'.[118] This, again, can be understood as a kind of historicism, 'a programme for robbing human history of its terrors by conceiving of history as a kind of human artefact'.[119] Moreover, it is consequentialism's historicist bent that represents its significant dissimilarity with classical teleological ethics, despite their being frequently grouped together in opposition to deontic approaches.[120] In consequentialism, classical teleology's 'value-ordering "for the sake of" has been replaced by a quite different "for the sake of", which means productive of'.[121] And while the consequentialist imagines that present acts totally determine the future, managerially choosing the prospective state of things, this is futile, because 'nothing will bind the future unless the future, for all its unpredictability, is already bound, by being the future of God's world, the history of his created order'.[122]

We can learn much here of O'Donovan's concern to secure moral agency in history over against any disempowering historical determinism. A purely consequentialist analysis ultimately undercuts action:

> All classical ethics, Christian and pagan, teleological and deontic, is challenged at its heart by the proposal to evaluate acts solely in terms of the consequences they tend to produce. Such a proposal can be understood only as a refusal to refuse to

---

[117] Ibid., 185.
[118] Ibid., 187.
[119] Ibid.
[120] Ibid. The reader may have noticed that when speaking of O'Donovan's integrative approach, I focused on the interplay of divine command and natural law. Later in this chapter, I address the place of character, virtue and community in his project. Missing, then, with these three facets listed, are non-classical teleological ethics of a utilitarian kind, which receive pretty short shrift from O'Donovan, and those he has influenced (often for very good reason). See O'Donovan, *Resurrection*, 138, 181–2, 187, 238. 46 Cf. O'Donovan, 'Augustinian Ethics', 46: 'Augustinian eudaemonism' – and we may take him to indicate his own ethic by extension – 'is not a teleological ethic in the modern sense, but a teleological metaphysical framework that serves to give intelligibility to ethics that are in substance command-based'. Theologians looking to integrate utilitarian perspectives would probably have to choose another exemplar than O'Donovan. In a previous generation, Catholic proportionalists might have been read to this end. For Protestants, perhaps, exemplars could come from among those more formed by the tradition of Reinhold Niebuhr than by Paul Ramsey, as O'Donovan is. That is not to say Ramsey cannot be seen, in his own way, as a Niebuhrian realist theo-politically – just that Ramsey's characteristic argumentation in his medical ethics in particular has a distinctly deontological flavour and includes numerous vigorous tussles with colleagues' consequentialist proposals. See *The Essential Paul Ramsey*, ed. William Werpehowski and Stephen D. Crocco (New Haven: Yale University Press, 1994), xx–xxii, D. Stephen Long, *Tragedy, Tradition, Transformism: The Ethics of Paul Ramsey* (Boulder: Westview Press, 1993), 1–2, and Eric Gregory, *Politics and the Order of Love: An Augustinian Ethic of Democratic Citizenship* (Chicago: University of Chicago Press, 2008), 180–8. Any outright attempt at integrating consequentialism into Christian ethics seems mistaken to me, but for illuminating *comparative* analysis see *God, the Good, and Utilitarianism: Perspectives on Peter Singer*, ed. John Perry (Cambridge: Cambridge University Press, 2014), and Charles Camosy, *Peter Singer and Christian Ethics: Beyond Polarization* (Cambridge: Cambridge University Press, 2012).
[121] O'Donovan, *Resurrection*, 187.
[122] Ibid., 188.

evaluate *acts* altogether. Indeed, we may go further and say that it is a proposal to abandon the *category* of acting altogether, for in reconstruing history as an artefact we abolish the only context in which acting can have any meaning. Acting implies risk. … To speak of acting implies a history *into which* we act.[123]

Wisdom is found in a proper understanding of novelty's relation to given, enduring order. That is not to say moral discernment is not partly about recognizing what is genuinely new, so that 'new moral decisions can be made'.[124] As O'Donovan writes in *Thirty-Nine Articles*, 'a biblical epistemology does not mean that thought must stand still. We have to grasp, appropriate, interpret and understand, and then we have to apply what we have learned to new problems'.[125] But beneath that is 'the perception that every novelty, in its own way, manifests the permanence and stability of the created order, so that, however astonishing and undreamt of it may be, it is not utterly incommensurable with what has gone before'.[126]

O'Donovan argues that this permanence and stability is a biblical concern. Dissatisfied with theologians' custom, more fashionable then than now, perhaps, of opposing 'the' Hebrew and/or early Christian cast of mind to 'the' Hellenistic metaphysical one, he writes: 'It has often been said, quite falsely, that Israel did not have the same sense of stability and eternity, set in opposition to change and history, that marked Greek thinking.'[127] Therefore it is mistaken to imagine that adopting Scripture's approach to morality would entail 'replacing the eternal stability of things with the arbitrary and historically determinate command of God'.[128] Scripturally, creation and history are not opposed:

> The joy of life-in-the-world was a gift given together with the joy of life-before-God. At the same time the arbitrary command of the transcendent Lord of history had assumed responsibility for ordered life. The God of Exodus and Conquest had shown himself as God of creation too. In *torah* the moral authority of created order and the transcendent authority of the electing God were made one.[129]

Again, in some ways a stronger contrast can hardly be drawn than between O'Donovan's interpretation and that of Robert Jenson – for whom O'Donovan's thought might be termed a divinity of *persistence*, yearning for the fleshpots of Egypt, theologizing about gods 'Continuity' and 'Return'![130] But we do not need to lurch so far in the opposite direction as Jenson to feel that O'Donovan says too much in claiming that 'the moral

---

[123] Ibid., 187–8.
[124] Ibid., 188.
[125] O'Donovan, *Thirty-Nine Articles*, 115.
[126] O'Donovan, *Resurrection*, 189.
[127] Ibid.
[128] Ibid., 190.
[129] Ibid.
[130] See e.g. Jenson, *Systematic Theology, vol. 1, The Triune God* (Oxford/New York: Oxford University Press, 1997), 66–8, which touches on the same Old Testament themes in a completely different way, contrasting theologies of 'persistence' with those of 'anticipation'. Might behind their disagreement partly lie differing mid- to late-twentieth-century positions in Old Testament theological interpretation concerning creation and redemption – could we roughly align Jenson's position

authority of created order and the transcendent authority of the electing God were made one'.[131] Surely there is a necessary asymmetry between these terms, such that if we grant that 'the transcendent authority of the electing God' does indeed imbue the created order with life-giving moral authority, we cannot thereby say that 'they were made one'.

What is important to see at this point is that O'Donovan's account of moral reason intends to allow space for the historically novel, and for divine freedom, in concert with an abiding affirmation of creation's consistency. He means to dissuade readers from concluding that his claims about the stability of unchanging morally normative goods owe more to philosophical commitments than biblical revelation. But, in keeping with Chapter 2, we might press whether there is space for the kind of *eschatological* novelty – which is not simply *historical* novelty – about which the canonical witness seems eager to instruct us. Again, we would not have to accept Jenson's posing of the problem (nor Pannenberg, Moltmann, or Jüngel's, for that matter) to think that O'Donovan may construe these things in a way that does veer towards imagination of an 'eternal stability of things'. That worry arises whether we think it is the product of undue influence from a 'Hellenistic' cast of mind, preoccupation with presuppositions of non-theological moral philosophy, the pressure of contextual discernments, all three or none. Before we move on to considerations of sin and knowledge, I want to draw attention to one further feature of O'Donovan's treatment of novelty.

In this book and elsewhere, the 'new' is a theme O'Donovan consistently negotiates with reference to Christology and pneumatology, and their ordered relation. Usually this underscores exactly the features we have already examined. But one or two tantalizing instances seem to press beyond the other passages, dovetailing notes of discontinuity and continuity in a way that suggests interest in genuinely *eschatological* novelty. Consider some lines from a sermon:

> The new cuts right across our existing framework of human experience. The new defies expectation, extrapolation, prediction, all those laws of change promising a certain stability within the flux of things. And yet it makes sense, not nonsense, of what we have experienced. It is discontinuity, yet it is fulfilment. Not any and every disruption in the course of things counts as something new, only that disruption which takes up the old, broken continuity into itself, and saves it as it destroys it.

---

with instincts of Gerhard von Rad and O'Donovan's with those of Claus Westermann or Bernhard Anderson?

[131] My own sense of a different approach to either Jenson or O'Donovan is represented fairly well by Francis Watson's comments on this part of Jenson's *Systematics* ('"America's theologian": An Appreciation of Robert Jenson's Systematic Theology, With Some Remarks about the Bible', *Scottish Journal of Theology* 55, no. 2 (2002): 201–23, 222–3). Though he recognizes Jenson's corrective instincts over against much modern theology, Watson troubles Jenson's exclusively eschatologizing hermeneutic by drawing attention to the character of the gospels as historical narratives – not apocalypses – and to the creed's centre of gravity being in the second article. Watson conveys a more unerring instinct for comprehension of the Christ event's genuinely pivotal character in its continuity and discontinuity than O'Donovan (who would seem sometimes to subordinate it to creation) and Jenson (who would seem sometimes to subordinate it to the eschaton). Of course, Watson will not here tell us what that might mean for ethics, nor much about the bearing upon the moral life of the kingdom of God that the gospel records as central to Christ's teaching.

> In the Acts of the Apostles the presence of the Holy Spirit is signalled by miracle. Miracle does not merely defy human expectations; it also satisfies the thread of hope within them. ... Miracle gives fulfilment to hopes lurking within the fabric of experience which have no claims on predictable experience. It is new. ... Yet the new is not easy to recognise. Precisely because it *is* new, we have no native capacity to see it, since recognition has to do with the familiar and the old. The new must force itself on us, evoking an act of faith, that is, an experienced discontinuity in our understanding. There is, Christians have dared to claim, one new thing lying at the heart of all new things: that Jesus is Lord. And *nobody can say 'Jesus is Lord' except by the Holy Spirit*.[132]

Here we seem to find a version of O'Donovan's major claims made in a form less susceptible to accusations of the collapse of creation and redemption, yet just as capable of describing their real relation, and of making good sense of the intimately related but non-exchangeable works of Christ and the Spirit in saving history. But this only presses the question again as to why the sense of unpredictable fulfilment evoked here is sometimes elusive in *Resurrection and Moral Order*. To venture a reason: Might it be because here, in a sermon, O'Donovan allows himself the rhetorical flourish to match the heights and depths of the gospel, where there the agenda is driven by what is seen as the pressing tasks of *ethics*, which cannot but be unsettled by this disjunction, by discontinuity? It may be O'Donovan's conception of those pressing tasks of ethics *qua* ethics, furthermore, which contributes to the book's checked recognition of sin – our next theme.

Sin and knowledge

Like 'The Natural Ethic', *Resurrection and Moral Order* postpones treatment of epistemological limitation and hindrance. O'Donovan does announce relatively soon that he is aware of the challenge: 'The *epistemological* programme for an ethic that is "natural", in the sense that its contents are simply known to all, has to face dauntingly high barriers.'[133] But his answer allows the account to move quite serenely on:

> [W]e are not to conclude from this that there is no ontological ground for an 'ethic of nature', no objective order to which the moral life can respond ... only ... that any certainty we may have about the order which God has made depends upon God's own disclosure of himself and his works.[134]

And the argument, of course, upholds the possibility of a fairly elevated degree of certainty about that order, based on a particular understanding of the disclosure of divine character and works. Yet Protestants routinely reject what O'Donovan calls

---

[132] O'Donovan, *Small Boats*, 46–7.
[133] O'Donovan, *Resurrection*, 19.
[134] Ibid.

the natural ethic, it seems to me, for two reasons. They reject it because of their impression of the obstacle that is *sin* and – a more recent trend, perhaps – because of their impression of the impediment of *creaturely finitude*. In this subsection, I consider O'Donovan's response to each of these two 'high barriers' in turn, before observing his approach to a third barrier: eschatology.

First, sin. O'Donovan's book usually explains human moral failure in terms of something like our disavowal of the created order, dissatisfaction with the value-bearing fixities that ought to shape our lives and govern our moral reasoning. We find less than we might expect about misperception of that order, or of the effects of sin upon it. Still, when epistemological hindrances are referred to overtly, they do nuance O'Donovan's natural ethic and its assertive moral realism. 'In speaking of man's fallenness', he writes, 'we point not only to his persistent rejection of the created order, but also an inescapable confusion in his perceptions of it … we must reckon also upon the opacity and obscurity of that order to the human mind which has rejected the knowledge of its Creator'.[135] Yet this kind of admission is almost always followed by the instant recollection that our rebellion and ignorance has been ineffective in degrading or damaging the natural order, outwith the moral state of the human creature. As Andrew Errington correctly observes, there is 'little talk of sin as involving a corruption of the conditions in which obedience takes place. The order itself is undamaged.'[136] All told, neither sin's effects on the human knower nor its effects on the known object and its self-disclosing value seem as serious as they might.[137]

O'Donovan's prioritization of creation, I think, seeks to outbid the Protestant worry about sin, in mapping a substrate of moral reality prior to any presupposition of the fall. If, as Bonhoeffer lamented, there are two kinds of Protestant failure to properly regard the penultimacy of 'the natural' – for some it was 'completely lost in the darkness of general sinfulness … for others it took on the brightness of primal creation' – *Resurrection and Moral Order* is more liable to be counted among the latter.[138] In a similar way, O'Donovan's cartography of moral action may also intend to outbid the threat of the doctrine of sin. Agency is grounded in created reality, and while O'Donovan of course recognizes that ethics takes place in a world become sinful, I think he proceeds with a sense of the ethicist's task as being to take agents' sin-stricken limitation for granted and rather to describe the shape of free (that is, restored) action in a good, vindicated order of creation.

Thus O'Donovan's epistemological caution is perhaps less about the difficulties of rightly perceiving the moral order because of sin than it is – here is the second 'barrier' – about the difficulties of finite creatures' knowledge of an order of creation of which they are themselves part. The objection to *Veritatis Splendor*'s rationalistic employment

---

[135] Ibid.
[136] Errington, *Every Good Path*, 152.
[137] Wannenwetsch's understanding is very similar to O'Donovan's. Nonetheless, he is sometimes a little clearer than O'Donovan about the effects of sin and therein the need for the disclosive work of the divine Word. See e.g. 'Creation and Ethics: On the Legitimacy and Limitation of Appeals to "Nature" in Christian Moral Reasoning', in *Within the Love of God*, ed. Anthony Clarke and Andrew Moore (Oxford: Oxford University Press, 2014), 216.
[138] Bonhoeffer, *Ethics*, 171.

of Thomistic natural law that we considered earlier might therefore owe more to the point about finitude than to any Protestant disquiet about sin and revelation[139] – nor any post-liberal point about cultural traditions' particularity, and revelation's primarily ecclesial reception.[140]

To see O'Donovan's understanding of this barrier of finitude, we need to familiarize ourselves with the main features of his account of knowledge, which are found in the final chapter of Part One, thus rounding off the treatment of 'the objective reality' of ethics. What knowledge, O'Donovan asks, is it that has the created order as its object? He finds answer in the term *participation*. Participation is no abstracted gaze, since it cannot be the kind of knowledge that rises above creation; rather it is knowledge from our position in the universe, 'from within … "existential" knowledge'.[141] As knowledge of the natural order 'it must … be knowledge of things *in their relations to the totality of things* … the "shape" of the whole'.[142] This consideration of participatory knowledge is not entirely removed from the consideration of sin, though, because such knowledge is not neutral, but always-already 'moral knowledge … co-ordinated with obedience'.[143] Or, stated with critical edge: '[T]he exercise of knowledge is tied up with the faithful performance of man's task in the world, and that his knowing will stand or fall with his worship of God and his obedience to the moral law'.[144]

A further feature of this account of knowledge is especially relevant for our question: it 'must be *ignorant of the end of history*':

> Whatever apprehension of created order may belong to man by virtue of his place within that order, the shape of history belongs to the secret counsel of the Lord of history. The creature must walk blindfold along the road of time, and may see only when he turns to survey that portion of the road which has already been traversed.[145]

Here we find O'Donovan revisiting the themes of the discussions of historicism, now with an epistemological focus, and foreshadowing the later discussions of novelty that we have already examined. It is no wonder, he suggests, that there is an unceasing 'search for a philosophy of history', since 'the question about the end of history is a matter of anxiety'.[146] To many philosophies the future appears as threat: 'To face novelty with confidence, they must be sure that what they have truly known as good in the past

---

[139] For a most pointed articulation of this disquiet (in combination with a bold estimation of the predominantly disjunctive character of the new), see Ziegler, 'The Fate of Natural Law at the Turning of the Ages', now republished in *Militant Grace*.

[140] For the post-liberal point see Hauerwas, *The Peaceable Kingdom: A Primer in Christian Ethics* (London: SCM Press, 1984).

[141] O'Donovan, *Resurrection*, 79. I do not focus on the question of epistemology and natural law in Chapter 5's exposition of *Ethics as Theology*, so note here rather than there a passage from *Entering into Rest* (63–4) where in terms coherent with *Resurrection* O'Donovan writes that natural law is 'not badly described by Pope Benedict XVI as a "blunt instrument"'.

[142] O'Donovan, *Resurrection*, 77.

[143] Ibid., 87.

[144] Ibid., 81.

[145] Ibid., 82.

[146] Ibid., 83.

cannot be invalidated by what they may yet have to know', but of this they know no guarantee.[147] Sympathy is evident here, as O'Donovan's 'they' becomes a 'we':

> In the fallen condition of the universe the created order is constantly put in question by the events of history, so that we have no assurance that the good which we have been given to know, and may still presume to know even though our knowledge is misknowledge, can and will sustain itself.[148]

Nevertheless, in truth the knowledge afforded to us is 'knowledge that is vindicated by God's revelatory word that the created good and man's knowledge of it is not to be overthrown in history'.[149]

A more detailed explanation follows:

> Such knowledge, according to the Christian gospel, is given to us as we participate in the life of Jesus Christ ... he is the one whose faithfulness to the created moral order was answered by God's deed of acceptance and vindication, so that the life of man within this order is not lost but assured for all time.[150]

I return below to the relationship between this knowledge, 'given' in Christ, and that knowledge 'vindicated by God's revelatory word'. But we may pause over the quotation's theological formulation.

The main point is well taken: Jesus's earthly obedience, as a human person within the world, makes possible renewed earthly life for the rest of humanity. The notion that Christ's faithfulness was 'to the created moral order' may surprise us, though, because it is perhaps not exactly a scriptural idiom – surely Christ's earthly career is said principally to show faithfulness to his Father. So we have to join the dots a bit to see how the claim works, which we can if we look to another passage: Christ, O'Donovan writes there, 'has been a faithful witness to the order in which we live, "faithful to him who appointed him"'.[151] And I think O'Donovan construes within Jesus's broader faithfulness to the created moral order a more particular disclosure of that witness: the 'works of healing and exorcism', which he mentions later, adding that his 'new teaching vindicated itself by vindicating and restoring the old creation'.[152] To conclude: Is it unfitting or imprudent to speak of Christ's faithfulness to the created moral order? Not necessarily, and for a Christian ethic attentive to creatureliness, this may be one of the morally noteworthy ways we can interpret Christ's obedience to

---

[147] Ibid.
[148] Ibid. The exegetical excursus on pages 84–5 rewards attention, culminating in interpretation of Revelation 4–5, the 'diptych', which both here and elsewhere O'Donovan considers a locus classicus of the threatening nature of history – 'the sealed scroll'. See beyond these few lines 'History and Politics in the Book of Revelation', in *Bonds of Imperfection: Christian Politics, Past and Present*, ed. Oliver O'Donovan and Lockwood O'Donovan (Grand Rapids: Eerdmans, 2004), a revised version of 'The Political Thought of the Book of Revelation', *Tyndale Bulletin* 37 (1986): 61–94.
[149] O'Donovan, *Resurrection*, 85.
[150] Ibid.
[151] Ibid., 150.
[152] Ibid., 137.

'the Father Almighty, maker of heaven and earth'. I have paused over the formulation here, then, but it should not trip us up too much – so long as we intend to speak just as much in idioms that draw out the more prominent ways Christology figures in New Testament ethical exhortation and much of the Christian moral tradition.[153]

At any rate, the general claim is there: true knowledge is not possible without Christ, and true participation in the created order requires participation in him. In a sense, it is therefore exclusive knowledge, and this exclusivity is 'an epistemological implication of the fallenness of man'.[154] However, following the same pattern of relating particular and universal we observed earlier, 'the object of this exclusive knowledge is inclusive: it is the whole order of things created, restored and transformed'.[155] In Chapter 2, we highlighted Wells and Quash's classification of O'Donovan's claims, and Errington also synopsises them well when he writes that for O'Donovan '"God's revelatory word" … given to humanity in Jesus Christ … is the particular, exclusive point of access to the inclusive field of vision of creation that moral knowledge seeks'.[156] Most basically, what O'Donovan wants to say, in keeping with his understanding of created order's utter objectivity, is this: 'It requires no revelation to observe the various forms of generic and teleological order', but 'such knowledge is incomplete unless the created order is grasped as a whole, and that includes its relations to the uncreated'.[157] If we object that the world itself seems less than perfectly orderly, he will reply that any disorder, 'like misknowledge, is attributable only to things which are in their true being ordered', and its brokenness is 'not merely unordered chaos' but 'the brokenness of order'.[158] Disorder is to be attributed to historical appearances, not creation's 'true being'.[159]

O'Donovan's stronger claims here seem difficult to maintain in view of the kinds of concerns that we saw well expressed by McKenny at the end of Chapter 2. Perhaps, again, O'Donovan's main point might be reformulated more modestly into one that, as Neil Arner details, has featured in other recent Protestant retrievals of natural law: that we should hold to an *extensive* rather than *intensive* notion of sin. So to say, sin's damage extends to every natural and human capacity (so has both epistemological and ontological effects), but does not destroy them.[160] That would preserve O'Donovan's argument: sin has not corrupted the created order such that human creatures cannot know its configuration to some extent without revelation.

However, the relation O'Donovan envisions between revealed and common or 'natural' knowledge, if indeed consistent, is certainly sometimes a little difficult to work

---

[153] There are plenty of 'therefore' exhortations consequent on Christological (especially soteriological) statements in the Epistles, none of which seem to me directly related to Christ's faithfulness to the created moral order as such. E.g. Rom. 6.4; 6.12; 12.1; 15.7; 1 Cor. 6.20; 15.58; Gal. 5.1; Eph. 5.1; Phil. 2.12, 4.1; Col. 2.6, 2.16, 3.5; 1 Thess. 4.18, 5.11; 1 Pet. 1.13; 4.1. That is not at all to say that other Christological statements are not ethically significant, nor that the apostles thought creation unimportant, or morally irrelevant. But the way Christology figures directly in these paraenetic sections is worth considering.
[154] O'Donovan, *Resurrection*, 87.
[155] Ibid., 85.
[156] Errington, *Every Good Path*, 149, initially quoting O'Donovan, *Resurrection*, 85.
[157] O'Donovan, *Resurrection*, 88.
[158] Ibid.
[159] The phrase is from 'Response to Craig Bartholomew' (see 113–14).
[160] Arner, 'Precedents and Prospects', 382.

out. He expresses it from different angles at different points, and it is no surprise that he has been taken to intend different things. One articulation in *Resurrection and Moral Order* seems to attempt a certain *via media*:

> revelation in Christ does not *deny* our fragmentary knowledge of the ways things are, as though that knowledge were not there, or were of no significance; yet it does not *build on* it, as though it provided a perfectly acceptable foundation to which a further level of understanding can be added. It can only expose it for not being what it was originally given to be.[161]

This is still clearly a middle way approached from the Protestant (or at least, Augustinian) side, and not from the Thomist one, because inasmuch as O'Donovan propounds a 'natural ethic' based on the doctrine of creation – taking Brunner's line regarding the orders of creation in the dispute with Barth – we might expect him to follow some Catholic theology in indexing the sense in which revelation in Christ 'exposes' our impoverished grasp of reality to the sense in which it clarifies, elevates and perfects our 'fragmentary knowledge'.[162] For, on a typical explanation of the different traditions, like that of Nigel Biggar:

> Moral theologians who follow Augustine – Luther, for example – tend to view the ravages of sin as grave, reason as crippled, and the need for intellectual and moral grace through Scripture as acute. Those, on the other hand, who stand in the tradition of Aquinas are inclined to think that the deliverances of reason remain valid in spite of sin, and are more in need of supplementation than correction.[163]

Yet here O'Donovan does not follow the latter line, instead leading with the note of judgement, of acute need. What, then, *does* 'revelation in Christ' bestow?[164]

'We are not', he writes a few pages later, 'to think of revelation as conferring upon man a knowledge of created order which he never possessed before.'[165] But 'it is true …

---

[161] O'Donovan, *Resurrection*, 89.
[162] Ibid., 86–7. See the wide-ranging Bruce D. Baker, *The Transformation of Persons and the Concept of Moral Order: A Study of the Evangelical Ethics of Oliver O'Donovan with Special Reference to the Barth-Brunner Debate* (PhD Diss. University of St Andrews, 2010). That O'Donovan's account of natural knowledge and epistemology is hard to grasp is evident in the disagreement between Baker and Hans Burger, who criticizes Baker's interpretation in 'Receiving the Mind of Christ: Epistemological and Hermeneutical Implications of Participation in Christ according to Oliver O'Donovan', *Journal of Reformed Theology* 10, no. 1 (2016): 52–71, 55, no. 11. Cf. Hans Schaeffer, *Createdness and Ethics: The Doctrine of Creation and Theological Ethics in the Theology of Colin E. Gunton and Oswald Bayer* (Berlin/New York: Walter de Gruyter, 2006), e.g. 209. As well as the Barth-Brunner debate, I wonder if it would also be illuminating to read O'Donovan against the backdrop of the Barth-Balthasar conversations.
[163] Nigel Biggar, 'Moral Theology', in *The Cambridge Dictionary of Christian Theology*, 323.
[164] I push on to discuss themes related to eschatology here, but on those left aside, see also Brian Brock, 'The Form of the Matter: Heidegger, Ontology and Christian Ethics', *International Journal of Systematic Theology* 3, no. 3 (2001): 257–79, which uses Barth to 'sharpen O'Donovan's account of natural knowledge, clarifying the relation between redeemed and natural understandings of the normativity of the form of the matter' (257).
[165] O'Donovan, *Resurrection*, 89.

that it confers a knowledge of the shape of *history* which he never possessed before'.[166] This confidence can seem puzzling, if we recall the earlier line that knowledge must be of a kind '*ignorant of the end of history*'. As before, the key to understanding this potentially confusing pair of statements is to see that O'Donovan's doctrine of revelation preserves a degree of eschatological reserve about history's direction, along with an eschatological confidence about the promise of nature's restoration. And perhaps concerning these questions, *Resurrection and Moral Order* is not entirely resolved.

How O'Donovan imagines that combination of eschatological reserve and confidence to work out in epistemology may be clearer in *Self-Love*. There, as elsewhere, the interpretations of Augustine tell as much about O'Donovan's theological principles as they do about the Bishop of Hippo. For Augustine, he says, eschatology represents 'a new, decisively Christian discontinuity':

> 'We walk by faith, not by sight', we do not yet see God, as the same apostle says, 'face to face'. Christian eschatology poses a serious threat to the prospect of a reason-based epistemology. It is characteristic of the mature Augustine that he will not, as once he might have done, evade the implications of eschatology.[167]

Augustine does not abandon reason-based epistemology entirely, though; rather, he attempts 'to develop a theory of knowledge-by-faith which has room' for eschatology – which shows 'a continuity between what may be known and loved now and what may only be known and loved then'.[168] 'Sure faith is the beginning of knowledge', he goes on: 'Only the beginning .... Yet it is no less than the beginning. For without some kind of sight, the deliveries of *auctoritas* could have no content'.[169] Put otherwise: 'Augustine is not pleading for a total discontinuity between the self that is and the self that will be. The negative stress in this distinction is balanced by the positive assertions of created goodness in the other.'[170] If '"faith" is the dominant discontinualist, *auctoritas*-oriented motif of the ascent', then this does not discount 'the chief force' for continuity, which is 'the desire for happiness' fundamental to any eudaimonistic scheme.[171]

I have said a little about O'Donovan's acknowledgements of 'the dauntingly high barriers' to a natural ethic – namely, sin, finitude and eschatological hiddenness – and have tried to get across something of the tensions involved in the way O'Donovan's epistemology deals with each. When we turn to the book's understanding of the moral life, as we are about to do, we will find some passages of greater resolution, but the same tension in the acknowledgement of sin, and the same combination of eschatological reserve and confidence: a tension and combination that are sometimes productive, and sometimes less so.

---

[166] Ibid.
[167] O'Donovan, *Self-Love*, 79.
[168] Ibid.
[169] Ibid.
[170] Ibid., 62.
[171] Ibid., 90.

Conversion and character

In this next subsection, I review *Resurrection and Moral Order*'s proposals regarding a conspicuous theme of contemporary Christian ethics – character – as well as one that contemporary Christian ethics neglects – conversion. I do so favourably, because these proposals seem to me some of the book's most attractive, and because they show well the import of a range of doctrines, including eschatology, for an understanding of the moral life.

We can begin exploring O'Donovan's approach to conversion and character by seeing how it unfolds from the book's earlier commitments. Following the commitment to moral realism, 'moral understanding is a grasp of the whole shape of things'.[172] Moral learning, therefore, must be more than 'a simple *accrual* of moral wisdom. ... To learn radically new moral truth is to change the shape of the whole outlook. One cannot *add* moral truth to moral truth; one can only *repent* false perceptions of the moral order and turn to truer ones'.[173] Repentance – indeed, conversion – is a basic feature of the moral life. As Daniel Westberg among others has observed, conversion is a neglected theme in moral theology, failing to appear in Protestant, even evangelical, ethics where one might expect it; O'Donovan, as Westberg says, is unusual in writing about it substantively.[174] When doing so in *Resurrection and Moral Order*, he follows once more a route *Self-Love* plotted, taking now as an illustration Augustine's depiction of the moral life:

> The mature Augustine was not interested in spiritual and moral progress as a matter for speculative theorising. True, he began where the ascetic theologians began, with the Platonic mystical ascent of the soul; like them, he worked this out in Christian terms as a pilgrimage toward the purification of the soul and the vision of God; like them, he believed that the Christian life was a protracted moral struggle. But for him there was no ladder of progress by which the soul's movement from one level of moral achievement to a higher one could be charted. The struggle rather consisted in a series of recapitulations of Adam's choice between good and evil.[175]

And indeed, the effort to recognize conversion's ethical significance is consistent through O'Donovan's work – I will further contemplate conversion's place in *Ethics as Theology* in Chapter 5.

This effort is never clearer than in *Resurrection and Moral Order*'s reflections on 'the function of an ethic of character' at the end of the tenth chapter, 'The Moral Subject'.[176] In passing, we ought to glance at the headline arguments of the chapter, which I do not in this study relay in much detail. Certainly O'Donovan's ethics, as we have seen, focuses upon moral *acts* and the moral *order* in which, and in response to which, acts

---

[172] O'Donovan, *Resurrection*, 92.
[173] Ibid.
[174] Westberg, *Renewing Moral Theology*, 106–10.
[175] O'Donovan, *Self-Love*, 150.
[176] O'Donovan, *Resurrection*, 224–5.

take place, before it focuses upon the moral character of the agent. But here O'Donovan turns directly to the relationship between 'act-evaluation' and 'agent-evaluation'.[177] To summarize a dense and exegetically rich series of arguments and interactions with scholarship, O'Donovan comes to insist upon 'an epistemological priority of act over character: the character is known only through the acts', and therefore to conclude that, while knowledge of an agent's character can contribute to '*evaluative* moral thought', it 'cannot contribute to *deliberative* moral thought'.[178] Finally, we should note that in view of statements like these, readers have interpreted O'Donovan's relation to the 'turn to character' or 'turn to virtue' quite differently. Daniel Westberg claims that O'Donovan's account can be squared wholly with Aquinas's approach to virtue: 'Because virtues are developed by a pattern and then a habituation of consistent right choices and actions, there is what … O'Donovan calls 'the epistemological priority of act', and this is clearly taught by Thomas Aquinas in his general principles of act and virtue'.[179] Jennifer Moberly, on the other hand, seeks to 'counter O'Donovan's statement that notions of character can only inform the evaluation of an act … not the decision of how to act' with a reading of Bonhoeffer's 'virtue-ethical motifs' that can still satisfy Protestant concerns, while offering prospective as well as retrospective help.[180]

That material and the question of its position within virtue ethics would reward much greater attention, but my real interest here is in the passage at the end of the chapter, where O'Donovan re-engages questions that pertain to our theme of character and conversion. He advocates three functions of a character-based approach, the first of which is expressly soteriological:

> An ethic of character … raises the question of salvation in relation to morality; that is why the Catholic tradition has been right to retain it. But it does not answer that question sufficiently; that is why the Protestant tradition has been right to suspect its possible pretensions. We shall not learn how to save our souls by talking about the formation of virtuous characters. Nevertheless, such talk may teach us better than anything else what it is for a soul to be lost or saved, and so teach us to care about it for ourselves and others.[181]

The second function accentuates the first: 'thought about moral character plays a central role in repentance', not least because it enables us to 'form judgments … on what kind of character our history has disclosed, and these, rather than judgments

---

[177] Ibid., 205.
[178] Ibid., 211, 215.
[179] Westberg, *Renewing Moral Theology*, 85. See also Westberg, 'The Influence of Aquinas on Protestant Ethics', in *Aquinas among the Protestants*, ed. Manfred Svenson and David VanDrunen (Chichester: Wiley-Blackwell, 2018).
[180] Jennifer Moberly, *The Virtue of Bonhoeffer's Ethics: A Study of Dietrich Bonhoeffer's Ethics in Relation to Virtue Ethics* (Eugene: Pickwick, 2013), 232. Moberly takes on *Resurrection*'s comparatively austere account of virtue in her concluding study (229–32). A valuable further comparison that I cannot pursue here would be with Elizabeth Agnew Cochrane, *Protestant Virtue and Stoic Ethics* (London/New York: T & T Clark, 2018).
[181] O'Donovan, *Resurrection*, 224.

on particular acts, are what will make us feel most acutely the need of salvation'.[182] O'Donovan continues: 'Of an ethic of character, then, we can say with particular point what Lutheran theology used to say about the moral law in all its forms, that by condemning us it drives us to seek the grace of God.'[183] In view of some theological under-determination within the wider turn to character and virtue in Christian ethics, we may therefore join with Adam Hollowell in appreciating 'significant early writings by … Oliver O'Donovan' that 'situate this turn within an explicitly Christian frame'.[184]

Though his soteriological convictions (besides his commitments to deontology) chasten the ethic of character appropriated here, O'Donovan by no means thinks conversion is all. In the earlier section he criticizes some Protestants so fixated upon conversion that they are tempted to fasten to the concept all talk of morality, undercutting any impression of moral growth.[185] Now, this critical claim is often made and certainly reflects *some* strands of Protestant theology, in which, as Gustafson writes, the moral life suffers from 'benign neglect',[186] because, as John Webster says, 'justification virtually leaves sanctification, ecclesiology and ethics in suspension'.[187] O'Donovan's targets go unnamed (we may expect that at least some are Lutheran, and that some general evangelical trends are also in question). If we assume that the charge may, when O'Donovan wrote, have stuck to some Protestant tendencies, does it still?

I am yet to encounter in person or print many contemporary Protestants who in fact conceive of morality so starkly, having the courage of any reductionistic soteriological convictions in their ethics – or lack of ethics. Many Protestant theologians develop or adopt conceptualities bespeaking moral growth, whether 'sanctification', some understanding of progressive 'discipleship', or more extensive language of character and virtue. At a popular level, preachers who do not – though virtually nobody seems to eschew them in one guise or another – hardly forego talk of holiness, for example, and can be just as moralistic as those who do (albeit haphazardly). The exception here are perhaps 'Radical Lutherans' like Gerhard Forde, and in his tradition, Steven Paulson and Mark Mattes, plus the radically Lutheran Episcopal Paul Zahl.[188] For the briefest but bracingly cask-strength indication of where their disagreements with perspectives like O'Donovan's might lie, consider Forde's review of Webster's introduction to the theology of Eberhard Jüngel, in which Forde reminds the reader, in view of Webster's trademark concerns for moral ontology and human action, that

---

[182] Ibid., 225.
[183] Ibid.
[184] Hollowell, *Power and Purpose*, 5. Hollowell writes that while the turn to virtue is 'largely attributed' to MacIntyre, Porter and O'Donovan contributed this theological definition. We can add to them the contributions of Josef Pieper, Romanus Cessario and Stanley Hauerwas.
[185] O'Donovan, *Resurrection*, 92.
[186] James M. Gustafson, *Protestant and Roman Catholic Ethics: Prospects for Rapprochement* (Chicago: University of Chicago Press, 1978), 10.
[187] John Webster, 'Christology, Imitability and Ethics', *Scottish Journal of Theology* 39, no. 3 (1986): 309–26, 320.
[188] See e.g. Gerhard Forde, *A More Radical Gospel: Essays on Eschatology: Authority, Atonement and Ecumenism*, ed. Mark C. Mattes and Steven D. Paulson (Grand Rapids: Eerdmans, 2004); Forde, 'The Christian Life', in *Christian Dogmatics*, vol. 2, ed. Carl Braaten and Robert Jenson (Minneapolis: Fortress, 1994); Paul Zahl, *Grace in Practice: A Theology of Everyday Life* (Grand Rapids: Eerdmans, 2007).

Pelagius was also British![189] Ultimately, for all that these radical Lutherans can teach us, I do think O'Donovan's account of conversion and growth – the second part of which we are about to relate – shows that they miss a great deal out.[190] I was careful, earlier, to say 'reductionistic soteriological convictions', and *not* 'reductionistic*ally* soteriological convictions', because the problem is not straightforwardly that the radical Lutherans cannot think otherwise than salvation. They are right to think theological ethics ought never to leave grace behind. Rather, they sometimes cannot think the grace upon grace of the Spirit's effective work in conforming human beings to Christ, beyond cursory indications that it will involve liberation for love. By contrast, I think it is possible to think from the precedence of divine being and action through to the sanctification of the pardoned sinner, and to explore the latter aspect at more leisure, without losing any grasp of the gratuity of salvation *extra nos*.

O'Donovan is keen to make clear his soteriological priorities: he maintains that he, too, holds that true moral knowledge begins with conversion, and that in order 'to proceed with seriousness it must be constantly renewed in repentance'.[191] But he does create room for a loftier understanding, espying 'a mode of learning, which is not accumulation on the one hand, not merely a sequence of repentings on the other'.[192] Yet as O'Donovan recognizes in a third comment on character ethics, Christian caution regarding speaking of growth in the moral life is not just the product of anti-Pelagian resolve – a concern that O'Donovan shares but does not allow to disqualify reception of biblical and traditional witness to that genuine 'mode of learning'. It also issues from an eschatological consideration.

The 'self-assessment' of character ethics does show how we 'stand under the law of God, which accuses', and leads to an assessment of others, too, 'because the moral law speaks generically'.[193] But these judgements are firmly provisional, because of the eschatological hiddenness of disclosure:

> Just as our favourable judgments on ourselves must be provisional ... so our favourable judgments on others are tempered by the knowledge that they, too, are open to temptation. More importantly, just as our critical judgments on ourselves must be provisional, lest we despair of repentance and transformation, so our critical judgments on others must be expectantly open to God's grace. And when we look at others we have to think not only of repentance and transformation that may yet take place, but of that which may possibly have already taken place, though without being disclosed to our view. Thus Solon's warning, to call no man happy until he is dead, is less cautious than Jesus' warning [not to judge, Mt. 7.1].

---

[189] Forde, review of Webster, *Eberhard Jüngel: An Introduction to His Theology*, Lutheran Quarterly 2, no. 4 (1988): 531–3.
[190] See also Michael Allen's recent critique (Allen, *Sanctification*, 30–3, 183).
[191] O'Donovan, *Resurrection*, 93. Cf. O'Donovan, *Thirty-Nine Articles*, 80–1.
[192] O'Donovan, *Resurrection*, 92. Gilbert Meilaender's recurring account is similar. See e.g. *The Limits of Love: Some Theological Explorations* (University Park: Pennsylvania State University Press, 1987), 35; endorsed by Hauerwas and Pinches: 'On Developing Hopeful Virtues', in *Christians among the Virtues: Theological Conversations with Ancient and Modern Ethics* (Notre Dame: University of Notre Dame Press, 1997), 116.
[193] O'Donovan, *Resurrection*, 92.

Even of the dead we do not know what hidden work of God may yet be shown us on the last day.[194]

Sometimes, the way the doctrine of creation and the doctrine of its eschatological perfection are interpreted in *Resurrection and Moral Order*, without adequate and formative reference to the moments of sacred history in between, yields what can appear a premature ethics of glory.[195] But in instances like this, O'Donovan does acknowledge constraints upon knowledge of the success or otherwise of the moral life, owed to finitude, sin and eschatological hiddenness. He sometimes concedes that the moral life itself will, in this order, be difficult (and this difficulty involves more than the hard thinking of moral reasoning). If O'Donovan can acknowledge the difficulty, then why, in his thought, is the concession fairly infrequent? In the next subsection, I identify and assess some of the theological convictions that may be the cause.

Obedience, flourishing and the cross

O'Donovan's acknowledgement of constraint and difficulty is, I want to suggest, theologically entwined with his meditation upon 'the meaning of the cross *in itself*.'[196] Christ's death, for O'Donovan,

> shows us the outcome of the encounter between the true human life and the misshapen human life, between the order of creation as God gave it to be lived and known and the distorted and fantastic image of it in which mankind has lived ... joyful and obedient participation cannot continue freely in the world but must conflict with disobedience and so be driven out.[197]

That, he continues, is the cross's meaning, 'presupposed by all further meanings which it assumes in the light of the resurrection.'[198] O'Donovan's paschal ethics, defined by the accent placed upon Easter Sunday vindication, is at last able to register something of Good Friday's moral-theological magnitude. While we 'confess that God reversed the crucifixion of the Son of man and vindicated the true against the false', O'Donovan can write in the preceding sentences, 'that does not alter the fact that the corrupted order had in itself the tendency and the capacity to destroy the uncorrupted.'[199]

Given the apparent reluctance elsewhere to admit the efficacy of creaturely rebellion, these sentences are noteworthy. It is clearer here, too, that the corrupted order after the

---

[194] Ibid.
[195] And not just to those radical Lutherans, though among contemporary theological sensibilities, it is theirs whose would likely anathematize O'Donovan's most severely – consider, for example, Forde's angular commentary on the Heidelberg Disputation, *On Being a Theologian of The Cross* (Grand Rapids: Eerdmans, 1997).
[196] O'Donovan, *Resurrection*, 92.
[197] Ibid.
[198] Ibid., 95.
[199] Ibid.

resurrection still has in itself that tendency, because O'Donovan derives *present* moral implication from the encounter epitomized in the cross. The record of the way things went for Christ, of goodness's rejection by a fallen world, is also an indication of the way things will go for the people called by his name, because it discloses the way things must always go in the corrupted order. 'We are not invited now to live in the created order as though there had been no cross.'[200] It might seem that here O'Donovan seems to imply that the created order was not 'restored and fulfilled' by the resurrection in as univocal a sense as he elsewhere maintains. He is able to make these claims as he does without implying that, though, by placing great weight on the distinction between the created order and 'the distorted and fantastic *image* of it in which mankind has lived', identifying 'the corrupted order' totally with the image. For O'Donovan, this ontologically insubstantial fabrication seems to be what is always intended by the New Testament concept of 'the world'.

I have quoted the book's most thoroughgoing sentiments regarding the cross's disclosure of the conditions of the moral life. In spite of these, however, it has been suggested that O'Donovan understates the cross's place in moral theology. Gustafson was incorrect in saying that 'crucifixion is absent from this book', but would he have been mistaken to say that it is often missing from the book's basic ethical approach? Stephen N. Williams saw that the cross was not absent, but pressed the query about the relation of resurrection and crucifixion, linking it to the marginalized place of suffering.[201] And in some ways, we should expect more evangelicals like Williams to query that relation in O'Donovan's thought.[202] When O'Donovan takes the resurrection as keynote of an evangelical ethics that 'proclaims the good news as one of its aspects', this means, in O'Donovan's words, that while there is 'an ascetic and disciplinary side to moral theology … it is not primarily an ascetic discipline, just as Christian discipleship itself involves participation in the cross of Christ but is not primarily crucifixion but resurrection'.[203] This perspective was and is, no doubt, therapeutic for some evangelical audiences. Yet it also means that while amplifying an evangelical accent on theology's proclamatory nature and task, he can tend to underplay the proclamation of the word of the cross. To venture an analogy, the force of O'Donovan's moral theology is more like Stanley Spencer's series *The Resurrection at Cookham* – which paints risen life in continuity with what went before, provoking us to contemplate our this-worldly responsibilities – than it is the finger of the Baptist pointing to the crucified One, in Barth's beloved Isenheim altarpiece.

The way different moral theologies relate cross and resurrection and their respective moral import can sometimes determine, or be determined by, adherence to one metaethical approach over another. Self-consciously or not, eudaimonism in ethics, we might say, must presume the resurrection's reaffirmation of the goods of creaturely life, and of natural teleology. An ethics of divine command and obligation may tend to see

---

[200] Ibid., 94–5.
[201] Williams, 'Outline for Ethics', 89. He also raised well-placed worries about O'Donovan's reading of 1 Peter, in this vein, and drew a pointed contrast with liberation theology.
[202] These same concerns are there in Chester's *Mission and the Coming of God*, which originates in a thesis supervised by Stephen Williams. See also Parry, 'Evangelicalism and Ethics', 183.
[203] O'Donovan, 'The Foundations of Ethics', 103.

the cross's revelation of the character of obedience in this age of death, sin and the devil as more paradigmatic. These characterizations cannot hold true for all moral theologies (Hauerwas would be hard to classify by this, for one), but it may help understand some of the kinds of links between dogmatic proportion and moral-theological atmosphere that we can detect in different presentations of Christian ethics. If that is true, then *Resurrection and Moral Order* is a good case study: O'Donovan's most extended meditations on the difficulties of obedience are also his most extended meditations on the cross, and they are different in tone from the large swathes of the rest of a book that bases its ethic upon the resurrection.

While these meditations on the cross's moral import do seem far less central to the book's moral vision than its meditations on the resurrection, some have valued the way O'Donovan brings the two together in their proper relationship. Daniel Westberg is one, and he makes a similar link to meta-ethical issues. Placing O'Donovan (and himself) in a trajectory of moral thought that sets out to communicate a vision of human flourishing, and subsequently to assimilate to it notions of obligation and duty, argues that this reflects the proper relationship between resurrection and cross.[204] A brief consideration of Westberg's argument helps us distinguish the profile of O'Donovan's moral theology better. Like *Resurrection and Moral Order*, Westberg's *Renewing Moral Theology* aims to incorporate within an essentially eudaimonistic whole an evangelical concentration upon the cross of Christ and related recognition of the power of obedience as a concept:

> The Christian life presented in the Scriptures, in the life of Christ and described in sermons and saints' lives is obviously a combination of duty and joy, of obligation and fulfilment. But which is more fundamental? Jesus in the garden of Gethsemane prayed that the cup of suffering might be avoided, but he accepted that God's will and not his own was to be done. On the other hand, the Epistle to the Hebrews says that our Lord, 'who for the sake of the joy that was set before him endured the cross, disregarding its shame' (Heb. 12.2), speaking of an ultimate joyful purpose.[205]

On this basis, Westberg goes on to situate ethical recognition of duty inside, as it were, an ethics based on teleological purpose:

> The assumption that an ethics based on duty is more 'ethical' or more Christian is understandable when we think of morality in the restricted sense of special decisions where we sense difficulty, confusion and especially conflict. It is especially in times of temptation when inclination and desire lead to a course of action more attractive to us, but if we are honest, we know that the right thing

---

[204] Westberg, *Renewing Moral Theology*, 32. This tradition that seeks to promote human flourishing, Westberg points out, is Protestant as well as Catholic: after all, he notes, isn't enjoyment central to the Westminster Catechism?

[205] Ibid. There are resonances with Arner's account of increasing Protestant interest in 'flourishing' (citing the diverse work of Mirsolav Volf, Ellen Charry, and Neil Messer), and of recent 'forthright defences' of eudaimonism (citing Eric Gregory and Jennifer Herdt). Arner, 'Precedents and prospects', 378.

to do is what we ought to do – that is our 'duty'. But if we expand morality from these special situations of doubt, conflict and temptation, and we accept that all of our conscious actions reflect our morality, then it is easier to see that the more fundamental picture of being attracted to good things (such as marriage, friends and career) and through them to the good itself is sounder philosophically, psychologically and biblically. The sense of duty is secondary to overall purpose. Laws and lists of duties, job descriptions, and responsibilities are important and essential, but they do not furnish fundamental motivation, except at certain stages of immaturity or training.[206]

We can appreciate much about this rejection of a 'hard cases' model for moral reasoning. I welcome its view of Christian ethics as reflection upon Christian life in its full span, and the manner it draws the widest possible circle around moral action. Furthermore, if some Protestant piety does indeed portray discipleship as a joyless struggle, or courts hyper-kenoticism – a valorization of sacrificial suffering for its own sake – then there is surely something again therapeutic or reparative for Protestant piety in relating flourishing and duty like this.[207] O'Donovan makes a very similar argument to Westberg in his article 'The Foundations of Ethics': 'The struggle of the cross is one which takes its calling solely from the joy that is set before it, the pattern of the resurrection life in its completeness.'[208] And Eric Gregory's summary of O'Donovan's thought certainly coheres with Westberg's: 'Obedience is not an end in itself, but a means to human flourishing in delight with God's will for the good of human beings as revealed and made possible through the saving work of Jesus Christ.'[209] Let us, therefore, examine in a little more detail some of the constitutive parts of claims, like these about obedience and flourishing made by Westberg and O'Donovan besides Gregory and others as part of burgeoning Protestant interest in eudaimonistic ethics.[210]

---

[206] Westberg, *Renewing Moral Theology*, 33. We might ask: what about obedience to Christ himself (Heb. 5.9), or to the teaching of the gospel about him (Rom. 6.17; 2 Cor. 9.13)? That is hardly a form of obedience to be left behind! For its place in the Christian life as described by Paul, see e.g. Rom. 2.8, Gal. 5.7, and, for commentary, John Barclay, *Obeying the Truth: A Study of Paul's Ethics in Galatians* (Edinburgh: T & T Clark, 1988) – cf. 1 Pet. 1.22.

[207] Judgments on the character of popular piety like this would be very difficult to make.

[208] O'Donovan, 'The Foundations of Ethics', 106.

[209] Gregory, '"The Spirit and the Letter": Protestant Thomism and Nigel Biggar's "Karl Barth's Ethics Revisited"', in *Commanding Grace*, 50-9.

[210] The place of eudaimonism within Protestant theological ethics is contested. Its compatibility with various Protestant commitments is long debated, including divine command, pride's sinful self-love, and the self-forgetfulness of Christian obedience. Many contemporary moral theologians, including Protestants, are adopting broadly eudaimonistic perspectives. That this adoption is thought desirable and possible, even necessary, relies in part on thoroughgoing – merited – critique of anti-eudaimonist arguments of Protestants like Nygren and Reinhold Niebuhr as well as renewed attention to the eudaimonistic character of classical Christian ethics (Augustine and Thomas Aquinas largely, but others besides), and, at best, detailed reflection on the ways in which Christian theological concerns modify philosophical eudaimonism. It also frequently involves dismissal of Reformational moral thought, especially Luther's. Or, more accurately, what is usually perceived as Luther's *lack* of moral thought. This part of the case seems more hastily prosecuted, not least because Luther wrote plenty and there is more than one interpretation of 'Lutheran ethics'. A precise consideration of eudaimonism and Christian ethics can be found in Frederick Simmons, 'Eudaimonism and Christian Love', in *Love and Christian Ethics: Tradition, Theory, and Society*, ed. Frederick V. Simmons, with Brian C. Sorrells (Washington: Georgetown University Press, 2016).

Ingredient in this placing of obligation 'within' a broader view of flourishing is the view, as widely espoused by Catholic theologians in their own recovery of virtue ethics, that in the 'first person' perspective 'the commandments are a pedagogical stage relative to the formation of the moral virtues'.[211] But the view is also increasingly common in Protestant theology, among those theologians like Westberg who embrace some form of eudaimonism. D. Stephen Long builds on MacIntyre's *After Virtue*, for instance, when he writes that 'the moral life begins with "our nature as it is in itself" ... and transforms it to "our nature as it should be". This movement is what helps us make sense of laws and commands. They are not ends in themselves; they are intelligible because of the ends to which they direct and form our nature.'[212]

We have not reviewed all of the passages in which O'Donovan treats law and command, but we have seen enough to know that he would likely be sympathetic to this attempt to contextualize them within a broader moral vision. Frederick Simmons would seem to support this sense when, in a precise, technical essay on 'Eudaimonism and Christian Love' that characterizes a variety of eudaimonisms, he associates O'Donovan's understanding in *Self-Love* with the kind that takes eudaimonism to be 'the doctrine that moral obligation is justified by its contribution to the eudaimonia of those who comply with it'.[213] (Of course we have established that in O'Donovan's case, the contextual intelligibility of law and command that he principally wishes to emphasize is their contextual intelligibility within the vision of a normative created order, rather than teleological intelligibility as penultimate within the life of virtue.) But at the same time I expect that O'Donovan may caution against exaggerating the sense in which divine commandments as such are simply pedagogical, and would urge us to distinguish the senses of law and commandment we intend – for instance, are we speaking of the Mosaic law, or of the general human experience of obligation, or finally 'the law of the gospel'? For all that we can speak of law, in the first sense, as 'a particular historical phase of Israel's experience of God' – or, in the second, as representing 'a universal existential situation in which an individual at any point of history may find himself before Christ has become a saving reality in his experience' – we must remember that 'the command of God is not to be dismissed as unevangelical *praeperatio evangelii*. It is not a crutch; it is a life-giving command, "Rise, take up your bed and walk!"'[214]

It is important to understand that O'Donovan and these other Protestant eudaimonists construct their theological ethics with an awareness of retrieving an older, holistic moral theology after a period of modern decline. Westberg's own espousal of

---

The collected volume, containing an essay by O'Donovan himself, is a kind of extended tribute to Gene Outka, whose 1970 Princeton class O'Donovan took, and which, he writes here, gave him the stimulus to return to Oxford intending to write about self-love in Augustine (under Henry Chadwick's supervision). That sojourn also provided the opportunity to learn from Paul Ramsey, from whom O'Donovan gained 'his understanding of how Christian ethics should proceed' (O'Donovan in Shortt, *God's Advocates*, 267).

[211] Melina, *Sharing in Christ's Virtues*, 136.
[212] D. Stephen Long, *Christian Ethics: A Very Short Introduction* (Oxford/New York: Oxford University Press, 2010), 18.
[213] Simmons, 'Eudaimonia', 190, 204 n. 5.
[214] O'Donovan, *Resurrection*, 152, 154.

eudaimonism is indebted to the account of Servais Pinckaers, and is predicated on Pinckaers' declension narrative of 'a major shift ... to a fundamental orientation of the moral life to law and obedience'; in this shift, 'prudence and the other virtues recede, or become aspects of an obedient will' and 'conscience becomes the source for moral reasoning, with the decision to act taken by the will, a decision which then takes on the character of obedience or disobedience'.[215] That narrative, I think, is compatible with one that we have found O'Donovan telling from the time of 'The Natural Ethic'.[216] And Westberg thinks that Pinckaers' critique of the Catholic post-tridentine tradition's reductionistic and austerely rigoristic interests in conscience, law and obedience – against which the recovery of eudaimonism is set – would also find something of a target in Protestant theological ethics, as well as in Anglican moral theology, which was directly influenced by Catholic ills.[217] And it may also hit home in the drily moralistic evangelical ethics Westberg also has in mind. I find the most part of Westberg's analysis persuasive, and he helps us see some of the problems that O'Donovan's resurrection-oriented account of human flourishing was designed to mend.

Yet – here is the point of my partial digression – for all the gains of these developments over against what may have gone before, is there not in this adoption of a 'morality of beatitude' (Pinckaers) sometimes a risk that it has travelled too far in the opposite direction? In the preface to *Resurrection and Moral Order*, O'Donovan writes of his suspicion that Hauerwas espouses 'crucimonism' – 'a tendency to privilege the crucifixion over the other moments of the Christ-event, in keeping with an emphasis on martyrdom and death as the normative expression of Christian witness'.[218] Perhaps that is true: a sympathetic reader of Hauerwas like Samuel Wells agrees that 'by over-emphasizing the cross and underplaying creation, Hauerwas falls short of his own

---

[215] Westberg, 'Influence of Aquinas', 277. For contemporary ownership of something like the view criticized see John Hare, *God's Command* (Oxford: Oxford University Press, 2015), e.g. 312.

[216] Though I cannot pursue the comparison further here (I hope to elsewhere), Pinckaers therefore makes an interesting Catholic counterpart to O'Donovan, as to Hauerwas. There is disagreement about the extent to which Pinckaers himself managed to integrate law and obedience within his retrieval of eudaimonism. (See Craig Steven Titus, 'Servais Pinckaers and the Renewal of Catholic Moral Theology', *Journal of Moral Theology* 1, no. 1 (2012): 43–68, 59–67, for references to the literature and a positive assessment.) But Pinckaers' reaction to what he saw as the negative shift – and to much 'manualist' Catholic moral theology – has a great deal to commend it, not least his turn to 'Sacred Scripture', his concern to give a theological 'redimensioning' to moral anthropology and an account of moral reason, and to reconnect moral with spiritual theology ('Theological redimensioning' is Melina's phrase – see e.g. Melina, *Sharing in Christ's Virtues*, 140).

[217] To be sure, Westberg knows classical Anglican theologians like Jeremy Taylor and Richard Hooker, and more recently Kenneth Kirk, have plenty to offer within and besides these topics. There is certainly debate about the extent to which the Caroline divines reformed scholastic casuistry when they absorbed it. Actually, Kenneth Kirk and Henry McAdoo's readings of the Caroline divines make them sound rather like Pinckaers himself, in terms of restoring the connection between moral and ascetic theology, and between Scripture and reason. See Kirk, *Some Principles of Moral Theology and Their Application* (London: Longmans, Green, & Co., 1920); McAdoo, *The Structure of Caroline Moral Theology* (London: Longmans, Green, & Co., 1949). That said, like Peter Sedgwick after him, McAdoo thinks that the Caroline divines align with, and indeed are 'a striking anticipation' of, the work of Catholic moral theologians like Häring and Fuchs (see Joyce, *Richard Hooker*, 7), whose sensibilities overlap with Pinckaers but the two of whom can be clearly distinguished, post-Vatican II.

[218] O'Donovan, *Resurrection*, xvi. Reinhold Niebuhr wrote similar things about Barth.

criteria ... failing to do full justice to the *narrative* form of Christian convictions'.[219] Wells thinks it is only later, by turning to Milbank's account of nonviolent creation, that 'Hauerwas can finally bridge the divide between creation ethics and kingdom ethics'.[220] But is there equally a danger on O'Donovan's side – and certainly for younger generations of O'Donovanians and Protestant eudaimonists – of constructing a vision of the journey of the moral life inadequately marked by consideration of disciples' need to be conformed to the cruciform way of Christ in the world?[221]

If we are, in the final analysis, to take up something like the broadly eudaimonistic understanding just entertained, we must be alert to the occasional trace of triumphalist overstatement in Westberg's case that can also be found in *Resurrection and Moral Order*. It threatens to weaken the sense in which creaturely life in this order is stricken by sin and suffering, and the related sense in which the life of creaturely flourishing that is the destiny of the children of God might as often as not be 'hidden with Christ' (Col. 3.3), awaiting disclosure. Granted, some Thomist moral theologians take the time to clarify that beatitude's 'subjective' side is more than simply a state of enjoyment, rooted as it is in its ultimate object – God.[222] But I would still emphasize that the subsumption of obedience under a eudaimonistic account of the virtues – whether act-oriented or agent-oriented – should not be enacted blithely, because here again the danger of an ethics of glory lies close at hand.[223]

Christ's incontrovertibly cruciform way is, as a *way*, ordered to a *telos* beyond the opposition and difficulty encountered in this world as this world is currently configured. But it knows no path around them – and we should reject any inference that Christ's obedience (for our sake) was necessary because he was at a certain stage of moral immaturity.[224] Recognition of Christ's way should encourage us to retain a strong sense of the moral life as a struggle for reasons more adequate and realistic than merely an overactive fascination with the difficulty of isolated moral decisions.[225] Much contemporary Christian ethics seems to coalesce around the thought that the commitments of an august 'morality of happiness', broadly construed, should once again be taken as the marrow of the Christian ethical approach, in this post-liberal age just as they were in patristic and medieval moral thought.[226] If the retrieval is theologically

---

[219] Wells, *Transforming Fate into Destiny*, 156.
[220] Ibid., 158.
[221] Cf. Mt. 16.24; Mk 8.34; Lk. 9.23.
[222] For instance Elliot, *Hope and Christian Ethics*, e.g. 16, there building on Pinckaers, and William C. Mattison, *The Sermon on the Mount and Moral Theology: A Virtue Perspective* (New York: Cambridge University Press, 2017).
[223] Language of obedience is hardly absent from Scripture. The link between obedience and blessing finds biblical support, too, throughout Old and New Testaments, though answers to the question of eschatological reward can be related in different ways to answers to the question of present flourishing.
[224] That would surely be a mistaken (subordinationist or adoptionist) way to read Heb. 5.8 ('Although he was a Son, he learned obedience through what he suffered ...').
[225] Cf. Hauerwas and Pinches, 'Is Obedience a Virtue?' in *Christians Among the Virtues*, 129-48.
[226] Pinckaers aims to demonstrate just how central it was – see *Sources of Christian Ethics*, 134-68. Despite the extensive making of distinctions in Thomistic moral theology, 'obedience', 'duty', 'obligation', 'law' and 'commandment' are not always as well defined in the turn to virtue as they might be, in the rush to make a case for virtue's supremacy. Likewise, 'obedience' and 'virtue' are sometimes effectively mapped onto an 'Old'/'New Law' scheme less carefully than might be

disciplined, then I see no problem with that. But to that end, I am expressing a concern (predictably Protestant) that *how* this classical tradition[227] is appropriated needs to be maximally rather than superficially informed by our understanding of the real situation of human creatures as disclosed by the gospel.

Finally, and to tie these reflections back in with our main theme, in terms of the relation of eschatology to ethics, these are especially apt matters for contemplation. After all, both flourishing and obedience are notions that, in part, derive their theological intelligibility from eschatology, as well as from Christology and soteriology – or, more precisely, often from the perceived relation of these tracts of Christian teaching. And notions of flourishing and obedience often achieve their power exactly by extension from a particular understanding of eschatology's relation to present conduct. Eschatology can sponsor strongly teleological narrations of the moral life based on imagination of Christian life as a present participation in the joy of beatitude; it can also sponsor narrations in a sense equally teleological but typically gloomier, based on imagination of the Christian life *in via* as dutiful endurance.

To make a very minimal claim, we would want to say that any account of eschatology's import for ethics should not dispense with the essential truth of either. It should affirm the presence even now, by the Spirit, of the blessedness of eternal life.[228] It should also grant the fleeting quality of the present experience of that blessedness in the face of the world's corruption, and in view of the temptations to betray its promise – against which biblical exhortations to perseverance and endurance are issued.[229] Coherently and persuasively relating these different dispositions of Christian ethics is a task for a theological narration of the Christian life that seeks to describe well the bearing upon that life of hope in the kingdom of God. What my study argues cumulatively can be stated more plainly here: this task requires attentiveness to the full range of theological *loci* that describe the realities in which the Christian life subsists, including the full range of eschatological aspects. Again, this is a modest criterion for theological ethics, but, I submit, a useful one.

I find the dialectical understanding of conversion and character in *Resurrection and Moral Order* persuasive, and I appreciate the way it is responsive to a full range of doctrinal *loci* as well as philosophically astute. But overall I have found the book's

---

desired. Melina *does* count 'humility, obedience, service' as 'new virtues', 'in reference to Christ' (135), but in general, 'obedience' is usually understood in terms of 'negative precepts' (often those in the Decalogue), and the realization that obedience seems to be also a feature of the 'New Law', exemplified Christologically, does not lead to much further reflection on the shape of 'virtue'. The riches of *ressourcement* have evidently put Catholic moral theology back in touch with Scripture in a serious way, but the moral visions that *ressourcement* has produced might still not be as closely canonically informed as Protestants might hope. Exceptions here in relation to the particular question could be the work of William C. Spohn, e.g. *Go and Do Likewise: Jesus and Ethics* (New York/London: Continuum International, 2007), in which the place of obedience in discipleship is well-observed, and Raniero Cantalamessa, e.g. *Obedience: The Authority of the Word*, trans. Frances Lonergan Villa (Slough: St. Paul, 2018), who shows the place of obedience 'in the Spirit'.

[227] See e.g. Julia Annas, *The Morality of Happiness* (New York/Oxford: Oxford University Press, 1995).

[228] Mattison stresses an 'intrinsic', 'continuous' relationship between eternal happiness and activity in this life in *The Sermon on the Mount and Moral Theology*, e.g. 39–40, 204–23. Whether Protestants with different convictions about merit may need to relate the two differently is a moot question.

[229] See e.g. Rom. 5.4; Col. 1.11; 2 Tim. 2.12; Heb. 10.23 (remembering 10.39) and 12.1; Jas 1.12; 1.25. Also Mt. 10.22; 13.21 (Mk 4.17); 24.13 (Mk 13.13).

evocation of the general mood of the moral life a touch less persuasive. The evocation of joyful flourishing is not illegitimate; it is based on an understanding of the created goodness of human life in the world, goodness secured through the work of Christ and realized by the Spirit in the life of discipleship. Yet it is less dialectical than it might be, because it demotes the way Christ's cross discloses how obedience must go in this order before the perfect fulfilment of eschatological consummation, and the way the Spirit testifies in our weakness and affliction as well as obvious triumphs.[230] Keeping these assessments in mind, we turn now to the ecclesiological passages in *Resurrection and Moral Order*, searching them for further persuasive proposals, and alert to this tendency.

Community and kingdom

We can arrive at O'Donovan's ecclesiology by following his continued explorations of the theme of freedom that we left off some time ago. A continuing pneumatological determination unites with an increasingly eschatological one. O'Donovan speaks of 'freedom to act in such a way that our freedom itself is affirmed and sustained, the freedom to achieve our supernatural end, which is the perfect liberty of the kingdom of God.'[231] This is dogmatically parsed in a now familiar pattern of ascription: 'It is Christ, the pioneer of renewed creation, who evokes this freedom in us, as the Holy Spirit makes the authority of his eschatological triumph subjectively present and immediate to us.'[232] And the account of human freedom opens out to ecclesiological horizons here, since it is not just individual liberty that is made possible:

> Our communal action, too, is made free by the work of Christ, who is the first of a community of brothers. Human freedom consists not only in the power to act alone, but in the power to act together, as a co-operating fellowship. Our humanity is destined, as the seer of the Apocalypse presents it, for the shared life of a city, a fulfilment, redeemed and transformed, of the collective existence of ancient Israel, the 'new Jerusalem, coming down out of heaven'. (Rev. 21.2)[233]

Freedom's communal dimension is available because of a promised – and pneumatologically present – eschatological reality.

Just as O'Donovan's ethics typically attends first to moral action (and his political ethics to the political 'act') but finds room for consideration of character, having attended to the individual moral agent, it now begins to address the community as the subject of moral reflection. He is able to pitch individual and communal moral subjects as non-competitive by following Augustine in speaking of 'the City of God, which eschatologically transcends the tensions between infinite individual aspiration

---

[230] Rom. 8.26.
[231] O'Donovan, *Resurrection*, 163.
[232] Ibid.
[233] Ibid.

and the limitations of collective structures'.²³⁴ And he is able to show how the freedoms of individual and community are necessarily different, but finally convergent:

> The freedom of the community to render corporate obedience to the gospel is the ground of its authority over the individual member. At the same time, his individual freedom to render obedience to the gospel in immediate responsibility to God defines the limits of the community's authority over him. It is obvious enough that these freedoms are liable to conflict. ... However ... . The conflict between them, when it arises, is only provisional, springing from sin or from misunderstanding. For both these freedoms are authorised by the same eschatological reality, the kingdom of God, in which every individual vocation is fulfilled and brought to perfection in harmony with the whole. This means that within the church's life the eschatological reconciliation of individual and collective can begin to be realised. There can be a partial experience, at least, of living together in love. Both the church's freedom and the individual's freedom consist in their finding fulfilment in each other, and so displaying in outline the lineaments of the kingdom of God.²³⁵

Later passages toe a similar line: we see a glimpse of the kingdom in 'the communitarian character of redemption', but this does not disaffirm individual vocation, an eschatologically derived requirement of solitude that values 'secret alms, private prayer, and concealed fasting'.²³⁶ That requirement reminds us of the dangerous possibility that 'public deeds of righteousness ... lose their eschatological reference'; that 'their horizon is entirely occupied by the demands and satisfactions of the religious community in the present'.²³⁷ The value of those private deeds 'is not spent upon the community of the present', but it 'can expect acknowledgment in the eschatological community of God's kingdom'.²³⁸

There is much to learn from O'Donovan about the way theology can speak convincingly about both individual and community, and, for ethics more particularly, much to learn about questions of freedom and agency, personal and ecclesial.²³⁹ (It is probably accurate for pedagogical purposes, as Malcolm Brown does, to classify O'Donovan along with Hauerwas, Milbank and Banner as 'communitarian' rather than 'liberal' Christian ethicists, but might O'Donovan's reflections on the individual-in-relation-to-community, throughout his work, evince a depth that tag would not always necessitate?)²⁴⁰ More to the point, we find here that O'Donovan's ethic encompasses an eschatological factor inasmuch as it has an ecclesial definition. That connection is not conflation; he is quick to discourage any 'angel ecclesiology' – unequivocal, over-realized identification of church with kingdom.²⁴¹ The church not only proclaims the

---

²³⁴ Ibid., 164.
²³⁵ Ibid., 169.
²³⁶ Ibid., 230.
²³⁷ Ibid.
²³⁸ Ibid., 231.
²³⁹ Not to say political theology – see *Desire*'s account of Christian and civil freedom.
²⁴⁰ Malcolm Brown, *Tensions in Christian Ethics: An Introduction* (London: SPCK, 2010).
²⁴¹ O'Donovan, *Resurrection*, 164.

kingdom and 'is, therefore, in its secondary movement, the kingdom's messenger'; first and characteristically, it 'hears God's word addressed to it, enters the kingdom of God by faith, and ... begins to be conformed to its life'.[242] If we speak of the church's authority, we first have to speak of it standing under another authority, and as such 'the church's authority is genuinely ecclesial only when it manifests the church's identity as a witness to the kingdom of God'.[243] With this appropriately deflationary caution, however, O'Donovan is willing to call the Christian community 'a true anticipation of the kingdom of God', as the portion of humankind that hears God's word.[244]

We can learn much about 'the true character of eschatological expectation' over and against 'enthusiastic attempts to invoke final judgment prematurely', O'Donovan suggests, from Luke the Evangelist.[245] The church's sign 'points, entirely symbolically, to the last judgment', and in this, symbolic witness is differentiated from political authorities.[246] Ecclesial authority is dialectically related to the eschatological disclosure of reality. On the one hand, its 'judgments are vulnerable to the hiddenness of the future', for 'nobody knows what an individual will become, nobody can speak a final word of judgment upon him' (recall the comments on character ethics).[247] On the other, 'a provisional disclosure of reality is given to us. The importance of this sign is that it takes the church's public life seriously as a sphere of action in which eschatological reality can be seen'.[248] On this basis, the church's authority can

> penetrate behind deception and render a judgment by the prophetic word which makes hidden things plain. This judgment derives its terrifying decisiveness from its relation to the final judgment of God, which seems to cast its shadow back across the penultimate judgments of men and make itself known in the midst of history.[249]

After appropriate checks and balances, then, O'Donovan's ecclesiology is unafraid to align the church with the city of God: it 'is only a witness to that reality, operating under the constraints and ambiguities of public life, nevertheless it is a witness which the Holy Spirit has authorized, and through which God's word has been made known, constraints and ambiguities notwithstanding'.[250] In a line that contains the kernel of an idea repeated in his political theology and ethics – and that finally flowers in *Entering into Rest* – he writes: 'A community of loving agreement in the truth can have existence, though fleeting and imperfect, in our midst, and can show us something of the life of heaven.'[251]

---

[242] Ibid.
[243] Ibid., 173.
[244] Ibid., 165.
[245] Ibid., 177.
[246] Ibid., 173.
[247] Ibid., 176.
[248] Ibid.
[249] Ibid., 178.
[250] Ibid., 176.
[251] Ibid.

I suspect that some readers may find in O'Donovan's ecclesiology traces of the triumphalism that troubled me in earlier narrations of the moral life, and there is no doubt that, seen in the context of the book, triumphalism could be inferred from the assured designation of church as witness to the kingdom. The general mood is perhaps one of certainty, 'constraints and ambiguities notwithstanding'. But while I recognize that danger, I find O'Donovan's ecclesiology more persuasive. This is partly because its use of the concept of 'witness' seems to keep us firmly in the era of the church militant, even as in our midst there may be by grace a foretaste of the Church triumphant. (As Webster writes, 'the notion of witness tries to express the permanently derivative character of the work of the church', 'the active visibility' of which 'consists in attestations of the Word and work of the God who is its creator, reconciler and consummator'; the church's active life is 'one long act of testimony'.)[252] However, we are still in search of a comparably persuasive instance in which O'Donovan shows eschatology's import for the moral life – a search that takes us to the book's final two chapters.

Love, faith and hope

We may orient ourselves to the themes of these chapters by beginning with a summary of the argument of *Resurrection and Moral Order* that John Berkman and Michael Buttrey present in an article critical of McKenny's interpretation, which we have already seen:

> To understand O'Donovan's theology of created order, of the 'beginning', we start with the end, both the end of creation in general, and with our individual ends as human persons specifically. O'Donovan refers to our end as the restored order of creation (or 'new creation'), which we as Christians participate in through a life of ordered love of God and neighbour. Indeed, this proper ordering of love is the chief task of Christian ethics.[253]

If we afford the priority to the claims of the earlier chapters of O'Donovan's book that they seem to demand for themselves, then this interpretation, including the decision to 'start with the end', amounts to Augustinian-Thomist streamlining of the book. I make this argument more fully in this chapter's conclusion. But here it serves to introduce the way *Resurrection and Moral Order*'s final two chapters contribute to the whole, just as McKenny's summary expressed the contribution of the earlier chapters.

---

[252] Webster, 'On Evangelical Ecclesiology', in *Confessing God: Essays in Christian Dogmatics II* (London/New York: T & T Clark International, 2005), 183, 175. Webster's clarity about the church's identity as witness is matchless, but we may find salutary affirmations in O'Donovan's ecclesiology that Webster's near-incessant deflationary instincts tended to suppress in fear of contemporary 'ecclesiocentrism'.

[253] John Berkman and Michael Buttrey, 'Theologies of Enhancement? Another Look at Oliver O'Donovan's Created Order', *Toronto Journal of Theology* 31, no. 1 (2015): 27–37, 30.

Chapter 11, 'The Double Aspect of the Moral Life', tells us more about the significance of love: 'the principle which confers unifying order both upon the moral field and upon the moral subject's character ... the moral law's fulfilment on the one hand, and the virtues' form on the other'; the rule of worship and of social life, admitting no conflict between active and contemplative, or between evangelism and works of mercy.[254] Once more, love is 'free conformity of our agency to the order of things which is given in reality. ... Love of the material world is good if it is built upon a recognition of what material goods are and what they are for'.[255] Love is this-worldly. Still, 'love of Christ must be viewed eschatologically, as the form which our moral obligations have taken in these last days, at the climax of God's redemptive work'.[256] Indeed love, 'like faith and hope, has an eschatological reference which belongs to it essentially'.[257] It, therefore, has a measure of *discontinuity*:

> What ... did Jesus mean when he taught it as a *new* command 'that you love one another' (Jn 13:34)? The point is that whenever we take love seriously, even within the perfectly 'natural' perspective of the twofold command of love to God and neighbour, we stand under the shadow of the last things. The order of love, the created moral order, does not have eternity in itself, but looks forward to a new creation to fulfil it and make it wholly intelligible.[258]

With this, O'Donovan augments the result of an exposition of 1 John in the previous chapter, and goes a little beyond it in a salutary direction. There he suggested that the commandment's 'newness ... is the eschatological newness of Christ's appearing; its oldness, correspondingly, the aboriginal oldness of created order which is vindicated as the dawning light floods the world'.[259] But here the 'newness' is the eschatological newness of 'new creation', of the last things, a fulfilment that seems to mean new wineskins as well as wine.

Chapter 12, 'The End of the Moral Life', goes on to show how understanding love's eschatological reference aright means considering the 'relations to the eschatological future' of faith and hope, too, 'dispositions which are quite without point if they are viewed in isolation from the end':

> If we have understood why love, the form of the moral life, is grouped, not with the spiritual gifts, which have their own intelligibility, but with faith and hope which depend for intelligibility upon the end of history, then we have grasped how morality is related to salvation, how it is that Christian ethics is evangelical. The moral life of mankind is a moment in God's dealing with the created order which

---

[254] O'Donovan, *Resurrection*, 226.
[255] Ibid., 236.
[256] Ibid., 242.
[257] Ibid., 245.
[258] Ibid., 247.
[259] Ibid., 243.

he has restored in Christ. Only as that restored order is fully disclosed can the meaning of human morality be comprehended.[260]

Hope and faith 'qualify' love in different ways, O'Donovan suggests, and I will dwell on these further reflections on the Pauline triad because his explanation of the three virtues' complementary functions illuminates and puzzles in equal measure.

Hope 'encourages us and sustains us by promising to our present experience, with all its ambiguity, a completion that will render it intelligible'; in it, 'future transformation' is made 'present to our minds by anticipation'.[261] It raises questions of love's reward and therein love's incompleteness in the current order, for the 'divine life of love', truly the supernatural end of humankind, 'quite surpasses the life of human love'.[262] But, O'Donovan says, we can confess that heavenly end without denigrating its earthy analogue, of which it is 'a renewal and perfection'.[263] For 'the life of love to God and neighbour is a true participation in the restored order of creation, a responsive love to the divine love in which the divine mode of life becomes our own'.[264] Still, the two must be distinguished, and the reasons given for this distinction are compelling ones that we would have been glad to find more readily repeated throughout the book. Our 'participation in the restored creation' must be conformed to a cruciform pattern if it is to 'point forward to the resurrection', and 'the present hiddenness of God's new creation demands its fulfilment in public manifestation, the *parousia* or "presence" of the Son of man to the cosmos in which God is to be all in all'.[265]

Faith conceives 'that future as something apart from our present, wholly independent of it and standing in judgment upon it'.[266] In view of it, the moral life is utterly dependent on 'God's final judgment of grace'.[267] Faith qualifies love by relating it to justification, revealing how love is ultimately consequent upon 'the one eschatological reality' of the moment of conversion: 'the one decisive transformation' that is successively reclaimed, and signified publicly in baptism.[268] All human lives, myriad in outward appearance, stand under the 'final question … what do they constitute for eternity?'[269] The criteria of that judgement, further, 'are not immanent to the created order itself but … come from beyond it, from its supernatural end', asking whether 'this life, this act, this character' belongs 'to the renewed and transformed world which God is bringing into being'?[270] This question reduces to 'a stark and awesome simplicity' the complex issues of morality 'as diverse as the created order which gives rise to them'; it can 'be answered only in terms of the relation to Christ in whom the transformed world is already present to us'.[271]

---

[260] Ibid., 243, 245–6.
[261] Ibid., 247.
[262] Ibid., 248.
[263] Ibid., 249.
[264] Ibid., 248.
[265] Ibid.
[266] Ibid.
[267] Ibid., 253.
[268] Ibid., 256–8.
[269] Ibid., 259.
[270] Ibid.
[271] Ibid., 260.

Eschatology absolutely does frame the narration of the moral life that O'Donovan gives in these last chapters, then. And he is aware of multiple other ways in which ethics' eschatological orientation has been voiced. We might 'speak of Christian morality in relation to the kingdom of God', of 'the Christian life as life *in Christ* ... "hidden" (Col. 3.3) and "waiting" (Heb. 10.13)', or of 'the Christian moral life as lived *in the Spirit*' who is 'a signpost to the future ... (Eph. 1.14)'.[272] It is a shame that a more prominent place is not found for each, though as we shall see, O'Donovan himself attempts just that in later writing. More troubling than the relative absence of these idiomatic expressions, though, is the relation between hope and faith that is posited in the final chapter.

In hope, we read, our contemplation begins 'from the problematic character of the present', turning 'gratefully to the future judgment of God which perfects the imperfections of the present and promises completion'.[273] In faith 'we move in the opposite direction', beginning with God's Yes to humankind's 'created life and love', and turning to the present, 'our appointed scene of action, to claim and enjoy that affirmation ... as an immediate reality'.[274] So far, so helpful. But we read on: faith 'takes two decisive steps beyond hope' since it 'corrects' hope's orientation to the ambiguous present, paying attention 'first to the objective completeness of the divine judgment', and, decisively, by moving '*to* the present rather than *away from* it', it gives 'practical "substance" to what is hoped for (Heb. 11.1)'.[275] Faith 'is thus at once more contemplative and more active'.[276] There is a logic to the account, but surely these conclusions are unsatisfactory. If hope *truly described* is, as the tradition has variously taught, not just a naturally arising attitude or disposition but one that is brought to fruition in the creature as a gift of God the Holy Spirit, then it should be incorrigible and inalienable Christian disposition. If we are speaking of Christian hope, the theological virtue, and we have no reason to think that O'Donovan is not, then why the need in a purportedly complementary account to imagine faith as improving upon hope – 'correcting' it, going 'beyond' it decisively on every count? I suppose it could be possible to argue that *the moral life* is more obviously served by faith, understood this way, whereas prayerful longing is nourished by hope. That itself would be mistaken: 'of its very nature hope is an aid to action'.[277] Yet even this division of labour is not O'Donovan's move; here, faith also trumps hope for contemplation.

This inadequate argument alerts us that in moral theology, sometimes the space afforded to eschatology contracts because of a prima facie concern that ethics be assured about the given, and by an inclination to evaluate aspects of Christian confession according to their apparent practicability. For O'Donovan, that assurance about the given is found subjectively in the justification faith knows, and objectively in the justified (that is, vindicated) created order to which love conforms. There is nothing as such mistaken about that, though, to repeat ad nauseam, the second part can be understood more or less subtly. But why, we may wonder, did St Paul risk including

---

[272] Ibid., 247.
[273] Ibid., 253.
[274] Ibid.
[275] Ibid.
[276] Ibid.
[277] Thomas Aquinas, *Summa Theologica*, Ia IIae, q. 40, a. 8.

hope as one of three if it is so likely to detract from the present, and if the Christian life could be better served by explication of faith? The inadequacy of O'Donovan's argument is especially mystifying since he has just argued convincingly that love's eschatological character does not diminish its this-worldly significance. Yet it seems to me that he does not quite trust his own argument on that point, which proves to be a neuralgic one through to later work.

That this is indeed a belief about which O'Donovan wavers might be further indicated by drawing attention to an influential and much-contested criticism he made of Augustine's earlier theology in an article published between *Self-Love* and *Resurrection and Moral Order*, and reaffirmed in the latter.[278] To simplify greatly, O'Donovan's worry there is that in *De doctrina Christiana*, Augustine holds to an unfortunately instrumentalizing model of Christian neighbour-love because he places the order of love within an eschatological framework, rather than within an ontological framework (that is, one based on creation). Within the eschatological framework, O'Donovan says, with its central motif of the moral life as 'pilgrimage' (*peregrinatio*), the neighbour is merely the earthly means to a heavenly end, whereas, within the ontological framework, the intrinsic value of the neighbour is secured. Yet as Sarah Stewart-Kroeker demonstrates, O'Donovan's critique establishes 'a false opposition between ontology and eschatology, neighbour and self, neighbour and God'.[279] Rather, 'The ontological and the eschatological aspects of Augustine's understanding of ordered love are integral threads bound together in a Christological understanding of love, richly developed in the *peregrinatio* image as a process of moral formation in loving God, self, and neighbour rightly'.[280]

Given O'Donovan's characteristic confidence in the ability of the Christian tradition's resources to reframe ethics theologically, the apparent loss of nerve over hope in *Resurrection and Moral Order* is conspicuous. And should either Stewart-Kroeker's reading of this earlier piece be correct or my reading of 'The Natural Ethic' be plausible – or both – then *Resurrection and Moral Order*'s difficulty with hope is illustrative of an ongoing struggle concerning the place of eschatology in ethics. That struggle is the subject of my concluding analysis.

Analysis and interpretation

Resurrection and Moral Order is not easy to engage. It is densely argued, intrepid in its proposals and light on references. In chapters 2 and 3, we have considered some central features, especially its concern for an objectively grounded moral realism, and for subjective freedom correlated to the authority of the objective created order. Perhaps most significantly, we have lingered over the claims epitomized by the book's title and

---

[278] O'Donovan, '*Usus* and *Fruitio* in Augustine, *De doctrina Christiana* I', *Journal of Theological Studies* 33, no. 2 (1981): 361–97. See O'Donovan, *Resurrection*, 235.

[279] Sarah Stewart-Kroeker, *Pilgrimage as Moral and Aesthetic Formation in Augustine's Thought* (Oxford: Oxford University Press, 2017), 243.

[280] Ibid.

subtitle, plumbing O'Donovan's claims about the resurrection's role as cardinal ('hinge') moment in securing created order, and the ways in which this represents good news for us as ethical agents. In all of these and in further related themes, besides, I have traced the treatment of eschatology in its moral implications. In closing, I draw out from the foregoing analysis a set of direct comments on that topic, volunteering additional support and interacting critically with a handful of other readers of O'Donovan's book.

Eschatology is not by any means totally occluded in the book's moral vision. It is present in at least two ways. An understanding that entertains thoughts of eschatological transformation is unquestionably found, though it often plays second fiddle. Besides this, a more continuous understanding is very much in evidence, coherent with generally un-interruptive salvation motifs of 'restoration' and 'vindication'. It is this continualist element that I have sought particularly to interrogate, because it seems to me to determine O'Donovan's fundamental moral theology more than the other. Envisioning a fundamentally realized 'already', it conceives that realized 'already' as inaugurating a new creation that is not just proleptically present in the moral order that confronts believers, but – inasmuch as it is substantially continuous with the reaffirmed created order – already *is* that moral order. Newness, then, appears absorbed to a high degree into a primarily continuous account of the created order. The tendency is to subordinate the commitment to an eschatological affirmation of transformation to the prior commitment to a classically contoured 'natural ethic'.

Interestingly, the key issues surface already in *Self-Love*'s conclusion, though there O'Donovan seems to answer them rhetorically rather than head-on. At the heart of it, again, lies his concern for comprehension of the proper relationship obtaining between creation and redemption. Witness the criticism of Nygren:

> It has sometimes been suggested that Nygren has no place for the doctrine of Creation, the ground on which Augustine would assert the continuity and stability of the created subject who is the object of God's grace. It could perhaps be argued that the reverse is the case: He has no room for anything other than the doctrine of Creation, since every movement from the divine centre has to be presuppositionless, *ex nihilo*, creative, bringing into existence something quite unprecedented. His rejection of 'philosophic *eros*' is not so much the rejection of Creation as the refusal to presuppose it. Creation is existential, never to be taken as read, never to be regarded as the foundation for subsequent movements, both of initiative and response, which will be differently characterised. When man's conversion is described as a 'new creation' the phrase is taken literally.[281]

We also see it in a more synoptic statement, which serves as a useful précis of a host of questions important for our investigation:

---

[281] O'Donovan, *Self-Love*, 158. Meilaender identifies these passages' description and criticism of neo-Lutheranism as capturing the kind of Lutheranism he was trained in, and what was wrong with it – see 'Hearts Set to Obey', in *I am the Lord Your God: Christian Reflections on the Ten Commandments*, ed. Carl E. Braaten and Christopher Seitz (Grand Rapids: Eerdmans, 2005), 263.

The heart of the quarrel between Augustine and his critics, then, is whether the creative work of God allows for teleology, and so for a movement within creation, which can presuppose the fact of creation as a given starting point, to a destiny which 'fulfils' creation by redeeming it and by lifting it to a new level. It is the meaning of salvation that is at stake: is it 'fulfilment', 'recapitulation'? If this is indeed the authentic Christian understanding of what God has done in Christ, then Augustine's critics will have to face this implication: Between that which is and that which will be there must be a line of connection, the redemptive purpose of God. We cannot simply say that agape has no presuppositions, for God presupposes that which he himself as already given in *agape*. However dramatic a transformation redemption may involve, however opaque to man's mind the continuity may be, we know, and whenever we repeat the Trinitarian creed with Saint Augustine we confess that our being-as-we-are and our being-as-we-shall-be are held together as works of the One God who is both our Creator and Redeemer.[282]

I accept most of these contentions. But as they play out in *Resurrection and Moral Order*, the weak transformation and strong continuity that 'redemption may involve' seem sometimes too transparent to the moral theologian's mind. And I worry that they appear too transparent for reasons as much generated by the ethical discourse's assumed need for confidence in natural order as by the encompassing reach of a unified doctrine of God 'who is both our Creator and Redeemer'.

Philip Lorish and Charles Mathewes, reading *Self-Love*, observe an 'insistence on a connection, some continuity between this life and the life to come', and 'a sturdy and durable (perhaps less Augustinian than [O'Donovan] thinks) insistence that things are *clear enough* – that, in fear and trembling, we can know at least something of what to do'.[283] The impetus for *Resurrection and Moral Order*, they suspect, was partly the attempt to get 'at the theological basis for that conviction'.[284] Their observation is purely descriptive and comes in a passage of deservedly fulsome commendation, but it also corroborates something like my reading.

Returning to the thought that eschatology is everywhere in O'Donovan but not everywhere the same – true of this book as well as of his *oeuvre* as a whole – it is no surprise that interpreters may find in it quite differently constructed schemes and may utilize them to quite different ends. At the most basic level, it is obviously a text susceptible of readings that pay more attention to the account of creation order and of those that take it to be thoroughly eschatological, a susceptibility I will illustrate by taking up a few examples of interpretation – six in all. In some appropriations of O'Donovan's thought, I will argue, a particular figuration of salvation history goes more untested than it might, were it exposed to a broader set of theological interlocutors. In others, it seems as though the interpretation rebalances the different parts of O'Donovan's theological architectonic – whether deliberately or not it is hard to tell.

---

[282] O'Donovan, *Self-Love*, 159.
[283] Lorish and Mathewes, 'Theology as Counsel', 723.
[284] Ibid.

First, Joshua Hordern's highly interesting work represents a sample of recent moral theology in which the theological sensibilities, and not simply topical ethical judgements or account of moral reasoning, are inherited very substantially from O'Donovan – *Resurrection and Moral Order* in particular. In Hordern's book *Political Affections*, 'Vindication' is the controlling cipher at any moment when substantive Christian teaching is mentioned, representing the whole economy of the gospel by synecdoche.[285] We read of 'God's good creation vindicated by the incarnation and resurrection of Jesus Christ'; of the 'coming of a new humanity vindicating the moral order and bringing coherence to the human experience of it'; of an objective moral order, 'created by God and vindicated by the incarnation and resurrection, as God's saving actions say "yes" to the goodness of that which was created from the beginning and destined for fulfilment in the new heavens and the new earth'; and very, very often of 'vindicated created order' or similar.[286] And, finally:

> Since ... dogmatic knowing is the beginning of ethics, the crucified and vindicated Christ is where Christian ethics must begin. Since the resurrection vindicates creation, it is also through such knowledge that the true moral order is discovered and the shape of the new heaven and the new earth is disclosed.[287]

The doctrinal substructure of Hordern's work, then, is wholly familiar from O'Donovan's book.

Hordern does acknowledge what he sees as Augustine's sense of the 'current corrupted state of the world', but supplements it quickly with O'Donovan's talk of 'redeemed creation', depicting epistemology once more as the only difficulty.[288] *Political Affections*' 'theological description' of reality 'speaks ... of a created, fallen, vindicated universe of generically and teleologically related features, whose stability is guaranteed by a transcendent God who became incarnate'.[289] (Notice that, much as in Waters' work, in Hordern's appropriation of O'Donovan's thought, the doctrine of the incarnation often secures the claims for the stability and normativity of created order besides the resurrection.) Most other instances, unfortunately, leave out the modifier 'fallen', and when they do, the implications are constrained. When we read, for instance, of 'the settled, attractive quality of the created though fallen order', the implication to be spelled out is this: 'Rather than rooting the instability in the world – which, though blighted by sin, is yet firmly established – our account calls people to examine themselves, their own unstable fragility, and their failure to be fitted to the cosmos as it is.'[290]

---

[285] Joshua Hordern, *Political Affections: Civic Participation and Moral Theology* (Oxford: Oxford University Press, 2013). This book originates in an Edinburgh PhD supervised by O'Donovan.
[286] Ibid., 5; 7; 83–4; 84, 87, 90, 93, 98, 101, 110, 112, 113, 118, 119, 121, 125, 161, 200, 201, 241, 272, 280, 282.
[287] Ibid., 277.
[288] Ibid., 92, 97.
[289] Ibid., 98.
[290] Ibid., 98–9.

Ultimately, what the doctrinal scheme from *Resurrection and Moral Order* produces in the constructive vision of Hordern's *Political Affections* is the conviction that 'Christ's incarnation and resurrection along with Pentecost vindicated the localized life of natural affections within the moral order, thereby reaffirming its mode of stability'.[291] I will return to *Political Affections* in Chapter 4, because it will give us both the opportunity to see how some of O'Donovan's theological convictions can inform theo-political claims, besides those made in O'Donovan's own political theology and ethics, and – perhaps surprisingly – it will show us that his own political theology and ethics is in fact rooted in a differently accented set of theological claims than his moral theology (and is therefore subtly different in tone than Hordern's politics).

Hordern, taking up O'Donovan's account of creation and redemption, does not entertain extant or possible challenges to it. Other readers of *Resurrection and Moral Order* do acknowledge potential challenges yet see in its account of the resurrection's two aspects an ample theological qualification of a purely natural ethic and thus, overall, an equally defensible proposal. An excellent example of this reading is found in Berkman and Buttrey's article, which I quoted earlier. They take McKenny to task for his apparent inability to see such qualification because of his focus on the 'first aspect' of O'Donovan's book:

> We fear that McKenny has neglected the architectonic significance of the resurrection and eschatology for O'Donovan's account of created order, where the resurrection vindicates the created order and eschatology fulfills the created order. While McKenny understands O'Donovan to derive his account of created order from the Genesis creation narratives ... we believe 1 Corinthians 15 and Colossians 3 are the decisive texts for O'Donovan's understanding of created order.[292]

Thus their own reading makes much of the 'second aspect' as the first's supplement:

> Jesus' resurrection vindicates creation in a 'double aspect': on the one hand it redeems and restores the original created order from its 'sub-natural' enslavement to sin and death (13, 55–57); on the other hand it points to creation's renewal and transformation (both actual and eschatological) towards its supernatural destiny. On O'Donovan's Trinitarian account of the created order, to act with an ordered love precludes an exclusive focus either on preserving the original creation or on bringing about the new creation; the ordered love to which we are called 'respects the natural structures of life in the world, while looking forward to their transformation'.[293]

Two possible responses suggest themselves. We could allow that McKenny overlooks the second aspect. But to miss it would be an easy mistake because the first aspect dominates the programmatic early chapters. The possibility of overlooking the recessive

---

[291] Ibid., 235.
[292] Berkman and Buttrey, 'Theologies of Enhancement', 31.
[293] Ibid., 34.

second aspect in itself connotes a challenge to the book's argument. For if they are right about 'O'Donovan's Trinitarian account', and the account is clear, why can such misreadings so easily arise? Perhaps, then, McKenny is in fact privy to at least some of the subtleties of the book – his reading of O'Donovan's position on nature's normativity suggests as much – and yet still does not think that the second aspect makes much of a difference to the its basic moral vision. (I would extend their criticism more happily to other readers of the book, who seem routinely to overlook those subtleties.)[294] More specifically, I argue that if the aspect of renewal and transformation did make more of a difference, then the aspect of vindication and restoration would not itself be articulable in such confident priority (even, at times, effective isolation) so as to be intelligible as a 'natural ethic'. If that is correct, McKenny would be quite justified in working on the assumption that the kind of commitment to stable created order seen in *Resurrection and Moral Order* represents O'Donovan's essential position. Even if this assumption may not do justice to the synthesis presented by Berkman and Buttrey, to observe that O'Donovan *can* give a more nuanced account of the resurrection's two aspects takes nothing away from the observation that he sometimes does not do so when arguing for a natural ethic. Andrew Errington agrees: 'O'Donovan does speak explicitly about transformation .... Yet, overall, the transformative side of the resurrection does less work than these statements lead us to expect, particularly in relation to the book's treatment of moral reasoning. The order to which morality conforms is fundamentally static'.[295]

Berkman and Buttrey's précis is entirely balanced, with respect to both theological claims and moral vision; by the same token, it is worth asking if that balance is actually there in O'Donovan's book – and perhaps, in view of that question with which 'The Natural Ethic' concluded, whether it is straightforwardly intended. Theologically, their presentation of the eschatological renewal of creation towards its supernatural end may interpret O'Donovan's account in the language of his more Augustinian-Thomist idiom[296] – a theological understanding that seems native to them – rather than O'Donovan's other, slightly different and more N. T. Wright-like, ways of speaking about new creation (Wright, we might think, would like their reconstruction less than he did O'Donovan's book). And it may be that Berkman and Buttrey relieve some of the tension exhibited in O'Donovan's book; I am not sure it is usually as clear about 'creation's renewal and transformation' so as to make a distinction between 'actual and eschatological' as they are. Morally, to say that acting with 'an ordered love precludes an exclusive focus either on preserving the original creation or on bringing about the

---

[294] An example here is Matthew Simpkins, 'The Church of England's Exclusion of Same-sex Couples from Marriage: Some Problems with Oliver O'Donovan's Influence and Arguments', *Theology* 119, no. 3 (2016): 172–84.

[295] Errington, *Every Good Path*, 151–2.

[296] There may, that said, be tensions between Augustinian and Thomistic eschatologies here, particularly in relation to Benedict XVI's encyclical *Spe Salvi* – perceived as austerely Augustinian – and its unfavourable reception by some Thomists. But the general trend of (conservative) contemporary Catholic theology seems to be to affirm the broad continuity of Aquinas's with Augustine's thought. See Matthew L. Lamb, 'Wisdom Eschatology in Augustine and Aquinas', in *Aquinas the Augustinian*, ed. Michael Dauphinais, Barry David, and Matthew Levering (Washington: Catholic University of America Press, 2007).

new creation' would seem to resonate more with O'Donovan's actual account on the latter point than the former, which we have seen is not pronounced.

Gilbert Meilaender's reading, I think, exegetes and exhibits similar balance when it notes the importance for O'Donovan's exegesis of 'the overarching account the Bible gives of humankind as claimed and graced by God in creation, reconciliation and redemption', going on to say that 'there is movement in this account. The end is not simply the restoration of the beginning'.[297] That is not necessarily an amelioration of O'Donovan's position – O'Donovan makes each of the points Meilaender republishes – though again it leaves to the side some of O'Donovan's less balanced statements. It is also worth noticing that Meilaender's Barthian parsing, in terms of creation, reconciliation and redemption,[298] is not quite how O'Donovan organizes his own thoughts about the canonical history's long course. I do not draw attention to this for the sake of pedantry, but because it allows us to see an interesting divergence among major theologians. O'Donovan's preface to the second edition, noting the publication of Barth's *Ethics*, does admit that Barth's adoption of the principle 'that Christian ethics must conform to the shape of salvation-history, and so has a threefold pattern corresponding to creation, reconciliation and redemption (i.e. eschatology) ... promises a fuller account of theological ethics than any monothematic programme based on creation, kingdom or even resurrection'.[299] But having observed the value in Barth's scheme, the preface's following pages of discussion identify 'instructive difficulties' for it: – the distribution of subject areas across the three headings 'can look quite arbitrary', and it lacks an additional 'advent moment' denoting Christ's incarnation and his ministry 'in fulfilment of the hopes of Israel'.[300] They eventuate in the defence of 'the *particular* significance of the resurrection' that we reviewed in Chapter 2.[301] That is not at all to say Meilaender and O'Donovan are far apart, here or in general; in his own thought, Meilaender characteristically blends a Barthian vision with another imaginary, more Augustinian-Thomist.[302]

---

[297] Meilaender, 'Ethics and Exegesis: A Great Gulf?' in *Royal Priesthood?* 262.

[298] Found throughout Meilaender's work and put to very good use in, for example, 'The Church: A Family of the Adopted', in *Church, Society, and the Christian Common Good: Essays in Conversation with Philip Turner*, ed. Ephraim Radner (Eugene: Cascade, 2017).

[299] O'Donovan, *Resurrection*, xvi.

[300] Ibid., xvi, xvii.

[301] Ibid., xviii.

[302] To be clear, by associating this 'transcendent' strand of eschatological affirmation with Augustine and Aquinas, I do not mean to suggest that they discount eschatological continuity. As Matthew Lamb describes Thomas's position: 'Eschatology is the teleology of redeemed creation in the fullness of the kingdom of God', indeed, 'as grace perfects nature, so the revelation of the last things perfects the finality of all creation'. Matthew L. Lamb, 'The Eschatology of St. Thomas Aquinas', in *Aquinas on Doctrine: A Critical Introduction*, ed. Thomas Weinandy, Daniel Keating and John Yocum (London/New York: T & T Clark, 2004), 225, 227. Cf. Carlo Leget, 'Eschatology', in *The Westminster Handbook to Thomas Aquinas*, ed. Joseph Wawrykow (Louisville: Westminster John Knox Press, 2005). Contemporary Thomists are almost as keen as O'Donovan to gainsay any doom-mongering prediction of eschatological destruction, no doubt worried about similar excesses in contemporary Christians' eschatological expectation. Any *discontinuity* 'from the viewpoint of this world', Lamb writes, is simply purification: 'The sapiential eschatology of Aquinas, building upon patristic eschatologies, understands the eschatological and apocalyptic passages in Scripture as revealing the transformation of the whole of creation so that it fully manifests the divine wisdom, beauty and goodness', not, therefore, 'as involving or portending widespread devastation or ultimate

Our next interpreters, Brent Waters and Luke Bretherton, seem to be as unconcerned (or unaware) of possible challenges to the approach of *Resurrection and Moral Order* as was Hordern, but they tend to foreground slightly less prominently the un-glossed appeals to normative created order as vindicated and restored, rather presenting them – as Berkman and Buttrey, along with Meilaender – in combination with the more eschatological claims. When speaking of 'the vindicated order of creation', for example, and drawing consistently on the gist of O'Donovan's thought, Waters adds that it 'cannot be seen, however, in isolation from the redemptive, providential, and eschatological dimensions of what is revealed in Christ's resurrection. ... The created and redeemed order is irreducibly eschatological, proleptic, and teleological'.[303] He then quotes the passage of O'Donovan's book where it is clarified that this is no 'mere restoration, the return of a *status quo ante*', and goes on: 'creation's pristine state is not recovered but transfigured into the new creation'.[304] A couple of pages earlier, Waters criticizes Herman Dooyeweerd for using '"creation" and "nature" as interchangeable terms', and thereby implying 'that redemption is more a recovery of creation's pristine origin than its transformation in Christ; more an attempt to restore the old than to be drawn into the new'.[305] Waters is correct, I think, but it does raise its own questions of the instances we reviewed in which O'Donovan himself speaks of redemption in terms of recovery.

Bretherton conscripts *Resurrection and Moral Order* (as does Hordern) to show the 'Distinctiveness of Christian Ethics' on precisely eschatological grounds.[306] O'Donovan is brought in to lend Christian specificity to a basic structure endowed by MacIntyre, and to reject Grisez's project as inadequately shaped by theological concerns. 'In effect', Bretherton writes, 'Grisez is saying that Christ simply republishes the moral law',

---

doom' (Lamb, 'Eschatology of St. Thomas Aquinas', 236.) That sapiential eschatology, at least as Lamb presents it, integrates creation and eschatology in a way not unlike O'Donovan's clearer statements. Nevertheless, I do not think Augustinian-Thomists need to share to the same extent the worry O'Donovan seems too often to have, that Christian hope that fastens itself to a promise of a world to come that is innovatively related to this world (as well as meaningfully continuous with it) will have morally distorting effects. They should be able to defend more strongly than he does a creaturely longing for that supernatural end to which creation is drawn in Christ – an end truly 'more than we can ask or imagine' (Eph. 3.20).

[303] Waters, *The Family*, 162.
[304] Ibid., 163.
[305] Ibid., 160. A glance at Jonathan Chaplin, *Herman Dooyeweerd: Christian Philosopher of State and Civil Society* (Notre Dame: University of Notre Dame Press, 2011), suggests that Dooyeweerd did understand redemption as 'radical and comprehensive restoration of creation', which it neither 'abrogates nor supersedes' (47–51). More generally, I wonder if the neo-Calvinist intention to avoid what it perceives as dualistic understandings of nature-grace, either in grace-annihilating-nature (Pietism) or grace-elevating-nature (Catholicism) leads to inadequate acknowledgement of either sin or transformation. The Dutch neo-Calvinist Hans Schaeffer realizes that the theology of marriage might be a litmus test for testing construals of the creation-eschatology axis, and he sees that certain New Testament texts (Mt. 22.30; 1 Cor. 7), and thereby the vocation of singleness, could pose challenges to his creation 'orders' or 'mandates' based moral vision (*Createdness and Ethics*, 275) – though, following Oswald Bayer, these mandates are by no means static entities. But when Schaeffer comes to discuss 'Creation, Eschatology, and Marriage' (331–42), and to mitigate (rightly or wrongly) the biblical texts' discontinuous tenor, singleness appears to vanish as a consideration. Bennett follows similar exegesis, but does a better job with singleness.
[306] Bretherton, *Hospitality*, 61.

and just so he 'fails to take seriously enough the implications of the resurrection and eschatology for ethics'.[307] What are these implications?

> Revelation does not merely enable enhanced intelligibility of an already existent morality. While it does do this, it does more than this as well. Revelation furnishes the Christian with a materially new content that entails distinct moral demands ... in Christ our fulfilment is already realised and this fulfilment can now, through the Holy Spirit, break into the present age. By implication, our participation in Christ, through the Holy Spirit, brings new insight, and calls (and enables) new kinds of responses to old problems. [308]

This means going beyond MacIntyre, too, since Bretherton perceives that O'Donovan has 'a very different conception of time and history': he 'understands there to be a single reality which itself is under transformation by the eschatological kingdom of God'.[309] In order to develop this line of critical comparison, then, Bretherton again seems to play up the second aspect of the two evident in O'Donovan's book. If MacIntyre lacks 'a distinctively Christian cosmology', O'Donovan's 'eschatological framework ... is able to account for the continuity and radical discontinuity between this age and the age to come. O'Donovan is thus able to account for the continuity and discontinuity between Christian and non-Christian approaches to morality'.[310] Consider Bretherton's thoroughly doctrinal summary of 'ethics for O'Donovan' as 'Trinitarian in nature', which places its accent at the same point:

> To be moral is to be judged and re-created by Christ and so free to direct oneself, through knowledge and actions, to one's eschatological transformation; which is being accomplished now through the priestly actions of Christ with the Father, in which we can participate through the actions of the Spirit.[311]

---

[307] Ibid., 54. It may be – this is not meant critically – that Waters, Song, Bretherton, Hordern and others saw in O'Donovan the moral-theological route for their ecclesial sensibilities (which I think would not be incorrectly identified as evangelical) to enter academic theological discourse. Certainly in Bretherton and Hordern's books quoted here directly, devotional language beyond O'Donovan's keeps company with the technical vocabulary of doctoral theses. In a review of *Political Affections*, Mathewes is descriptively correct if a little unfair when he writes: 'One might be forgiven for wondering why Hordern does not notice that the two idioms do not smoothly flow together, nor are they neatly sutured together'. *Journal of the American Academy of Religion* 84, no. 1 (2016): 272–6, 275. In addition, I wonder if this evangelical identification, along with the academic trajectory of scholars in Christian ethics whose first degrees were often not in theology, means that O'Donovan likely appeared a singularly powerful *doctrinal* as well as ethical and ecclesiastical voice. Again, I do not mean to be critical: each ethicist brings different insights from their other disciplinary backgrounds and O'Donovan is a serious dogmatic theologian even if he does not typically identify as one by trade (though note that his position at Wycliffe College, Toronto, was in Systematic Theology). But it might lead – as in other cases – to a more uncritical appropriation of a leading figure's thought.
[308] Bretherton, *Hospitality*, 54, 55.
[309] Ibid., 81.
[310] Ibid., 88, 87.
[311] Ibid., 74.

Or, again,

> Christ's resurrection has the double aspect of being resurrection from sin and death (thus healing and restoring creation) and glorification at God's right hand (thus looking forward to the eschatological transformation and perfection of creation as a new creation, as distinct from a revolutionary or teleological transformation of existing creation). By contrast, MacIntyre's ethics appears closed to the possibility of this kind of newness or transformation.[312]

Bretherton follows Hauerwas here in asking 'whether MacIntyre's teleology is compatible with Christian eschatology' and in raising 'an important and largely unexplored question as to what the relation may be between Paul's eschatology and the teleology insisted upon by MacIntyre'.[313] To extend the point a little further, in closing, we may ask what the relation is between Paul's eschatology and the teleology sometimes insisted upon by O'Donovan.

Conclusion

As it happens, Hauerwas raised a connected query about *Resurrection and Moral Order*. O'Donovan himself quotes it in the preface:

> The connexion that I made between resurrection and created order allowed some commentators, and by no means unfriendly ones, to conclude that I was using resurrection simply as a way back to creation ethics. 'What I think O'Donovan seeks is an account of natural law which is not governed by the eschatological witness of Christ's resurrection', Stanley Hauerwas wrote. 'We cannot write about *Resurrection and Moral Order* because any order that we know as Christians is resurrection.'[314]

O'Donovan responds by outlining where he thinks their projects overlap and diverge. First, 'we walk together in agreement about the non-self-evidence of created order. But where I turn to the Christ-event and to the apostolic witness, he turns first to the practices of the church'.[315] Then there is the 'parting of the ways, with Hauerwas, focusing on Good Friday, following the Western tradition, and myself, focusing on Easter Sunday, the Eastern'.[316] To be fair to Hauerwas, are we so sure as O'Donovan that

---

[312] Ibid., 83. Cf. 81.
[313] Ibid., 81. Cf. Wells, *Transforming Fate into Destiny*, 153. One answer to that question – that they are essentially identical – is given in Colin D. Miller, *The Practice of the Body of Christ: Human Agency in Pauline Theology after MacIntyre* (Eugene: Pickwick Publications, 2014). Unfortunately I do not find the argument at all convincing.
[314] O'Donovan, *Resurrection*, xvi. For Hauerwas's comments in full, see *Dispatches from the Front: Theological Engagements with the Secular* (London/Durham: Duke University Press, 1995), 175.
[315] O'Donovan, *Resurrection*, xv.
[316] Ibid.

they do agree about the non-self-evidence of created order, in view of what were (at least for a long time) their different stances on natural law? And to be fair to O'Donovan, let us affirm against Hauerwas that on O'Donovan's own terms, the intention absolutely *is* to discipline an account of the natural order's moral relevance with an eschatologically inflected account of Christ's resurrection. Then again, Hauerwas could put the line about *Resurrection and Moral Order* in a slightly different and more piquant way: 'Too much moral order, not enough resurrection'.[317] Along with some of that book's many insights, what my exposition has illustrated, I hope, is that Hauerwas was on to something.

---

[317] Quoted in William Cavanaugh, 'Stan the Man: A Thoroughly Biased Account of a Completely Unobjective Person', in *The Hauerwas Reader*, 25.

4

Territory

Desire of the Nations and *Ways of Judgment*

Introduction

O'Donovan's political theology and ethics merits far, far more space than I can afford it here. It would have been possible to centre a study of the import of eschatology for ethics on the role it plays in *Desire of the Nations* alone, not least in the first part's narration of the scriptural and traditional development of political conceptualities. It would be hard to miss the well-worked and warranted prominence of themes like the rule of God or the Lordship of Christ in O'Donovan's theo-political vision. Yet having chosen *Resurrection and Moral Order* as this investigation's nub, here, I need to home in on just a few features, largely following leads through this material that were set in earlier chapters. Accordingly, I do not make very much of the strictly 'political' in treating O'Donovan's theo-political vision in this chapter. First, in exposition of the trope of 'Restoration' found in *Desire of the Nations*, I show the continuities with the earlier book in respect of the predominance of the resurrection's backwards-looking aspect. Second, I reflect on the discernment of the times inherent in O'Donovan's theo-political, as well as moral-theological projects. Observing what appear to be its contextual oversights, I suggest that these oversights both conditions and are conditioned by theological presuppositions. Third, I demonstrate how eschatological themes once again figure strongly in O'Donovan's ecclesiology, and how they now figure in his account of political life. Finally, engaging debate among commentators, I offer some comments on the way different doctrinal *loci* – creation, sin, providence, salvation and eschatology – are drawn upon to various effects in O'Donovan's political as compared with moral theology.[1]

---

[1] In general, this part of his work seems to have attracted more commentary than others, though some contemporary conversations in political theology do not engage his thought as much as one might expect. I interact with a few pieces of commentary here, though aspects I cannot engage include the important ongoing conversation regarding 'rights' between Lockwood O'Donovan and O'Donovan on the one hand, and Wolterstorff among others on the other. I also cannot treat O'Donovan's earlier *Peace and Certainty: A Theological Essay on Deterrence* (Oxford: Clarendon Press, 1989) or later *The Just War Revisited* (Cambridge: Cambridge University Press, 2003), though these represent major interventions.

Inevitably, I must pass over many of the historical details within O'Donovan's political theology and ethics, which are funded by a thoroughgoing theo-political *ressourcement* achieved in partnership with Joan Lockwood O'Donovan.[2] I also leave unmentioned many (hundreds!) of the constructive claims, and my engagement with O'Donovan's theo-political reading of scripture can only be piecemeal, though arguably this is just as fundamental to his project as the retrieval of a 'Great Tradition' and is intriguingly dovetailed with it.[3]

I treat *Desire of the Nations* and *Ways of Judgment* together – books O'Donovan describes as 'two phases in an extended train of thought'.[4] In the preface to the second, he reflects on the whole project's positioning:

> The enterprise is superficially similar to, but very different in spirit from, a line of enquiry promoted under the title 'political theology' in the second half of the twentieth century, which also argued for the correlation of theological and political concepts, but made the former depend on the latter. After showing how theologians of the past had been the stooges of the political forces that made use of them, political theology set out to reorder our theological concepts to the service of a suitably liberal world-view. The proper political orientations were taken to be well understood, the shape of our theological beliefs indefinitely negotiable. I start from diametrically the opposite assumption. The Gospel proclamation I take to

---

[2] The historical texts ingredient in this return *ad fontes* are gathered in a sizeable volume edited by O'Donovan and Lockwood O'Donovan: *From Irenaeus to Grotius: A Sourcebook in Christian Political Thought* (Grand Rapids: Eerdmans, 1999), a publication accompanied by the essays contained in *Bonds of Imperfection*. Their retrieval of the 'Great Tradition' has attracted (inescapable) concerns about its partiality: see e.g. Arne Rasmusson, 'Not All Justifications of Christendom Are Created Equal: A Response to Oliver O'Donovan', and Christopher Rowland, 'Response to *the Desire of the Nations*', *Studies in Christian Ethics* 112, no. 2 (1998): 69–76, and 77–85 respectively, and O'Donovan's reply: 'Response to Respondents: Behold the Lamb!' (91–110 of the same edition). Note O'Donovan's suggestion that the sourcebook was compiled in response to the 'falsified Christian history' produced by John Howard Yoder (Shortt, *God's Advocates*, 255).

[3] The reader may remedy this lack, however, by consulting *Royal Priesthood*, a volume of essays (including responses from O'Donovan) addressing precisely his scriptural interpretation, especially in *Desire*. As already noted, prominent in O'Donovan's theo-political reading of scripture is his suggestive reading of Revelation. With that in mind, I suggest that those who with some good reason imagine essential methodological agreement between O'Donovan and Nigel Biggar would do well to heed the differences as to respective trajectories of their thought. Consider O'Donovan's comments on Biggar's most recent book:

> Biggar is a theologian who … can usually remind us of a detail we had forgotten or a document we had missed. He is interested in history … His opinions are often forceful, and glory in their unfashionability … We may sometimes be puzzled, however, as to what distinguishes his contribution to these themes as a theological one. The use of theological sources is only occasional, and rather at arm's length … is it not curious for a theologian to discuss empire without once touching on the reflections on that topic which the author of the Apocalypse drew from the book of Daniel?

(Review of *Between Kin and Cosmopolis: An Ethic of the Nation*, *Theology* 119, no. 1 (2016): 42–3, 43)

[4] O'Donovan, *Ways*, ix.

be, in its essential features, luminous, the political concepts needed to interpret the social and institutional realities around us obscure and elusive. The work of political theology is to shed light from the Christian faith upon the intricate challenge of thinking about living in late-modern Western society.⁵

O'Donovan's approach, then, is decidedly confessional in this domain, just as it was in the broader moral-theological one that *Resurrection and Moral Order* represents. The purpose of *Desire of the Nations* was to show 'how the political concepts wrapped up in Jewish and Christian speech about God's redemption of the world still had political force, generating expectations for political life that found one type of expression … in the political ideals of "Christendom".⁶ *Ways of Judgment*, for its part, is 'a Christian political ethics', though one 'the agenda of which' was 'set by political rather than by theological questions'.⁷ Accordingly, though it is a fascinating book, and cited here when relevant, much of *Ways of Judgment* is less immediately germane to the limited kind of enquiry begun here – chiefly moral-theological *qua* moral-*theological* and, subsequently, political-theological *qua* political-*theological*. Going through, I draw also from *Common Objects*, which like the two major books from this period was quoted earlier when relevant, but belongs to this period of thought.⁸

I also treat this period as in general marking no great departure from *Resurrection and Moral Order*. Indeed the sequence of theo-political works is carried through in self-conscious continuity with it.⁹ As O'Donovan writes elsewhere:

> Knowledge of the moral order can be a common knowledge, the possession of a community shared through the activity of tradition. It can be the subject of discussion, or persuasion, of agreement; and so it can form the basis of free common action. Within the objective moral order is given the possibility of rational community. This is the necessary path that leads from ethics to politics, a path that I took subsequently to *Resurrection and Moral Order* though following lines I had already indicated there.¹⁰

To be sure, the theo-political works deliver many expanded treatments of particular themes, and certain features of O'Donovan's argument in them represent modifications

---

⁵ Ibid.
⁶ Ibid. Should a reader be tempted to think that O'Donovan's agenda represents uncritical retrieval, we must note that he has quite adamantly denied it: 'I am not interested in the restoration of Christendom', he says, in interview. Shortt, *God's Advocates*, 249 – see also 255.
⁷ O'Donovan, *Ways*, ix.
⁸ I draw on a particular passage of *Ways* in Chapter 5, where it is especially pertinent to a discussion lying outside this chapter's purview. *Common Objects* is brimming with insight, but not especially connected to my topic. The book occasionally touches on the question, though, ubiquitous as it is in O'Donovan's thought: '[H]ow is creation vindicated in the coming of God's Kingdom? And how is the Kingdom seen to make creation new?' (46).
⁹ Cf. O'Donovan, *Resurrection*, xx.
¹⁰ 'What Can Ethics Know about God?' 40. Cf. O'Donovan, *Desire*, 19–20. Note there especially the line which follows rehearsal of *Resurrection*'s core theses: 'as true ethics is grounded in *that* history because it is a history of the vindication of creation order, so it is also grounded in *that* politics … the politics of the divine rule'.

of those initially propounded in the earlier book (for example, the account of authority).[11] These works do also have a tangibly different tonality, as the final part of this chapter explores. But, besides that, the elements that demand this study's concentration are not especially novel at this point.

Restoration

We read in *Desire of the Nations* that there is 'some truth in the suspicion that political theology has gained a following among those who have grown tired of talking about God'.[12] O'Donovan is quite self-consciously not among those 'suffering from metaphysical exhaustion'.[13] He is adamant that all substantive 'topics that responsible theology attends to' must inform political theology and themselves should in turn be illumined by it.[14] Listed as 'repentance and forgiveness, the Incarnation, the sharing of the life of the Godhead in the Spirit, justification and adoption, creation and the renewal of the world, the life of the Church and its ministry of word and sacrament', these are an admirably ambitious set of theological themes to expect political theologians to entertain.[15] Following our earlier analysis, O'Donovan's own construction and construal of these terms is of interest, and, given our exposition of *Resurrection and Moral Order*, particularly the paired terms 'creation and the renewal of the world'. Within the list, the latter phrase is, I take it, soteriological and eschatological shorthand. Of course the scope of that wholly unobjectionable phrase is not straightforwardly identifiable; perhaps in the context of the list, it is a placeholder for a range of aspects proper to eschatology – perhaps not. At any rate, the use of 'renewal' rather than 'vindication' in a compressed statement might lead us to think the earlier shortcomings will be avoided here in the political theology. Yet even as we appreciate *Desire of the Nations* and its exceptionally well-furnished theological conceptuality, we may find that it does not always escape the tendency identified previously. This is apparent in the theological grammar that surfaces most plainly in its ecclesiological fifth chapter.

In order to proceed in making the case that vindication may in fact again predominate in such a way as to occlude something of the other aspects of redemption, I need to note that much in *Desire of the Nations* is arranged by way of a scheme based on scriptural portrayal of the Christ event. 'The moments of the representative act' are four: 'Advent, Passion, Restoration and Exaltation'.[16] In a move also recognizable from earlier works, the church is rendered transparent to these moments in pneumatological

---

[11] O'Donovan, *Ways*, 142–3.
[12] O'Donovan, *Desire*, 3.
[13] Ibid.
[14] Ibid.
[15] Ibid.
[16] Ibid., 133. Constraints of space mean that I can only indicate here a potential comparison with the three 'focal images' – cross, community and new creation – of Hays' *Moral Vision* (see 193–206). While *Desire*'s scheme is admittedly heuristic and at times has something more of the ad hoc about it compared to the earlier account of the three facets of Yhwh's rule, it informs the rest of the book. O'Donovan responds to reviewers' confusion about the status of 'the four-moment analysis of the history of Christ', explaining its exegetical validity as 'a simplified summary, not as a detailed

recapitulation. (It could be an interesting further enquiry to establish whether our earlier slight apprehension about how certain moments of scriptural narrative or of creaturely life were appropriated to Son or Spirit is assuaged here.)[17] The basic fourfold pattern yields an account of four marks of the Church and (boldly!) four sacraments. It also corresponds to themes in the Old Testament and in Jesus's ministry; creatively, it also corresponds both to four praiseworthy features of liberal society, which has 'the narrative of the Christ-event stamped on it', and four parodic features of the same society's Antichristic pretence.[18]

O'Donovan's stated intention in identifying these moments of the *Heilsgeschehen* is not to sever them from one another, atomizing the act of salvation, which is properly 'one drama of redemption, not a series'.[19] His provocative list of ideal-type ecclesiologies, which foreground one moment above the others, illustrates the problems that isolating each produces. O'Donovan stresses that the church's pneumatological participation in these moments must be ultimately unified – and the sacraments, too, have a certain unity (whether two, four or seven). Yet he worries that when ecclesial thinkers have sought to bind them together, they have employed 'external narratives' in order to render the succession intelligible, for instance 'dissolving the signs of church identity into rites of passage'.[20] Much as we saw in the earlier case for the centrality of the resurrection, here, O'Donovan's own reading seeks 'the *inner* logic of the sequence', which is a thoroughly eschatological cogence: 'the logic of the dawning Kingdom of God which the sequence itself makes plain'.[21] In particular, among the four – Advent, Passion, Restoration and

---

analysis', and its intention to 'facilitate' the reading of text, as well as the subsequent use theory can make of it, in 'Behold the Lamb!', 98.

[17] A preliminary reflection: towards the end of *Ways*, in an ecclesiological chapter, O'Donovan offers explanation of the theological difference between the church's sacraments and its pastoral, didactic, and missionary ministries – a difference obscured by the neo-Aristotelian moral-theological interest in 'practices' as such. To do so he offers a distinction of them in terms of the missions of Son and Spirit formally familiar from *Resurrection*, but now applied. He writes of those ministries:

> Their authority is secondary in the same sense that the work of the Holy Spirit is secondary to the work of Christ, not implying ontological difference, merely a proper sequence in the order of salvation, where the once-for-all event that saved the world leads on to its manifestation in the church. The sacraments are Christologically determined, the church's communications and ministries are Pneumatologically determined. (266–7)

It is not quite clear how this last distinction, however tenable, quite relates to the sense in which *all* moments of the church's existence entail pneumatic recapitulations of the christic, as suggested earlier. It may be a defensible exercise of identifying the distinctive operation of Son and Spirit, respectively, within affirmation of the unicity of the divine persons in each of the works fittingly appropriated to each. A reminder of that mutuality and collaboration might be seen in terms of the sacraments, when we consider the place of (pneumatological) *epiclesis* in the gracious presence of Christ in the Eucharist, or the teaching that Christ's baptism is one 'with the Holy Spirit and fire' (Mt. 3.11).

[18] O'Donovan, *Desire*, 283. See the Appendix in Paul G. Doerksen, *Beyond Suspicion: Post-Christian Protestant Political Theology in John Howard Yoder and Oliver O'Donovan* (Eugene: Wipf and Stock, 2009), 217, which charts the whole set. Doerksen's study originates in a thesis supervised by P. Travis Kroeker, building on Kroeker's excellent 'Why O'Donovan's Christendom Is Not Constantinian and John Howard Yoder's Voluntareity Is Not Hobbesian: A Debate in Theological Politics Redefined', now reprinted as ch. 7 of *Messianic Political Theology*.

[19] O'Donovan, *Desire*, 191.
[20] Ibid.
[21] Ibid.

Exaltation – the third and fourth moments of recapitulation, restoration and exaltation, are the passages where we would expect to find eschatology's ecclesio-political import. I return to exaltation later, but first we can consider restoration.

If the earlier critical analysis of some usage of the term 'restoration' in *Resurrection and Moral Order* was at all percipient, then it will be worth pausing again over O'Donovan's choice of the word as shorthand term for the element signifying Christ's resurrection. Seen against the interpretation the earlier book presented of that event's double-aspect, to sum up resurrection under the aspect of restoration again seems to make primary the 'backward-looking' element, perhaps suggesting that the forward-looking element can be integrated under that heading well enough. No doubt O'Donovan does so partly because, with the term exaltation, signifying Christ's ascension, he names with the subsequent moment part the main aspect of the reality construed as forwards looking. (In *Resurrection and Moral Order*, O'Donovan criticized Barth for failing to emphasize this and therefore for neglecting the resurrection's 'backwards-looking' aspect.)[22] Again, the fourfold narration of the Christ event in *Desire of the Nations* is intended precisely to bring forward different aspects, and thereby to elicit a fuller picture of their manifold implications for human life – in particular political life. Still, might this treatment of the resurrection as restoration threaten to give up on the attempt *Resurrection and Moral Order* made, however strained, to combine notions of restoration and transformation under the rubric of resurrection? Does it return us to the lop-sidedness of 'The Natural Ethic'? A closer look at O'Donovan's explanation of restoration in *Desire of the Nations* is necessary if we are to discover a fair answer to that.

The church's correspondence to Christ's resurrection is found in its character as a 'glad community'.[23] A small-print exposition of the opening verses of 1 Peter that caught O'Donovan's attention – twice – in *Resurrection and Moral Order*, subsequently delineates the way in which 'Easter gladness' is connected to the moral life.[24] That connection is seen not least in 'joy, even in the face of suffering ... the decisive characteristic of the resurrection life': life lived in an 'eschatological frame, with the resurrection behind us and the full appearance of salvation ahead of us'.[25] This line of interpretation seems a more spacious approach to the text's eschatological themes than the more limited of the two earlier exegeses, allowing, like the other earlier other exposition, more room for the breadth of the epistle's subject matter. The challenge issued by its author, says O'Donovan, is to 'set your hope to the full upon the grace

---

[22] O'Donovan, *Resurrection*, 57, Paul Molnar defends Barth stoutly against O'Donovan's criticism on this point. See Molnar, *Incarnation and Resurrection: Toward a Contemporary Understanding* (Grand Rapids: Eerdmans, 2007), 337, n. 31.

[23] O'Donovan, *Desire*, 181. Typographical error here in copies of *Desire* seems to print 'Exaltation' instead of 'Restoration' as the *third* point as well as fourth. Unfortunately Bretherton was misled by this, and – relaying the scheme – calls the third moment 'Exaltation', worrying that 'O'Donovan seems to conflate two distinct moments within his third mark', which should instead correspond 'only to Christ's resurrection'. Bretherton, *Hospitality*, 104 (also 142). Though the typo obscures it, O'Donovan's third point *does* correspond to resurrection: my worry is that Restoration as the third moment itself conflates what were, in *Resurrection*, the resurrection's two distinct (though certainly inseparable) aspects.

[24] O'Donovan, *Desire*, 182.

[25] Ibid.

which is coming to you (1:13)', though it 'remains an open question for these members of the church whether their lives will be shaped by that exalted delight which is participation in the new creation of God, or whether they will be shaped by the old and habitual dispositions of the affections'.[26]

Yet the passages on gladness adjacent to this promising excursus explain it almost entirely in terms of the backwards look. O'Donovan suggests, in short, that by the Spirit, the ecclesial analogue to Christ's resurrection is its 'glad recovery of creation order'.[27] So if we perceive in *Desire of the Nations*' (essentially wonderful) account of resurrection joy something akin to the account of delight in creation found in *Resurrection and Moral Order*'s treatment of love, it is not misheard:

> When we say that the church is glad in the resurrection of Christ, we point to the meaning of that event as the *recovery of creation order*. Gladness belongs essentially to the creature, as glory belongs to the creator. There is something to say about the glory of the church, too, and mankind's exaltation to participate in God's rule; but we need know nothing of that as yet. It is enough that Adam has recovered the original joy with which he greeted the creator's glory. If the church's gladness is the gladness of creation, that means it is the gladness of Jesus himself; for this renewed order of creation is present in him. He was the 'first-born of all creation ... in whom all things hold together', and consequently, in his resurrection 'the first-born from the dead that in everything he might be pre-eminent'. (Col. 1.15, 18)[28]

Further elaboration of the response of a joyful heart continues in much the same style. We may learn from O'Donovan here much about the place of affective (and doxological) dimensions of creaturely response to God's work of redemption, and of these dimensions' crucial significance in the faithful moral life.[29] 'Gladness', for example, is described as 'a moral attitude, a disposition of the affections appropriate to the recognition of God's creative goodness'.[30] In Chapter 3, I indicated similarities between O'Donovan's understanding of wisdom, delight and joy and that offered by David Kelsey, in the section of his *Eccentric Existence* concerning creation (rather than those concerning reconciliation or consummation, which for Kelsey generate their own reflections on other dispositions). Those similarities are again clear here, and raise once more the question of whether they might push out due reflection on the other aspects of resurrection joy.

O'Donovan's account may again, despite its richness, seem to resolve the stated emphasis on joyful apprehension of God's *redemptive* goodness – found in 1 Peter, which O'Donovan seemed here to recognize – into an inextricable, but not identical, joyful apprehension of God's goodness in creation. For O'Donovan joy – as love, in *Resurrection and Moral Order* – sets in motion our true participation in the created

---

[26] Ibid.
[27] Ibid., 174.
[28] Ibid., 181.
[29] We could explore a strong resonance in these emphases with Brian Brock, *Singing the Ethos of God: On the Place of Christian Ethics in Scripture* (Grand Rapids: Eerdmans, 2007).
[30] O'Donovan, *Resurrection*, 181.

order, placing us within it, and 'by our gladness' making it complete.[31] Despite the mention of the Christian life's eschatological frame, it turns out that its love, gladness and joy, even if part of the eschatological renewal of human subjectivity, 'that exalted delight which is participation in the new creation of God',[32] seem to have their only objective referent in the order of creation. What happened, then, to setting our hope on the full appearance of salvation that is to come? Is the 'new creation of God' exhausted in the renewal of our affections within this order? Granted, it is not less than that – speaking of persons 'in Christ', we can say that 'there is' (already) 'new creation' (2 Cor. 5.17) – but, in putting things as O'Donovan does, there must be another eschatological element left unsaid, which especially pertains to the *awaited* remaking of this order.

One reader, Daniel Carroll R., raised just this challenge to O'Donovan's understanding of joy – that it seems tied mostly to creation in a manner that underplays joy's eschatological orientation.[33] That challenge O'Donovan undertook to answer:

> My account of joy, according to Carroll, is exclusively related to creation and history, not the future. The reasons for this lie with the subjective conditions for the experience of joy. Gladness is a subjective condition, objectively caused. The subjective condition must lie in a correspondence between the object and the subject, and where the object is future, in a correspondence between future and present. Without that, the future could not be a joyful one *for us*, however joyful it might be for God and the angels. Gladness lies in the vindication and confirmation of what is already given and loved. 'Pure' future is always terror. That we may find joy in what is still unrealised is true, but it is a truth not about joy as such, but about faith and hope, which become the basis of joy.[34]

The insights here about the affective experience of apprehending the future are familiar from earlier writing, but the response seems to me still a little unclear – it might be another instance of the attempt to relate the eschatological future to the moral present while being unsure about accrediting any genuine objectivity to that future, apart from its already manifest vindication of creation in past history. In any event, there is no problem with relating joy, as O'Donovan does, to the 'already' and 'now' of salvation in Christ as experienced in the church – that seems biblically responsible. Nevertheless, I am not sure creation as such or even its vindication is always so immediately the object of joy there, so much as salvation. And I am not sure we can follow what seems to be O'Donovan's inference that the deliverances of faith and hope in which joy is found are constituted primarily by apprehensions of creation and its vindication; to see what it means to 'rejoice in hope' (Rom 12.13),[35] we must follow the related Pauline thought

---

[31] Ibid., 182.
[32] Ibid.
[33] M. Daniel Carroll R., 'The Power of the Future in the Present: Eschatology and Ethics in O'Donovan and Beyond', in *Royal Priesthood*. Finding Carroll's essay, I located something of a kindred reading (and even a similar title).
[34] O'Donovan, 'Response to Daniel Carroll R.', in *Royal Priesthood*, 143–6, 145.
[35] A theme taken up to good effect in chapter 3, 'Rejoicing in Hope', of Elliot, *Hope and Christian Ethics*.

that '*the kingdom of God* is righteousness and peace *and joy* in the Holy Spirit' (Rom. 14.17).[36]

The critical point I am entertaining here is that discussion of restoration, a moment that ostensibly takes its lead from Petrine emphasis upon 'the eschatological frame' of the Christian life, becomes one that, while gilding that frame's 'behind us', neglects to embellish its 'ahead of us'. This cannot just be because *Desire of the Nations*' fourfold scheme parcels up the eschatological and pushes it along the line to the fourth moment, exaltation, though that was surely the force of O'Donovan's comment, quoted earlier, that 'we need know nothing of that yet'. *Resurrection and Moral Order* suggested that the raising of Christ from the grave entailed both aspects intrinsically. *Desire of the Nations*' explanation of the resurrection's moral implications by speaking of restoration, then, may be another sign of the tendency to imply that when dealing with the central matters of ethics 'we need know nothing ... yet' of the eschatological horizon. Because there is little doubt that the moment of restoration, in *Desire of the Nations* as elsewhere, outweighs Advent, Passion or Exaltation (it is the longest section), and brings into play more themes already central to O'Donovan's ethical vision than the others.

We may see this indirectly, too, if we consider the second moment, 'Passion', and then how O'Donovan relates joy in restored creation to the church's experience of suffering – in terms reminiscent of *Resurrection and Moral Order*'s comments on cross and resurrection. Passion receives the shortest of the four treatments. Nevertheless, here there is an important description of the church 'as a *suffering community* engaged in conflict with the principalities and powers that Christ has overcome', and of its true martyr-consciousness.[37] If meditations on the cross's significance in O'Donovan's writing may typically entail reflection on the cruciform shape of individual lives rather than the Christian community, the fourfold scheme's passion moment is to a certain extent the exception. Aspects of the moral life O'Donovan typically correlates with the cross are usually connected to particular discernments of personal vocation rather than the generic obligations of morality; here, the account of the suffering community, in its 'authority to confront and overcome resistance to God's saving will by enduring suffering in whatever form', definitively ascribes them to the ecclesial assembly.[38]

The passion moment, however, must lead to that of restoration: 'No re-enacting of Christ's death by the suffering church could be without its affirmation of divine victory.'[39] The ecclesial response to Christ's resurrection, in its identity and activity as glad community, is, among other things, 'an essential qualification to the martyr-consciousness of the church':

> For communities that find their identity in the fact that they have been unjustly treated come to depend upon the injustice of others ... what stands between the church and this pathology is the conscious joy it takes in the resurrection life. 'The Spirit of him who raised Jesus from the dead' dwells within it. From this

---

[36] On the link between the Holy Spirit and joy cf. Ps. 51.10-12; Acts 13.52; Gal. 5.22; 1 Thess. 1.6.
[37] O'Donovan, *Desire*, 178. Cf. *Ways*, 294, 'The Foundations of Ethics', 104–5.
[38] O'Donovan, *Desire*, 179.
[39] Ibid., 181.

position of strength it has no need of the oppressor's impotent oppression, and so can offer reconciliation. Forgiveness is the sign that all rebellion against God has been defeated, so that the enemy, too, is liberated from its power.[40]

Again, O'Donovan contrasts his position with Hauerwas's, from whose understanding of martyrdom and its place in Christian witness he diverges, contending that 'readiness for martyrdom is not the only form the church's mission must take. Since true martyrdom is a powerful force and its resistance to Antichrist effective, the church must be prepared to welcome the homage of the kings when it is offered to the Lord of the martyrs.'[41] These are significant passages, providing the detailed subtexts to the headline contestation of 'Constantinianism' in the theo-political debate bubbling away between O'Donovan and Hauerwas, besides others.[42] They illustrate the far-reaching implications for political as well as moral theology of differing construals of cross and resurrection: though I cannot take up that debate here, I hope that my reconstruction and evaluation of O'Donovan's thought could in a minor way inform it.[43]

Certainly, O'Donovan is suspicious of what in *Ways of Judgment* he again calls a 'characteristically Western concentration on the cross at the expense of the resurrection'.[44] The explanation there further discloses why 'restoration' assumes significantly more ethical and political weight:

> While the cross discriminates between God's righteous servant and the world that rejects him, and brings every question down to the point of which side we stand on, it is the resurrection that vindicates the pattern of humanity that Christ lived for us and commanded us to follow. The resurrection does not leave God's judgment as a mathematical point without dimensions, but unfolds it and expounds it in the life of the Second Adam. That life, though not wholly disclosed, is not undisclosed either: 'Thy judgments have been revealed' (Rev. 15.4). Here there is a prescription we may embrace as a promise, a prescription that wholly presupposes that God has given us back our human powers of active life renewed.[45]

As we have already established, the handful of treatments of the cross in O'Donovan's work, to which we can add these, ought to prevent us from saying simply that the cross is absent from it. But given the pattern of exposition within them, and the more common silence about the cross, the reader might be led to think that the events of Good Friday are to be understood by theology and ethics as merely epiphenomenal to the central matter of the Christian mysteries. I do not think that O'Donovan actually regards the cross as a preamble to proclamation – a necessary, negative presupposition

---

[40] Ibid.
[41] Ibid., 215.
[42] Cf. O'Donovan, 'The Foundations of Ethics', where, asking how the church can 'sustain Easter joy in conflict', in the 'struggle of the cross', a 'struggle … against the principalities and powers', O'Donovan says it 'can do so by forgiving its enemies', 'an eschatological sign of the resurrection of the human race' (106–7).
[43] Cf. Doerksen's sound comparative work in *Beyond Suspicion* (71–85).
[44] O'Donovan, *Ways*, 85, speaking of Luther.
[45] Ibid., 85–6.

for the *euangelion* of resurrection; he does intimate that along with the other moments it is constitutive of God's work of salvation, and that it is disclosive, in itself, of the truth about the way faithfulness will go in this order. But, again, might the tendency to recalibrate what are taken to be lopsided traditions of dogmatic and moral teaching lead to an insufficiently dialectical account? The tendency to over-realize eschatological restoration as regards created order, in description of the resurrection victory, can seem to suppress a little the moral-theological and theo-political significance of the way of the cross in a world of *ongoing* sin and suffering. (And we can find more of a place for the normativity of the life and cross of Jesus than O'Donovan does without being reductionistically 'Jesuological' – a worry O'Donovan expresses about some political theology.)[46]

Leaving the moment of 'Passion' behind, we can further see that among the four moments, it is 'Restoration' that encompasses the major themes of O'Donovan's ethics by noticing that, of them all, 'Restoration' is said to cover 'the *moral life of the church*'.[47] (Lest that seem to represent a newly ecclesiocentric moral turn, note that 'Restoration' is also the moment that corresponds to 'natural right' – sometimes 'natural order' – comprising natural equality, structures of affinity, universal humanity and creaturely cohabitation.) O'Donovan summarizes this morality as follows:

> This is a morality of new creation in Christ, the life of a new community constituted by God's acceptance of Christ, promising a world made new in Christ and fit for human beings to live and act in. On the other hand, the Gospel is not simply 'apart from' God's law. The Mosaic Law, the possession of Israel, contained the promise of an active life, awaiting fulfilment in an Israel with the law written on its heart. That fulfilment is now offered. In Christ we may live and act acceptably to God.[48]

Unfortunately, I am not sure whether this summary, attractive as its moral vision is, goes much towards resolving some of the ambiguities in *Resurrection and Moral Order*: What does the 'new creation in Christ' signify? Is the promise of 'a world made new in Christ and fit for human beings to live and act in' fulfilled in the present? (The drift of the account would seem to suggest that.) Interestingly, the passage reads as though it was as much the world that needed making new in order for it to be the place of true human life and action, where elsewhere it had usually seemed that what needed renewal was primarily humankind, not least our perception of that still good world.

The context, which we have already seen, does little to clarify matters. However, the context is helpfully clear in demonstrating both the scriptural reasoning undergirding O'Donovan's presentation of an ethics oriented to 'Restoration', and his sense of crafting this presentation in contrast to 'contemporary liberal assumptions':

---

[46] On this, see again Doerksen, *Beyond Suspicion*. And we can do so without the needlessly anti-metaphysical stance of Nathan R. Kerr, *Christ, History, and Apocalyptic: The Politics of Christian Mission* (Eugene: Wipf and Stock, 2009), which despite its many fine proposals, is held back by this diffidence, both in its reading of Barth (and to a certain extent Hauerwas) and its constructive claims.

[47] O'Donovan, *Desire*, 183.

[48] Ibid.

As the church participates in Christ's resurrection it is authorised to live joyfully in the order God has made, and to recover it from oppressive and exploitative corruptions. The church of the New Testament self-consciously claimed the created structures of life and work in community, as we may see especially (but not only) in the so-called 'household codes', a common model of ethical catechesis underlying passages in Colossians, Ephesians and 1 Peter. These have sometimes been thought a disappointingly conservative sequel to the proclamation of the Kingdom of God. The reasons for discomfort are various: it arises from direct quarrels between contemporary liberal assumptions and the convictions expressed in the text ... but it arises also from a failure to appreciate what these texts undertake to do. They do not treat household structures merely as part of an unnegotiable social context with which the church has to get along somehow. They repudiate aspects of them, and claim back other aspects.[49]

The comment here overlaps significantly with those on 1 Peter in *Resurrection and Moral Order*. In *Desire of the Nations* too, then, we find a concerted attempt to do justice to 'created structures of life and work in community', over and against those who are tempted to take the notion of the kingdom of God as an excuse for the condescension of posterity towards biblical morality. But it is the effects of this attempt, when we view the shape and proportion of the argument as a whole, which gives me pause. Again, O'Donovan seems so concerned in fighting the fires of historicism that the effort issues in a disappointing disinclination, within the passages that represent key movements of his moral thought, to offer substantial readings of the genuine proclamation of the kingdom of God in regard to those eschatological themes not directly translatable to the 'recovery of created order'. When we read, in *Ways of Judgment*, that 'the order of creation is the only point of reference to judge what is good for created beings to do', we may wonder if in these books the other moments of the Christ event, and of the divine economy as a whole, have again been denied any weight as morally determinative.[50]

That is not at all to say that the eschatological in O'Donovan's theo-political works is exhausted by the exposition of 'Restoration' (simply that this seems to carry the most moral weight). For one thing, O'Donovan goes on describe the significance of the fourth moment, 'Exaltation', which bespeaks truly eschatological realities. In a moment, I will turn to that description and some related passages, in an appreciative reading. Before I do, however, I want to reflect further on the relationship between O'Donovan's prudential judgement concerning the contemporary situation, on the one hand, and the theological architectonic both conditioning that circumstantial judgement and conditioned by it, on the other.

---

[49] Ibid. Cf. Francis Watson's comments on Richard Hays' *Moral Vision*, in which, despite its other fine intuitions, 'the pastoral epistles are seen as marking a decline from the exhilarating radicalism of authentic Pauline ethics into a dull traditionalism that has learned to accommodate itself to the social status quo'. Review, *Studies in Christian Ethics* 10, no. 2 (1997): 94–7, 96.

[50] As emblematic of my broader concern, we should ask of a statement like this what sense could be made of vocations to singleness if it were true, without the addition of other considerations related to other moments of the divine economy.

Discernment of the times, revisited

What I seek to do here is to test out a concern that emerges in reading both *Desire of the Nations* and *Ways of Judgment* by drawing attention to it here in a very specific way. In short, the concern is this. First, that the discernment of the times made in these books, like the one found in 'the Natural Ethic', tilts the scales towards a creation ethics less affected by eschatology than it should be. Second, that despite the contextual discernment's partial accuracy, this tilting of the scales in turn produces lapses in attentiveness to pressing moral challenges.

Articulating my concern requires brief consideration of O'Donovan's treatment of what he terms the 'Southern school' of political theology, or in other words, political theologies of liberation. Early on, *Desire of the Nations* declares that despite its merits, that school lacks a concept of authority – it expresses a philosophically idealist suspicion against the notion itself – and, by such an omission, builds itself 'on an acephalous idea of society, dissolving government in deconstructive scepticism'.[51] Ultimately, it lacks 'a point of view which can transcend given matrices of engagement'.[52] For critical readers of O'Donovan's political theology, these particular statements are often a lightning rod for broader uneasiness about O'Donovan's 'patrician', perhaps 'legitimating', tone and the lack of radicality exhibited by his political thought – responses, we should note, that O'Donovan professes to be surprised by.[53] What I want to observe is one of O'Donovan's claims in particular: 'This rejection' – of authority – 'has tended to restrict the immediate usefulness of political theology influenced by the Southern school to questions faced in the North'.[54] 'The Northern democracies', O'Donovan suggests, present different questions than the Southern – questions that require 'detailed attention to the structures of authority which undergird their unruly democratic culture'.[55] The Northern questions are listed as follows:

> Can democracy avoid corruption by mass communications? Can individual liberty be protected from technological manipulation? Can civil rights be safeguarded without surrendering democratic control to arbitrarily appointed courts? Or stable market-conditions without surrendering control to arbitrarily appointed bankers? Can punishment be humane and still satisfy the social conscience? Can international justice be protected by threats of nuclear devastation? Can ethnic, cultural and linguistic communities assert their identities without oppressing individual freedoms? Can a democracy contain the urge to excessive consumption of natural resources? Can the handicapped, the elderly and the unborn be protected against the exercise of liberty demanded by the strong, the articulate

---

[51] O'Donovan, *Desire*, 16.
[52] Ibid. Cf. O'Donovan, 'Political Theology, Tradition and Modernity', in *The Cambridge Companion to Liberation Theology*, ed. Christopher Rowland (Cambridge: Cambridge University Press, 1999).
[53] E.g. Timothy Gorringe, 'Authority, Plebs, Patricians', *Studies in Christian Ethics* 11, no. 2 (1998): 24–9; Andrew Shanks, review of *Royal Priesthood*, *Theology*, 107, no. 836 (2004): 145–6.
[54] O'Donovan, *Desire*, 18.
[55] Ibid.

and the middle-aged? Should the nation-state yield place to large, market-defined governmental conglomerates?

Accordingly, for O'Donovan 'philosophically motivated "modernity-critics" who have concentrated on the philosophical character of technology … and of modern moral and political thought' are more enlightening on these issues than political theologians.[56] To my mind, there is nothing inherently disagreeable in this, and we have benefited much from O'Donovan's expansions upon their analyses. It surely also true to say, as Christopher Insole does, that attractive in O'Donovan's thought 'is a prudential determination to judge in a way that is sensitive to the particularities and contingencies of a time and a place'.[57] We need to press on a little further in analysis of O'Donovan's judgements, then. We can gain further purchase on them by recalling and comparing O'Donovan's earlier explanation of the reasons the polarized 'naturalist and historicist camps' formed:

> We have to proclaim the gospel in different cultural and philosophical contexts. Many of us have deep sympathy with the problems of the Third World, tyrannical regimes, oppressive family and tribal structures, maldistribution of resources, and so on, and, speaking authentically to the static naturalisms which have produced and aggravated such problems, will talk eschatologically of transformation, even with a daring but possible expropriation of language, of 'revolution'. Others of us are concerned chiefly with the problems of the Western world, the abuses of technology, the threat to the family, the dominance of financial power, and so on, and find themselves needing constantly to point to the *data* of created nature. No doubt there is a temptation here: it is easy for the one group to think of the other as 'conservative' or 'radical'. But whenever we do this we exclude one side of the nature-history balance, and condemn our own stance to being less Christian for lack of that balance.[58]

Unsurprisingly, there is strong overlap between the kinds of concerns assigned to 'the Western world' in the earlier piece and to 'the Northern democracies' later on, and a more implicit consistent sense of 'the Third World' issues, addressed by 'the Southern school'. Yet reflecting on these two texts together does not just show us O'Donovan's consistency of judgement; I think it also aids our perception of the relationship between his circumstantial judgements and theological architectonic, as follows.

If O'Donovan sees concern for *both* contexts as authentically Christian, given the construal of both impulses in 'The Natural Ethic', then we have to regard his diagnosis of the issues facing us and his deployment of pertinent theological resources as purely pragmatic. The rationale would go something like this: we have a duty to understand and utilize the theological resources applicable to our situation, which enable proclamation in the here and now. As I observed in Chapter 1, O'Donovan's attraction

---

[56] Ibid.
[57] Christopher Insole, 'Seek the Wrong', *Times Literary Supplement* 5427 (2007): 9.
[58] O'Donovan, 'The Natural Ethic', 31.

to the natural ethic can be seen as a discernment in this light – a reading fortified by what we read in *Desire of the Nations*. But from both texts, it is still unclear just how misguided or not he considers other attempts to draw, therapeutically, on different theological emphases for different cultural maladies. Because while it seems as though O'Donovan was content to give some credence to the instincts of those who correlated creation with 'North' and kingdom with 'South', at the same time, he located his own theological architectonic as comprehensive, integrating and transcending both poles – and continues to do so in the theo-political writings.

In these books, O'Donovan does seem similarly to give credence to those whose response to pressing 'Southern' issues leads them to foreground different theological concepts. In *Desire of the Nations*, he records a 'word of honour … due to Gustavo Gutierrez', who has devoted his career 'to clarifying the authentic shape that theology must take in his own cultural situation'.[59] In *Ways of Judgment*, too, rehearsing three 'over-simplified' construals of sin, O'Donovan credits liberation theology by name (as 'least misleading'!) for its insights into the way 'the envy of the primal sin may be worked out in *excluding structures*'.[60] And O'Donovan does so at the point in that book when he himself begins to 'make contact with the long tradition of Christian concern for the poor'.[61] (Though announcing a rewarding set of reflections, it is hard not to think that needing to 'make contact' with that tradition suggests O'Donovan's own reflections begin elsewhere, perhaps returning to other apparently more exigent matters beyond this interlude.) In *Desire of the Nations*, he discounts a particular charge of political theology's 'influential critics' because 'it fails to recognise the inspiration of the movement, which has been to take up the cause of the poor *as a theologically given mandate*'.[62] O'Donovan goes on: 'If the question of the poor is, quite specifically, the question of Latin Americans because it arises in their context, it is, at the same time, a question for everyone because it arises from scriptural warrants to which we must all attend.'[63] Liberation theology's 'true weakness lies not in taking up the cause of the poor in a preferential manner, but in partially concealing the theological warrants for doing so in order to conform the historical dialectic of idealism'.[64]

O'Donovan is not as such inattentive to 'Southern' or 'Third World' issues, then, nor is he entirely unimpressed by political theologies of liberation; neither is he unaware that some of the questions for liberation theology are questions 'for everyone'. But we should, just so, mark the two lists' confidence in adjudicating which questions are matters for Christian deliberation in 'Northern democracies'. Are the demarcations at risk of tidying away manifestations of sin plaguing 'Northern democracies' into a list of items proper for deliberation by 'Southern' Christians? Looking back to 'The Natural Ethic', we remember that the audience was not made up of two groups from disparate contexts. The fact that *British* Christians were exercised about the kinds of issues O'Donovan allocates there to 'the Third World' might have been a hint that different

---

[59] O'Donovan, *Desire*, 12.
[60] O'Donovan, *Ways*, 82.
[61] Ibid., 45.
[62] O'Donovan, *Desire*, 10–11.
[63] Ibid., 11.
[64] Ibid.

discernments about their immediate context were being made, too. Yet the assumption seems to be that their interest was in those problems as manifested *there,* never here.

At the very least, even if O'Donovan's impressions of the main features of cultural situations are to a greater degree accurate, it has been the experience of some Western Christians that their concern for the problems of 'the Third World' alerted them to *universal* features of sin: features found in their own societies. In a not dissimilar vein, O'Donovan writes of *Veritatis Splendor* that, while there is no detectible 'conscious intent to respond to the challenges of liberation theology ... clearly the Pope is ready, in squaring up to the more dehumanizing determinants of Northern civilization, to learn from that source and to imitate the spirit of Christians who have confronted oppressive structures in the South'.[65] (It is not clear whether we should learn just to imitate their spirit, or whether we can also learn to confront oppressive structures, should there be any evident in 'Northern civilization'.) Admittedly, European political theologians' accounts of particular instantiations of the universal features of the moral field sometimes lack subtlety. Neither do they attain the exegetical or conceptual sophistication of O'Donovan's political theology and ethics. But as he himself has given us reason to expect, they can be based on scriptural warrants as well as social analysis.

I would suggest that features of life in 'Northern democracies' fit into O'Donovan's category of those constitutive of 'the Third World', and in the terms of our study, this raises the following question: Do these features demand that we draw more on eschatological vocabulary to address them? In a way, O'Donovan would be right to reject this inference, if he wants to maintain the claim that Christian ethics' centre of gravity should be established prior to the pressures of context that produce disequilibrium in a Christian metaphysics for morals. But O'Donovan would seem to have to accept the inference, given that the contextually derived concerns he does take up seem to him to require primarily attention to the order of nature, and are addressed on the basis of a strongly creation-oriented account of salvation as predominantly restoration. Accepting that latter point, though, would seem to mean admitting more than we have seen O'Donovan do, that 'kingdom ethicists' could have rightly intuited the doctrinal resources to draw upon, since they saw the moral challenges differently. But as we will find again in *Ethics as Theology*'s critique of Moltmann, O'Donovan is still very far from that admission.

In other words, O'Donovan might make a more particular argument than he lets on, exactly in the way he structures his putatively universal claims – yet he seems to criticize others for not assuming those same universal claims. There is an admirable reach in his thought: both an effort to outline a credibly universal account of moral and political life, *and* a stated sensitivity to the circumstance-derived heterogeneity of Christian moral reason's practical exercise. But I do think the relation between the two is vexed. The ambitions are belied by the contextual oversight that is found here, an oversight that keeps company with the inability of O'Donovan's natural ethic to take into account, as fully determinative for moral theology, a broader range of theological affirmations.

---

[65] O'Donovan, 'A Summons to Reality', 43.

Granted, it is partly true to say, as O'Donovan himself does, that 'where we live' – meaning the Northern democracies as such – 'the location of true poverty is hidden behind a veil of widespread wealth'.[66] 'The church's identification with the poor', he goes on, 'has to be the goal, not the presupposition, of social reflection in the North'.[67] But true poverty is not veiled in all places 'we' live in Northern democracies, nor are the Northern assemblies of the Christian community all completely remote from the poor (thank God).

I do not mean by all this to raise suspicion only or reductively in terms of the sociology of knowledge; it is valuable, but not sufficient to point out theological views' unavoidably habituating socioeconomic locations. Tim Gorringe's review of Joshua Hordern's *Political Affections*, which I will quote some milder comments of in a moment, is a fierce example of that.[68] Rather – and this might be to say both less and more – the observation to be made is that actual losses of perspectival range occasioned by this academic and ecclesial locatedness are not unrelated to the diminishment of *theological* resources necessary for the discovery of the lost insights. What that might mean in this connection is that specifying what seems not to be seen by O'Donovan is to specify precisely those challenges the discernment of which was earlier taken to have been better served by 'kingdom ethics' than 'creation ethics'.

Rowan Williams is right to say that O'Donovan's work 'has been marked by the patient, coherent assemblage of a viewpoint thoroughly permeated by primary theological convictions', and that this 'is why he is so hard to characterize as a thinker of "left" or "right" – and why he is so hard to dismiss and so necessary a presence'.[69] In seeking to take up O'Donovan's thought as a resource, it is therefore imperative that we interrogate what seem to be these failures of perception theologically as much as sociopolitically, searching in and under the presenting issues for the precipitating oversight. Too few critics have done so.[70] In a way, O'Donovan's description of Christian ethics' polarization and the different moments of doctrinal teaching each side draws upon

---

[66] O'Donovan, 'Response to Peter Scott', in *Royal Priesthood*, 374–6, 375.
[67] Ibid., 376.
[68] Gorringe, review of *Political Affections*, *Journal of Theological Studies* 64, no. 2 (2013): 868–70. Gorringe overstates his case drastically, but I think there is more than a molehill there, in Hordern's work, for Gorringe to have made a mountain out of: *Political Affections'* reading of the times and approach to poverty in the UK can, among other judgements, with straight face hold up Iain Duncan Smith's 'Antiochene experience … in Easterhouse, Glasgow' as heralding a revolution in 'the tone and leadership of the United Kingdom Conservative Party since 2005 with regard to poverty', which is to be understood credulously as exemplary instance of 'Christian affections'' ability to 'disturb, renew, or correct patterns of social trust, renewing and challenging political loyalty and representation' (271). If there is an element of truth to this, formally, it seems to me a completely wrongheaded example to choose, given the effects of that Party's policies when in government (already tragically evident by the time *Political Affections* was published).
[69] Williams, 'Foreword', viii. Malcolm Brown observes that 'Williams's social theology and O'Donovan's evangelical political theology may not be so far apart after all'. 'The Case for Anglican Social Theology Today', in *Anglican Social Theology*, 23.
[70] Whatever one makes of the critics' complaints, it is both lamentable that many of them seem to misread O'Donovan *and* that he continually seems to invite reproaches and misreadings by his compressed, even gnomic style and occasionally aloof tone, as well as by incautious examples and turns of phrase, some of which are justly picked up on by commentators. This goes beyond the theo-political works. See e.g. the generally fair comments of Doug Gay – review of *Finding and Seeking*, *Theology* 118, no. 5 (2015): 364–5.

itself gives us the beginnings of a response. What we have come to see, however, is that his own project does not seem to have overcome that polarization sustainably. If anything, the claim to have overcome such corrosive dualisms (echoed *verbatim*, for instance, by Hordern) might have led to complacency about the scope of political and social reality in 'Northern democracies' that demands theological attention.

We might speculate further about why, as the late John Hughes wrote, 'O'Donovan does not have so much to say about social and economic questions'.[71] Perhaps it is the simple fact that in view of his manifold other interests, O'Donovan recognized his own relative lack of expertise in these areas, especially while contemporaries wrote extensively about such questions. (Even from this remove it does seem that socioeconomically concerned theologians were certainly prominent in Christian 'social ethics' during O'Donovan's career – in the UK alone, we may think of Ronald Preston, John Atherton and Duncan Forrester.) However, the oversights of discernment cannot claim that as sufficient excuse, even if it explains, in part, the scope of O'Donovan's treatment of social and economic questions.[72] But let us now move on to a reading of some of those places within O'Donovan's theo-political project where eschatological themes seem to yield greater insight.

The church, the kingdom of God, and politics

It is to the description of 'Exaltation' and some related passages that I turn now, showing how eschatology figures in the ecclesiology of these books and how it sets the terms for politics.

Recalling that each recapitulation of the representative act yields corresponding ecclesial dimensions, we find that the church's participation in Christ's exaltation is that it 'is a community *that speaks the words of God*'.[73] It does so in prayer and in prophecy, and corresponding to this fourth moment is the speculatively proposed

---

[71] John Hughes, 'After Temple? The Recent Renewal of Anglican Social Thought', in *Anglican Social Theology*, 86. The context here is Hughes' positioning of the work of O'Donovan and Milbank as parallel developments (Anglican evangelical and Anglo-Catholic, respectively) of MacIntyre and Hauerwas's critiques of enlightenment liberalism. While O'Donovan 'does not have so much to say about social and economic questions ... his evangelical account of natural moral order and his constitutionalist defence of the legitimacy of the use of political power and law have been very influential on the current generation of Anglican social thinkers, particularly among evangelicals'.

[72] It is interesting to see that with Waters' *Just Capitalism: A Christian Ethics of Economic Globalization* (Louisville: Westminster/John Knox, 2016), we now have an economic ethics from one of O'Donovan's students, though (at first glance) not one that would satisfy the critics of O'Donovan's theo-politics who have themselves worked on socioeconomic themes. That said, as have seen, Sean Doherty's *Theology and Economic Ethics* also shows O'Donovan's influence in parts, though to make a related case in an essay entitled 'The Kingdom of God and the Economic System: An Economics of Hope' Doherty relies on other sources. That volume (*Theology and Economics: A Christian Vision of the Common Good*, ed. Jeremy Kidwell and Sean Doherty (New York: Palgrave MacMillan, 2015), carries a brief response by O'Donovan to four essays (not Doherty's), of characteristic analytical precision but not many constructive clues. *Desire*'s comments on poverty (98, 165, 207) and *Entering into Rest*'s comments on markets (50–1) suggest that O'Donovan does have more to say about socioeconomic questions, if nowhere addresses them programmatically.

[73] O'Donovan, *Desire*, 189.

fourth sacrament: the laying on of hands. By this O'Donovan means to capture the common significance lying behind a range of church practices, including ordination and prayer for bestowal of the Spirit at confirmation. These all in some way secure a place for the recognition in community of the individual and their vocation. (Again we might note the interesting pattern that a connection is made between the most eschatological element of the narration of the economy and the individual vocation, whereas the centre of gravity of the Christ event is connected again with general moral order.) We need not dwell on O'Donovan's intriguing suggestion here apart from noting that part of his case for it rests upon the observation that 'in the New Testament … it signifies the church's privilege of invoking 'the powers of the age to come', and especially the bestowal of the Holy Spirit':

> The prayers of the church seek one thing only, the final manifestation of God's rule on earth. Nevertheless, because it is called into existence in order to witness to that coming manifestation through its own life and word, it prays also for God's power at work within itself. Prayer is invocation of the Spirit, calling upon God's power now to witness to God's power then.[74]

In witness, then, the church is a political community as 'the community of God's rule, manifesting his Kingdom for the world'.[75] In this way, as in *Resurrection and Moral Order*, O'Donovan makes some quite fulsome statements about the *ecclesia* as instantiating witness to the Kingdom:

> In Jesus' proclamation the duality of Babylon and Israel has become a frontier in time. He stands at the moment of transition between the ages where the passing and coming authorities confront one another. … The same frontier in time occupies the apostolic proclamation, with this expansion: the future age now has a social and political presence. A community lives under the authority of him to whom the Ancient of Days has entrusted the Kingdom.[76]

So too in *Ways of Judgment* O'Donovan writes that 'the church differs from all societies that we know otherwise in representing the kingdom of heaven'.[77] The socially communicative quality of life beyond judgement – truly a taste of the eschaton – infuses ecclesial life:

---

[74] Ibid., 190, 189.
[75] Ibid.
[76] Ibid., 158.
[77] O'Donovan, *Ways*, 254. Rowans Williams writes of *Ways*: 'In this as in all his books, Oliver is developing a full-blooded doctrine of Church, ministry, and sacraments in the course of discussing what we might mistakenly have thought at first to be issues quite alien to this agenda' (Foreword, viii). O'Donovan, I suggest, is a major ecclesiological thinker – and this aspect of his thought might be relatively neglected, possibly because he does develop it in the course of discusses so many other topics. It seems that his interest in ecclesiology developed through teaching – see his comments in Shortt, *God's Advocates*, as well as the reflections of two former students: Michael Nai-Chiu Poon, 'Recovering a Sense of Place', *Living Church* (Spring 2012): 9–11, 9; and Peter Widdicombe, 'Patient Teacher to All', *Living Church* (Spring 2012): 11–13, 12.

As the model for the communication of the Spirit in the world, the church is defined as the community that 'judges not', but bears witness to a final judgment ... it is the bearer of a discourse that defers judgment, seeking further reflection and a discourse 'between the times' in the moment of God's patience. This discourse is its life, both as an announcement and as a lived display. For the church is the community within which the Spirit is 'given', representing the eschatological identity of humankind, and embodying it provisionally for all to see and enter.[78]

The church is itself possessed of backward- and forward-looking aspects by virtue of its social character: 'In the church we look forward to the sociality of the human race gathered around the throne of God and of the Lamb, and we look back upon the given sociality of the race in its creation, apart from sin and the necessity of human rule.'[79] Thus in the present, the church 'both is and is not a "political society"': it judges not, and is as such 'counter-political', yet it is judged.[80]

If, as we shall see, O'Donovan intends to put politics in its proper place in view of the city of God, it is not that he wants the church to preen itself on account of its individuating witness. Recognizing the true character of the church militant, we find, is really about understanding its *time*:

But the counter-political witness of the church, too, is constrained by that 'not yet'. It points to the future appearing of the one representative, and to the decisive judgment he will give. It models the eschatological community. But it is not simply identical with the eschatological community that will live without structure or form other than the immediate presence of God and the Lamb in its midst.[81]

Again, these quotations – and the question of the church's eschatological continuity and the current legitimacy of governmental judgement – provide grounds upon which interesting conversation between the emerging traditions of O'Donovan and Hauerwas could be staged (especially if we entertain Wells's proposal to modulate Hauerwas's earlier largely spatial claims into ones more about time).[82]

---

[78] O'Donovan, *Ways*, 254.
[79] Ibid., 241.
[80] Ibid., 318.
[81] Ibid., 261.
[82] See Wells, *Transforming Fate*, ch. 7, 'From Space to Time'. In a way, William Cavanaugh's somewhat Hauerwasian reading of Augustine gets us a certain distance towards this end, and provides a staunch critique of the legitimation of dualities that are spatialized according to a spurious parsing of eschatological 'already' and 'not yet' – see 'From One City to Two: Christian Reimagining of Political Space', *Political Theology* 7, no. 3 (2006): 299–321. Christopher Insole's reply to Cavanaugh's piece identifies this challenge, but also the somewhat problematic irresolution in Cavanaugh's proposal (Insole, 'Discerning the Theopolitical: A Response to Cavanaugh's Reimagining of Political Space', 323–35, of the same issue). Insole's push for clarity about the present status of government and his further development of the temporal dimension are both largely coherent with O'Donovan's work. However, Insole seems to press the anti-ecclesiocentrism line a little harder than O'Donovan would. This difference is seen directly in Insole's worries about *Ways* expressed in 'Seek the Wrong'. Actually, the way Insole understands the eschatological 'disruption of our false "already" by God's already' (Insole, 'Discerning', 332) to trouble the post-liberal turn to communal practices and virtuous habit is not dissimilar to the ways in which some current exponents of apocalyptic

O'Donovan is attentive to the ways in which the church's eschatological orientation relates to the political as such. Central among these is that it calls into question the hubristic, self-aggrandizing tendencies of earthly rule. Rulers and ruled must never forget: 'The kingdom of God can have no concrete representation upon earth except the indirect one afforded by the church'.[83] This is not to say that eschatology has no relation to earthly affairs. As *Desire of the Nations* puts it, 'Justice is to have a new, evangelical content'.[84] *Ways of Judgment*, as O'Donovan's volume of political ethics, pursues the same thought, perhaps best summarized in this line: 'Our membership in the kingdom of God may be transcendent, but it can be gestured towards in the way we do our earthly justice'.[85]

That O'Donovan means to take that gesture seriously is perhaps easiest to comprehend when placed in the relief that he wishes us to see. Critical comments in *Ways of Judgment* on Luther's political theology re-present in this political connection the critical comments I introduced earlier on law-and-gospel ethics. In a chapter considering 'Punishment', O'Donovan understands his own commitment to the moral reach of Christ's victory ('the triumph of the kingdom') to necessitate following Augustine's lead instead of Luther's, when it comes to the present relevance of the gospel for practices of judgement. Unlike Luther, Augustine could see 'no other context for exploring this than the church's mission of reconciliation and redemption'.[86]

Yet it is also characteristic of O'Donovan to stress that recourse to eschatology in political thought can turn pernicious. For instance: 'Actually to project an ideal of eschatological equality onto the political order of secular society produces a tyrannous idealism, for social reality as we encounter it is always shaped by representation and judgment one way or the other. Eschatological equality belongs to the "not yet" of the kingdom.'[87] As Eric Gregory writes, for O'Donovan, 'though politics can be in the service of the church, we do not build the kingdom of God through revolutionary action, even as we long for that promise to be fulfilled and pray for it come'.[88] Or again:

> No reader of O'Donovan – or Augustine for that matter – could underestimate this cautious, non-apocalyptic realism flowing from recognition of the fallen human

theology (Nathan Kerr, David Congdon) seek to puncture what they see as the hypertrophy of ecclesiality in otherwise kindred theologies. I have some sympathy with some of this de-emphasis – and recognize the point about the pervasiveness of sin – but for reasons related to the theology of grace, and less to do with any untheological pessimism about the church, or any revalorization of liberal individualism, a night in which all secular and ecclesial cows appear black, and which may be too determinative in Insole's piece.

[83] O'Donovan, *Ways*, 214–15.
[84] O'Donovan, *Desire*, 201. Cf. Wannenwetsch, *Political Worship*, 251–60, which interacts with drafts of *Desire*.
[85] O'Donovan, *Ways*, 215.
[86] Ibid., 89. Compare O'Donovan's earlier comment that Augustine's 'distinctly Christian approaches to the administration of justice should not be described (H.R. Niebuhr) as "transforming" earthly institutions, for they do not anticipate the eschatological kingdom but assert the created order of loving equality as the context in which juridical coercion should be interpreted. In the final peace of God itself there will be no human dominion.' O'Donovan, 'Augustinian Ethics', 48.
[87] O'Donovan, *Ways*, 261.
[88] Eric Gregory, 'The Boldness of Analogy: Civic Virtues and Augustinian Eudaimonism', in *The Authority of the Gospel*, 73.

condition, the contingency of history, and the mystery of providence. Civic virtues have their proper ends, ones chastened by the future rather than present dimensions of salvation. In fact, judiciousness is the virtue of an eschatological patience that knows the 'not yet' of any human achievement. Here we find something like an apophatic political theology, veiled in the ambiguity of exilic pilgrimage and sin-stained temporality. … Our compromised politics are not the kingdom of God.[89]

Yet as Gregory himself describes it, for O'Donovan, 'relieved of the pressure to be salvific, politics is set free to pursue its provisional and relative tasks. Such politics, like our experience of grace, operates more in the modality of healing than elevation. It tempers imperfection rather than tutors perfection'.[90] As 'Buckle Street', O'Donovan's poem that prefaces *Ways of Judgment*, has it, 'Grace' is 'the invader', and though its work is 'scornful of gravity', righting what has gone wrong, to do so it 'Follows the traces left by our interdicts / Scoops out from hard-core legal strictures / Runnels of kindly communication'.

That poem's topic of judgement is fundamental to O'Donovan's project, and through it runs an eschatological thread, though it cannot be examined in any detail here.[91] Neither can more than a word be said about secularity, another aspect of his metaphysically ambitious account of political reality and history that the thread runs through.[92] Deeply suggestive, though, is the line in *Common Objects*: 'Western society has forgotten how to be secular. Secularity is a stance of patience in the face of plurality, made sense of by eschatological hope; forgetfulness of it is part and parcel with the forgetfulness of Christian suppositions about history'.[93] And, in a wonderful earlier passage of that book:

> Secular social reality, we may say, is constantly subverted by a conspiracy of nature and grace. The community-building love that the Creator has set in all human hearts, and that makes even Hell a city, will always need redemptive love if it is to realise its own capacities. Secular community has no ground of its own on which it may simply exist apart. It is either opened up to its fulfilment in God's love, or it is shut down, as its purchase on reality drains away.[94]

---

[89] Ibid.
[90] Ibid.
[91] See Guido de Graaff, 'To Judge or Not to Judge: Engaging with Oliver O'Donovan's Political Ethics', *Studies in Christian Ethics* 25, no. 3 (2012): 295–311.
[92] Brian Brock finds the form of eschatology – final judgement – which shapes O'Donovan's understanding of secularity too limited. He goes on to make a case, following Wannenwetsch, for the political 'fertility' of eschatological hope in a 'secularity generated by … present experience of reconciliation' rather than '"unfulfilled promise"'. (Brian Brock, '"What Is the Public?" Theological Variations on Babel and Pentecost', in *The Authority of the Gospel* ed. Robert Song and Brent Waters (Grand Rapids: Eerdmans, 2015), 168). De Graaff's article also represents a modification of O'Donovan's theo-politics influenced by Wannenwetsch's ecclesial vision.
[93] O'Donovan, *Common Objects*, 69. On the difference between O'Donovan and Milbank's evaluations of secularity, see Gregory, *Politics and the Order of Love*, 146.
[94] O'Donovan, *Common Objects*, 24.

Politics for O'Donovan, then, is firmly this-worldly. This-worldly in the *created* sense of the natural, dignified limitations and contingencies of social life; in the *fallen* sense of the pretensions of powers and principalities openly rebelling against divine rule; and in the providential sense of the necessity of the acts of judgement that restrain evil. But it is never entirely without analogy to the ways of divine judgement, untouched by the ways of divine grace.[95]

Conclusion

Jonathan Chaplin has remarked well what he calls *Desire of the Nation*'s 'panoramic, Augustinian eschatological vision of political history' and that remark lends the theme on which I conclude.[96] Lorish and Mathewes were not misled when they wrote that O'Donovan's 'has been a distinctively *Augustinian* judiciousness':

> One attuned to the complexities and paradoxes of a sin-riddled creature, immured in this world but longing for a divine happiness that never has more than a fugitive presence here, and all the ironies and necessary compromise attendant on such a creature's existence in our world.[97]

Nor was Gregory, when he wrote that their statement 'nicely captures the anthropology and eschatology of an influential strand of political Augustinianism':

> It is governed by what O'Donovan names as a 'threefold metaphysic of a good creation, an evil fall and an end of history which negates evil and transcends the

---

[95] O'Donovan, *Ways*, 100.
[96] Jonathan Chaplin, 'Political Eschatology and Responsible Government: Oliver O'Donovan's "Christian Liberalism"', in *Royal Priesthood?* 275.
[97] Lorish and Mathewes, 'Theology as Counsel', 722. They write that *Desire* 'simply recast the field of "political theology"':

> ... Up until that work, discussion of "church and state" issues had largely been occupied by a running debate between ecclesially minded "narrative theologians": of Hauerwasian and Yoderian varieties, on the one hand, and those "public theologians" for whom the Christian's presence in a liberal society was a given fact that needed to be acknowledged: the former saw the latter as perniciously collaborationist, while the latter saw the former as hopelessly sectarian ... O'Donovan's book rearranged the categories for everyone, both taking scripture and church if anything *more* seriously than the narrativists, and also engaging in the public order more constructively and collaboratively than the public theologians. (725)

Gregory writes: 'Deliberativeness is another way of identifying this judiciousness' they appreciate in O'Donovan, 'one that marks O'Donovan's distance from the oscillation between prophetic jeremiad and secularist punditry which can be found in Anglo-American theological ethics' (Gregory, 'The Boldness of Analogy', 73). There's something essentially right in both sets of comments, though it seems to me too crude to characterize Hauerwas's mode as simply prophetic jeremiad, not least since he has done as much as anyone to *propose* a particular social ethic, and to commend specific practices, sometimes in conversation with non-theological interlocutors. More to the point, arraying the options in this way, thereby portraying one's exemplars and oneself as, for example, neither left nor right, can be a comfortable way of fending off the sharp end of Hauerwas's jeremiads (granted, he pens a few!).

created good'. So understood, politics is theologically located in the flux of history in the time between the times (*in hoc saeculo*), not in created nature.[98]

Insole too makes a similar assessment, writing that *Ways of Judgment* shows no exception to the 'Augustinian sense of our imperfectibility' that 'provides the pedal note under all of O'Donovan's work'.[99]

This sense so identified may indeed be sustained throughout O'Donovan's work, but given my reading of 'The Natural Ethic' and *Resurrection and Moral Order*, I want to suggest some specification. An assessment of the sobriety of O'Donovan's eschatological reserve in political theology, history, and ethics has to be accompanied by an assessment of the confidence of his eschatological realization in moral theology. This reading is itself supported by Lorish and Mathewes's comments cited earlier, the drift of which was that *Resurrection and Moral Order*'s conviction about moral clarity is less 'Augustinian' than O'Donovan might think. Developing this assessment is not straightforward, though, because as we have seen, that book itself seemed to meld different strands of eschatology. On one hand, it seemed to envisage sturdy continuity between creation and new creation, which makes possible strong knowledge in the present of the form of created goods (renewed knowledge that may, in O'Donovan's 'flatter' accounts of restoration, be coterminous with new creation). In this kind of epistemic confidence, there might be something not quite 'Augustinian'.[100] But, on the other hand, O'Donovan held even there an austere view about the possibilities of knowledge of the moral import of the eschatological future, of the kingdom of God, besides creation's already-eschatologically achieved vindication.

In his political theology, in distinction, O'Donovan strikes me as a more singularly 'Augustinian' thinker. Apophatic reserve takes hold more strongly: the relation of earthly to eschatological reality is by analogy; current reality seems more marked by sin; current perception seems more provisional; and current possibilities of perfection seem more fragile, even absent. The peace and justice obtained in the necessary compromises of Christian engagement with the *saeculum* are, for O'Donovan, as for Augustine, 'merely shadows of what will obtain after this life'.[101] And whatever appellation we might use, O'Donovan's sobriety concerning earthly politics is why other moral and political theologians who otherwise share many instincts can find him unduly pessimistic. Finding the relation too equivocal, the echo too distant, they wish for a more univocal relation between heaven and the earth in particular moments or movements of worldly activity.[102] Yet when that judgement is considered, it must be borne in mind that O'Donovan's political theology has also been criticized for an 'overrealized' eschatology, which is understood to sponsor its Constantinianism. And

---

[98] Gregory, 'The Boldness of Analogy', 73.
[99] Insole, 'Seek the Wrong', 9.
[100] I realize that to say 'Augustinian' is to raise almost as many questions as it settles, inviting engagement with critical debates not mentioned directly, while literature related to competing readings of *City of God* continues to proliferate.
[101] Carol Harrison, *Augustine: Christian Truth and Fractured Humanity* (Oxford: Oxford University Press, 2000), 213. Cf. O'Donovan, 'Augustine of Hippo', in *From Irenaeus to Grotius*.
[102] E.g. Gregory, 'The Boldness of Analogy' and *Politics and the Order of Love*; Brock, 'What Is "the Public"?'

that claim has force, if not necessarily precision.[103] Again, it seems that if eschatology is everywhere in O'Donovan's political theology, it is not everywhere the same.

In O'Donovan's thought, the givens of (redeemed) creaturely life and its goal are always already given. They seem to dictate the mood of his moral theology. Though that mood strongly permeates the treatment of 'Restoration' and its ecclesial parameters in *Desire of the Nations*, for the most part, the atmosphere of the theo-political work is subtly different. In it, the unknowns of life in this order, owed both to sin and to the 'not yet' of the kingdom, are an ever-present bulwark upon which human reasoning breaks, and must be respected. Gregory's remark was to the point, that when seen in terms of the threefold metaphysic O'Donovan espoused in *Resurrection and Moral Order*, 'politics is theologically located in the flux of history in the time between the times … not in created nature'. Gregory, I think, probably means that description of O'Donovan's theo-political vision as continuous with the salvation history of O'Donovan's moral vision – that's why he takes up an earlier formulation in defining it. But, for *Resurrection and Moral Order*, ethics, by contrast with politics, seemed to be theologically located more resolutely in created nature, at times too far removed from historical flux. As I wrote in the Introduction, when vindication or restoration becomes the shorthand for the aspects of eschatological reality that appertain to creaturely life, O'Donovan often announces eschatology and expounds creation. (Again the trend is partly present here, too, inasmuch as the foregrounded notion of 'Restoration' underpins the account of the church and its moral life.) Yet in a dimension distinct from this, in O'Donovan's theo-political work, it is the kingdom of God and the last judgement that come to the fore, besides the 'already' and 'not yet' of Christ's triumph over earthly powers, and which represent the transcendent and delimiting horizon of human affairs.[104]

An intriguing further realization might follow. In broad terms, if Hordern's theo-politics takes up what I earlier called *Resurrection and Moral Order's* over-realized strand of eschatology, then O'Donovan's own theo-politics actually seems more informed by other, the more transcendent and apophatic strand. When Gorringe writes (let us leave aside the mentions of Hitler and Mussolini) that Hordern's book is 'very much in the school of [O'Donovan] … drawing on his work as a principal source', he means principally that 'Hordern accepts O'Donovan's contention that there is an objective moral order'.[105] But that is, of course, a contention not especially central to

---

[103] Kroeker ('Why O'Donovan's Christendom …') critically assesses the adequacy of that claim as made by Yoder. It is one repeated by Hauerwas and Fodor, and by Cavanaugh ('Church', in *The Blackwell Companion to Political Theology*, ed. William Cavanaugh and Peter Scott (Oxford: Blackwell, 2004), 404). Cf. J. Alexander Sider, *To See History Doxologically: History and Holiness in John Howard Yoder's Ecclesiology* (Grand Rapids: Eerdmans, 2011), ch. 1, Doerksen, *Beyond Suspicion*, 104–8, and D. Stephen Long, *The Goodness of God: Theology, Church, and the Social Order* (Grand Rapids: Brazos, 2001), 89–104.

[104] Like Brock, Carroll considers O'Donovan's eschatological interest too much spent on final judgement.

[105] Gorringe, review of *Political Affections*, 868, 9. He continues:

> We can readily agree with this. The problem, of course, is how we know it, and what aspects of it we identify. Ulysses, in Shakespeare's *Troilus and Cressida*, articulates just such an order, which one suspects would not be unsympathetic to Hordern, but which for much of the past century and a half has been subject to an ideology critique of which Hordern is innocent.

O'Donovan's own account of *politics*. In O'Donovan's theo-political work, the account of created order's restoration only lends a baseline of reality to political life, most easily described as social life, and most fully explicated in terms of the moral life of the church. Saying this, I do not deny that Hordern also holds to 'the eschatological, Augustinian distinction between an Eden without human politics, the present where political authority serves society, and the coming Kingdom', which 'enables the insight that that the givenness of social life is not made by political authority but discovered by it'.[106] But, for example, Hordern does seem to allow an analogy to be drawn more closely between the affective participation in worldly order generated by the experience of salvation in Israel and the church, and affective participation in the status quo of political life as such.

It is true that O'Donovan's political theology also fundamentally relates particular and universal, inasmuch as its universal account of political authority is hewn from the canonical history of God's works.[107] All political authority, in some way, is located in divine providence, and rightly for him, an understanding of that must be won through attending to the story of God's ways with God's people. Yet in *Desire of the Nations* and *Ways of Judgment* there is an ecclesial particularity to the fuller appropriation of restored creation. That, I think, produces some tension with O'Donovan's earlier moral theology, and seemingly with Hordern's less restrained theo-politics.

Scholars have often attributed O'Donovan's restraint to his 'dispensationalist' grounding of politics in providence and his rejection of the idea that politics is, instead, moored in creation.[108] (In this way O'Donovan is perhaps classifiable as Augustinian rather than Thomist, with the caveat that this distinction, in his own thought and the thought of others, is not quite as secure as it might have previously seemed.)[109] That is exactly right, since for O'Donovan politics 'belongs within the category of history, not of nature': '[P]olitical order is a *providential* ordering.'[110] Judgement, after all, the

---

Gorringe levels the same charge at O'Donovan, by implication. For Hordern, I think, 'natural law' seems more straightforwardly considered in purely positive terms than for O'Donovan, where Christological concentration exerts more conceptual control. I mean this critically, but should note that Peter Scott intends to extend *Desire*'s motif of 'Restoration' and corollary account of 'natural right' further, indeed basing that 'further' on claims about nature's eschatological fluidity, in order to remedy the features of O'Donovan's political theology I too worry about. He writes: '[T]hose who live "closest" to nature, or who are the principal mediators of nature to society, or who are denied access to natural goods, may be those who are best able to speak of this dynamic order'. 'Return to the Vomit of "Legitimation"?' in *Royal Priesthood*, 361.

[106] Hordern, *Political Affections*, 245.
[107] In a different way, *post*-apostolic history too, itself subject to divine activity – a strong notion of providence across the centuries that is markedly different from the implication of a 'fall' into Constantinianism found elsewhere.
[108] See Chaplin's theoretically precise challenge (Chaplin, 'Political Eschatology', 296–304).
[109] O'Donovan wrote earlier: 'It was at this point that Aquinas sharply diverged from the Augustinian tradition to re-establish the connection, carefully severed by Augustine, between earthly politics and humanity's final good'. 'Augustinian Ethics', 48. Later, at least, O'Donovan sees their divergence as not insurmountable (see O'Donovan, *Ways*, 60), but would not go quite so far, I think, as recent attempts to find a 'naturalness' to political authority in Augustine, and by so doing to draw him closer to Aquinas, found in Gregory and Joseph Clair, 'Augustinianisms and Thomisms', in *The Cambridge Companion to Political Theology*.
[110] O'Donovan, 'Deliberation, History and Reading: A Response to Schweiker and Wolterstorff', *Scottish Journal of Theology* 51, no. 1 (2010): 127–44, 137.

core of O'Donovan's proposal, presupposes an actual wrong, and therefore the fall.[111] Some readers, among them Jonathan Cole, have presented this providential grounding contrastively against O'Donovan's own embryonic political theology, for instance *Resurrection and Moral Order*'s brief mention of 'institutions of government' among a list of 'natural structures of life in the world', taken to mean that 'politics might in fact have prelapsarian origins'.[112] (From our reading of 'The Natural Ethic', we can see that this too enthusiastically understands 'natural' to mean 'created'; natural, for O'Donovan, has always included *post-lapsum* historical provisions.) In saying this, Cole recognizes the distinctions within Chaplin's interpretation of O'Donovan's mature position, in which 'salvation *restores and vindicates* the created orders of *society*, but *restrains and disciplines* the providential order of *government*'.[113] But Cole wants us to 'locate the *esse* of political authority in the created order', as he thinks *Resurrection and Moral Order* did, and 'to locate its *bene esse* in Christ's redemption of the whole created order, which is to say in the providential realm of history'.[114] By placing politics more squarely in the scheme of created order and its redemption, Cole intends also to recognize a middle term, the *male esse* of creatures' perversion of creation's form, in order to help O'Donovan ward off the impression that by grounding politics in providence alone the evil of tyranny is ascribed to God.[115]

Cole's concern with Chaplin's 'distinction between the redemption of society and the taming of political authority' – which I think is an accurate reading of O'Donovan – is that it is not clear how it 'can resolve the question of how O'Donovan's providentialist account of the ontology of political authority can explain its ability to evoke a free and intelligible human response if it is not grounded in the regularity of the created order like other authorities'.[116] With that grounding, Cole means to create space in political theology for an extended notion of the common good, besides remedial judgement.[117] Much as, I think, do those 'Augustinian' political theologians who read Augustine as more proximate to Aquinas and therefore government as 'consisting in organising and facilitating social life as much as protecting it against wrong'.[118] I am not unsympathetic. Yet it is worth seeing that the same grounding in creation and new creation, without the kind of careful specifications that Chaplin's analysis, for instance, would demand,

---

[111] That is not to say O'Donovan means 'judgement' purely in the sense of retrospective condemnation, though critical readers seem to have assumed it. As de Graaff says, for O'Donovan judgement 'consists in forward looking policy', too ('to Judge or not to Judge', 299). Cf. O'Donovan, *Ways*, 8–10, 61–3.

[112] Jonathan Cole, 'Towards a Christian Ontology of Political Authority: The Relationship Between Created Order and Providence in Oliver O'Donovan's Theology of Political Authority', *Studies in Christian Ethics* 32, no. 3 (2019): 307–25, 316 – quoting *Resurrection*, 58.

[113] Ibid., 322, quoting Chaplin, 'Political Eschatology', 296. Chaplin thinks that for O'Donovan liberal society's structures of 'natural right' (which correspond to 'Restoration'), are 'evidently parallel to the varying manifestations of "natural authority"' in *Resurrection*, but that these are distinct from government in the purest sense of the execution of right, 'needed in our present age, but … not grounded in created order in the same way that natural social structures are' (296–7).

[114] Cole, 'Towards', 322.

[115] Ibid., 324.

[116] Ibid., 323.

[117] Cf. Biggar, 'On Defining Political Authority as an Act of Judgment: A Discussion of Oliver O'Donovan's *The Ways of Judgment* (Part I)', *Political Theology* 9, no. 3 (2008): 273–93.

[118] De Graaff's description (300), though he also does not enter the debate.

can equally open up possibilities like those Gorringe sees as actualized in Hordern. If Gorringe projects those possibilities upon more dubious tendencies of Hordern's book indiscriminately, it does not mean that a worry that problematic use may be made of the ascription of naturalness to political authority is unfounded (nor, for that matter, a worry that equivalent problematic use may be made of natural law in ethics).

Perhaps that is only as much as to say that the doctrine of creation, as hamartiology and eschatology, to name but two others, can be appealed to in political theology for diverse ends. That is a rather lame conclusion, but its implication is that we should be careful to specify what exactly we wish for, if we want O'Donovan to relate creation or eschatology more directly to political life (that is, positively rather than by negation).[119] Furthermore, if we would aim – like a Mathewes or a Gregory – for a closer analogy between the life of heaven (the life, that is, of love) and the life of the secular, earthly polis, we would do well not to lose our grasp of the other Augustinian commitments O'Donovan holds besides those shared by 'political Augustinianism', namely Christ-centredness and confidence in Christ's distinctive presence in his body, the church.[120]

I do not engage theo-political debates further; this study's purview is necessarily limited. In a sense, the case I have been making is the inverse of what Cole proposes: not so much that O'Donovan should ground politics in creation, instead of providence and the particularity of Israel and the church[121] – nor for that matter simply in eschatology[122] – but that O'Donovan give us an ecclesially determined *ethics* as duly attentive to sin, providence and the kingdom as it is to creation. That, I think, would yield a modified political theology, but that is not my focus here. In the next chapter, I explore how *Ethics as Theology* both frustrates and fulfils the development of a moral vision along the lines I have pointed towards thus far.

---

[119] Gregory shows how doctrines of eschatology – in its 'reserve' – and sin are important for the Augustinian realism of Niebuhr and Markus (Gregory, *Politics and the Order of Love*, 93).

[120] Stewart-Kroeker takes a lead from Gregory here, but advances upon it. See *Pilgrimage*, chapter 5, 'The Body of Christ: Church as the Site of Formation'. The Christological and ecclesiological determination can be emphasized without the conflations of Milbank, to which Gregory rightly reacts in *Politics and the Order of Love* – perhaps overreacts.

[121] Cole's interesting article might be a little unguarded regarding that implication, and perhaps could have made it clearer that we do not have to play the two off against each other (if, as I hope, that is what he too thinks).

[122] As refreshing as Doherty's 'The Kingdom of God and the Economic System' is, that is a worry.

5

Remapping

Ethics as Theology

Introduction

In an illuminating autobiographical note in the preface to *Self, World, and Time*, the first of three volumes that make up *Ethics as Theology*, O'Donovan recounts an experience of waiting in Canterbury Cathedral for a ceremony to begin, meditating upon the book he brought with him in order to while away the time – Thomas à Kempis's *The Imitation of Christ*. Contemplating it, he writes, 'created a healthy disturbance in my mind. ... I was prompted to ask further about the gift of the Spirit and its implications for the forceful moral objectivism of my *Resurrection and Moral Order*. A "Pentecost and Moral Agency", perhaps?'[1] This asking further began 'yet another turn around the floor with that "bad idea" ... Christian Ethics'.[2]

What we have before us, then, is a return to moral-theological first things. (In that return – indeed in the whole sweep of O'Donovan's literary production – we find something like the arc O'Donovan himself saw in the *oeuvre* of Paul Ramsey.)[3] *Ethics as Theology* revisits the themes of *Resurrection and Moral Order*, but it modulates them into a new key. The task of this chapter is therefore to stimulate discussion about the ways in which it does so, especially as regards the place of eschatology.

As with the previous chapter, our focus – plus the constraints of space – requires that much be left aside. What is forfeited is at least as great as before, and probably greater. *Ethics as Theology* includes passages of constructive comment upon just about every major question of fundamental moral theology, passages of deepened engagement with particular conversation partners (Cicero or Kant; Milbank or Lacoste) and contributions to particular ethical issues, especially in *Entering into Rest*'s chapters on work, friendship and truthfulness. Many of these aspects, regrettably, I cannot touch on. And what is also forfeited is further reflection on the new *mode* of moral-theological work that O'Donovan is crafting here. His late style has a meandering quality, though in its own way, this project is systematic as well as digressive. Might it be an 'irregular

---

[1] O'Donovan, *Self, World, and Time*, xii.
[2] Ibid., vii.
[3] Bookended first by *Basic Christian Ethics* and last by research on Jonathan Edwards, an 'opportunity to return to the theological roots of ethics'. 'Paul Ramsey: 1913–88', 90.

Christian ethics', akin to Barth's description of 'irregular dogmatics'? It is unfortunately true that 'the reader ... may sometimes feel forgotten, even lost, within a labyrinthine internal monologue'.[4] It is also true that in these books, more so than ever before, O'Donovan seems to consider his work something other than mere scholarship: an approach that is balm to some and irritation to others. For one of the latter, *Self, World, and Time* seems to 'hold itself in significant ways in isolation from the debates of the Church at large and from the etiquette of the contemporary academy'.[5]

Whatever that judgement's veracity, much in *Ethics as Theology* does take it beyond theoretical brilliance, and into the realm of spiritual and devotional classics (if of a rarefied kind!). The trilogy's second volume, *Finding and Seeking*, one reader observes, 'combines scholarly precision in ethics with a richness of ... spiritual wisdom unfolding a vision of life in the Spirit'.[6] To read it, says another, 'is to sit with a wise, compassionate and toughminded spiritual director through a meditation on the business of gaining a self. This is a profound, pastoral, almost parental preparation for Christian action in the world'.[7] A dust jacket recommendation of the third volume, *Entering into Rest*, describes it as 'a profound encouragement on our pilgrimage to the God of love'.[8] 'Were I a bishop', a final theologian tells us, *Ethics as Theology* 'would be a primary examination text in pastoral care for all seminarians in my charge'.[9]

It follows, then, as with earlier chapters, that the proportions of this chapter of my critical investigation *by no means* reflect the ratio of material that I find deeply illuminating in relation to that about which I am less convinced. Of necessity, I select a handful of topics pertinent to my theme, and select texts that best display their dimensions. I begin by asking further after O'Donovan's understanding of the developments *Ethics as Theology* represents upon *Resurrection and Moral Order* – developments not incidental to the question of eschatology's import. Chief among the developments, on my reading, are twin advances in conceiving the moral life's subjective, lived character. Fresh insights into self and time now take their place alongside a finessed construal of world. The fruitful correlation of these terms with the three theological virtues – self (the agent) with faith, world (the order of values) with love, and time (the horizon before which we deliberation on action) with hope – yields a host of insights, including, as their shadow, accounts of sins against self, world (and the other) and time.[10] It also finds a more fitting role for hope in particular than the etiolated one it seemed to occupy in O'Donovan's earlier work.[11]

---

[4] Clare Carlisle, 'Cry for Wisdom', *Times Literary Supplement* 5837 (2015): 28.
[5] Samuel Wells, review of *Self, World, and Time*, *Theology* 117, no. 5 (2014): 392–4, 393–4.
[6] David Cloutier, review of *Finding and Seeking*, *Pro Ecclesia* 26, no. 3 (2017): 333–6, 336.
[7] Doug Gay, review of *Finding and Seeking*, 365. Similar sentiments are expressed in Cloutier's review – *Pro Ecclesia* 26, no. 3 (2017): 333–6.
[8] From Hans Boersma's dust jacket recommendation of *Entering into Rest*.
[9] Nicholas M. Healy, review of *Finding and Seeking*, *Studies in Christian Ethics* 29, no. 3 (2016): 359–62, 362.
[10] Again, an interesting comparison could be drawn with Kelsey's threefold account of sins 'against' – both O'Donovan and Kelsey in this regard provide fine-tuned variations upon an essentially Barthian theme.
[11] The intensified attention to temporality and its phenomenological texture are partly owed, I think, to the fruitful engagement with Lacoste.

Yet some of the old habits may persist, and in some ways the marginalization of eschatology in O'Donovan's model of moral reason is, curiously, more patent in *Self, World, and Time* and in *Finding and Seeking* than earlier. That occlusion, I argue, is also seen in the apparently largely formal bearing of the kingdom of God on present action, an abstraction that may explain O'Donovan's continued incomprehension of Moltmann's ethical priorities, as well as the lapses of attention in his interpretation of the biblical book of James. In search of further reasons why this occlusion might inhere in O'Donovan's thought, I turn next to the definitional demarcation of doctrine and ethics expressed and evolving throughout O'Donovan's career and again apparent in *Ethics as Theology*. Ruminations on this theme lead into a final section in which I find, in *Entering into Rest*, a fuller reckoning with eschatology's moral import, once again interlaced with ecclesiological explorations – and wonder how this knits with what has gone before.

'A necessary complement'

I have already intimated that O'Donovan considers *Ethics as Theology* as something of a return to first principles, an opportunity to re-imagine – to remap, as I have put it – the foundations of moral theology that *Resurrection and Moral Order* laid out earlier. But now that O'Donovan has made this return, how does he think that the two fit together? In *Self, World, and Time*'s fifth chapter, 'The Task of Moral Theology', the question is addressed directly. It is worth hearing the context in which it comes up, because now O'Donovan locates the relationship of the two projects in a movement of thought central to the theological argument of *Ethics as Theology*. Here he is discussing one of the newly expanded foci, the agent-self:

> If ... we inquire how the agent is centred in him- or herself, competent and empowered, exercising freedom in self-identity, the answer can only be that the agent is centred also upon this absolute centre, the moment of history at which the name 'Jesus Christ' was made known for the redemption of the world ... Jesus' resurrection from the dead .... With the self made sure upon that historical centre, the agent is free to move in either of the two directions practical reason requires, towards world and towards time ... in one direction from the empty tomb of Easter to the beauty and order of the life that was the creator's gift to his creation and is restored there ... in the other direction from the empty tomb to a new moment of participation in God's work and being ... . The risen life of the last Adam gives hope to the first Adam in the midst of God's created work. The risen life of the last Adam inaugurates the Creator's purpose to consummate all life, past, present, and future, in the reign of life. In the empty tomb we are shown heaven and earth, we are promised that they shall be restored, not destroyed and brought to nothing, and we are taught to look for new activity, new deeds, new possibilities that prepare the way for a new heaven and a new earth. These two directions are not alternatives, to one or the other of which Christian thought might equally

well turn, adopting a 'conservative' or a 'radical' posture to taste. Neither are they sequential directions, that we should satisfy the demands of created order first and newness second afterwards. ... The two directions are mutually reinforcing angles of vision that depend for their intelligibility upon each other.[12]

At this point, the relation between this and the earlier work is treated explicitly. O'Donovan explains that *Resurrection and Moral Order* 'adopted an angle of vision that looked principally towards the objective order of created goods and the restoration of human agency by the resurrection of Christ'.[13] This perspective seemed important, he continues, and still does, 'in the light of the civilisation's forgetfulness of created order, which persists, "green" issues notwithstanding, to the present day'.[14] It was not just wider societal amnesia that demanded that approach, though, but theological forgetfulness:

> The neo-orthodoxy that put Christ at the centre without putting him *at the centre of the created world* gave birth to an Ethics that danced like an angel on the head of a needle, wholly lacking worldly dimensions and focused solely on a conversion encounter with the cross. The sublation of Ethics into faith ... was founded on the simply assurance that the worldly content of Ethics was blandly self-explanatory and needed no interrogation, but only to be situated in relation to theology. A generation which saw the normalization of nuclear weapons and biotechnology could hardly sustain that assurance, unless with its eyes tightly shut. *Resurrection and Moral Order*, therefore, undertook to validate the interest of Theological Ethics in elucidating worldly order.[15]

O'Donovan's own reading of that earlier work's goal coheres well enough with my depiction of it, and his account of the discernment of the times that sponsored its emphasis also supports what has been argued. The identity of this unreferenced 'neo-orthodoxy' is a little elusive, though, and it seems to me that this lack of specification hinders the case somewhat. Whose writings and influence is meant: Barth or Bonhoeffer? Bultmann – certainly it is often the existentialist aspects that are at issue – or Brunner? Reinhold Niebuhr? In some ways, the grounds for criticism recalled in *Self, World, and Time* do seem similar to those that motivate O'Donovan's criticism of Lutheran law-and-gospel theology in earlier works. The clearest sense of what O'Donovan sees at issue is, however, found not in relation to any of these figures – though there are rewarding cameos for Bonhoeffer and Barth in the book[16] – but in relation to the less influential figure of P. T. Forsyth. Named in the full passage, Forsyth is also mentioned earlier, in the context of a discussion of 'Authority', where

---

[12] O'Donovan, *Self, World, and Time*, 92–3.
[13] Ibid., 93.
[14] Ibid.
[15] Ibid.
[16] If not much engagement with recent scholarship concerning Barth's ethics. There is one reference to Nigel Biggar's earlier *The Hastening that Waits* (Oxford: Clarendon Press, 1996) in *Finding and Seeking*.

O'Donovan writes that Forsyth fails 'to give sufficient weight to the purpose and moral order of the world *as creation* ... . Forsyth's concept of the ethical never really broadens out beyond a pinpoint moment of motivation, never takes in the breadth and scope of wisdom as it is spoken of in the Old Testament'.[17] That may be so,[18] but without further specification, we have to take on trust O'Donovan's implicit suggestion that 'neo-orthodoxy' was sufficiently productive of moral-theological confusion to occasion that strong objectivism.

At any rate, O'Donovan's defence of *Resurrection and Moral Order*'s theological coherence and timeliness leads to an explanation of the present work's aims:

> What follows may now be regarded as a necessary complement to it, its angle of vision turned principally towards the subjective renewal of agency and its opening to the forward calling of God. The restored agent is also the renewed agent, filled with the life of God poured out within the world. In comparing the two books in this way, I speak only of their general directions. Much must be said here about the objective order of created goods; rather more was said there about the renewal of human agency than was apparent.[19]

It is a neat, attractive explanation, though the claim that *Resurrection and Moral Order* adopted a particular angle of vision does seem to smooth over its own self-presentation as *An Outline for Evangelical Ethics*: a complete primer. Similarly, while coherent with the notion that this 'Pentecost and Moral Agency' is a sequel, what we read here seems to mitigate the force of the question that O'Donovan says he was prompted to ask – surely something more like a revision than a supplementary perspective is being entertained when speaking of the 'implications for the forceful moral objectivism' of the earlier book. Certainly, some of the differences between the two simply reveal different emphases within a consistent undertaking. And there are certainly plenty of points of continuity. But there are also points at which decisive departures are made from the earlier work.

One example would be the topic of freedom and authority. Self-consciously, O'Donovan espouses a more nuanced view than in *Resurrection and Moral Order*, now defining authority as 'an *event in which a reality is communicated to practical reason by a social communication*' – as 'mediated' to a greater extent than was acknowledged

---

[17] O'Donovan, *Self, World, and Time*, 58.
[18] Other scholarship supports O'Donovan's designation. In fact, one assessment of Forsyth's thought draws on *Resurrection* to criticize Forsyth on similar grounds. See Jason Goroncy, *Hallowed Be Thy Name: The Sanctification of All in the Soteriology of P.T. Forsyth* (London/New York: Bloomsbury T & T Clark, 2013), 76–7. Note, though, that while Goroncy follows the gist of *Resurrection*'s case for the resurrection's 'vindication of the providential unfolding of created order within history', the passage concludes thus: '[W]e may anticipate the redemption of creation as its renewal and completion, but not its restoration; for Christian hope is placed not in a renovated Eden but in a hallowed new heaven and earth.' (Goroncy does not seem to realize that in this he places the accent in a different place than did *Resurrection*).
[19] O'Donovan, *Self, World, and Time*, 93.

before.[20] He still believes, to my mind correctly, that freedom and obedience must correspond, and he maintains that authority is the objective correlate of freedom:

> All this must be said, and yet freedom is a *wider category* than authority, so that my phrase was too loose to make a satisfactory definition. Not every exercise of freedom is, directly at least, a response to authority. Authority is not simply vested in the world, self, and time as soon as we awake to them. That would collapse the dialectic of freedom and authority onto a flat plane, reducing all authority to self-evidence, all obedience to commonsense … . And that is why my account of 'moral authority' in *Resurrection and Moral Order* was flat and this-worldly. In studying *political* authority subsequently … I laid more emphasis on authority's lack of perspicuity, and this emphasis must now be accommodated within the general theory. … Authority, we must say, is a *focused disclosure* of reality, one that demands we turn our attention away from everything else and concentrate it in this one place.[21]

We should welcome what we find here and throughout *Ethics as Theology*: the threefold attentiveness to self, world and time that allows O'Donovan to shade with greater subtlety the depicted realities of the moral life. Even more interesting for my purposes than the question of freedom and authority, though, is whether and how the consideration of *hope* is another aspect of development, or even one of departure.

Hope

O'Donovan has by no means become a utopian or an apocalypticist. He is ever ascetical in his attitude to philosophizing or theologizing about the future, and to its moral value. There are, he says, in *Self, World, and Time*, many kinds of future, each with its own ontic status, and they are not equally pertinent for ethics. There is 'the future we imagine, prompted by fears or hopes or lazy presumptions of regularity. Such projected futures are easy enough to construct in imagination, but ontologically they are shallow; they make little claim on our belief'.[22] There is a theologically genuine 'absolute future', too, 'that winds up future, present and past in the appearing of Christ and the judgment of God on history'.[23] That future, we might say, marked much of the horizon in *Desire of the Nations* and *Ways of Judgment*. Since it 'has the ontic status of a promise', however, it is 'partially accessible to knowledge as the promise is heard and believed'.[24]

But, '[o]ur responsibility is not to any of these futures, real or imaginary, any more than it is for the past'.[25] Why not – and what future is our responsibility?

---

[20] Ibid., 53.
[21] Ibid., 53–4.
[22] Ibid., 16.
[23] Ibid.
[24] Ibid.
[25] Ibid.

We do not attend to any of these futures, any more than we attend to the past, *deliberatively*. I reflect, but cannot deliberate, on what I ought to have done in the past week. I imagine, but cannot deliberate about what my life will be like many years hence. I may hope for, but cannot plan to bring about, the coming of the Kingdom of God. Reflection on things remembered, anticipation of things projected, feed and shape my actual deliberations, for prudence, the virtue proper to deliberation, weighs up existing states and projected outcomes. But the focus of deliberation is not on these futures but on the immediate future, the forward-looking present, the future as it beckons to the present, the present as it opens to the future. To define this moment more precisely: it is the *available* future, the possibility that lies open to our action.[26]

The insights formed by this understanding of the 'available' future are abundant. But we are bound to ask about the way in which the ultimate future is kept at bay in the sphere of ethics. O'Donovan is alert to the question: 'Does the Kingdom of God, then, not overshadow the available future and make it possible? Is the remote future merely "absolute"? Or does it, as in the first proclamation of Jesus, "draw near"?'[27] O'Donovan's answer sets the terms for eschatology's presence in *Ethics as Theology*:

> Certainly it draws near, and in that there lies the importance of *hope* to deliberation. But we must not think we can reach out and grab it. Our first thought must be to allow the horizon to be the horizon, to resist the temptation of taking over the ultimate and managing it. Practical reason is not a way of organizing the future.[28]

The ethicist's vocation – or, better, the vocation of any responsible agent – demands disavowal of prediction as much as projection:

> 'I am no prophet, nor a prophet's son!' (Amos 7.14) is a motto for every moralist, professional and amateur. If we knew the story of the future hidden in God's foreknowledge, we should be beyond deliberation, beyond action, even beyond caring. 'The kingdom of God is not coming with observation' (Lk. 17.20). Even of the Son of God through whom God acts in history it is said that the day and the hour are not revealed to him. The price of agency is to know the future only indirectly, that we may venture on it as an open possibility. The future of prediction, dreary with anxiety or buoyant with hope, has to be held at bay, so that we may use this moment of time to do something, however modest, that is worthwhile and responsible, something to endure before the throne of judgment.[29]

If eschatology is certainly here in the sober horizon of judgement, once more, and newly drawing near in hope, then O'Donovan hyper-sensitivity to hope's potential to mislead is still evident. Its buoyancy is to be avoided if it issues in prediction, and it is

---

[26] Ibid., 16–17.
[27] Ibid., 17.
[28] Ibid.
[29] Ibid.

placed parallel to a vice (anxiety) in a way he would be unlikely so directly to do with the theological virtues of faith or love.

Pairing hope with a single vice might be thought curious, too. After all, at least on a Thomist telling, there are vices either side, as it were, the theological virtue, and the one paired with anxiety (or despair) is presumption. Granted, as David Elliot writes, presumption is 'false and bloated hope' that 'subverts moral agency' and is 'often confused with theological hope itself'.[30] But O'Donovan again seems to risk their conflation. And lest we be misled by that mention of 'bloated' into thinking that one can have too much hope, we must emphasize that presumption is not true but *false* hope. Again, if real hope is a gift of God (a 'theological virtue' in the true sense), then there is no problematic 'excess' beyond any 'prudent' mean; it knows no excess to be avoided because its revealed object is the giver of the gift, God, who is perfect plenitude.[31]

I have focused on what may be an indicatively distrustful mention of hope, there, which is reminiscent of O'Donovan's earlier work. But in *Ethics as Theology*, O'Donovan does generally clarify the place of genuine hope in the moral life. The importance of hope to deliberation – to framing action at 'the opportune time'[32] – represents a seam to follow through the work, there in the final chapter of *Self, World, and Time*, and coming to fruition in *Finding and Seeking*. A good part of *Finding and Seeking*'s treatment re-presents the first volume's treatment,[33] but the account is extended, and it informs the superb reflections on deliberation and discernment that comprise the book's two final chapters.[34] So prominent is hope within *Ethics as Theology*'s account of moral reason, and so convincing the articulation of how the future horizon becomes 'an opening for reasonable action',[35] that it may seem churlish to maintain reservations about O'Donovan's handling of eschatology. Yet I do still have reservations, which are best explained via close readings of a few particular passages of *Finding and Seeking*.

Moral reason and the kingdom of God

A lengthy excursus on the twelfth chapter of Luke's gospel allows O'Donovan to further distinguish hope from anticipation, observing 'how largely such a critique' – of anticipation – 'figures in Jesus' own teaching about the ultimate future'.[36] Having sifted out anticipation, O'Donovan says, the gospel's teaching is precisely about 'the

---

[30] Elliot, *Hope and Christian Ethics*, 111. On presumption, see also Josef Pieper, *On Hope* (San Francisco: Ignatius Press, 1986), 65–72. In terms of popular-philosophical attempts to grasp hope's promise in this regard, a fascinating pair to compare here are Terry Eagleton, *Hope Without Optimism* (New Haven/London: Yale University Press, 2015), and Roger Scruton, *The Uses of Pessimism* (London: Atlantic Books, 2010).
[31] On this boundlessness of the theological virtues, see Long, *Christian Ethics*, 21.
[32] O'Donovan, *Finding and Seeking*, 146–7.
[33] See e.g. O'Donovan, *Finding and Seeking*, 150–2.
[34] For a fine reading of these, see Errington, *Every Good Path*.
[35] Ibid., 215. Cf. 233.
[36] Ibid., 152.

great eschatological redirection of practical reason'.[37] We are eager to ask what this might mean, and so too, it appears, is O'Donovan: '[H]ow does hope transform the immediate horizon?'[38] But the answer he finds in the text is 'astonishingly spare' – it is simply the demand for 'watchfulness'.[39]

The parable O'Donovan has in mind, 'of the servants who stay up for their master's return', 'is one that echoes through the teaching of Jesus'.[40] Yet whereas 'Mark's version mentions a variety of duties' and 'Matthew's the duty of the household steward', here in Luke's version 'the servants do nothing at all but stand around in their household clothes ready for their chores whenever the knock on the door shall come'.[41] O'Donovan takes from this 'striking adaptation' that it 'highlights the *formal contentlessness* of the practical task given to us':

> No definite thing, or things, must be done in the light of the promised future. The single category that embraces all the many things we may have to do is waiting, attending wholly and with concentration focused on what is *not yet* happening, so that whatever *is* happening is handled with a mind supremely bent on something else. That gaze into the distance, causing all intervening action, as it were, to disappear, is Luke's key to life lived hopefully.[42]

This Lukan 'formal contentlessness', then, may serve to reify O'Donovan's characteristic way of exhibiting eschatology's import: God's future sheds light on the moment of action, on the path before our feet – but it does not determine it. In *Ethics as Theology*, this aspect is brilliantly expounded with reference to the Holy Spirit, the one whom we ask in prayer 'for the reconstruction and re-attunement of our moral imaginary, bringing the world before our eyes as created, redeemed, and destined for fulfilment'.[43] Yet is there not something a little unsatisfactory about this, not unrelated to the discomfiture that I and others have felt about O'Donovan's work more broadly? (What, for one thing, of the normative force of Mark and Matthew's content-full wakefulness, which seem to be passed by?) Reflecting upon the treatment of Moltmann in the following pages of *Finding and Seeking* can help us flesh this worry out further.

At this point, O'Donovan turns aside to note with bafflement a pair of contradictory pieces of Moltmann's thought. Moltmann acknowledges, O'Donovan says, that eschatology cannot be based on extrapolation, given hope's basis in God's promise. But Moltmann also insists on anticipatory 'intrinsic possibilities', and it is from these that he has developed his 'ethico-political program for the life of hope in the world'.[44] And this mistakes hope's moral function:

---

[37] Ibid., 154.
[38] Ibid.
[39] Ibid.
[40] Ibid.
[41] Ibid.
[42] Ibid., 154–5.
[43] Ibid., 127.
[44] Ibid., 164.

Hope cannot be the answer to any question of the form, 'what shall we do next?' It is the *condition* on which that question can be raised and answered – answered on its own terms according to criteria of practical reasonableness. Hope … cannot ground the program Moltmann elicits from it: the struggle for economic justice, the struggle against political oppression, the struggle for solidarity against alienation.[45]

Now, I agree that there is some reason to be baffled at a contradiction between the recognition that eschatology cannot be based on extrapolation and the assertion that there are eschatological 'intrinsic possibilities' (depending on what that latter statement means). But, as I will seek to show very simply in what follows, I also think there is good reason to be unsettled by O'Donovan's incomprehension of the more basically defensible elements of Moltmann's project. There may also good reason to be baffled at a contradiction in a piece of O'Donovan's own reasoning, which is connected to this incomprehension, and to which we will turn subsequently.

O'Donovan finds nothing objectionable in 'the political clothes in which Moltmann has dressed his doctrine of hope', finding them 'respectable, neatly cut, and fashionable', if bearing the appearance of having 'been slept in'![46] But, O'Donovan cautions immediately: 'No agenda for practical Christian witness can have universal and timeless validity',[47] and we therefore have 'to ask how the elements of this program, with its distinctive priorities, were come by. The suggestion that they were found on the straight road from the resurrection of Christ and the promise of the Kingdom is frankly unbelievable'.[48]

I do not doubt that plenty of suggestions in Moltmann's theology and ethics, or in particular his *Ethics of Hope*, are less than carefully asserted.[49] Yet, as before, I find something unsatisfactory about O'Donovan's assessment of Moltmann, and want to trouble it in an exploratory but focused way.[50] To this end, I suggest we consider these passages alongside O'Donovan's moral-theological commentary on the letter of James in *Finding and Seeking*'s immediately preceding chapter. Contemplating O'Donovan's interpretation of scripture helps us see better why his worries about Moltmann

---

[45] Ibid., 165.
[46] Ibid.
[47] A similar point is, in fact, made by Moltmann – see *Ethics of Hope*, xii.
[48] O'Donovan, *Finding and Seeking*, 165.
[49] Nor do I doubt – as O'Donovan has been known to remark – that it is suspicious how similar Moltmann's vision of the kingdom of God looks to an achieved political programme of the *Socialdemokratische Partei Deutschlands*, or the like. (A similar congruence might be remarked between Hordern's vision of vindicated creation and the British Conservative Party, of course, just as one was remarked between Niebuhr's 'Heavenly City' and the United States – so Wilson Carey McWilliam, quoted in Gregory, *Politics of Love*, 18.)
[50] Compare O'Donovan's expression of incredulity about Moltmann's way of grounding ethics eschatologically to Ronald Preston's professed cynicism about the strand of the World Council of Churches' theology named 'eschatological realism' (Ronald H. Preston, *Confusions in Christian Social Ethics: Problems for Geneva and Rome* (London: SCM Press, 1994), 140–2). This ecumenical programme is one Moltmann self-consciously takes his bearings from (Moltmann, *Ethics of Hope*, xii), and though it was certainly rather incautiously broad in some of its theological brushwork, the far-reaching cynicism Preston expresses tells as much about his peculiar commitments – overriding concern for a certain understanding of the public rationality of Christian ethics, admitted agnosticism about biblical eschatology – as about any WCC document.

arise. Beside this, it advances our understanding of why O'Donovan fails to see how Moltmann can hold that a biblical-theological framework might lend certain priorities, principles or patterns to contextual moral deliberation: aids that may in fact have some kind of 'universal and timeless validity', and that authentically nudge Christians (like Moltmann) in particular directions of historically specific discernment, even as they do not stipulate particular moral policies.[51] Let us turn to O'Donovan's exegesis.

James, he says, is 'a moral treatise' that 'begins where a doctrinal treatise would end', with joy.[52] (I will return to that contrast later.) In this tract of ethical instruction, then, 'themes of Christology and redemption are notably absent'.[53] It is, in fact, an exemplary moral treatise: 'Moral teaching at its best addresses generic truths specifically, focusing on typical points of urgent need', and James' letter is 'addressed throughout to all Christians everywhere, in their most universal moral needs'.[54] Its focus is 'the paradigmatic human oppositions that generate moral need: rich and poor, sick and well, hesitant and confident'.[55] The epistle's examples 'take us to situations that typify the moral life', and *Finding and Seeking*'s largely persuasive reading ranges very widely among them (the index notes twenty-four references to the book, ranging from the first chapter to the last).[56] Of these situations, O'Donovan takes poverty and wealth as a prime illustration. He finds 'the two presented in a surprisingly parallel manner', though he does goes on to note (very briefly) James's other comments (in 4.1-6 and 5.1-6) 'on the slippery slope of wealth'.[57]

This assessment seems that they are parallel seems a little surprising to me. And in a very straightforward way, it is accordingly striking that O'Donovan fails to mention, across all of his references to the epistle, the first part of its second chapter. Consider a few lines from it:

> My brothers and sisters, do you with your acts of favouritism really believe in our glorious Lord Jesus Christ? For if a person with gold rings and in fine clothes comes into your assembly, and if a poor person in dirty clothes comes in, and if you take notice of the one wearing the fine clothes and say, 'Have a seat here, please', while to the one who is poor you say, 'Stand here', or 'Sit at my feet', have you not made distinctions among yourselves, and become judges with evil thoughts? Listen, my beloved brothers. Has not God chosen the poor in the world to be rich in faith and to be heirs of the kingdom that he has promised to those who love him? But you have dishonoured the poor. Is it not the rich who oppress you? Is it

---

[51] The way Moltmann sometimes undiscerningly constructs a counter-tradition that promotes marginal(ized) religious figures as the true bearers of Christian eschatological hope should not put us off the straightforward exegetical basis of some his claims (e.g. Moltmann, *Ethics of Hope*, 39–41). The present moral bearing of the kingdom of God is well borne out by readers of Moltmann who do not carry all of his baggage – see, e.g. Bauckham and Hart, *Hope against Hope*, 159–68.
[52] O'Donovan, *Finding and Seeking*, 142.
[53] Ibid.
[54] Ibid.
[55] Ibid.
[56] Ibid., 143
[57] Ibid.

not they who drag you into court? Is it not they who blaspheme the excellent name that was invoked over you? (Jas 2.4-7)

I am no New Testament specialist, but these verses' subject matter seems to include a few features that we were told we would not much find in the book: moral chastisement appears here in and with ecclesiological determination, alongside theological and specifically Christological reference besides a markedly asymmetrical treatment of poverty and wealth, and the relating of all this to the eschatological horizon of the kingdom of God. It is difficult to see this passage, on my reading, as descriptive of 'the formal contentlessness of the practical task given to us … in the light of the promised future'.[58] If the epistle *is* universal in ethical intent, then this passage too must have (determinate) normative force of some kind. O'Donovan's only way to deny that, given his characterization of the letter, would be to paint it as an aside – perhaps an incongruous interpolation? – comprising less-than-generic hortatory material addressed to particular churches at a particular time. But it would be decidedly unlike O'Donovan to deny normative value to such passages of situational paraenesis, and he has already told us that it 'is addressed throughout to all Christians everywhere'.[59]

My point is this: even if apparently minor, this difficulty crystallizes a few features I have paused over in earlier chapters as well as this. It is hard not to think that it is occasioned by the priority afforded to a generalizing account of ethics as concerning universal features of moral reason, an account that sometimes seems to originate in deliberate remotion from the realities Christian faith is given to believe, other than the reality of creation. (Not least, remotion from those realities of Christ, his kingdom and its concerns, his church, and the structural sur-realities of sin that oppose his reign: each present in these verses of James.) What this means is that O'Donovan's depiction of the ethical moment of obedience may have been achieved in abstraction from the content of obedience those theological particularities would give it. Relatedly, I would argue that concern for the poor is a prominent – perhaps the prominent – aspect of the formation of Christian obedience-in-action in light of the kingdom. Here in James, it appears by negation: oppression of the poor is highlighted as a particular kind of sin against God's ordering of the kingdom. If O'Donovan overstated the matter a little when he wrote that 'themes of Christology and redemption are notably absent' in James, then he followed it with a line that could have provided a clue to the way they are present there: 'Yet of all the New Testament texts none follows so closely the teachings of Jesus of Nazareth, and especially the Sermon on the Mount.'[60] Might not

---

[58] Ibid., 154.
[59] Ibid., 142.
[60] A similar kind of oversight afflicts Biggar's treatment of Barth's *The Christian Life* in *The Hastening that Waits* and 'Karl Barth's Ethics Revisited'. He cannot see the inner link between Barth's ethically suggestive notion of the hastening that waits – language Biggar likes – and Barth's governing rubric of 'revolt' – language Biggar does not. Biggar recruits the purported realism of eschatological restraint and opportunity for action in the 'messy reality' of the world, but not the directions to which Barth would have that action go. Yet I venture that those directions are more than tangentially related to Holy Scripture, despite Biggar's doubts. For a reading alert to the inner link, see Ziegler, '"To Pray, To Testify, and to Revolt"' – introduction to the recent edition of Barth, *The Christian Life* (London/New York: T&T Clark International, 2017).

the passages of James overlooked here represent one of the points at which its teaching most resonates with those teachings – which are not exactly 'astonishingly spare' taken together – and with that sermon that has been called the 'charter of the Christian life'?[61]

It is true that it would require extensive further argumentation to work from these scriptural passages, or the countless others that are congruent in conviction, to something like Moltmann's contemporary agenda (should we want to). That further argumentation cannot be pursued here – though an engagement with O'Donovan could be a good place to push it to a high level of clarity. But I think it is possible. And, to put it the other way around, it seems probable that O'Donovan's bafflement about Moltmann's claims for his ethico-political agenda is not unconnected to the way that O'Donovan's project is apparently unable to reckon fully with scriptural passages (and a long tradition beyond them) that would allow Moltmann to think he has grounds for it.[62]

It may be that here O'Donovan's exaggerated demarcation of 'moral treatise' and 'doctrinal treatise' (here, James and Romans) contributes to the oversight.[63] O'Donovan's distinction is between texts, but we might compare the similar intra-textual kind of distinction attempted by New Testament scholar David Horrell in his *Contemporary Reading of Paul's Ethics*.[64] Horrell writes that 'Paul's ethics are thoroughly grounded

---

[61] So Augustine, in his commentary. Quoted in Mattison, *Sermon on the Mount*, 1.

[62] As I was in the very last stages of finalizing the manuscript of this study, a set of essays responding to *Ethics as Theology* was published in the journal *Modern Theology*, accompanied by a response by O'Donovan. Among much interesting analysis, some of which I have latterly integrated in this chapter, Sarah Coakley's essay contains a comment which is worth relating here:

> this magisterial, but profoundly *cerebral*, undertaking in theological ethics … has already spawned, in this special journal book symposium, certain predictable criticisms of O'Donovan for failing to take on more explicitly some of the most challenging moral problems in today's society (those associated with gender and sexuality, with 'race' or racism, with the escalating division between rich and poor). [Here Coakley cites the essays by Jennifer Herdt and Charles Mathewes] But O'Donovan is by nature a "conservative" thinker, in the best sense; and seemingly these contemporary Siren voices are not ones which he wishes to allow to divert him from his core theological progression. In what follows I deliberately eschew the 'cheap' course of chiding him for these apparent oversights from an assumed position of liberal egalitarian rectitude, let alone of moral superiority. On the contrary, what I … wish to explore – in the form of a sensitive immanent critique – is what it is about the core structure of O'Donovan's theological vision that makes it hard for these particular concerns to leap to the forefront of his thinking.

Sarah Coakley, 'A Response to Oliver O'Donovan's *Ethics as Theology* Trilogy', *Modern Theology* 36, no. 1 (2020): 186–92, 187. As with my readings of earlier works of O'Donovan, I hope that the queries I raise in this section – not unrelated to 'the escalating division between rich and poor' – do not represent that 'cheap' course: the scriptural aspect to my argument is partly designed to avoid it, as is the overall attempt to attend to what Coakley calls 'the core structure of O'Donovan's theological vision' in connection with moral problems. Interestingly, Coakley herself writes, later: 'I cannot help pressing the question whether [O'Donovan's] primary adherence to the *Pauline* vision of faith, hope and love in this work finally remains undisturbed by the more challenging and radical requirements of *Jesus's* teaching on attention to the poor and dispossessed' (188). The concluding comments resonate, too: 'it is surely impossible to dissociate the life and prayer of Jesus from his urgent longing for his 'Father', for the kingdom of heaven, and for the healing and restitution of the poor, despised and dispossessed. And much of this substance is already vibrantly present in O'Donovan's trilogy, however much certain other elements seem to tame or check its radicality. Thus to do full justice to this work would take a much longer essay' (192).

[63] O'Donovan, *Finding and Seeking*, 142.

[64] David G. Horrell, *Solidarity and Difference: A Contemporary Reading of Paul's Ethics*, 2nd edn (London/New York: Bloomsbury T&T Clark, 2016).

in the myth which constitutes Paul's "theology", the story which establish the worldview and the ethos he promotes. His reflective moral arguments also depend upon this theology for their content and motivations' – particularly Christology.[65] But, Horrell continues:

> I have not, however, unlike many studies in Pauline ethics, given space to outlining specifically how eschatology, the Spirit, and so on function as motivating bases for ethical exhortation. This is in part because these represent aspects of the mythology rather than the ethics themselves; thus they convey motivations for acting ethically rather than indications as to what *constitutes* ethical action. ... It is also in part because in attempting to engage Pauline ethics in a conversation with other approaches to ethics I have sought to express the exhortations of these ethics in terms that our meaningful outside the bounds of theological discourse.[66]

I am not making any comment here on Horrell's endeavour (the book is full of insight), but I would suggest that O'Donovan's conception of his own work's task would not usually be expressed in terms quite like these, and that, therefore, we should ask how and why a similar demarcation seems to obtain in passages like those we addressed earlier. Even if it were a genuinely available distinction to make vis-à-vis Paul (I have doubts), surely it would – or should – be nigh on impossible to make with regard to Christian theological interpretation of the prophets, the evangelists and John of Patmos, the testimonies of each of whom are, rightly enough, authoritative for O'Donovan's constructive Christian ethics.

It is unavailable, I would claim, because for Christian theology, and thus ethics, the present bearing of the kingdom is not just an initial impetus for Christian morality, a formal source of intentions or basis of motivation. It does not just open up the ground before our feet for action determined wholly by other criteria that can be filled out in a way entirely intelligible beyond the Christian church. If scripture and much tradition are right, it makes perceptible demands upon that morality, too: 'formed references', in the Barthian phrase. And that means that in concrete history, faithful moral deliberation and discernment can be tracked not only in its moral-psychological operations but also in the particular direction of its attentions and the peculiar shaping of its affections. The kingdom of God, to put it technically, is for Christian ethics action-motivating *and* action-guiding. All of that is not to gain say that very often indeed those criteria that determine faithful Christian action will be shared with others, or at least rationally accessible to them – to a high degree, even. But Christians have reasons to think that their moral deliberation can and should be open to concrete policies made uniquely intelligible by the revelation of eschatological reality and, to make the bolder claim, by its presence in the Spirit.

It seems that defining the demarcation between doctrinal and moral in a more exclusive way than might be appropriate is necessary for O'Donovan, given certain commitments he holds about ethics as a discipline, drawn in contrast to doctrine.

---

[65] Ibid., 306.
[66] Ibid., 307.

Though at certain other moments of his writing O'Donovan shows himself exemplary in his awareness of the potential moral significance of the whole array of scriptural genres – to earlier examples I would add here a wonderful recent piece on Galatians – this disciplinary distinction derives from a more bifurcating reading (or, as I have said, requires it).[67] The particular description of James vis-à-vis Paul here fits neatly O'Donovan's characteristic dispersal of tasks to theology and ethics, a pattern that we find across his writing, and it is to his construction of that disciplinary distinction that we turn now, with an eye to its effects on the place given to eschatology.

Doctrine and ethics

Analysis of the place of eschatology in O'Donovan's moral theology has proved knottily entangled with general questions about the relation of doctrine and ethics. Here, I approach the theme from the other end, addressing the general questions directly and only subsequently eschatology's part in them. While all of O'Donovan's work presupposes an operative account of that relationship, *Ethics as Theology*, as the title suggests, represents his mature position. *Self, World, and Time* in particular distinguishes the two schematically, and I begin here with the relevant passages, introducing some comparable recent treatments: an essay on 'The Trinity and the Moral Life' and a review essay responding to the systematician Nicholas M. Healy's critical reading of Hauerwas and entitled, tellingly, 'What Shall We Do?'[68] Appraising ourselves of the key features of the disciplinary demarcation and interrelationship O'Donovan conceives in these pieces will help us contextualize our broader study. Yet I find nothing particularly objectionable within them, and much to appreciate. Moreover, it seems to me that the account we find in these texts does not really explain the ongoing difficulties with the handling of *eschatological* doctrine. Nor, alone, does an earlier piece 'How Can Theology Be Moral?', though examining it will help us discover the rudimental form of the distinction, essentially contiguous with the later treatments. My hunch is that the fault line is most easily seen in another earlier essay: 'What Can Ethics Know about God?' (Perhaps the titles of these latter pieces already give something away.)

In 'What Can Ethics Know about God?', O'Donovan shows himself aware of the charge that he neglects eschatology, and sets out to address it directly. But to a striking degree, this essay shows him unable or unwilling to overcome it, for reasons that will be familiar from our earlier chapters and intelligible given the other articulations of ethics' disciplinary tasks in distinction from doctrine – but that are stated most baldly here. Some sense of O'Donovan's struggle towards a more adequate account of the relationship between doctrine and ethics is seen in passages from the final essay that I

---

[67] See 'Scripture and Christian Ethics', and 'The Moral Authority of Scripture'. For the reading of Galatians, see O'Donovan, 'Flesh and Spirit', in *Galatians and Christian Theology: Justification, the Gospel, and Ethics in Paul's Letter*, ed. Mark W. Elliot, Scott J. Hafemann, N. T. Wright and John Frederick (Grand Rapids: Baker Academic, 2014).

[68] O'Donovan, 'The Trinity and the Moral Life: *In Memoriam John Webster*', in *A Transforming Vision: Knowing and Loving the Triune God*, ed. George Westhaver (London: SCM, 2018); O'Donovan, 'What Shall We Do?' *Times Literary Supplement* 5831 (2014): 24.

consider here, 'Sanctification and Ethics', which overlaps with slightly revised material in the contemporaneous *Finding and Seeking*.[69] We will need to jump around a bit chronologically, but I believe taking the texts in this order will help us gain further traction with regard to the question at hand. Let us turn to our first text.

Self, World, and Time's section 'Moral Theology and the Narrative of Salvation' begins with a laudable concern for what we might call the doxological excess of dogmatics:[70]

> What can and must be sung and said in praise ... must be sung and said on its own terms. A Christology that could be cashed out wholly in terms of moral reason ... could hardly be adequate to the miracle of God's presence in human nature. There is an excess of divine action over human which can only be acknowledged.[71]

But, O'Donovan says, for a moral theologian the treatment cannot terminate with that recognition:

> There is also something like an excess of human action, something not – or not yet – included in the announcement of God's being and works. When those who heard Saint Peter's sermon on the day of Pentecost asked themselves, 'Men and brethren, what are we to do?' (Acts 2.37), it was a *next thing* that they asked about, not something they had already been told of in Peter's proclamation. There can be ways of framing doctrine which have had the effect of shutting the door in the face of that next thing, swallowing up the 'what are we to do?' in the irrevocable gift and calling of God.[72]

I am sympathetic to O'Donovan's point and to the critical characterization of those framings of doctrine that do not adequately recognize the realm of morality, but I am slightly curious about this way of putting things. Presumably what is meant is that the 'next thing' is a sphere of human freedom, and that ethics, as the discipline that reflects upon that reasoning-to-action, is an intellectual realm with its own dignity. It is not to be (as O'Donovan writes earlier in the book) absorbed wholesale 'into the theological construction of reality'.[73] But might it be a little incautious to speak of an 'excess of human action'? If action is truly consequent upon the proclamation to which it is a response, then that action must be conceived as founded, encompassed, directed and brought to completion by the sovereign work of God. Far from swallowing up the moment of deliberation, the doctrine of election is right the way along determinative for ethics, because it is what establishes free action, or, to put it another way, what grounds and shapes those 'good works, which God prepared beforehand to be our way of life' (Eph. 2.10).

---

[69] O'Donovan, 'Sanctification and Ethics', in *Sanctification: Explorations in Theology and Practice*.
[70] For a meditation on this theme, see the postscript to this study.
[71] O'Donovan, *Self, World, and Time*, 82.
[72] Ibid.
[73] Ibid., viii.

Still, O'Donovan knows that dogmatics and ethics, understood aright, are non-competitive. As he writes in 'The Trinity and the Moral Life', an essay written in dialogue with the work of John Webster, there is a 'mutual service of dogmatics and ethics in theology'.[74] The two have a 'complementary and non-exchangeable relation', as *Self, World, and Time* expresses it.[75] On one hand, this means we must avoid conflating the two – a danger O'Donovan illustrates by describing how he understands each discipline to treat sin (a topic that I cannot focus upon here, but that I believe would be an interesting further case study of this demarcation's effects.).[76] On the other hand, it also means that we must avoid completely separating the two. The illustration provided for this separation focuses on two examples: post-Tridentine Catholic moral thought, the 'pastoral ambitions' of which were laudable, but which devised moral theology as 'regulative system for ordering the conduct of the faithful'; and 'twentieth-century adventures that aligned Moral Theology with political agenda, whether of radical social change or of conservative resistance'.[77]

The temptations to conflation and total separation arise, we are told, because moral theology does by nature 'reach out in both directions, towards the doctrinal and towards the practical. It accompanies the course of Christian practical reasoning all the way from its apprehension of the truths of the creed to its practical discernment of the opportunities and duties opening up before its feet.'[78] The active, dynamic nature of

---

[74] O'Donovan, 'The Trinity and the Moral Life', 225. For the suggestion that 'Webster's approach to moral theology greatly parallels that sketched by Oliver O'Donovan, "Sanctification and Ethics"', see Michael Allen, 'Toward Theological Anthropology: Tracing the Anthropological Principles of John Webster', *International Journal of Systematic Theology* 19, no. 1 (2017): 6–29, 25, n. 99. That may be almost entirely true, but there are some subtly important differences, which I hope to examine more closely elsewhere. A further study would incorporate O'Donovan's own recent reflections: 'John Webster on Dogmatics and Ethics', *International Journal of Systematic Theology* 21, no. 1 (2019): 78–92, which I am not able to treat here.

[75] O'Donovan, *Self, World, and Time*, 82.

[76] Cf. O'Donovan, *Finding and Seeking*, 17–18; O'Donovan, *Entering into Rest*, 65–71. The way O'Donovan articulates the kind of knowledge ethics should have of sin could be brought into conversation with other understandings. For O'Donovan, while Christian doctrine may know of ultimate (that is, original) sin, ethics, for its part, as an essentially practical discipline concerned with freedom, is given to know only the possibility of the sins that lurk at the door (akin to what the tradition calls 'actual' sin) – in order to avoid them in the next moment of action. This instinct coincides with an emphasis upon the way in which sin represents a possibility for the individual actor. Theologians impressed by the 'apocalyptic' reading of St Paul, on the other hand, urge full cognisance of the radical scope of the power of Sin (the capital 'S' is quite deliberate); indeed, they are so struck by its constriction of free action that 'ethics' itself is placed under a question mark. By the same token, some such thinkers display a lively sense for the structural realities of sin. Both positions clearly share, up to a point, a theological analysis of the relation of sin's ultimacy to human action, but seem to express essentially dissimilar convictions about its deployment in Christian ethics. Kelsey's *Eccentric Existence* could be harnessed in an initial attempt to negotiate the two, since it sustains (in triplicate!) an attempt to characterize both 'Sin' and 'sins' in terms of mis-response to God's gracious relating to create, consummate, and reconcile respectively. (In fact, Kelsey's account of Sin in relation to consummation draws explicitly on the apocalyptic reading of St Paul). Yet Kelsey does not supply a thoroughgoing account of their integration or their mutual implication, nor a discernment of their significance for Christian ethics. This is not, of course, necessarily to mark for blame, since he is not himself offering a theological ethics; what does need to be said about Christian ethics' knowledge of sin, then, must be found or offered elsewhere.

[77] O'Donovan, *Self, World, and Time*, 88.

[78] Ibid., 89.

the metaphor is important: moral theology must not 'forget how to make the journeys of thought entrusted to it between heaven and the circumstances'.[79] (Interestingly, O'Donovan describes the task of preaching in similar terms.)[80] Moral theology is informed by description, since it 'is bound to be realist', making 'what God has said and done the ground of normative judgments'.[81] But it cannot terminate in moral reflection: '[E]thical realism cannot mean that the directive and regulative role of moral thinking is irrelevant or unnecessary. ... Discipleship is not merely to be admired, but taken up as a task'.[82] As O'Donovan writes in 'The Trinity and the Moral Life', ethics is dependent upon the description 'that is the dogmatician's responsibility in theology', but should not pretend to take it over – and it has its own role to play.[83]

Further defence of this dynamic sensibility beyond description is found in O'Donovan's review of Nicholas M. Healy's *Hauerwas: A (Very) Critical Introduction*. Though he finds much of value in Healy's commentary, O'Donovan intimates that it is, in essence, 'a sketch of what Hauerwas might have been if he had been a dogmatic theologian' – perhaps even the 'revenge' of 'school theology' against an occasional essayist and practically oriented thinker.[84] That is, Healy fails to see that Hauerwas is a *moral* theologian, interested in belief's 'inextricable relation to authentic action'; accordingly Healy overlooks the fact that 'the Church, in Hauerwas's understanding, is a category of moral reason ... even ... his version of Kant's categorical imperative. It underlines the plural pronoun in the formal question of deliberative thought, "What shall we do?"'[85]

Very much presuming and defending the emphasis upon ethics' deliberative character was the much earlier article 'How Can Theology Be Moral?' (1989), an early pass over the topic of the two disciplines' identities and relation couched in terms redolent of *Resurrection and Moral Order*. The title raises a challenge to be worked through, for 'tension exists between the disciplines of theology, which seeks to discern the rational order of what is believed and to impose intellectual discipline on its presentation, and moral thought which is practical in nature, thought-towards-action'.[86] They seem 'incompatible partners', an incompatibility that can be formulated in 'three antinomies', of which I relay the first and third here.[87] (The second posits that if theology is 'evangelical', moral thought is 'problematic', having to do 'with confronting

---

[79] Ibid.
[80] See O'Donovan, *Small Boats*, 4. For a winsome appreciation of O'Donovan's understanding and practice of preaching, see John Webster, 'One Under Authority', his contribution to a 'Symposium in Honor of Oliver O'Donovan', *Living Church* (Spring 2012): 8–18, 14–15.
[81] O'Donovan, *Self, World, and Time*, 89.
[82] Ibid. O'Donovan, *Self, World, and Time*'s account of the roles of description and prescription are employed by John Perry in a compelling evaluation of contemporary 'empirical ethicists' vis-à-vis historic Christian moral sense theory. See Perry, 'Jesus and Hume Among the Neuroscientists: Haidt, Greene, and the Unwitting Return of Moral Sense Theory'. *Journal of the Society of Christian Ethics* 36, no. 1 (2016).
[83] O'Donovan, 'The Trinity and the Moral Life', 227.
[84] O'Donovan, 'What Shall We Do'. Compare Webster's review of Healy's book: 'Ecclesiocentrism', *First Things* 246 (2014): 54–5, which unfortunately shows no sign of O'Donovan's qualifications.
[85] O'Donovan, 'What Shall We Do'.
[86] O'Donovan, 'How Can Theology Be Moral', 81.
[87] Ibid., 83.

difficulties rather than with announcing solutions'.[88] O'Donovan's response to this antinomy is entirely coherent with *Resurrection and Moral Order*, and we have dwelt upon it.)

The first antinomy is between theology's 'declarative' and moral thought's 'deliberative' characters. Theology 'must consider the merits of action proposed rather than the facticity of action accomplished .... The traditional formula distinguishing the *de*scriptive from the *pre*scriptive utterance, crisp and simple-minded though it may be, has its own validity'.[89] The 'opposition of knowledge and will' underlies the tension.[90] If deliberation is 'oriented towards an act of will, a decision to do something ... which brings new reality into the world', how can that 'be conditioned by knowledge of reality that existed prior to it?'[91] Yet the New Testament shows a 'progress of thought from proclamation to prescription, rotating on the word "therefore"'.[92] That progress is possible, then, and if not by deductive inference, then still rationally; we speak inductively 'of the "appropriateness" or "inappropriateness" of given acts to the realities which the mind contemplates'.[93] An act of will is a new but never '*dissociated*' reality: '[O]ur behaviour takes on the meaning of a response to what is there before it, an acceptance or rejection of the world into which we act.'[94] Because of this, a 'command cannot evoke rational obedience unless it discloses some aspect of reality': 'Reality is authoritative and action-evoking, and nothing else is. The possibility of moral theology is founded on the dependence of rational action upon reality, of will upon knowledge.'[95]

The third antinomy is perhaps most pertinent. If 'theology is Christocentric, moral thought must be generic. To speak about what ought to be done is ... to speak about what ought to be done by anybody at any time in the relevant circumstances. The "ought" of moral discourse does not allow for sheer particularity.'[96] How does moral theology get to grips with this difficulty? O'Donovan's first move, familiar from *Resurrection and Moral Order*, is to 'begin to explore this opposition from another opposition', one 'essential to the Gospel, between the particularity of the Incarnation and the universality of the reign of Christ'.[97] Yet he notes that 'faith in the universal itself demands concrete witness':

> The church in each limited time and place is committed to discerning the implications of Christ's future and universal rule for its own worldly experience ... it attempts to grasp its experience both generically and particularly: generically, in terms of the structures of worldly order such as family, political community, economic relations and so on, because the world which is claimed for Christ's rule is an ordered universe; particularly, in terms of the vocation of this or that

[88] Ibid.
[89] Ibid., 82.
[90] Ibid., 84.
[91] Ibid.
[92] Ibid., 85.
[93] Ibid.
[94] Ibid.
[95] Ibid., 88.
[96] Ibid., 83.
[97] Ibid., 91.

community or individual in this place or that time, because the world is a universe of particulars.[98]

Here, O'Donovan makes an unexpected and additional disciplinary distinction: 'In the first of these two tasks of concrete interpretation we locate the work of moral theology, in the second the work of pastoral theology.'[99] (There was no sign that pastoral theology was in question before this point, but it may also help to recall that at Oxford O'Donovan was Professor of Moral *and Pastoral* Theology.) Still, 'these two cannot meaningfully be separated in practice. For moral theology, as a deliberative discipline, always has as its end the venturing of the actions or the forming of the attitudes which are the vocation of a given believer or community of believers.'[100] And, as we have already seen, 'to discern a vocation ... is already to fulfil a generic duty which rests on all who act, and it presupposes an understanding of the moral order by which the acts and attitudes to which we believe ourselves called will be judged positively or negatively.'[101] Moral theology's 'generic orientation ... is not a refusal of the particular, but is in dialectical correspondence with it.'[102]

O'Donovan realizes that with his disciplinary demarcations, he wanders 'perilously close to some kind of ontic absolutising of the purely conventional distinctions which we observe between different branches of theology'.[103] But the intention is 'not to freeze the lines of demarcation', and the notion of 'dialectical correspondence' used here I take to be definitive of O'Donovan's thoughts about the nature of Christian ethics as it exists between theology and moral thought as such:

> Theology by its very nature must move in certain directions and meet up with the concerns of moral thought, while moral thought, if ... undertaken in relation to Christian belief, must move back again and find its centre in the primary proclamation of theology ... this both authorises Christian moral thought and disciplines it.[104]

The details of this authorization and disciplining of Christian moral thought by theology's 'primary proclamation' are worth noticing: they mark his thought indelibly.

Theology disciplines Christian moral thought 'by requiring an acknowledgment of the ambiguity that surrounds any form of worldly order, historical or natural'.[105] It asks questions about these, but not 'sceptically, as though it knew there was no purpose in history, no normativity in nature, and that every pretence at objective order was a sham':

---

[98] Ibid., 91–2.
[99] Ibid., 92.
[100] Ibid.
[101] Ibid.
[102] Ibid.
[103] Ibid.
[104] Ibid.
[105] Ibid.

Theology asks them precisely because it knows that there *is* order, in nature and in history; that the shape of the final order is not yet visible save in outline; and that therefore every apparent element of order must be tested by that outline for its authenticity. The rule of Christ is the measure of order, and 'we do not yet see everything in subjection to him; but we see Jesus ... crowned with glory and honour' (Heb. 2.8f.). The moralist's love of the appearances of order which present themselves in the world must be challenged and tested by faith and hope.[106]

If we recall the interpretation of these verses from Hebrews in *Resurrection and Moral Order*, we will anticipate the 'but' shortly to arrive. But, O'Donovan says, theology also 'authorises the moralist's love of order':

The light shed by the sacred particulars will illumine the forms of order which condition the life of our civilisation. Because of this the moral theologian can interest himself in the detailed description of those forms and learn from whatever source he may to understand them more clearly.[107]

Nevertheless, there is no value-neutral mode of describing the order which is found in reality:

Scientists and technologists, too, are interpreters. ... It is here that theology appropriately exercises its normative function, by testing the adequacy and the right of these conceptions against what is given, and by opening them to encounter the horizon of faith, hope, and love, the rule of Jesus Christ.[108]

This last line surely suggests that both creation – 'what is given' – and eschatology – 'the horizon of faith, hope, and love, the rule of Jesus Christ' – ought to be normative, criterial, in that testing.

In this light, we might say that *Resurrection and Moral Order* went further in testing the adequacy and right of scientific and technological conceptions against what is given than it did in opening them to encounter with that horizon. In a certain sense, the theo-political works did indeed confront certain non-theological conceptions in exactly this way. We were still waiting, however, for a more concerted *moral-theological* attempt at encounter with the horizon of faith, hope and love – 'the rule of Jesus of Christ'. From what we have seen so far, *Ethics as Theology* has gone some way towards that, but it has sometimes seemed to balk at a fuller encounter. As it turns out, in *Entering into Rest*, O'Donovan is able to perform a subtly different variation on his consistent theme, and in so doing, to pursue precisely that encounter; in the final part of this chapter, we can see the shape of this new interpretation. The earlier articulation in 'How Can Theology Be Moral' already provided an understanding within which it could be achieved, yet frequently in the intervening years, O'Donovan seems to have

---

[106] Ibid., 93.
[107] Ibid.
[108] Ibid.

been reluctant to follow through with it. We find a prime example, I think, in the article 'What Can Ethics Know about God?'.

The basic argument of this essay is entirely unobjectionable. In fact, it is very similar to that made in *Self, World, and Time*. O'Donovan sets out to 'explore ... the cooperation within theology' of doctrine and ethics:

> All Christian thought must prove itself as theology, and Christian thought about ethics must prove itself as 'moral theology'. ... Yet at the same time theology is a complex of intellectual undertakings. Ethical questions are not the same as doctrinal questions; the old [Barthian] slogan that 'ethics is dogmatics' was intolerably high-handed. But since doctrine has a central place in theology, moral theology is bound to acknowledge and define its relation to the questions of dogmatics, and especially to the central doctrines of God and Christ.[109]

Ethics ought not 'bid for independence', for although 'discussions of the being and work of God ... are someone else's special task ... without them the moral task would lose its coherence and integrity'.[110] Neither ought it to 'imagine that ethics can lay down its terms to doctrine as an equal or even senior partner'.[111] The first temptation – ethics' bid for autonomy – afflicted Protestants 'in the seventeenth and eighteenth centuries' and 'some Catholic Christians in the twentieth'; the second – moralizing doctrine – is 'characteristic of nineteenth- and early twentieth-century idealism', especially 'the Ritschlian school'.[112] Though 'conscious of recapitulating some classic idealist moves' in his own argument, O'Donovan is keen to avoid this temptation. He distances himself from it as follows:

> In theology talk about God and Christ has priority. Dogma is *doxa*, an act of praise, in which the being and work of God is the first and last thing on our lips. ... Ethics belongs in between this first and that last word of praise; its significance is derived from its mediating position. Its task is to inform, out of praise and for the sake of praise, the deliberative reasoning which determines practical human undertakings. Yet although ethics has no equal partnership with dogmatics, the communication between the two is reciprocal. Doctrinal implications can be drawn from ethical premises, ethical implications from doctrinal premises.[113]

On this construal, two procedures are available. 'Dogmatics ... can appeal to ethics to clarify a point, and ethics can appeal to dogmatics.'[114] O'Donovan subsequently engages in three exercises as examples of the first kind, 'in which appeal to ethical

---

[109] O'Donovan, 'What Can Ethics Know about God?' 33. Cf. O'Donovan, *Self, World, and Time*, 81, for criticism of the Barthian slogan.
[110] O'Donovan, 'What Can Ethics Know', 33.
[111] Ibid.
[112] Ibid.
[113] Ibid., 34.
[114] Ibid.

premises supports doctrinal conclusions'.[115] He asks, respectively, 'what moral theology may contribute' to analogical predication of moral attributes to God; what it may contribute to 'statements about the saving work of God'; and what it may contribute to statements 'about the trinitarian being of God'.[116] The second concerns us here, in which O'Donovan turns deliberately 'from the first article of the creed to the second and third', wondering whether 'anything comparable [can] be said'.[117] Behind this interest lies 'a personal reason':

> When ... I wrote a book called *Resurrection and Moral Order*, some critics doubted the seriousness of the work done by the resurrection in its programme. I could invoke the resurrection to secure ethics, but could not, they thought, allow that resurrection made any difference to ethics.[118]

O'Donovan again mentions Hauerwas's memorable one-liner, and observes that 'others have kindly undertaken to defend' that book 'against Hauerwas's criticism'.[119] (Who he has in mind is unclear.)[120] But he does 'want to respond constructively to his doubt – which of all possible doubts about the programme of that book seems to me the one most worth taking seriously'.[121]

Thus Hauerwas's doubt invites, for O'Donovan, a question: 'What might an "ethics of redemption" look like?'[122] (That is to say, an ethics both responding to the doctrine of redemption and so also contributing to it.) Exactly, we might think: at last. What we read next, though, does not seem to amount to any new attempt:

> When Christian doctrine speaks of redemption, it speaks of the redemption *of the created world*. To ask what ethics 'knows' of this redemption is not to ask that it should know anything *besides* the created moral order, but that it should know that moral order also in and through its historical and eschatological destiny. Here I am at one with Hauerwas; though his incautiously phrased remark, 'any order we know as Christians is resurrection', could be mistaken to intend a polarity between a Christian resurrection-ethic and a non-Christian creation-ethic. My suspicions in *Resurrection and Moral Order* were directed against those who sought to champion eschatology in opposition to created order.[123]

This statement again corroborates my earlier instincts. But I do not think it takes us further towards the actual 'ethics of redemption' that O'Donovan had promised to attempt; it seems to swerve away from it once more under the pressure of the same

---

[115] Ibid.
[116] Ibid., 35.
[117] Ibid., 39.
[118] Ibid.
[119] Ibid.
[120] One example I am aware of is Werpehowski, *American Protestant Ethics*, ch. 4 'Politics, Creation, and Conversion', 104.
[121] O'Donovan, 'What Can Ethics Know', 39.
[122] Ibid.
[123] Ibid.

worries concerning 'kingdom ethics'. Unfortunately, on my reading, the rest of the subsection that follows makes little progress towards it, either. Crucially, I think, this is owed to the way O'Donovan's exposition is governed by an instinct we are now acquainted with: about 'what ethics does not know but must be told'.[124] Determinative here is the conviction that ethics 'knows nothing by itself of human sin, and nothing of the fact that God has redeemed us ... what ethics may and should know is that the moral order is present to the world *objectively*'.[125]

What should we make of these claims? On one level, it is plausible that ethics *qua* ethics may and should know that 'the moral order is present to the world objectively' (though the evidence of twentieth-century moral philosophy suggests otherwise). And indeed it does seem to be 'ethics' simply as 'ethics' that the essay is concerned with, just as the previous essay was concerned with 'moral thought' simply as 'moral thought', and only then moved to negotiate a role for moral theology. What is on closer inspection critically unclear in both texts, I think, is the extent to which O'Donovan thinks *Christian* ethics can go on *etsi doctrina non daretur*. Certainly even here he says all the right things about the need for Christian moral thought to prove itself as theology; later he is clearer still. But the starting point is consistently this putatively neutral ethics (who does this neutral 'ethics' – do Christians? – and why does this 'ethics' natively have no 'theology' of any kind, secular or otherwise?). It seems to me that O'Donovan's difficulties with eschatology are partly caused by that first principle.

By my lights, for Christian ethics, the distinction between what doctrine knows and what ethics knows – and does *not* know, but must be told – is untenable, and in fact redundant. To underline the point: the book in which this second essay is published is called *The Doctrine of God and Theological Ethics*. That is, not *The Doctrine of God and Philosophical Ethics* or *The Doctrine of God and Commonsense Ethics*. What those who confess the creeds are given to know is the whole sequence of Christian teaching on God's gracious ways with God's good creation. It may be, of course, that some Christian ethicists *choose* – tactically, not strategically – to speak in public without direct reference to these teachings.[126] Granted, there is certainly precedent for appealing to the implicit affirmations downstream of one doctrine in particular in the case for speaking in public, or more saliently here for moral reasoning in general; I presume that the assumptions O'Donovan imagines 'Ethics' to have about moral objectivity are in some sense licensed by natural law implications derived from a doctrine of creation. (And a doctrine of creation

---

[124] Ibid.
[125] Ibid. The final passage (45) might suggest that ethics cannot know much of the cross, either.
[126] The distinction between tactics and strategy is de Certeau's – see Wells, *Transforming*, 114–15, and thereafter Joseph L. Mangina, *Karl Barth on the Christian Life: The Practical Knowledge of God* (New York: Peter Lang, 2001), 187. Nigel Biggar seems to operate with what he imagines is an expressly counter-Hauerwasian distinction between deliberately 'distinctive' Christian moral arguments, and 'responsible', 'useful' moral arguments still having 'Christian integrity' and 'authenticity'. See especially *Behaving in Public: How to Do Christian Ethics* (Grand Rapids: Eerdmans, 2011). In practice, does Biggar always remember the difference between tactics and strategy? Has he remembered to continue 'labouring in the quarry' for 'theological fragments'? (Duncan Forrester, *Truthful Action: Explorations in Practical Theology* (Edinburgh: T&T Clark, 2000), 155–6).

conceived of as containing deliverances more accessible to reason by other means than special revelation, compared to other Christian teachings.)[127] But to make these moves in any more than a circumstantially tactical way (and even that seems to me risky) would seem to me to pretend not to have heard the whole prophetic and apostolic declaration of the *magnalia Dei*: 'God's deeds of power'.[128] At this point O'Donovan seems to turn a form of apologetic tactic into a foundational principle.

If, as Bonhoeffer might tell us, the church (and its moral theology) knows the beginning from the end, making this first move itself would mean pretending not to know how we come to know at all well the form given in the beginning.[129] I think O'Donovan's own affirmation of the doctrine of creation by tying it to the 'vindication' entailed in salvation and the renewal entailed in redemption itself presses this question. The only order we know must be subject to sin and salvific divine action, not neutrally 'natural order' as such. It would be no moral realist who, having been told, bracketed out the Christological and eschatological determination of the real; that would be knowledge of 'the world', an abstraction, in O'Donovan's own terms.[130] What we see in this article, I think, is the desire to give a hearing to the full scope of Christian doctrine in Christian ethics, but irresolution about how exactly that might be achieved without destabilizing the baseline of 'Moral Thought' which is presumed to carry over into Christian ethics. For further clues as to why that irresolution is found in O'Donovan's work, we need to turn to our final example of his reflections on dogmatic and moral theology, the relatively recent piece 'Sanctification and Ethics'.

In this article, O'Donovan sets out to ascertain 'whether and how ethics as a theological discipline may be located within a scheme of doctrines'.[131] Ethics 'cannot renounce its interest in any of the three theological virtues', and this means that 'if we follow Barth's alignment ... ethics [lays] claim to a view of all three doctrines of salvation, namely, justification, sanctification, and vocation'.[132] This understanding augurs well, but how does it fit with what went before? O'Donovan tells us directly. *Resurrection and Moral Order* 'proposed that the proper location of ethics lay with the

---

[127] That is, of course, debatable. Reinhard Hütter once wrote: 'Creation is only intelligible as doctrine, as part and parcel of the proclamation of the Gospel ... the redemptive story of God with Israel and with/in the life, death and resurrection of Jesus of Nazareth. The functional location ... of the doctrine is the theological, doxological, and ethical life of that community which was and constantly is created by the One whom this community confesses to be the Creator of Heaven and Earth.' Hütter, 'Creatio ex nihilo: Promise of the Gift. Remembering the Christian Doctrine of Creation in Troubled Times', in *Some Christian and Jewish Perspectives on Creation*, ed. Robert A. Brungs and Marianne Postiglione (St. Louis: ITEST Faith/Science Press 1991), 3.
[128] Acts 2.11.
[129] Dietrich Bonhoeffer, *Creation and Fall: A Theological Exposition of Genesis 1-3: Dietrich Bonhoeffer Works*, vol. 3, ed. John W. de Gruchy, trans. Douglas S. Bax (Minneapolis: Fortress Press, 1997), 21-2. An essentially identical point is made by Hauerwas in 'The End Is in the Beginning: Creation and Apocalyptic', 3.
[130] O'Donovan himself articulates this kind of 'world' well at *Ways*, 231.
[131] O'Donovan, 'Sanctification and Ethics', 152.
[132] Ibid.

doctrine of the *resurrection of Christ*, in which the created order, to which our active life was bound, was vindicated and delivered from threat of dissolution':

> The question I was trying to answer was how moral teaching could be evangelical, not an appendage to faith in the gospel but integral to it. If the work of Christ were understood solely from the point of view of the cross, as negation of the world, or from the point of view of the ascension, as transcendence of the world, or even from the point of view of the incarnation, as assumption of the world into the being of God, moral norms, which have *human* action in view within the created world, could not be conceived evangelically. They could be a law that condemned us, an old order we left behind, or a precondition for realising the birth of God; but only when salvation was conceived as gracious restoration of the world from threat of dissolution could moral norms be a gift that made the path before our human feet a celebration of the coming of God. In locating ethics at that moment in Christology ... I argued ... the centrality of this moment. That said ... there remains to be explored the relation of the Holy Spirit to ethics, of the church, of the doctrine of the last things. For redeemed action is not solely a matter of *world*-redemption, but also of the redemption of subjectivity and of time. ... I have to correct, then, any inference that might be drawn from my proposal that theological ethics ... relates to dogmatics at this sole point in the dogmatic scheme. To put it another way: moral theology does not locate itself by reference to a distinct dogmatic theme. Ethics is a reflective mode of *practical reason* ... thought undertaking not to conclude in *knowledge* but in *action*.[133]

These paragraphs show the same self-understanding as 'What Should Ethics Know of God?', but they now promise a better attempt at overcoming the earlier constriction. And they announce the agenda of *Ethics as Theology* at its best. O'Donovan continues:

> We should avoid the suggestion that doctrine, whether in whole or in part, may be *ethicised*. ... Ethics cannot replace, or improve on, dogma. Dogmatic statements must simply be grasped and believed – by a moral theologian as by any other Christian. ... What ethics can do is reflect on how those statements, once believed, shape and transform practical reason. It thinks ... *around* dogmatic statements and *out from* dogmatic statements, but not *about* dogmatic statements ... since the revelation that dogma attests is essentially a single truth of God's action, not a series of truths, ethics is in no position to choose among dogmas and declare itself more at home with one (let us say, creation or the incarnation) than another (let us say, Christ's heavenly session at God's right hand). There may, however, be a *route through* the one truth of God's action that is especially conducive to pursuing the questions that arise in reflection on practical reason. Even dogmatics ... does not always follow the trinitarian order of the Apostles' Creed. And that is how my proposition in *Resurrection and Moral Order* is best understood, I now think: as

---

[133] Ibid., 153.

identifying *a dogmatic starting point* that will allow moral theology to unfold in a comprehensible and ordered way.[134]

This is highly illuminating. Yet the point I would like to make, predictably by now, is that if 'ethics is in no position to choose among dogmas and declare itself more at home with one … than another', but may plot 'a *route through* the one truth of God's action', it must still show that each of the dogmatic points that it passes through on its journey genuinely determines its 'reflection on practical reason'. Certainly, it ought not do so mechanically, or simply for the sake of it – and that is why concerns about the relative doctrinal proportions of any Christian ethics do not yet tell us whether it represents a rounded thinking 'around' and 'out from' Christian dogma. But in conceiving the 'route', we should be careful not to prejudge 'the questions that arise in reflections on practical reason' in such a way as to downplay the sense in which dogmatic statements 'shape and transform practical reason' itself.

It seems to me that one of the reasons for the particular shape of practical reason's journey through the one truth of God's action, as O'Donovan plots it, is an ambition perhaps imperfectly but suggestively described as apologetic.[135] *Ethics as Theology* is constructed very skilfully so as to lead the reader to the realization that 'wider wisdom is required if we are to hold … the wisdom of morality, in its place: Christ the centre of the world, the bridegroom of the self, the turning-point of past and future'.[136] As the trilogy's title suggests, the narration is designed to show how 'Ethics opens up towards theology'.[137] As we shall see as we turn to *Entering into Rest*, eschatology is very much part of the theology that ethics *eventually* opens up to, once we 'have reached the limit of a theory of moral reason'.[138] I do think that *Ethics as Theology*'s phenomenological texture is in part an aesthetic and, relatedly, apologetic method. It provides, at the first level, a general phenomenology of ethical experience that serves as a propaedeutic to the explicit claims of moral theology, which it insinuates into the unfolding of moral reason's search for wisdom as that search strains towards ultimate horizons.

It may be rewarding to compare the approach of *Ethics as Theology* with O'Donovan's interpretation of the work of Rowan Williams as in its own way apologetic. In 'a Williams train of thought', O'Donovan suggests:

> The Kingdom of God is always slipping its hand surreptitiously into the doubter's back pocket and replacing the wallet and credit cards with a better-funded set. His

---

[134] Ibid., 153–4.
[135] Having described it in this way, I now notice that Charles Mathewes, in his recent review essay, entertains a similar thought about *Ethics as Theology* but describes it as 'not exactly apologetic but dialogical', and later as 'the opening of the terrain of moral experience as a space of dialogue (not directly apologetics, let alone polemics)'. Mathewes, 'A Response to Oliver O'Donovan's *Ethics as Theology* Trilogy', *Modern Theology* 36, no. 1 (2020): 165–72, 167, 168. I think there is something to that, but I also suspect that O'Donovan may be less nervous about the implications of 'apologetics' than Mathewes might be, for whom 'dialogue' might denote the mode of interaction he wishes primarily to appreciate in O'Donovan's late work. A further exercise might compare e.g. Linda Zagzebski, 'Does Ethics Need God?' *Faith and Philosophy* 4, no. 2 (1987): 294–303.
[136] O'Donovan, *Self, World, and Time*, 9.
[137] Ibid.
[138] O'Donovan, *Finding and Seeking*, 239.

engagements with ethics and politics tend to be night-time raiding parties, less interested in knowing how they work than in finding out where they break down, and not with any idea of repairing them, either .... I have learned something from the apologetics of fracture, perhaps under Rowan's influence. But I don't want to stay my eye on that cracked glass, but through it pass and then the heaven espy.[139]

O'Donovan's *Ethics as Theology*, to draw the contrast, is deeply interested in how ethics and politics work, and is designed exactly as an assignment of repair. If this trilogy uncovers where moral and political thought and life break down, then it is perhaps less to do with exposing the fracture of sin than with pressing at the limitations of finitude. Moreover, it ends precisely, as we shall see in *Entering into Rest*, by espying heaven. In O'Donovan's late work, then, the kingdom of God certainly replaces – or perhaps renews – the resources of the moral and political actor who doubts or is yet to believe; but the comprehensive scope with which this is conceived means that O'Donovan's engagements with ethics and politics here are thus less night-time raiding parties than a Trojan horse at break of dawn.

Sarah Coakley interprets O'Donovan's trilogy in a similar way: '[A]s I read it a second (and third) time, I begin to see it as a sort of veiled 'natural theology' of agency itself, in which the unashamed God-claims creep up on us out of the rich phenomenology of moral existence.'[140] Coakley, I think, means this is a commendation – and as a departure from what she sees as O'Donovan's earlier Barthianism – and I am also to a certain extent willing to be won over by *Ethics as Theology*'s ground-up, earth-to-heaven and even cradle-to-grave apologetic.[141] But it is worth raising questions that arise from its approach. Is what occurs in the conversion of moral reason simply the Christological 'thematisation of what has always been the case'? (A criticism of Rahner's perspective, for instance).[142] For all its phenomenological richness and perceptiveness about the everyday experience of moral agency in the world, does *Ethics as Theology*'s way of recounting the process in which moral perception is honed marginalize the starkness of at least some biblical impressions of moral ontology? (Are they, like the more ultimate aspects of the doctrine of sin, to be left for dogmatics?) Put otherwise, does it prioritize wisdom traditions at the expense of a closer tracking with the dramatic heights and

---

[139] Shortt, *God's Advocates*, 268.
[140] Coakley, 'Response', 187.
[141] In her contribution to the recent *Modern Theology* symposium, Jennifer Herdt also offers a reading along these lines:

> What *Ethics as Theology* achieves with extraordinary skill is the performance of a Gospel-normed ethics that dwells in a loving way on the shape of natural moral experience and the practical questions of ordinary people, including those for whom theological categories are alien or dead .... O'Donovan readily grants that there is no necessity in the movement from the experience of responsible agency to God. His communication might fail: 'the reference to God in this train of thought is not inescapable' (O'Donovan, *Finding and Seeking*, 31). Yet he proffers it as a persuasive induction.

Herdt, 'Oliver O'Donovan's *Ethics as Theology* and the Struggle for Communication', *Modern Theology* 36, no. 1 (2020): 159–64, 160, 163.

[142] Christopher Steck uses the phrase to describe misperceptions of Rahner's view. Steck, *Ethical Thought*, 100.

depths of the drama of salvation portrayed in the New Testament? We might recall O'Donovan's comments on Nygren quoted earlier, whose mistakes apparently included his having 'taken literally' scriptural instances when 'conversion is described as a "new creation"'. The criticism of Nygren is, there as here in *Ethics as Theology*, well-merited and instructive. But, as O'Donovan knows, the way in which the scriptural witness links creation and redemption is absolutely to draw analogy between the two acts (e.g. 2 Cor. 4.6), and this can be expressed in terms that do seem designed to bring the ex nihilo quality of creation to mind when we contemplate election and salvation (so Rom. 4.17).[143]

Now, this does not mean to say that the divine works of free grace are 'presuppositionless' in the sense of being opposed to God's loving covenant faithfulness to creation. Rather, it means that our trust in God's ability to redeem sinners – as utterly unable to make ourselves new as to create ourselves in the first place – is based on confession that in the beginning, God (alone) created from nothing and so can, does, and will (alone) make new. And it is true that when, for instance, Kathryn Tanner writes in a noticeably direct affirmation of what O'Donovan rejects, that 'this movement is something like our literal recreation', she does so speaking as a dogmatic theologian, without necessarily having to construe immediately the moral implications.[144] O'Donovan's approach towards moral conversion 'from below' also seems, quite obviously, to distance it from dogmatic approaches 'from above' (though it certainly proceeds hand-in-hand with his account of 'Spirit', as we find it in *Ethics as Theology* without the definite article).[145] However, the sharp biblical portrayal of disjunction between 'the old self with its practices' and 'the new self, which is being renewed in knowledge according to the image of its creator' (Col. 3.9-10) does not seem to be presented scripturally as, for instance, doctrinal or spiritual hyperbole without correspondingly stark moral import; the moral import follows on (so Col. 3.11-15). Renewal in knowledge is, in magnificently imagined detail, the subject matter of *Ethics as Theology*, but not necessarily with such sharpness.

I also wonder whether it is, in part, O'Donovan's precisely *evangelical* interest in conversion (in the broader and perhaps narrower senses of the word 'evangelical') that gives the account the apologetic cast and angle of vision 'from below' it possesses. My impression is that if O'Donovan's *political* theology is about articulating the character of political judgement so as to invite recognition that the central categories of Western political thought can be seen as in truth lucent with theological realities, then his *moral* theology, especially in the later work, is about articulating moral reason in such a way that it can be seen as latent with religious commitments. On that view, moral theology, as O'Donovan wrote about the conception of it found in *Veritatis Splendor*, 'is a pastoral and evangelistic response to the existential question constantly thrown up by the human agent who needs to find a ground and end of action'.[146] I will not dwell further upon this avenue of investigation here (though it is another that I think could rewardingly

---

[143] See John Barclay, *Paul and the Gift* (Grand Rapids: Eerdmans, 2015), 132, 140, 461, 479-92.
[144] Kathryn Tanner, *Christ the Key* (Cambridge: Cambridge University Press, 2010), 64-5.
[145] See e.g. O'Donovan, *Finding and Seeking*, 95-6.
[146] O'Donovan, 'A Summons to Reality', 41.

be pursued).[147] Now we can turn directly to *Entering into Rest*, which represents among other things O'Donovan's response to the existential question about action's end. As he wrote in *Finding and Seeking*, looking forward to the final volume: 'The end of action … directs our love of the created world towards the Kingdom of Heaven. Here Ethics is shaped by an eschatology that it cannot take direct responsibility for.'[148]

De finibus

If the first instalment of *Ethics as Theology* was about the study of moral thinking, and the second about the progress of moral thinking, then *Entering into Rest* turns its attention to moral thinking's 'object': 'the forward horizon with which moral thinking engages'.[149] O'Donovan invokes a classical division of moral philosophical tasks to describe 'the two aspects' under which these three parts can be considered, the first corresponding to 'classical discussions *de officis*, "on duties"', and now the second corresponding to treatises '*de finibus*, "on ends of action"'.[150] Though the distinction is improperly worked out in modern ethics in the split between deontological and teleological approaches, there is some benefit, he says, to concentrating attention upon agents' responsibility, on the one hand, and the goals and ends of their action, on the other. According to this scheme, *Entering into Rest* represents O'Donovan's own *de finibus*.

This last movement imparts to the earlier works' outlook a new perspective: it is 'a view of the climax of the Pauline triad in the sovereignty of love'.[151] As with the resurrection motif in earlier works, O'Donovan recognizes that 'there could be other possible starting points' than the Pauline sovereignty of love for this work, too: '[T]he Sermon on the Mount suggests itself, framed as it is by declarations of the moral significance of the ultimate future, for the teleology of classical ethics is drawn, in a Christian context, inexorably into the magnetic field of eschatology.'[152] That starting point is arguably one taken by Hauerwas – and certainly by writers like Glen Stassen and David Gushee; we can only wonder what material difference it might have made to O'Donovan's enterprise.[153]

---

[147] Luke Bretherton, review of *Self, World, and Time*, *Studies in Christian Ethics*, 27, no. 3 (2014): 365–9, 367. Cf. James King, 'Moral Theory: Response to Chapter Four', *Scottish Bulletin of Evangelical Theology*, 33, no. 1 (2015): 86–91, and O'Donovan's response (104–8 of the same edition).

[148] O'Donovan, *Finding and Seeking*, 239. Commending Archbishop Sentamu's Advent book to those who do not share his faith, O'Donovan writes: 'To attend to what is involved in living in the world teaches us to ask about the love that moves all things and has the power to renew them'. O'Donovan, 'Foreword', to John Sentamu, *Wake Up to Advent!: The Archbishop of York's Advent Book 2019* (London: SPCK, 2019).

[149] O'Donovan, *Entering into Rest*, vii.

[150] Ibid.

[151] Ibid. (A number of reviewers of the trilogy thus far seem to have wondered this aloud, too.)

[152] Ibid.

[153] David P. Gushee and Glen H. Stassen, *Kingdom Ethics: Following Jesus in Contemporary Context* (Downers Grove: IVP, 2003), though for startling loss of confidence in this project, see now David P. Gushee and Codi D. Norred, 'The Kingdom of God, Hope, and Christian Ethics', *Studies in Christian Ethics* 31, no. 1 (2017): 3–16. It becomes bracingly clear that, while becoming laudably engaged

Still, the 'moral significance of the ultimate future' directly occupies the *de finibus* that O'Donovan actually wrote, too. Its basic lineaments in that respect are as follows. Fundamentally, the Pauline recognition of the sovereignty of love demands a reassembly of the triad. Earlier formulated in the sequence faith, love and hope, it is now configured as faith, hope and *love* (here O'Donovan meditates upon 1 Corinthians 13). With this reconfiguration, the horizon of 'accomplishment' is perceived: '[T]he satisfaction of moral agency in its end ... a point of rest on the far side of deliberation to which practical reason may look as its goal, not alien to practice or superseding practice, but pushing its horizon back to the accomplishment that life itself is offered.'[154] Newly evident, too, are love's crowning gifts to the 'character of life in community', and thus an ultimately ecclesiological setting for the perfecting of moral action.[155]

In a moment, I will explore these final contributions of love in more detail. First let us observe that up to this point in *Ethics as Theology*, we may have worried that the ecclesiological element of this new moral theology was somewhat attenuated. That is, in itself, worth noting, because as we have seen, O'Donovan has sometimes been counted among those post-liberal theologians who have helped us regain confidence in doctrinal and ethical speech about the church, a classification that is surely not wholly incorrect. Against this background, the ecclesially underdetermined character of *Self, World, and Time* in particular did not go unremarked. Though Samuel Wells counts a little stingily when writing that he 'only picked up one reference to "church" in the book' – there are a handful more – his remark is substantively to the point.[156] I have also argued, throughout, that in O'Donovan's work, it is relation to the church that eschatology's import for the moral life is most often exhibited. Does that mean, therefore, that eschatology's place has been attenuated up until the final volume of *Ethics as Theology*, too? Not straightforwardly, as we have seen. While the link is prominent in *Resurrection and Moral Order*, and especially in *Desire of the Nations*, it is almost absent from the first two books of *Ethics as Theology*. When eschatological themes are present in the discussions of hope in *Self, World, and Time* and in *Finding and Seeking*, they are largely uncoupled from ecclesiology, and are instead focused on the possibility of agents' free action. In *Entering into Rest*'s schematic reorientation, however – a deliberate one internal to *Ethics as Theology* – both areas, earlier curtailed, are once more inextricable from one another. And they are front and centre, in this last idiosyncratic meditation upon love.

---

in social concern, the 'evangelical left' in this intellectual expression seems to have reproduced the immanentism of the Social Gospel, turning the eschatological confessions of the creed into functions of ethical action – and in the face of contraindications to earthly (read: American) progress, their hope has burned out.

[154] O'Donovan, *Entering into Rest*, 2.
[155] Ibid.
[156] Wells, review of *Self, World, and Time*, 393. O'Donovan's response, I imagine, might be essentially to reiterate the sentiment he expresses in *Self, World, and Time*, in commentary on Schleiermacher's 'Ethics conceived as *religious* description', which is silent 'about the ordered and structured beauty of the created world': 'There can be no objection, of course, to the idea that Moral Theology is a practice located within the church ... its form as well as its context. ... But the church is not the object *about which* it raises questions, nor the presupposition on which it does so' (86–7).

For O'Donovan, love, as understood in 1 Corinthians, describes 'a moment when the urgent need to act is postponed in the interest of others' actions'.[157] He intends something quite precise by this: not contemplation leaving behind 'the sphere of action', rather, an 'active-passive disposition', which as rest is specifically '"resting in" others' labours'.[158] When placed at the 'summit' of the three, therefore, love 'is a statement about the finality of the community'.[159] This ecclesiological point is pregnant with eschatological resonance. Placed there, love is also 'a statement about the end of time … now placed on the far side of hope, the virtue that "anchors" the endurance of time in a future of promise'.[160] Hope needs this further love, then, and just so *ethics* needs it:

> An Ethics that had never heard tell of such a future could only end tentatively, in an uncertain hope of endurance for any further goal there may or may not be. Hope acquires its assurance with the word, 'The time is fulfilled, and the Kingdom of God has drawn near' (Mark 1:15). Yet though anchored in the promise, hope cannot draw the Kingdom near enough to be talked of and experienced, for hope lives only in the dark. An Ethics that concluded in hope would be apophatic, gesturing towards a goal of which it could not speak. The same evangelical logic that brings assurance to hope, then, also implies that hope cannot pronounce the last word in Ethics. The Gospel confirms, but also reorders, practical reason. The Kingdom's drawing-near offers agency a provisional view of the final point of rest.[161]

As in *Resurrection and Moral Order*, then, there is a sense in which hope is superseded. However, here, hope may be 'gone beyond' in a more theologically satisfactory manner. Certainly, O'Donovan is still hypersensitive to the difficulty moral reason has in reckoning with the kingdom, and eager to underline the particular manner in which it may come to know of it:

> The drawing-near of the Kingdom is a reality that has first to be announced. It is not merely *teleological*, projected forward by the logic of moral experience, but *eschatological*. Ethics must be told of it, and then learn to refer to it in terms of moral reason. But the moral reference is possible only if the Kingdom, which lies beyond the goods of world and time, can somehow be represented within the goods of world and time.[162]

Just that representation, we might think, is what in previous statements O'Donovan has seemed to deny. Yet here he announces that there is a reliable way of representing the Kingdom 'within the goods of world and time': that of St Paul, which is to speak

---

[157] O'Donovan, *Entering into Rest*, 2.
[158] Ibid. 3.
[159] Ibid.
[160] Ibid.
[161] Ibid.
[162] Ibid.

again of love, 'what Ethics has already known'.¹⁶³ O'Donovan's elaboration of this way is dense, and difficult to parse in relation to earlier articulations:

> Love's *métier* is a world of meaning and goodness. Love is focused on an object, finding its rest in an objective world. ... God could have responded to the moral loss of mankind by making new worlds of which mankind was not part; instead, he has restored the world of which we are part, making it responsive to our purposive action. The logic of Paul's inverted triad, then, is the logic of salvation and eschatology; no eschaton could be a Kingdom of God *for us*, if it were not also a redemption and recovery of the created work of God we are. As we are offered love as the climactic moment in our moral thinking, concluding, ordering, and making sense of what has gone before, we know it as familiar, and yet we have never encountered it before *like this*. To discover the sovereignty of love is to discover created good given as a foretaste of the Kingdom of God, as the future appearing in a present familiarity, the past reappearing with a new message of what God will do.¹⁶⁴

The explication of eschatological novelty in terms of renewed apprehension of this 'restored ... world of which we are part', in order to secure 'our purposive action', is a familiar one. As O'Donovan writes, 'at the end of a hope that sprang out of love we have not taken one step beyond love' – and love defined with a familiar this-worldly orientation to created good.¹⁶⁵

O'Donovan's description of the *form* of that love, though, entails as confidently material a description of eschatology's import for ethics as we are likely to find in his work. In other words, the 'never ... before *like this*' begins to make a difference. 'If hope', he writes, 'narrows deliberation to the moment of opportunity and adventure', then 'love now leads out into a world, not the final world of the Kingdom of God but a genuine anticipation of it'.¹⁶⁶ It is nothing other than 'many agents living and acting with one common agency'.¹⁶⁷ We cannot call it 'the eschaton *tout court*', but it is 'more broadly "eschatological", announcing God's future'; 'the experience of redemption includes the representation of ourselves to ourselves as living wholly with, for, and in dependence upon, one another'.¹⁶⁸ Put otherwise, boldly, 'Community alone can tell us of the universal order yet to arrive ... . To act that another may act well: that is to seek an end which carries the assurance of God's Kingdom within it'.¹⁶⁹

Though ethical 'content' was earlier apparently denied to hope in response to the way in which Moltmann filled out the virtue, O'Donovan does offer something substantive here – in the eschatological character of *caritas*. Thus if hope cannot pronounce ethics' last word, charity does not 'make an end of hope', since, 'so long

---

¹⁶³ Ibid.
¹⁶⁴ Ibid. 4.
¹⁶⁵ Ibid.
¹⁶⁶ Ibid.
¹⁶⁷ Ibid.
¹⁶⁸ Ibid.
¹⁶⁹ Ibid., 5.

as we are situated in time', charity 'does not exhaust the content of promise'.[170] As a 'token of the promised final rest', charity's 'rest in community' is provisional. And that means hope still has a place. In it 'we return to deliberation, confident of finding in community the authoritative form of our own further acts'.[171]

Recalling the Pentecostal character (in the original sense of the word) of O'Donovan's constructive ecclesiology in earlier works, we may expect a pneumatological explication of this social 'foretaste'.[172] Indeed, though we did not focus upon it, the narration of the 'forward-looking' aspect of the resurrection in *Self, World, and Time* majors even more on the 'step forward into the life of Spirit' than earlier works: if we are 'to speak of an eschatological elevation without being left gesturing, contentless, pointing towards indefinable and indescribable empty space', we will have to 'speak of Pentecost'.[173] And now, here in *Entering into Rest*, O'Donovan draws an equation between 'acting together and thinking as one' (Phil. 2.2) and a 'communion of the Holy Spirit' (2 Cor. 13.13).[174]

The pneumatological provenance of this *genuine* anticipation is brought out most clearly in passages in this final volume that take the fifth chapter of Romans as their basis (a chapter in which O'Donovan finds further confirmation of his reading of the 'rearranged triad of virtues').[175] There, we learn: '"Hope will not disappoint, since God's love is poured out in our hearts by the Holy Spirit that is given us"' (Rom. 5.5).[176] O'Donovan comments: 'Love offers the final validation of moral reason ... love not as a demand, but as a present reality, as sure sign of the presence of the divine, reflectively completing and evoking hope, an eschatological anticipation made real by the presence of the Holy Spirit.'[177] He continues in this vein, paying attention the tenses used by Paul:

> If faith has its object in the *past* acts of God, the death and resurrection of Christ, and hope has its in the *future* judgment and salvation to be wrought through Christ, the tense of love is the present tense, representing what we possess and know already, in this time of love's 'pouring out'. Love's 'now' is a viewpoint which can take cognisance of all time ... spanning the gap that divides the accomplished from the still-to-be-accomplished, and situating the present situation, with its experience of the Holy Spirit and its practical tasks of service and endurance, in between these two temporal poles. For this is a *second* reflection of love, not merely upon the world God has redeemed, but upon the temporal movement of our salvation, emerging from and proceeding towards the purposes of God in time.[178]

The inversion of the triad, then, seems to promise the development of an account of the present bearing of eschatology in the life of love, beyond that 'merely' – owed to love's first reflection – and beyond the apophasis of hope.

---

[170] Ibid., 19.
[171] Ibid.
[172] O'Donovan, *Self, World, and Time*, 95.
[173] Ibid.
[174] O'Donovan, *Entering into Rest*, 5.
[175] Ibid., 6.
[176] Ibid.
[177] Ibid., 7.
[178] Ibid., 7–8.

What does this mean for practical reason? First, we are presented with 'an *eschatological extension* of practical reason, an extension implied by the drawing near of the Kingdom of God'.[179] While practical reason can conceive of action's ends, it needs 'a disclosure to bring to light what it is groping after', which gives back 'what natural practical reason "had" in its abstract ideality, and conferred what it "could not have" apart from promise'.[180] Here a familiar pattern is applied: 'The destiny of practical existence is governed by the logic of the resurrection: restoring the world, and opening up a world made new'.[181] Second, this eschatological extension implies 'an *ecclesiological orientation* of practical reason'.[182] This eschatological extension and ecclesiological orientation seem, therefore, to fulfil the latent yearnings of moral reason.

All told, we find what we have consistently found: O'Donovan is absolutely capable of bringing these eschatological and ecclesiological dimensions to the fore, but certain convictions about the presuppositions of 'a life that remains to be lived on the ground' seem at times to segregate them from some of his moral theology's core claims.[183] *Entering into Rest*'s formulations may make one wonder again, too, about the ambiguous theological specificity of the account of moral thinking in the first two volumes. This might very well be viewed positively – Eric Gregory writes in his endorsement of this third book that 'by stretching categories of religious and secular thought with eschatological horizons, it has something constructive to say to our spiritual and intellectual lives and the communities that sustain them'. But the strength of its ultimate ecclesiological and eschatological convictions may just as well raise questions about just how coherently possible the earlier abstracted accounts in fact were: questions this study has been inclined to answer more negatively. And even here, at the end, eschatology's contribution to ethics seems itself for the most part formal, and a touch abstract.

At this point, having traversed more than forty years' worth of O'Donovan's writings – almost overwhelming in their cumulative contribution and in the craftsmanship that they display – we can proceed to an evaluation of salient aspects of his thought using a wider-angle lens, and to making a set of tentative suggestions in view of the whole.

---

[179] Ibid., 8.
[180] Ibid.
[181] Ibid.
[182] Ibid.
[183] O'Donovan, 'Some Reactions from the Ground', *Modern Theology* 36, no. 1 (2020): 193–200, 200.

Conclusion

Which parts of O'Donovan's approach should we adopt – and which should we not? How should we adapt those elements that seem broadly generative, but not exactly right? In what ways might O'Donovan's work be related to other more-or-less contemporary projects in doctrinal, moral and political theology? What overall should we say about eschatology's place in ethics – and what is the case to be made for that place? Throughout the foregoing five chapters, I have indicated the beginnings of an answer to each of these questions, which I will not repeat here. Readers interested in a further exercise to range O'Donovan's work in the context of other contemporary theologians' work may consult the Appendix to this volume, which comprises an impressionistic sketch. But the additional thoughts with which I wish to conclude the study concern the final question just raised: about the case to be made for the place of eschatology in moral reasoning.

On eschatology and ethics

My argument here is fairly simple. I can begin with O'Donovan's own proposal that we 'grasp the Christian metaphysic in its wholeness and realise its significance for ethics'.[1] This is an entirely salutary suggestion, for our understandings of the moral life must be contextualized within the economy of the gospel, the proclamation of which details moral action's 'environment' or 'arena'.[2] By marginalizing any core Christian doctrine, ethics cannot but close itself off from the light that divine teaching might shed upon considerations of creaturely conduct.

Affirming this point is not simply about suggesting the reliance of ethics on doctrine nor about encouraging moralists to say something about each dogmatic affirmation for the sake of a kind of creedal courtesy. The need to demonstrate deliberate attention to each moment of the church's confession does not (or should not merely) arise from the systematician's demand that ethicists adhere to dogmatic theology's aspirations in terms of comprehensiveness, proportion and *taxis*, valuable as those considerations can be. I think it may arise, instead, from the requirement – or, better, happy possibility – that Christian ethics might be true to the worship of the church. If this means, as has become popular to suggest, that Christian ethics 'must incorporate sustained reflection

---

[1] O'Donovan, 'The Natural Ethic', 31.
[2] The terms are, respectively, Paul L. Lehmann's and Balthasar's. See Lehmann, *Ethics in a Christian Context* (London: SCM Press, 1963) and Steck, *Ethical Thought*.

on the liturgical prayer of the church',[3] then it will certainly mean incorporating sustained reflection on eschatological themes. There is, undeniably, an overwhelming preponderance of eschatological expression in Christian hymns and songs, prayers, poetry and iconography.[4]

Whatever the fortunes of eschatological reflection among the professional theologians and ethicists of any given period, it seems to have been ever-present in all major traditions of Christian piety, one of the wellsprings of everyday Christian worship, and, because of that, one of the animating forces of the Christian life.[5] While not a few theologians have been tempted to think of traditional eschatological expectations as the workings of 'the simple mind' (Paul Althaus),[6] Christians in fact engage in complex and deeply compelling processes of reasoning when they seek to act in light of these commitments. It seems to me that all kinds of believers *display* much better than trained theologians will essentially ever explain, how 'hope for the future is an inseparable, integral dimension of Christian faith' and just so – without necessary competition – 'the implied condition of possibility for responsible Christian action in the world'.[7] When it comes to hope, it seems to have been especially hard for professionals to 'recapture *in modo cognitionis*, what the faithful heart of any old woman already knows' (one of Aquinas's definitions of theology).[8] One of the reasons why this is so, I think, is because professional ethicists and morally minded theologians in particular have been for some significant reasons highly attuned to the potential *dangers* of eschatological longing.

Sometimes resistance to eschatology's formative role in the Christian moral imagination is owed to the apparently false consolation it presumes to offer.[9] Sometimes it resolves into a concern that the wild diversity of eschatological beliefs among Christians might undermine any unified basis for social ethics.[10] In both instances

---

[3] Vigen Guroian, *Ethics after Christendom: Toward an Ecclesial Christian Ethic* (Eugene: Wipf and Stock, 2004), 7. Cf. Vigen Guroian, 'Liturgy and the Lost Eschatological Vision of Christian Ethics', *The Annual of the Society of Christian Ethics* 20 (2000): 227–38, the entire *Blackwell Companion to Christian Ethics*, and O'Donovan, *Liturgy and Ethics: Grove Booklets E: 89* (Bramcote: Grove Books, 1993).

[4] See paragraph 11 'The Law of Prayer is the Law of Belief', of the document of the International Theological Commission entitled *Some Current Questions in Eschatology* (1992), http://www.vatican.va/roman_curia/congregations/cfaith/cti_documents/rc_cti_1990_problemi-attuali-escatologia_en.html (accessed 26 April 2020). Cf. Peter C. Phan, 'Roman Catholic Theology', in *Oxford Handbook of Eschatology*, ed. Jerry L. Walls (Oxford: OUP, 2008).

[5] See Brian E. Daley, *The Hope of the Early Church: A Handbook of Patristic Eschatology* (Cambridge: Cambridge University Press, 1991).

[6] Quoted in Markus Mühling, *T&T Clark Handbook of Christian Eschatology*, trans. Jennifer Adams-Massmann and David Andrew Gilland (London: Bloomsbury T & T Clark, 2015), 262.

[7] Daley's conclusion to his survey of Patristic eschatology: *The Hope of the Early Church*, 217.

[8] Bruce D. Marshall, '*Quod Scit Una Uetula*': Aquinas on the Nature of Theology', in *The Theology of Thomas Aquinas*, ed. Rik Van Nieuwenhove and Joseph Wawrykow (Notre Dame: University of Notre Dame Press, 2005), 26.

[9] So Timothy P. Jackson, *Love Disconsoled: Meditations on Christian Charity* (Cambridge: Cambridge University Press, 1999) – an account influenced by Richard Rorty, and convincing to Jeffrey Stout (*Democracy and Tradition* (Princeton: Princeton University Press, 2004), 256, 336, n. 43). For theological responses to Jackson, see Elliot, *Hope and Christian Ethics*, 75–85, Levering, *The Betrayal of Charity: The Sins That Sabotage Divine Love* (Waco: Baylor University Press, 2011), 42–60, and Gregory, *Politics of Love*, 111–12.

[10] So Stephen N. Williams, with an essay response by Miroslav Volf, *The Limits of Hope and the Logic of Love: Essays on Eschatology and Social Action* (Vancouver: Regent College Publishing, 2006).

referred to here, interestingly enough, what emerges is a compensatory and almost monistic stress on the surpassing value of charity as action-motivating and action-guiding, without much support from its companions in the Pauline triad. For others, the worry is that eschatological hope, when it feeds (or becomes) a social gospel, burns bright and burns out. 'We've been through this business of the Kingdom before', said Reinhold Niebuhr.[11] Yet we must surely counter, with David Elliot, that 'theological hope is ... not a parasite or deadweight, but something which makes a real contribution to Christian love',[12] and does so sustainably; that hope is, in fact, to be closely associated with the perseverance that forms characters who do not grow tired of doing the good.[13] O'Donovan indisputably agrees – but does he occasionally waver? Are his concerns about the over-heated 'calculations or prognostications'[14] of anticipation a little too determinative of what he is able to say, positively?

Reservations about eschatology's ethical import have by no means put theologians off trying to make moral sense of it, however. And so convinced have some been that eschatology is indeed irrevocably central to Christian practice that they have declared that 'theological ethics is eschatological or it is nothing'.[15] (That is not quite true: theological ethics divested of eschatology is not nothing; it is very often something like natural law.) Yet there are few contemporary theologians who eschew it entirely. Perhaps more pressing – strange to say in a study advocating eschatology's abiding relevance to morality – is what Rowan Greer calls 'the risk that the last things have often become no more than a way of talking about the meaning of the here and now'.[16] That is, the risk of moralism.

So it is not the case that eschatology is usually absent. In much of today's theology, all of the main elements of Christian teaching are generally in play, to some extent or other, in any given theologian's work. The task of analysis is therefore to see how these elements relate, how certain *loci* are thought to be of more use than others in the development of an account of human action, and how particular areas of 'applied' ethics are understood to fall most fittingly under which dogmatic headings. (There are certainly now no generally accepted criteria for establishing which doctrines practitioners should reach for when approaching any given 'issue', if there ever were.) I have tried to pursue something of this task here, in relation to O'Donovan. It has been a difficult assignment, insofar as his work is complex, but a rewarding one, insofar as he too thinks directly about these questions, and offers a set of powerful answers. Some theologians make seeing the connections even easier: Markus Mühling, for instance,

---

[11] Reinhold Niebuhr, *An Interpretation of Christian Ethics* (New York: Harper & Bros., 1935), 59.
[12] Elliot, *Hope and Christian Ethics*, 85.
[13] Rom. 5.4; Gal. 6.9.
[14] The phrase is Ben Witherington III's: 'The Conquest of Faith and the Climax of History', in *The Epistle to the Hebrews and Christian Theology*, ed. Richard Bauckham, Daniel R. Driver, Trevor A. Hart and Nathan MacDonald (Grand Rapids: Eerdmans, 2009), 436. Witherington is defending actual eschatological hope, but it is not hard to find scholars who conflate all future eschatological hope with these over-heated predictions. They are, for example, entirely determinative of the astonishingly creative 'counter-apocalyptic' of Catherine Keller. See e.g. *Apocalypse Now and Then: A Feminist Guide to the End of the World* (Minneapolis: Augsburg Fortress Press, 2004).
[15] Helmut Thielicke, *Theological Ethics*, vol. 1 (Philadelphia: Fortress Press, 1966), 47.
[16] Rowan A. Greer, *Christian Hope and Christian Life: Raids on the Inarticulate* (New York: Crossroad, 2001), e.g. 3.

intersperses moral and pastoral topics among particular aspects of eschatology in particular – a kind of Barthian move at the micro-level.[17] For others, we would have to look a little more closely and to analyse at risk of artificially unravelling something deliberately woven, in order to see which doctrines are doing what work (to put it a little crudely).[18]

Leaving aside that task for now, we may ask, finally, what contribution the doctrine – or doctrines – of eschatology should make to Christian ethics. To put it for now in a necessarily abstracted, formal way, we can do worse than to base an answer upon Pannenberg's notions of eschatology's 'critical' and 'constructive' functions.[19] I have reservations about speaking of 'function', and would maintain that this tract of Christian teaching, like any other, is finally irreducible to any practical effect (I argue as much in the postscript to this study). But the proposal captures much that is important to capture. First, as O'Donovan and many others can teach us, the horizon of eschatology stands over current states of affairs, as a 'critical comparative',[20] serving a 'negative, interrogative'[21] purpose. And, second, hope in the fulfilment of that heavenly state of affairs here on earth has a 'positive and transformative' role to play, too.[22]

I have argued that O'Donovan has not made quite enough of this second aspect. But we must make much of in a particular way. It will always need repeating that Christian ethics is not in any cause and effect manner the means of producing the kingdom of God. Eschatological hope does not pass by the world, even as it goes beyond it,[23] but *we* do not, in any self-standing sense, 'build the kingdom'; 'real transformation of our estate is vested in God rather than human being'.[24] Yet 'relieved of final responsibility', we are 'called instead to steadfastness, alertness and expectancy', and to 'hopeful Christian action'.[25]

The action that moral theology seeks to commend *may*, then, be understood as really and meaningfully linked to the kingdom of God, but we will have to describe carefully the general character that 'link' possesses. There are no doubt many different kinds of words and phrases we might employ to do so; the basic rule for their validity will be whether they can be seen as coherent with the prayer 'Our Father … your kingdom come, your will be done'. To list just a few, we can legitimately say, I think, that human moral action can be an *annunciation* of God's kingdom, a *witness*, token

---

[17] Mühling, *T & T Clark Handbook*.
[18] One way in which we might do that is by employing an analytical tool, and one analytical tool that might be leveraged towards this end, it seems to me, is the hyper-systematic structure of David Kelsey's book *Eccentric Existence* (much like Barth's *Church Dogmatics* is often used, and especially its threefold logic of creation, reconciliation and redemption). For my attempt to do this, see the Appendix.
[19] Wolfhart Pannenberg, 'Constructive and Critical Functions of Eschatology', *Harvard Theological Review* 77, no. 2 (1984): 119–39. Cf Moltmann, *Theology of Hope*, 335.
[20] Eberhard Jüngel, *Theological Essays*, trans. John Webster (London/New York: Bloomsbury T & T Clark, 2014), 183.
[21] John C. McDowell, *Hope in Barth's Eschatology: Interrogations and Transformations Beyond Tragedy* (Aldershot: Ashgate, 2000), 180–213, 202.
[22] Ibid.
[23] Hans Urs von Balthasar, *Theo-Drama: Theological-Dramatic Theory, vol. V: The Last Act*, trans. Graham Harrison (San Francisco: Ignatius Press, 2003), 176.
[24] O'Regan, *Theology and the Spaces of Apocalyptic*, 56, paraphrasing Bulgakov.
[25] Webster, 'Hope', 214.

and *ensign* of redemption; that moments and patterns of creaturely behaviour can be seen, by the Spirit, as *analogies* to it or *parables* of it; and that the kingdom drawing near elicits our *corresponding* action, even as it is the reality under which we stand and the destiny to which we are drawn.

Finally, this study has suggested that scripture and tradition can give fuller indications of what kinds of action might constitute such witness than O'Donovan sometimes appears to think. I have been necessarily selective in following through on those suggestions here. Nevertheless, I have particularly wanted to press the point that concern for the poor is perhaps principal among those kinds of actions, although that example is not quite as clear a test case as the calling to singleness, to which I have also sought to draw attention. (It is not such a clear test case because concern for the poor can and should also be derived from a creation demand, whereas singleness is rendered intelligible by consideration of the eschatological moments of the divine economy.) In the final analysis, qualifications of O'Donovan's approach like this are important, but they only serve to specify further a conviction I am sure that he shares and on which I will end. It is, as O'Donovan's old friend Hauerwas puts it, that for the sake of the world, the church 'assembles reminders of the kingdom of God in subtle, seemingly trivial and insignificant ways'.[26]

---

[26] Stanley Hauerwas and William H. Willimon, *Resident Aliens: Life in the Christian Colony* (Nashville: Abingdon Press, 2014), 96–7.

Postscript

The end of ethics

This study has been about the import of eschatology for morality. But when we are thinking about eschatology, the last word cannot go to ethics, for a simple but spiritually crucial reason of which O'Donovan is aware. It is this: as regards the practice of the moral life, there is a profound superfluity to eschatological hope, an inassimilable '*more*'.

Before I invoke that surplus any further, let me be quite clear, again, that I think that hope is not only not inimical to action but itself a 'a busy and active thing' (as Luther described faith). It gives boldness (2 Cor. 3.12) and renews strength (Is. 40.31). 'To abound in hope by the power of the Holy Spirit (Rom. 15.13)', as Webster says, 'is not only to look to a prospective benefit but also to receive appointment as a certain kind of agent'.[1] To confess the Creeds' eschatological claims is to enlist for service, for all 'Christian statements of hope are unavoidably self-involving'.[2] And it bears repeating that to affirm these things is not to render eschatology a function of human projects or a matter of mere projection. It is true that visions of God's kingdom have been and will continue to be extraordinarily generative of ethical practice, and that the scriptural portrayal of that kingdom may encode many human aspirations in such a way as to suggest that they are (also) policies of action. But the ways in which biblical narratives regarding the kingdom do indeed serve to enable and form moral action are theologically utterly dependent upon those narratives' 'realist' function as references to – descriptions of – the mighty acts of God: already achieved, even now coming to pass, and yet to come.

The hope that realist faith produces, then, is truly fit 'for the densest of earthly settings', for situations of injustice, oppression and suffering.[3] Yet while it is present and powerful in these earthly situations, eschatological hope – as a non-reductively realist hope – reaches beyond them, too.[4] It does so because its object is the Coming

---

[1] Webster, 'Hope', 290.
[2] Nicholas Adams, 'Hope', in *The Oxford Companion to Christian Thought*, ed. Adrian Hastings, Alistair Mason and Hugh Pyper (Oxford: Oxford University Press, 1999), 310. For Thomas, among the three theological virtues hope loves God as our *personal* good, so possesses a particularly self-involving or existential character.
[3] Lifting this phrase from Ivor J. Davidson, 'Salvation's Destiny: Heirs of God', in *God of Salvation*, 169, where he uses it, profoundly, of the 'Abba' cry of the Lord Jesus.
[4] See Sonderegger, 'Towards a Doctrine of Resurrection', in *Eternal God, Eternal Life: Theological Investigations into the Concept of Immortality*, ed. Philip G. Ziegler (London/New York: Bloomsbury T & T Clark, 2016). Cf. Medi-Ann Volpe, *Rethinking Christian Identity: Doctrine and Discipleship* (Chichester: Wiley-Blackwell, 2013), 238: '[D]octrine points the way forward ... so that through the tribulations we can discern ... the kingdom of God toward which we hasten in hope'.

One who entered into the very depths of the creaturely life of earth, triumphed over evil on its own ground and is now raised victorious in the heavenly places. Fixed as it is upon him, 'our blessed hope' (Tit. 2.13), the Christian doctrine of eschatology has an ultimately doxological excess.[5] And, correspondingly, Christian hope – 'sure and steadfast anchor of the soul' (Heb. 6.19) – is finally irreducible to its ethical import, and cannot be exhausted in praxis. The 'God of hope' (Rom. 15.13), on this view, cannot be reduced to a postulate of practical reason necessary for morality, nor is God's kingdom just a principle of action, a regulative ideal rather than a promise the fulfilment of which we long for.[6] To be seen and lived as true, the Christian doctrine of eschatology does not need to be resituated wholesale in the realm of morality as though certain modern strictures upon speech about the 'beyond' successfully evacuated it of any content in dogmatic or spiritual theology.[7] This cluster of teachings does and should have critical and constructive ethical 'styles' and implications, but its primary 'style' will be first and last contemplative and 'celebratory'.[8]

O'Donovan is right: theological ethics ought not 'attach itself sluggishly to one of its poles ... *always* singing the praises of God in heaven or *always* picking over the practical possibilities of action in difficult circumstances': rather, it should 'make the journeys of thought entrusted to it between heaven and the circumstances'.[9] Yet as he also knows well, as such, ethics is only a 'middle' movement of Christian theological reason. It is true that this middle movement is an unavoidable responsibility in this age, and so too reflection upon it: 'Theological moral criticism is nothing but an endless trade in critique and revision until Christ comes' (John Bowlin).[10] Just so it is true, as Jennifer Herdt writes, that moral theology must be open, 'in and through its listening to the Word of God, to being disrupted by the alien character of the neighbor, particularly those on the margins of power', and that this 'is never a task that can be completed once and for all, this side of the eschaton. We are not yet, any of us, "entering into rest". We are called to be disturbed.'[11] But even in this life, even if everything bears moral implication, not all is ethics. And, as O'Donovan knows well, with 'all our busy activities over and done with' – even the busy activities of moralists – 'the only thing that will remain will be *alleluia*'.[12]

---

[5] On this see Adam, *Our Only Hope*, and Greer, *Christian Hope and Christian Life*.
[6] The language here is, of course, meant to invoke something of a Kantian understanding. See e.g. Immanuel Kant, *Religion Within the Boundaries of Mere Reason: And Other Writings*, trans. and ed. Allen Wood and George di Giovanni (Cambridge: Cambridge University Press, 1998), 137. Whether or not Kant's moral postulates should be read in this immanent way is contested. See Frederick C. Beiser, 'Moral Faith and the Highest Good', in *The Cambridge Companion to Kant and Modern Philosophy*, ed. Paul Guyer (New York: Cambridge University Press, 2006), 620.
[7] On this, see intriguingly John E. Thiel, *Icons of Hope: The "Last Things" in Catholic Imagination* (Notre Dame: University of Notre Dame Press, 2013).
[8] Adapting, here, some terms employed by Rowan Williams. See *On Christian Theology* (Oxford: Blackwell, 2000), xiii. Benedict XVI's *Spe Salvi* (2007) makes a somewhat similar argument to the one I am outlining in this postscript. However, he would seem to consider a greater quantity of political and liberation theology to fall foul of the argument's critical edge than I do.
[9] O'Donovan, *Self, World, and Time*, 89.
[10] Bowlin, 'Protestant Thomism', 251.
[11] Herdt, 'O'Donovan's *Ethics as Theology*', 164.
[12] Augustine, Sermon 255, in *Sermons: The Works of St. Augustine: A Translation for the 21st Century*, III.7 (230–272B), ed. John E. Rotelle, trans. Edmund Hill (New York: New City Press, 1993), 156. Italics added.

Appendix

Cartography with O'Donovan and friends

I said, in the introduction, that writing about O'Donovan analytically is not straightforward: it is much easier to reproduce his thought or simply to dismiss it. One of the aims of this study has been to map, patiently, the topography of O'Donovan's moral vision so that it might be more conveniently brought into wider discourse. To some extent, I hope, the passing references made to other theologians throughout have already begun to do just that. What I seek to do here in this appended and all-too-schematic reflection is to provide a skein of brief suggestions that are not to be considered definitive, but that might serve to invite further conversation, and to lay the foundations for further constructive work. One way in which we might do this is by employing an analytical tool, and the analytical tool that I attempt to leverage towards this end here is the hyper-systematic structure of David Kelsey's book *Eccentric Existence*.

Introducing Kelsey's grid

There are all kinds of material points of striking resonance and dissonance between Kelsey's *Eccentric Existence* and O'Donovan's work, some of which I have touched upon. But the point of using Kelsey's scheme of creation, consummation and reconciliation as scaffolding (the surprising order of the latter two terms is owed to Kelsey's supralapsarian conviction, but that does not need to detain us now) is that it might give us a formal grid with which to record O'Donovan's contribution to Christian ethics' *theological* presuppositions. And, second, a grid with which to relate it to other construals of moral theology's doctrinal coordinates more generally, and eschatology's import more specifically. In keeping with the admittedly tenuous analogy employed throughout the study, we might imagine this as an exercise in 'comparative cartography'.

To be clear, I am *not* suggesting that Kelsey necessarily gets things right – it does not matter whether he does or does not, for the purposes of this exercise. Nor am I suggesting that his style of hyper-systematicity is a goal worth striving for in ethics or, for that matter, in doctrine (I worry that this comparative exercise is otherwise another kind of school-theology revenge upon practical reasoners). But what Kelsey represents, in the clearest possible way – three hefty sections addressing each theme respectively – is commitment to thinking through the implications of each moment of the divine economy. What I am aiming at by employing the grid, then, is enriched thinking about the dogmatic presuppositions of different approaches in contemporary theological ethics. What follows is a rapid and selective tour of the horizon of contemporary moral theology, in which I use the terms 'creation, consummation, and reconciliation' to capture some differences of emphasis. It will be, by necessity, observational and assertoric, and restricted in its main figures to Protestant theology. And, once again, this way of going about the reception of O'Donovan's thought cannot directly assess his particular treatments of moral and political issues, or that of any other thinker engaged – and that, in itself, means the exercise is probably susceptible to the charge of formalism I occasionally made earlier!

First and very straightforwardly, we can see that O'Donovan, like Kelsey, affirms the doctrine of creation, and its place in moral theology. The significance of this cannot be underestimated, in view of cultural practices (in which Christians are complicit) that are at best inhospitable to the moral claims of the Christian theology of creation, and at worst participate in what Willie James Jennings describes as the 'abiding mutilation of a Christian vision of creation and our own creatureliness'.[1] (We might think here of structural sins like racism, sexism and the degradation of the environment.) As I have indicated, this places O'Donovan in the company of various Christian thinkers who have recently sought to retrieve the doctrine of creation for various ends. Moreover, that this is retrieval is now widespread should not blur recognition that O'Donovan was a pioneer. When Joseph Ratzinger wrote his own book on creation in the 1980s, he worried that 'the creation account is noticeably and nearly completely absent from catechesis, preaching, and even theology'.[2] And from Christian ethics, too, if we notice what Colin Gunton wrote a decade later, introducing an edited volume on the doctrine: besides Barth's 'treatment of the ethics of creation ... other recent treatments, with the exception of Oliver O'Donovan's seminal *Resurrection and Moral Order*, are thin on the ground indeed'.[3]

In theory at least, O'Donovan is able to show – just as Kelsey does, who provides doctrines of consummation and reconciliation besides creation – that salvation and eschatology can be thought alongside protology 'without elimination'. Yet in a sense, Kelsey's painstaking articulation of the three elements places in relief a tendency in O'Donovan's thought to slide into a salvation-historical monism: in which all that really matters morally is creation's form, 'the old, made explicit' (certainly given, restored and enduring, but essentially the same). Interestingly, as I noted, the kind of ethos promoted by Kelsey's doctrine of creation actually exhibits many of the same details as the one that O'Donovan intends to foster with his understanding of the resurrection. This observation may underscore a lack of properly eschatological definition in O'Donovan's view of the resurrection, to be sure; if the qualities he places under that

---

[1] Willie James Jennings, *The Christian Imagination: Theology and the Origins of Race* (New Haven: Yale University Press, 2010), 293.

[2] Joseph Ratzinger, *'In the Beginning...': a Catholic Understanding of the Story of Creation and the Fall*, trans. Boniface Ramsey (Grand Rapids: Eerdmans, 1995 [German ed. 1986]), ix.

[3] Colin E. Gunton, 'Introduction', in *The Doctrine of Creation: Essays in Dogmatics, History, and Philosophy*, ed. Colin E. Gunton (London/New York: T & T Clark International, 1997), 5.

rubric are almost without remainder found under Kelsey's rubric of creation then what ethical weight does the resurrection's forward-looking aspect in fact carry?

Yet it may provide a way of receiving and elaborating upon some of O'Donovan's material insights while uncoupling them from his apparent flattening of eschatology's import. In Chapter 2, I sought to query the way language of 'restoration' was used and to probe the element of strong continuity O'Donovan's eschatology displays. Moreover, I suggested that his account's ethical gains (including concern for the body, and for ecological issues) could just as well be obtained by other perspectives without these particular dogmatic emphases – and Kelsey's might be one.[4] As subsequent points will clarify, I do not mean by this modification to imply that creation should be viewed uneschatologically – O'Donovan's attempts to relate creation to Christology and eschatology are to be preferred to many current Protestant retrievals of natural law – rather that his account of restoration is not the only way to relate the two.

If we turn to the doctrine of eschatological consummation, and glance at the *content* of Kelsey's account, we find divergence here, too. In this area, Kelsey draws on the apocalyptic reading of Paul (as does Hauerwas, in his criticism of O'Donovan's focus on creation). This reading yields a more discontinuous, disjunctive vision and – though Kelsey claims not to be doing ethics – he embraces the broadly liberationist moral and political vision attendant on such a reading.[5] The apocalyptic sensibility clashes with O'Donovan's in a pronounced way, and I shall enlist it as a conversation partner for the rest of the chapter because it seems to me that the friction may be productive. Furthermore, that this sensibility does so sharply diverge from O'Donovan's is not surprising – apocalyptic theology's most vocal contemporary critic is N. T. Wright, and on occasion, apocalyptic critics of Wright have taken O'Donovan to task, too.[6]

'Apocalyptic' theology

To say that 'apocalyptic' theology has little invested, ethically, in a doctrine of creation is to underline the clearest of distinctions between O'Donovan and that sensibility. Moreover, that Kelsey himself, like O'Donovan, does take the time to explore the doctrine of creation and its implications, does represent a straightforward advance on many of the apocalyptic theologians who would approve of Kelsey's account of consummation. However, though Kelsey presents both aspects – creation and consummation – he gives relatively little help in seeing how the apocalyptic eschatology and doctrine of creation might relate. In fact, Kelsey's account of creation seems to be

---

[4] This shared concern for the moral implications of creaturely life in this space and time might be extended further by engagement with Ephraim Radner (*A Time to Keep: Theology, Mortality and the Shape of a Human Life* (Waco: Baylor University Press, 2016), and John Swinton (*Becoming Friends with Time: Disability, Timefullness, and Gentle Discipleship* (Waco: Baylor University Press, 2016)).

[5] Whether or not we accept Kelsey's denial does not affect my use of the scheme here, but I do think his theological anthropology (like any) is ethically primed. I hope to write more fully elsewhere about the ways in which *Eccentric Existence* might both inform and be challenged by a moral-theological reading. For a beginning, see Paul Dafydd Jones' review essay, *Journal of the American Academy of Religion* 80, no. 3 (2012): 787–800, 797–8.

[6] See the reference to the work of Samuel Adams, above.

decidedly non-teleological – and apparently based on Wisdom literature rather than on Genesis in order to deliberately *elude* implications of teleology – and therefore appears static in a slightly different way than O'Donovan's. Thus Kelsey (perhaps like Kathryn Tanner), however insightful the individual accounts of each *locus*, tends to sever the links between creation, providence, salvation and eschatology. This leads to widely observed tensions in his scheme between the moments of the divine economy.[7] More the point for this study, it leaves serious questions about how the multiple elements should inform *ethics*.

After all, if what we are presented with by Kelsey is three distinct stories, how might they inform moral deliberation? Granted, there is also the danger of reductionism in a single story reduced to one essential point – 'vindication', perhaps – but with this other route, there is the threat of incoherence. Perhaps they are different resources to be drawn upon as reflection demands (akin to a suggestion Francis Watson makes about ecclesial discernment regarding deployment of James' sense of created order and Pauline apocalyptic).[8] O'Donovan's sense of the relation of creation, providence, salvation and eschatology is obviously more integrated because, more teleological, and though in some way *over*-integrated, it is preferable to Kelsey's, and the more disjointed moments of Barth's, inasmuch as it answers the question of the significance of these elements' interrelation as a 'unified metaphysic' for morals. Yet that is only a major gain if O'Donovan is able to demonstrate sensitivity to the ways each of the dogmatic moments shapes the Christian ethos distinctively, which Kelsey tries to do discretely – to a fault.

Returning to the 'apocalyptic' theologians, I find that though often failing to account satisfactorily for creation, unlike Kelsey and O'Donovan, they do typically represent an advance on O'Donovan in one respect. Accounts based on logics of 'coming to pass/ passing away' (Christopher Morse)[9] or 'perpetual advent' (David Congdon, interpreting Bultmann),[10] I argue, can offer a heightened sense of eschatology's *present* import that is not always as pronounced in O'Donovan. In fact, Christopher Holmes' apocalyptic interpretation of the notion of *Christus praesens* in his book *Ethics in the Presence of Christ* is given doctrinal definition in direct criticism of O'Donovan's *Resurrection and Moral Order*, and his proposals can be compared here.[11] Holmes's approach has many merits, not least its concerted effort to see dogmatic Christology shape an understanding of ethics, and in such a way as to nourish commitment to reflection on Jesus's ministry and teaching, besides his death, resurrection, ascension and coming

---

[7] This leads to widely observed tensions in his scheme. For an overstatement of them, see Catherine Pickstock's assessment: 'The One Story: A Critique of David Kelsey's Theological Robotics', *Modern Theology* 27, no. 1 (2011): 26–40.

[8] Francis Watson, '"Every Perfect Gift": James, Paul and the Created Order', in *Muted Voices of the New Testament: Readings in the Catholic Epistles and Hebrews*, ed. Katherine M. Hockey, Madison N. Pierce and Francis Watson (London/New York: Bloomsbury T & T Clark, 2017). That suggestion might fit quite well with what we find in James Wm McClendon, *Ethics: Systematic Theology*, vol. 1 (Nashville: Abingdon, 2002).

[9] Christopher Morse, *The Difference Heaven Makes: Rehearing the Gospel as Good News* (London/New York: T & T Clark International, 2010).

[10] David W. Congdon, *Rudolf Bultmann: A Companion to His Theology* (Eugene: Cascade Books, 2005).

[11] Holmes, *Ethics*, 95–7.

in glory. If ethics that treat exemplarity do typically reflect on these, Protestants who ground ethics in Christology – including apocalyptic Christology – are seldom so committed to the practice of attention to the content of scripture's depiction of Christ as is Holmes. His approach, in terms of Christ's reality-making contemporaneity, nicely sharpens one element of *Resurrection and Moral Order*'s vision with the critical eye of a Barthian systematic theologian. But as a perspective, it seems to remain monocular: while we are advanced beyond *Resurrection and Moral Order* in terms of *one* of ethics' theological bases, we are not much informed about how we should think of the others, if at all.[12]

O'Donovan's focus upon judgement does resonate with some of this apocalyptic stress, and the awareness of moral action and identity being enacted and constituted *coram Deo* is there in his work, too. The sense of moral answerability – responsibility – in the present is important. O'Donovan does not, however, seem to bring out so much as these thinkers the way in which the presence of the kingdom in our midst even now – 'a concrete messianic *irruption* of history itself', in Nathan Kerr's representative terms – creates particular forms of liberative action.[13]

Some interpretations of apocalyptic theology are especially alert to moral dimensions,[14] deploying their eschatological emphases in a different kind of 'Augustinian' political theology than O'Donovan's (P. Travis Kroeker), and leveraging it against ethical turns to natural law (Philip G. Ziegler) or virtue (Morse). But those few with what might be called an apocalyptic sensibility for disjunction who *do* recognize creation's moral import as well as that of 'the new' (for example, Eberhard Jüngel) are elusive about what that might mean morally.[15] And while apocalyptic theology announces itself as thoroughgoing eschatology, it sometimes fails to account satisfactorily for *future* hope. Completely de-temporalizing eschatology in order to articulate it in purely spatial terms, as some do, is in the end, I worry, doctrinally, morally and pastorally irresponsible, and it cannot but betray authentic Christian

---

[12] That might also be considered a distinct limitation of Kerr's *Christ, History, and* Apocalyptic, despite its promise. My worries about Kerr's book – concerns amplified in terms of Congdon's work – are comparable to those expressed in D. Stephen Long, *Hebrews* (Louisville: Westminster John Knox, 2011), 198–213. Holmes now appears to develop implications more in terms of creation, while maintaining covenantal particularity: 'Just as Jesus Christ is the one who completes torah and temple he, as the agent of creation, is the very fulfillment of the created order'. (*The Lord Is Good: Seeking the God of the Psalter* (London: Apollos, 2018), 155). He is not primarily an ethicist, but interesting, perhaps, that his sensibility has shifted as he has moved away from apocalyptic theology, and in his own description 'through' Bonhoeffer and Barth: to an approach more informed by Augustine and Thomas, and among recent theologians Webster and Sonderegger. Interesting, too, that interpretation of the Psalms in Augustinian and Thomist idiom yields throughout formulations more in keeping with O'Donovan's than before.

[13] Kerr, *Christ, History, and Apocalyptic*, 188.

[14] E.g. Nancy Duff, 'The Significance of Pauline Apocalyptic for Theological Ethics', in *Apocalyptic and the New Testament: Essays in Honor of J. Louis Martyn*, ed. Joel Marcus and Marion L. Soards (Sheffield: JSOT Press, 1989); Douglas Harink, *Paul among the Postliberals: Pauline Theology beyond Christendom and Modernity* (Grand Rapids: Brazos, 2003); and *1 and 2 Peter* (London: SCM, 2009).

[15] See the deeply enigmatic Eberhard Jüngel, 'The Emergence of the New', in *Theological Essays II*, trans. Arnold Neufeldt-Fast and J. B. Webster (Edinburgh: T & T Clark, 1995), and more recent, 'New – Old – New: Theological Aphorisms', trans. R. David Nelson, in Nelson, Darren Sarisky, and Justin Stratis, eds. *Theological Theology* (London/New York: Bloomsbury T & T Clark, 2015).

hope.[16] It also fails thereby to fully overcome the immanentist, progressivist eschatology of the Social Gospel, which apocalyptic theology in its origins (J. Louis Martyn) in some way formulated itself over and against – though maintaining the Social Gospel's moral and political commitment.

Though I would wish to preserve something of the angularity of apocalyptic theology's construal of eschatology and its radical import for ethics, I think for it to contribute to a full-orbed moral theology, it must be modified by reparative arguments, for instance those made by Grant Macaskill and Cyril O'Regan, which begin to show how it can be integrated in a wider frame more like O'Donovan's, attentive to creation and the coming kingdom as well as the present day of salvation.[17] I would argue that it is certainly possible to maintain a heightened sense of the 'today' of Christian faith – a stress upon the drawing near of the kingdom, and the presence of judgement – alongside an elaboration of longing for the heavenly city. Kelsey at his best rightly sees no reason to oppose consummation or reconciliation to creation, nor within his considerations of eschatology any reason to oppose future hope and the existential immediacy of the 'even now'.[18] Ultimately, the best reason not to oppose any of these elements to one another is Christological: 'Jesus Christ, the same yesterday, today, and forever' (Heb. 13.8).[19]

Having found apocalyptic theology especially well suited to chasten O'Donovan's position, then, I have found it inherently limited as a perspective that one might want to adopt, and recurrently turned to Kelsey's schematic to chart the different elements and to show their essential compatibility. But, as already mentioned, I find Kelsey's schematic itself insufficiently integrated to serve moral theology as well as might be wished, and deficient in that respect compared to O'Donovan. What we are looking for, then, are *appropriately* integrated visions of ethics' theological bases that take on board creation, reconciliation and consummation – and more particularly, in terms of this study's specific topic, different aspects of eschatology's import. One promising candidate here is the sensibility associated with the 'Erlangen Luther' interpretation: Hans G. Ulrich, Bernd Wannenwetsch, Brian Brock and now Michael Laffin.[20]

---

[16] This is also a real issue with Kathryn Tanner, 'Eschatology and Ethics', in *The Oxford Handbook of Theological Ethics*. Cf. the final chapter of Kathryn Tanner, *Jesus, Humanity and the Trinity: A Brief Systematic Theology* (Minneapolis: Fortress Press, 2001).

[17] See Macaskill, 'History, Providence, and the Apocalyptic Paul'; O'Regan, *Theology and the Spaces of Apocalyptic*, and 'Two Forms of Catholic Apocalyptic Theology', *International Journal of Systematic Theology* 20, no. 1 (2018): 31–64.

[18] A further (unexpected) source of guidance here might be Jean Danielou, who, quoting Bultmann, emphasizes the former, and argues that it fits alongside the latter. See Jean Danielou, *The Lord of History: Reflections on the Inner Meaning of History*, trans. Nigel Abercrombie (London: Longmans, Green and Co, 1958), 32–3.

[19] On this see Katherine Sonderegger, '"Response"', to Christopher Morse, *The Difference Heaven Makes*', *Theology Today* 68, no. 1 (2011): 64–8, 66.

[20] See e.g. Hans G. Ulrich, *Wie Geschöpfe leben: Konturen evangelischer Ethik* (Münster: LIT Verlag, 2007); Wannenwetsch, *Political Worship*, Brock, *Christian Ethics in a Technological Age*, Michael Laffin, *The Promise of Martin Luther's Political Theology: Freeing Luther from the Modern Political Narrative* (London/New York: T & T Clark, 2016). We might also include the earlier Hütter (his doctoral supervisor was Ulrich).

'Erlangen' Lutheranism

Indeed, moral-theological integration of the apocalyptic sensibility about eschatology's present import with a concern for creation is effected explicitly in the thought of Hans Ulrich,[21] drawing on a particular line of Luther interpretation held in common with Oswald Bayer.[22] Ulrich, moreover, shares with O'Donovan a sense of the link between eschatology and pneumatology (again, one that Kelsey also recognizes, explicating pneumatology in the section on 'consummation', if again hermetically demarcating the *topoi*). Ulrich grounds an eschatologically inflected but firmly this-worldly account of the Christian life in pneumatology, sometimes constructing this account in direct conversation with O'Donovan's thought. Furthermore, because of his integrated theological vision, Ulrich's account of divine and human agency is also more promising than the apocalyptic account, and complements O'Donovan's. Besides this, Ulrich and those in his tradition have a different way of registering the significance of the doctrine of creation than O'Donovan – as O'Donovan himself notes[23] – and therefore offer a different presentation of nature's normativity than O'Donovan – one perhaps typically more subtly sensitive to the effects of sin and to the historical and social shaping of human life and action. Here they show some unexplored affinities with John Bowlin's Protestant Thomism, though, as with Bowlin's project, there are still questions to be asked about how exactly the material form of creation is to be evaluated, if it is to be indeed understood as place where God's call may be directly heard and responded to.[24]

Unfortunately, however, it seems as though to this point the 'Erlangen Lutheranism' can sometimes exhibit a certain allergy to futural eschatology because of its potential for distraction from ethical concern. It may thereby have a tendency to neglect the aspect of eschatological affirmation, the spiritual correlate of which is longing and hope. And, perhaps allied to an overreliance on presentist aspects of messianic eschatology (like some apocalyptic theology), the proper concern for integration may lead to a risk that eschatology and protology are conflated in an undifferentiating Lutheran theology of encounter with the creative Word. Thus to parse out the three aspects of eschatology's import, the Erlangen Lutherans do justice (a) to eschatology's reaffirmation of creation, and (b) eschatology's present coming-to-pass, but not so much (c) to its production of hope in what is to come. Actually, as in O'Donovan, it seems that this potential oversight is driven by moral-theological concerns rather than simply dogmatically watertight reasons; it is in fact the one area where these theologians may seem to court more doctrinal revisionism than they would be happy doing elsewhere.

---

[21] See especially Hans G. Ulrich, 'The Messianic Contours of Evangelical Ethics', in *The Freedom of a Christian Ethicist: The Future of a Reformation Legacy*, ed. Brian Brock and Michael Mawson (London/New York: T & T Clark, 2016). Cf. Hans G. Ulrich, *Eschatologie und Ethik: die theologische Theorie der Ethik in ihrer Beziehung auf die Rede von Gott seit Friedrich Schleiermacher* (München: Kaiser-Verlag, 1988).

[22] See e.g. Oswald Bayer, *Freedom in Response. Lutheran Ethics: Sources and Controversies* (Oxford: Oxford University Press, 2007).

[23] O'Donovan, 'The Object of Theological Ethics', *Studies in Christian Ethics* 20, no. 2 (2007): 203–14.

[24] See McKenny's review of Brock, *Christian Ethics in a Technological Age*, *Studies in Christian Ethics* 25, no. 3 (2012): 372–5.

Finally, it may be that that among prominent contemporary theological ethicists, it is Gilbert Meilaender whose work, when mapped onto Kelsey's grid, would most closely resemble O'Donovan's.

Gilbert Meilander

Meilaender, though Lutheran, does not necessarily share the apocalyptic sensibility of more 'radical' Lutheran thinkers. But while approximating O'Donovan's thought in the respects of concern for salvation's this-worldly significance *and* ultimately eschatological horizon, Meilaender seems sometimes to more successfully blend a concern for creatureliness (owed in his case to Lutheran and Barthian influences) with a transcendent eschatological vision of consummation (owed to Augustinian-Thomist influences such as Josef Pieper). He is also perhaps more sensitive to the effects of sin than O'Donovan, in his account of reconciliation and redemption. Moreover, while Meilaender's Lutheran instincts secure the significance of faith, and his Augustinian instincts a role for love – both crucial for O'Donovan, too – his Thomist vision engenders a more developed impression of the creaturely life *in via* than O'Donovan's, and he therefore seems to find a more consistently significant role for hope.

Conclusion

I could go on, registering the particular theological shape of other contemporaries on something like Kelsey's grid, but I will leave it there. Together, these comments, I hope, show the many rewarding avenues that might be pursued by further analysis. As Basil Mitchell wrote:

> The same factors that make for a distinctively Christian ethic will also make for distinctively different patterns of Christian ethics. Hence in trying to formulate a Christian view upon a contemporary moral issue it is often necessary to debate questions which are not, strictly speaking, ethical at all, but concern doctrine, hermeneutical principles and, in a broad sense of the word, philosophy.[25]

That is true, though I am also aware of not having added in the additional factor of moral and political 'issues' – doing so would develop this comparative exercise further. What this appendix does suggest, taken together, is that further work is always needing to be done to develop non-reductive moral theology attentive to the whole range of Christian doctrinal affirmations – the full scope of Christian worship. And, concurrently and thereafter, further work is always needing to be done working out the significance of all this for the living of Christian lives.

---

[25] Basil Mitchell, 'Is There a Distinctive Christian Ethic?' in Basil Mitchell, *How to Play Theological Ping-Pong: And Other Essays on Faith and Reason*, ed. William J. Abraham and Robert W. Prevost (Grand Rapids: Eerdmans, 1990), 55.

Bibliography

O'Donovan

O'Donovan, Oliver. 'Towards an Interpretation of Biblical Ethics'. *Tyndale Bulletin* 27 (1976): 54-78.
O'Donovan, Oliver. 'The Natural Ethic'. In *Essays in Evangelical Social Ethics*, edited by David F. Wright, 19-35. Exeter: Paternoster Press, 1978.
O'Donovan, Oliver. *The Problem of Self-Love in St. Augustine*. New Haven/London: Yale University Press, 1980.
O'Donovan, Oliver. '*Usus* and *Fruitio* in Augustine, *De doctrina Christiana* I'. *Journal of Theological Studies* 33, no. 2 (1981): 361-97.
O'Donovan, Oliver. *Transsexualism and the Christian Marriage*. Bramcote: Grove Books, 1982.
O'Donovan, Oliver. 'Transsexualism and Christian Marriage'. *The Journal of Religious Ethics* 11, no. 1 (1983): 135-62.
O'Donovan, Oliver. 'Review of Pannenberg, *Ethics*'. *The Journal of Theological Studies* 35, no. 1 (1983): 358-64.
O'Donovan, Oliver. 'Review of Gustafson, *Theology and Ethics*'. *The Journal of Theological Studies* 35, no. 1 (1984): 275-9.
O'Donovan, Oliver. *Begotten or Made?*. Oxford: Clarendon Press, 1984.
O'Donovan, Oliver. 'Augustinian Ethics'. In *A New Dictionary of Christian Ethics*, edited by James F. Childress and John Macquarrie, 46-9. London: SCM/Westminster: John Knox, 1986.
O'Donovan, Oliver. 'The Political Thought of the Book of Revelation'. *Tyndale Bulletin* 37 (1986): 61-94.
O'Donovan, Oliver. 'Paul Ramsey: 1913-88'. *Studies in Christian Ethics* 1, no. 1 (1988): 82-90.
O'Donovan, Oliver. 'Review of Mahoney, *The Making of Moral Theology*'. *The Journal of Theological Studies* 39, no. 1 (1988): 348-50.
O'Donovan, Oliver. 'How Can Theology Be Moral?'. *Journal of Religious Ethics* 17, no. 2 (1989): 81-94.
O'Donovan, Oliver. *Peace and Certainty: A Theological Essay on Deterrence*. Oxford: Clarendon Press, 1989.
O'Donovan, Oliver. 'Review of Fuchs, *Christian Morality: The Word Becomes Flesh*'. *The Journal of Theological Studies* 40, no. 1 (1989): 331-7.
O'Donovan, Oliver. 'Review of Milbank, *Theology and Social Theory*'. *Studies in Christian Ethics* 5, no. 1 (1992): 80-6.
O'Donovan, Oliver. 'Evangelicalism and the Foundations of Ethics'. In *Evangelical Anglicans*, edited by R. T. France and A. E. McGrath, 96-107. London: SPCK, 1993.
O'Donovan, Oliver. *Liturgy and Ethics: Grove Booklets E: 89*. Bramcote: Grove Books, 1993.

O'Donovan, Oliver. 'A Summons to Reality'. In *Understanding Veritatis Splendor*, edited by J. Wilkins, 41–5. London: SPCK, 1994.
O'Donovan, Oliver. *Resurrection and Moral Order: An Outline for Evangelical Ethics*. 2nd edn. Leicester: Apollos/Grand Rapids: Eerdmans, 1994.
O'Donovan, Oliver. 'Christian Moral Reflection'. In *New Dictionary of Christian Ethics and Pastoral Theology*, edited by David J. Atkinson and David H. Field, 122–8. Downer's Grove: IVP, 1995.
O'Donovan, Oliver. 'Response to Respondents: Behold the Lamb!'. *Studies in Christian Ethics* 112, no. 2 (1998): 91–110.
O'Donovan, Oliver. 'Political Theology, Tradition and Modernity'. In *The Cambridge Companion to Liberation Theology*, edited by Christopher Rowland, 235–47. Cambridge: Cambridge University Press, 1999.
O'Donovan, Oliver and Joan Lockwood O'Donovan. *From Irenaeus to Grotius: A Sourcebook in Christian Political Thought*. Grand Rapids: Eerdmans, 1999.
O'Donovan, Oliver. *The Desire of the Nations: Rediscovering the Roots of Political Theology*. Cambridge: Cambridge University Press, 1999.
O'Donovan, Oliver. 'Where Were You … ?'. In *The Care of Creation: Focusing Concern and Action*, edited by R. J. Berry, 90–3. Leicester: IVP, 2000.
O'Donovan, Oliver. 'Review of Porter, *Natural and Divine Law*'. *Theology* 104, no. 817 (2001): 60–1.
O'Donovan, Oliver. *Common Objects of Love: Moral Reflection and the Shaping of Community*. The 2001 Stob Lectures. Grand Rapids: Eerdmans, 2002.
O'Donovan, Oliver. 'Response to Craig Bartholomew'. In *A Royal Priesthood? The Use of the Bible Ethically and Politically: A Dialogue with Oliver O'Donovan*, edited by Craig G. Bartholomew, Robert Song, Jonathan Chaplin and Al Wolters, 113–15. Carlisle: Paternoster Press, 2002.
O'Donovan, Oliver, 'Response to Daniel Carroll R.'. In *A Royal Priesthood? The Use of the Bible Ethically and Politically: A Dialogue with Oliver O'Donovan*, edited by Craig G. Bartholomew, Robert Song, Jonathan Chaplin and Al Wolters, 143–6. Carlisle: Paternoster Press, 2002.
O'Donovan, Oliver. 'Response to Peter Scott'. In *A Royal Priesthood? The Use of the Bible Ethically and Politically: A Dialogue with Oliver O'Donovan*, edited by Craig G. Bartholomew, Robert Song, Jonathan Chaplin and Al Wolters, 374–6. Carlisle: Paternoster Press, 2002.
O'Donovan, Oliver. 'Archbishop Rowan Williams'. *Pro Ecclesia* 12, no. 1 (2003): 5–9.
O'Donovan, Oliver. *The Just War Revisited*. Cambridge: Cambridge University Press, 2003.
O'Donovan, Oliver and Joan Lockwood O'Donovan, eds. *Bonds of Imperfection: Christian Politics, Past and Present*. Grand Rapids: Eerdmans, 2004.
O'Donovan, Oliver. *The Ways of Judgment*. The Bampton Lectures, 2003. Grand Rapids: Eerdmans, 2005.
O'Donovan, Oliver. 'What Can Ethics Know about God?'. In *The Doctrine of God and Theological Ethics*, edited by Alan J. Torrance and Michael Banner. London/New York: T & T Clark, 2006.
O'Donovan, Oliver. 'Scripture and Christian Ethics'. *Anvil* 24, no. 1 (2007): 21–9.
O'Donovan, Oliver. 'The Object of Theological Ethics'. *Studies in Christian Ethics* 20, no. 2 (2007): 203–14.
O'Donovan, Oliver. *Church in Crisis: the Gay Controversy and the Anglican Communion*. Eugene: Wipf & Stock, 2008.

O'Donovan, Oliver. 'The Moral Authority of Scripture'. In *Scripture's Doctrine and Theology's Bible: How the New Testament Shapes Christian Dogmatics*, edited by Markus Bockmuehl and Alan J. Torrance, 165–75. Grand Rapids: Baker, 2008.
O'Donovan, Oliver. 'Foreword'. In *On Rowan Williams: Critical Essays*, edited by Matheson Russell, ix–xi. Eugene: Wipf and Stock, 2009.
O'Donovan, Oliver. *The Word in Small Boats: Sermons from Oxford*, edited by Andrew Draycott. Grand Rapids: Eerdmans, 2009.
O'Donovan, Oliver. 'Deliberation, History and Reading: A Response to Schweiker and Wolterstorff'. *Scottish Journal of Theology* 51, no. 1 (2010): 127–44.
O'Donovan, Oliver. *On the Thirty-Nine Articles: A Conversation with Tudor Christianity*. London: SCM, 2011.
O'Donovan, Oliver. *Self, World, and Time: Ethics as Theology vol. 1. An Induction*. Grand Rapids: Eerdmans, 2013.
O'Donovan, Oliver. *Finding and Seeking. Ethics as Theology vol. 2*. Grand Rapids: Eerdmans, 2014.
O'Donovan, Oliver. 'Flesh and Spirit'. In *Galatians and Christian Theology: Justification, the Gospel, and Ethics in Paul's Letter*, edited by Mark W. Elliot, Scott J. Hafemann, N. T. Wright and John Frederick, 271–84. Grand Rapids: Baker Academic, 2014.
O'Donovan, Oliver. 'Sanctification and Ethics'. In *Sanctification: Explorations in Theology and Practice*, edited by Kelly M. Kapic, 150–66. Downers Grove: IVP, 2014.
O'Donovan, Oliver. 'What Shall We Do?'. *Times Literary Supplement* 5831 (2014): 24.
O'Donovan, Oliver. 'Thoughts on Work'. In *On Rock or Sand? Firm Foundations for Britain's Future*, edited by John Sentamu, 111–31. London: SPCK, 2015.
O'Donovan, Oliver. 'Review of Biggar, *Between Kin and Cosmopolis*'. *Theology* 119, no. 1 (2016), 42–3.
O'Donovan, Oliver. *Entering into Rest: Ethics as Theology vol. 3*. Grand Rapids: Eerdmans, 2017.
O'Donovan, Oliver. 'The Trinity and the Moral Life: *In Memoriam* John Webster'. In *A Transforming Vision: Knowing and Loving the Triune God*, edited by George Westhaver, 218–27. London: SCM, 2018.
O'Donovan, Oliver. 'Foreword'. In *Wake Up to Advent!: The Archbishop of York's Advent Book 2019*, edited by John Sentamu, i–iii. London: SPCK, 2019.
O'Donovan, Oliver. 'John Webster on Dogmatics and Ethics'. *International Journal of Systematic Theology* 21, no. 1 (2019): 78–92.
O'Donovan, Oliver. 'Some Reactions from the Ground'. *Modern Theology* 36, no. 1 (2020): 193–200.

Other authors

Adam, Margaret B. *Our Only Hope: More than We Can Ask or Imagine*. Cambridge: James Clarke & Co., 2014.
Adams, Nicholas. 'Hope'. In *The Oxford Companion to Christian Thought*, edited by Adrian Hastings, Alistair Mason and Hugh Pyper, 309–11. Oxford: Oxford University Press, 1999.
Adams, Nicholas. 'Sacred and Profane: The Effects of Philosophy on Theology in Pannenberg, Rahner and Moltmann'. *International Journal of Systematic Theology* 2, no. 3 (2000): 283–306.

Adams, Samuel V. *The Reality of God and Historical Method: Apocalyptic Theology in Conversation with N.T. Wright*. Downers Grove: IVP Academic, 2015.
Allen, Michael. 'The Visibility of the Invisible God'. *Journal of Reformed Theology* 9, no. 3 (2015): 249–69.
Allen, Michael. *Sanctification*. Grand Rapids: Zondervan, 2017.
Allen, Michael. 'Toward Theological Anthropology: Tracing the Anthropological Principles of John Webster'. *International Journal of Systematic Theology* 19, no. 1 (2017), 6–29.
Allen, Michael. *Grounded in Heaven: Recentering Christian Hope and Life on God*. Grand Rapids: Eerdmans, 2018.
Annas, Julia. *The Morality of Happiness*. New York/Oxford: Oxford University Press, 1995.
Aquinas, Thomas. *Summa Theologica*, 61 vols. London: Eyre & Spottiswoode/New York: McGraw-Hill Book Company, 1964–80.
Arner, Neil. 'Ecumenical Ethics: Challenges to and Sources for a Common Moral Witness'. *Journal of the Society of Christian Ethics* 36, no. 2 (2016): 101–19.
Arner, Neil. 'Precedents and Prospects for Incorporating Natural Law in Protestant ethics'. *Scottish Journal of Theology* 69, no. 4 (2016): 375–88.
Aspray, Silvianne. 'Louis Bouyer and the Metaphysics of the Reformation'. *Modern Theology* 34, no. 1 (2018), 3–22.
Augustine of Hippo. *Sermons: The Works of St. Augustine: A Translation for the 21st Century, III.7 (230–272B)*, edited by John E. Rotelle, translated by Edmund Hill. New York: New City Press, 1993.
Austin, Victor Lee. *Up With Authority: Why We Need Authority to Flourish as Human Beings*. London/New York: T & T Clark International, 2010.
Austin, Victor Lee. *Christian Ethics: A Guide for the Perplexed*. London/New York: Bloomsbury T & T Clark, 2012.
Ayres, Lewis. 'In the Path of thy Judgments'. *Reviews in Religion and Theology* 4, no. 4 (1997): 25–34.
Ayres, Lewis. *Nicaea and Its Legacy: An Approach to Fourth-Century Theology*. Oxford: Oxford University Press, 2004.
Baan, Adrian W. *The Necessity of Witness: Stanley Hauerwas's Contribution to Systematic Theology*. Eugene: Pickwick, 2015.
Baker, Bruce D. *The Transformation of Persons and The Concept of Moral Order: A Study of The Evangelical Ethics of Oliver O'Donovan with Special Reference to the Barth-Brunner Debate* (PhD Diss. University of St. Andrews, 2010).
Balthasar, Hans Urs von. *Theo-Drama: Theological Dramatic Theory vol. 5: The Last Act*. Translated by Graham Harrison. San Francisco: Ignatius Press, 2003.
Banner, Michael. *Christian Ethics and Contemporary Moral Problems*. Cambridge: Cambridge University Press, 1999.
Banner, Michael. *Christian Ethics: A Brief History*. Chichester: Wiley-Blackwell, 2009.
Banner, Michael. *The Ethics of Everyday Life: Moral Theology, Social Anthropology, and the Imagination of the Human*. Oxford: Oxford University Press, 2014.
Banner, Michael. 'Review of *The Authority of the Gospel*', edited by Song and Waters. *Theology* 119, no. 3 (2016): 208–9.
Barclay, John. *Obeying the Truth: A Study of Paul's Ethics in Galatians*. Edinburgh: T & T Clark, 1988.
Barclay, John. 'Believers and the "Last Judgment" in Paul: Rethinking Grace and Recompense'. In *Eschatologie – Eschatology*, edited by Hans-Joachim Eckstein, Christof Landmeser and Hermann Lichtenberger, 195–208. Tübingen: Mohr Siebeck, 2011.

Barclay, John. *Paul and the Gift*. Grand Rapids: Eerdmans, 2015.
Barclay, John. 'Apocalyptic Allegiance and Disinvestment'. In *Paul and the Apocalyptic Imagination*, edited by Ben C. Blackwell, John K. Goodrich and Jason Maston, 257–74. Minneapolis: Fortress Press, 2016.
Barnes, Michel René. 'Ebion at the Barricades: Moral Narrative and Post Christian Catholic Theology'. *Modern Theology* 26, no. 4 (2010), 511–48.
Barth, Karl. *Church Dogmatics*, 4 vols. Edinburgh: T & T Clark, 1956–75.
Barth, Karl. *Ethics*, edited by Dietrich Braun, translated by Geoffrey W. Bromiley. Edinburgh: T & T Clark, 1981.
Barth, Karl. *The Christian Life*. Translated by Geoffrey W. Bromiley. London/New York: Bloomsbury T & T Clark, 2017.
Bartholomew, Craig G. 'A Time for War and a Time for Peace: Old Testament Wisdom, Creation, and O'Donovan's Theological Ethics'. In *A Royal Priesthood? The Use of the Bible Ethically and Politically: A Dialogue with Oliver O'Donovan*, edited by Craig G. Bartholomew, Robert Song, Jonathan Chaplin and Al Wolters, 91–112. Carlisle: Paternoster Press, 2002.
Bartholomew, Craig G., Robert Song, Jonathan Chaplin and Al Wolters, eds. *A Royal Priesthood? The Use of the Bible Ethically and Politically: A Dialogue with Oliver O'Donovan*. Carlisle: Paternoster Press, 2002.
Bartholomew, Craig G. *Contours of the Kuyperian Tradition: A Systematic Introduction*. Downers Grove: IVP, 2017.
Barton, John. 'Virtue in the Bible'. *Studies in Christian Ethics* 12, no. 1 (1999), 12–22.
Bauckham, Richard and Trevor Hart. *Hope against Hope: Christian Eschatology in Contemporary Context*. London: Darton, Longman, and Todd, 1999.
Bavinck, Herman. *Reformed Dogmatics I: Prolegomena*, edited by John Bolt and translated by John Vriend. Grand Rapids: Baker Academic, 2003.
Bayer, Oswald. *Freedom in Response. Lutheran Ethics: Sources and Controversies*. Oxford: Oxford University Press, 2007.
Behr, John. *Irenaeus: Identifying Christianity*. Oxford: Oxford University Press, 2013.
Beiser, Frederick C. 'Hegel's Historicism'. In *The Cambridge Companion to Hegel*, edited by Frederick C. Beiser, 270–300. Cambridge: Cambridge University Press, 1993.
Beiser, Frederick C. 'Moral Faith and the Highest Good'. In *The Cambridge Companion to Kant and Modern Philosophy*, edited by Paul Guyer, 588–629. New York: Cambridge University Press, 2006.
(Benedict XVI, Pope. *Spe Salvi* (2007), http://www.vatican.va/content/benedict-xvi/en/encyclicals/documents/hf_ben-xvi_enc_20071130_spe-salvi.html (accessed 26 April 2020).
Bennett, Jana Marguerite. *Water Is Thicker than Blood: An Augustinian Theology of Marriage and Singleness*. Oxford/New York: Oxford University Press, 2008.
Bennett, Jana Marguerite. *Singleness: A New Theology of the Single Life*. New York: Oxford University Press, 2017.
Berkman, John and Michael Buttrey. 'Theologies of Enhancement? Another Look at Oliver O'Donovan's Created Order'. *Toronto Journal of Theology* 31, no. 1 (2015), 27–37.
Biggar, Nigel. 'Evangelicalism and Social Ethics'. In *Evangelical Anglicans: Their Role and Influence in the Church Today*, edited by R. T. France and A. E. McGrath, 108–19. London: SPCK, 1993.
Biggar, Nigel. *The Hastening that Waits: Karl Barth's Ethics*. Oxford: Clarendon Press, 1996.

Biggar, Nigel. 'On Defining Political Authority as an Act of Judgment: A Discussion of Oliver O'Donovan's *The Ways of Judgment* (Part I)'. *Political Theology* 9, no. 3 (2008): 273–93.

Biggar, Nigel. 'Karl Barth's Ethics Revisited'. In *Commanding Grace: Studies in Karl Barth's Ethics*, edited by Daniel L. Migliore, 26–48. Grand Rapids: Eerdmans, 2010.

Biggar, Nigel. *Behaving in Public: How to Do Christian Ethics*. Grand Rapids: Eerdmans, 2011.

Bjørndal, Silje Kvamme. *The Church in a Secular Age: A Pneumatological Reconstruction of Stanley Hauerwas's Ecclesiology*. Eugene: Pickwick, 2018.

Black, Rufus. *Christian Moral Realism: Natural Law, Narrative Virtue, and the Gospel*. Oxford: Oxford University Press, 2000.

Blowers, Paul M. and Robert Louis Wilken. *On the Cosmic Mystery of Christ: Selected Writings from St Maximus the Confessor*. Crestwood: St. Vladimir's Seminary Press, 2003.

Bockmuehl, Markus. *Jewish Law and Gentile Churches: Halakhah and the Beginning of Christian Public Ethics*. Grand Rapids: Baker, 2003.

de Boer, Martinus C. *Galatians: A Commentary*. Louisville: Westminster John Knox, 2011.

Boersma, Hans. *Seeing God: The Beatific Vision in Christian Tradition*. Grand Rapids: Eerdmans, 2018.

Bonhoeffer, Dietrich. *Creation and Fall: A Theological Exposition of Genesis 1-3*. Dietrich Bonhoeffer Works vol. 3, edited by John W. de Gruchy, translated by Douglas S. Bax. Minneapolis: Fortress Press, 1997.

Bonhoeffer, Dietrich. *Ethics*. Dietrich Bonhoeffer Works vol. 6, edited by Clifford J. Green, translated by Reinhard Krauss, Charles C. West and Douglas W. Scott. Minneapolis: Fortress Press, 2005.

Bowlin, John. 'Contemporary Protestant Thomism'. In *Aquinas as Authority*, ed. Paul van Geest, Harm Goris and Carlo Leget, 235–52. Leuven: Peeters, 2002.

Bowlin, John. 'Notes on Natural Law and Covenant'. *Studies in Christian Ethics* 28, no. 2 (2015): 142–9.

Braaten, Carl. *Eschatology and Ethics: Essays on the Theology and Ethics of the Kingdom of God*. Minneapolis: Augsburg Publishing House, 1974.

Bretherton, Luke. *Hospitality and Holiness: Christian Witness Amid Moral Diversity*. Farnham: Ashgate, 2010.

Brock, Brian. 'The Form of the Matter: Heidegger, Ontology and Christian Ethics'. *International Journal of Systematic Theology* 3, no. 3 (2001): 257–79.

Brock, Brian. *Singing the Ethos of God: On the Place of Christian Ethics in Scripture*. Grand Rapids: Eerdmans, 2007.

Brock, Brian. *Christian Ethics in a Technological Age*. Grand Rapids: Eerdmans, 2010.

Brock, Brian. 'Christian Ethics'. In *Mapping Modern Theology: A Thematic and Historical Introduction*, edited by Kelly Kapic and Bruce McCormack, 293–319. Grand Rapids: Baker Academic, 2012.

Brock, Brian. '"What is the Public?" Theological Variations on Babel and Pentecost'. In *The Authority of the Gospel*, edited by Robert Song and Brent Waters, 160–78. Grand Rapids: Eerdmans, 2015.

Brock, Brian and Michael Mawson, eds. *The Freedom of a Christian Ethicist: The Future of a Reformation Legacy*. London/New York: T & T Clark, 2016.

Brock, Brian and Stanley Hauerwas, *Beginnings: Interrogating Hauerwas*, edited by Kevin Hargaden. London/New York: T & T Clark, 2017.

Brown, Malcolm. *Tensions in Christian Ethics: An Introduction*. London: SPCK, 2010.

Brown, Malcolm. 'The Case for Anglican Social Theology Today'. In *Anglican Social Theology: Renewing the Vision Today*, edited by Malcolm Brown, with Jonathan Chaplin, John Hughes, Anna Rowlands and Alan Suggate, 1–27. London: Church House Publishing, 2014.
Bultmann, Rudolf. *History and Eschatology: The Presence of Eternity*. New York: Harper & Row, 1957.
Burger, Hans. *Being in Christ: A Biblical and Systematic Investigation in a Reformed Perspective*. Eugene: Wipf & Stock, 2009.
Burger, Hans. 'Receiving the Mind of Christ: Epistemological and Hermeneutical Implications of Participation in Christ according to Oliver O'Donovan'. *Journal of Reformed Theology* 10, no. 1 (2016): 52–71.
Burridge, Richard. *Imitating Jesus: An Inclusive Approach to New Testament Ethics*. Grand Rapids: Eerdmans, 2007.
Calvin, John. *Institutes of the Christian Religion*, edited by John T. McNeill. Louisville: Westminster John Knox, 1960.
Cameron, Andrew J. B. 'How to Say YES to the World: Towards a New Way Forward in Evangelical Social Ethics'. *Reformed Theological Review* 66, no. 1 (2007), 23–36.
Cameron, Andrew J. B. *Joined-up Life: A Christian Account of How Ethics Works*. Nottingham: IVP, 2011.
Camosy, Charles. *Peter Singer and Christian Ethics: Beyond Polarization*. Cambridge: Cambridge University Press, 2012.
Cantalamessa, Raniero. *Obedience: The Authority of the Word*. Translated by Frances Lonergan Villa. Slough: St Paul, 2018.
Carlisle, Clare. 'Cry for Wisdom'. *Times Literary Supplement* 5837 (2015): 28.
Cavanaugh, William T. 'Stan the Man: A Thoroughly Biased Account of a Completely Unobjective Person'. In Stanley Hauerwas, *The Hauerwas Reader*, edited by John Berkman and Michael Cartwright, 18–32. London/Durham: Duke University Press, 2001.
Cavanaugh, William T. 'Church'. In *The Blackwell Companion to Political Theology*, edited by William T. Cavanaugh and Peter Scott, 392–406. Oxford: Blackwell, 2004.
Cavanaugh, William T. 'From One City to Two: Christian Reimagining of Political Space'. *Political Theology* 7, no. 3 (2006): 299–321.
Cessario, Romanus. *Introduction to Moral Theology*. Washington: Catholic University of America Press, 2001.
Cessario, Romanus. *Theology and Sanctity*, edited by Cajetan Cuddy. Ave Maria: Sapientia Press, 2014.
Chaplin, Jonathan. 'Political Eschatology and Responsible Government: Oliver O'Donovan's "Christian Liberalism"'. In *A Royal Priesthood? The Use of the Bible Ethically and Politically: A Dialogue with Oliver O'Donovan*, edited by Craig G. Bartholomew, Robert Song, Jonathan Chaplin and Al Wolters, 265–308. Carlisle: Paternoster Press, 2002.
Chaplin, Jonathan. *Herman Dooyeweerd: Christian Philosopher of State and Civil Society*. Notre Dame: University of Notre Dame Press, 2011.
Chaplin, Jonathan. 'Evangelical Contributions to the Future of Anglican Social Theology'. In *Anglican Social Theology: Renewing the Vision Today*, edited by Malcolm Brown. London: Church House Publishing, 2014.
Chaplin, Jonathan. 'Editorial'. *Crucible: The Journal of Christian Social Ethics* (April 2017): 3–10.

Chester, Tim. *Mission and the Coming of God: Eschatology, The Trinity and Mission in the Theology of Jürgen Moltmann and Contemporary Evangelicalism*. Milton Keynes: Paternoster, 2006.
Clough, David. *On Animals vol. 1 Systematic Theology*. London: Bloomsbury T & T Clark, 2013.
Cloutier, David. 'Review of *Finding and Seeking*'. *Pro Ecclesia* 26, no. 3 (2017): 333–6.
Coakley, Sarah. 'A Response to Oliver O'Donovan's *Ethics as Theology* Trilogy'. *Modern Theology* 36, no. 1 (2020): 186–92.
Cochrane, Elizabeth Agnew. *Protestant Virtue and Stoic Ethics*. London/New York: T & T Clark, 2018.
Cole, Jonathan. 'Towards a Christian Ontology of Political Authority: The Relationship Between Created Order and Providence in Oliver O'Donovan's Theology of Political Authority'. *Studies in Christian Ethics* 32, no. 3 (2019): 307–25.
Colish, Marcia L. *Ambrose's Patriarchs: Ethics for the Common Man*. Notre Dame: University of Notre Dame Press, 2005.
Collier, Charles M., ed. *The Difference Christ Makes: Celebrating the Life, Work, and Friendship of Stanley Hauerwas*. Eugene: Cascade, 2015.
Congar, Yves. *I Believe in the Holy Spirit*, 3 vols, translated by David Smith. New York: Herder and Herder, 2015.
Congdon, David W. *Rudolf Bultmann: A Companion to His Theology*. Eugene: Cascade Books, 2015.
Couenhoven, Jesse. 'Against Metaethical Imperialism: Several Arguments for Equal Partnerships between the Deontic and the Aretaic'. *Journal of Religious Ethics* 38, no. 3 (2010): 521–44.
Curran, Charles and Richard McCormick, eds. *Readings in Moral Theology, vol. 2: The Distinctiveness of Christian Ethics*. New York: Paulist Press, 1980.
Daley, Brian E. *The Hope of the Early Church: A Handbook of Patristic Eschatology*. Grand Rapids: Baker Academic, 1991.
Daniel Carroll R. M. 'The Power of the Future in the Present: Eschatology and Ethics in O'Donovan and Beyond'. In *A Royal Priesthood? The Use of the Bible Ethically and Politically: A Dialogue with Oliver O'Donovan*, edited by Craig G. Bartholomew, Robert Song, Jonathan Chaplin and Al Wolters, 116–43. Carlisle: Paternoster Press, 2002.
Danielou, Jean. *The Lord of History: Reflections on the Inner Meaning of History*, translated by Nigel Abercrombie. London: Longmans, Green and Co, 1958.
Davidson, Ivor J. 'Salvation's Destiny: Heirs of God'. In *God of Salvation: Soteriology in Theological Perspective*, edited by Ivor J. Davidson and Murray Rae, 155–75. Farnham: Ashgate, 2011.
Davidson, Ivor J. 'Gospel Holiness: Some Dogmatic Reflections'. In *Sanctification: Explorations in Theology and Practice*, edited by Kelly Kapic, 189–211. Downers Grove: IVP, 2014.
Dean, Robert J. *For the Life of the World: Jesus Christ and the Church in the Theologies of Dietrich Bonhoeffer and Stanley Hauerwas*. Eugene: Pickwick, 2016.
Doerksen, Paul G. *Beyond Suspicion: Post-Christian Protestant Political Theology in John Howard Yoder and Oliver O'Donovan*. Eugene: Wipf and Stock, 2009.
Doherty, Sean. *Theology and Economic Ethics: Martin Luther and Arthur Rich in Dialogue*. Oxford: Oxford University Press, 2014.
Dorrien, Gary. *Social Ethics in the Making: Interpreting an American Tradition*. Oxford: Wiley-Blackwell, 2010.
Dudley-Smith, Timothy. *John Stott: The Making of a Leader*. Downers Grove: IVP, 1999.

Dudley-Smith, Timothy. *John Stott: A Global Ministry*. Downers Grove: IVP, 2001.
Duff, Nancy. 'The Significance of Pauline Apocalyptic for Theological Ethics'. In *Apocalyptic and the New Testament: Essays in Honor of J. Louis Martyn*, edited by Joel Marcus and Marion L. Soards, 279–96. Sheffield: JSOT Press, 1989.
Eagleton, Terry. *Hope Without Optimism*. New Haven/London: Yale University Press, 2015.
Elliot, David. *Hope and Christian Ethics*. Cambridge: Cambridge University Press, 2017.
Eliot, T. S. *Four Quartets*. London: Faber & Faber, 2001.
Elmen, Paul. 'Anglican Morality'. In *The Study of Anglicanism*, edited by Stephen Sykes, John Booty and Jonathan Knight, 364–78. London: SPCK/Minneapolis: Fortress Press, 1988.
Errington, Andrew. 'Authority and Reality in the Work of Oliver O'Donovan'. *Studies in Christian Ethics* 29, no. 4 (2016): 371–85.
Errington, Andrew. *Every Good Path: Wisdom and Practical Reason in Christian Ethics and the Book of Proverbs*. London: T & T Clark, 2020.
Evans, C. Stephen. *Kierkegaard's Ethic of Love: Divine Commands and Moral Obligations*. Oxford/New York: Oxford University Press, 2004.
Farley, Margaret and Serene Jones. *Liberating Eschatology: Essays in Honor of Letty M. Russell*, edited by Margaret A. Farley and Serene Jones. Louisville: Westminster John Knox Press, 1999.
Felker Jones, Beth. *Marks of His Wounds: Gender Politics and Bodily Resurrection*. New York: Oxford University Press, 2007.
Fergusson, David, 'Interpreting the Resurrection'. *Scottish Journal of Theology* 38, no. 3 (1985): 287–305.
Fergusson, David and Marcel Sarot, eds. *The Future as God's Gift: Explorations in Christian Eschatology*. London: T & T Clark, 2005.
Flipper, Joseph F. *Between Apocalypse and Eschaton: History and Eternity in Henri de Lubac*. Minneapolis: Augsburg Fortress Press, 2015.
Forde, Gerhard. 'Review of Webster, *Eberhard Jüngel*'. *Lutheran Quarterly* 2, no. 4 (1988): 531–3.
Forde, Gerhard. 'The Christian Life'. In *Christian Dogmatics*, vol. 2, edited by Carl Braaten and Robert Jenson, 391–470. Minneapolis: Fortress, 1994.
Forde, Gerhard. *On Being a Theologian of The Cross*. Grand Rapids: Eerdmans, 1997.
Forde, Gerhard. *A More Radical Gospel: Essays on Eschatology: Authority, Atonement and Ecumenism*, edited by Mark C. Mattes and Steven D. Paulson. Grand Rapids: Eerdmans, 2004.
Forrester, Duncan. *Truthful Action: Explorations in Practical Theology*. Edinburgh: T & T Clark, 2000.
Francis, Pope. *Laudato Si* (2015), http://www.vatican.va/content/francesco/en/encyclicals/documents/papa-francesco_20150524_enciclica-laudato-si.html (accessed 26 April 2020).
Furnish, Victor P. 'How Firm a Foundation? Some Questions about Scripture in *The Desire of the Nations*'. *Studies in Christian Ethics* 11, no. 2 (1998): 18–23.
Gavrilyuk, Paul. *The Suffering of the Impassible God: The Dialectics of Patristic Though*. Oxford: Oxford University Press, 2006.
Gay, Doug. 'Review of O'Donovan, *Finding and Seeking*'. *Theology* 118, no. 5 (2015): 364–5.
Goroncy, Jason. *Hallowed Be Thy Name: The Sanctification of All in the Soteriology of P.T. Forsyth*. London/New York: Bloomsbury T & T Clark, 2013.

Gorringe, Timothy. 'Authority, Plebs, Patricians'. *Studies in Christian Ethics* 11, no. 2 (1998): 24–9.
Gorringe, Timothy. 'Review of Hordern, *Political Affections*'. *Journal of Theological Studies* 64, no. 2 (2013): 868–70.
de Graaff, Guido. 'To Judge or Not to Judge: Engaging with Oliver O'Donovan's Political Ethics'. *Studies in Christian Ethics* 25, no. 3 (2012): 295–311.
Grabill, Stephen J. *Rediscovering the Natural Law in Reformed Theological Ethics*. Grand Rapids: Eerdmans, 2006.
Greenman, Jeffrey P. 'Anglican Evangelicals on Personal and Social Ethics'. *Anglican Theological Review*, 94, no. 2 (2012): 179–206.
Greer, Rowan. *Christian Hope and Christian Life: Raids on the Inarticulate*. New York: Crossroad, 2001.
Gregory, Eric, *Politics and the Order of Love: An Augustinian Ethic of Democratic Citizenship*. Chicago: University of Chicago Press, 2008.
Gregory, Eric. 'The Spirit and the Letter: Protestant Thomistm and Nigel Biggar's "Karl Barth's Ethics Revisited"'. In *Commanding Grace: Studies in Karl Barth's Ethics*, edited by Daniel L. Migliore, 50–9. Grand Rapids/Cambridge: Eerdmans, 2010.
Gregory, Eric. 'The Boldness of Analogy: Civic Virtues and Augustinian Eudaimonism'. In *The Authority of the Gospel: Explorations in Moral and Political Theology in Honor of Oliver O'Donovan*, edited by Robert Song and Brent Waters, 72–85. Grand Rapids: Eerdmans, 2015.
Gregory, Eric and Joseph Clair. 'Augustinianisms and Thomisms'. In *The Cambridge Companion to Christian Political Theology*, edited by Craig Hovey and Elizabeth Phillips, 176–96. New York: Cambridge University Press, 2015.
Griffiths, Paul. *Decreation: The Last Things of All Creatures*. Waco: Baylor University Press, 2014.
Gunton, Colin E. 'Introduction'. In *The Doctrine of Creation: Essays in Dogmatics, History, and Philosophy*, edited by Colin E. Gunton, 1–15. London/New York: T & T Clark International, 1997.
Guroian, Vigen. 'Liturgy and the Lost Eschatological Vision of Christian Ethics'. *The Annual of the Society of Christian Ethics* 20 (2000): 227–38.
Guroian, Vigen. *Ethics after Christendom: Toward an Ecclesial Christian Ethic*. Eugene: Wipf and Stock, 2004.
Gustafson, James M. *Protestant and Roman Catholic Ethics: Prospects for Rapprochement*. Chicago: University of Chicago Press, 1978.
Gustafson, James M. 'Review of O'Donovan, *Resurrection*'. *The Journal of Religion* 68, no. 1 (1988): 131–3.
Haas, Guenther. 'The Significance of Eschatology for Christian Ethics'. In *Looking into the Future: Evangelical Studies in Eschatology*, edited by David Baker, 325–41. Grand Rapids: Baker, 2001.
Haas, Guenther. 'Calvin's Ethics'. In *The Cambridge Companion to John Calvin*, edited by Donald McKim, 93–105. Cambridge: Cambridge University Press, 2004.
Hall, Amy Laura. *Conceiving Parenthood: American Protestantism and the Spirit of Reproduction*. Grand Rapids: Eerdmans, 2008.
Hall, Pamela M. 'The Old Law and the New Law'. In *The Ethics of Aquinas*, edited by Stephen J. Pope, 194–206. Washington: Georgetown University Press, 2006.
Harink, Douglas. *Paul among the Postliberals: Pauline Theology beyond Christendom and Modernity*. Grand Rapids: Brazos, 2003.
Harink, Douglas. *1 and 2 Peter*. London: SCM, 2009.

Harrison, Carol. *Augustine: Christian Truth and Fractured Humanity*. Oxford: Oxford University Press, 2000.
Harvie, Timothy. *Jürgen Moltmann's Ethics of Hope: Eschatological Possibilities For Moral Action*. Farnham: Ashgate, 2009.
Hauerwas, Stanley. *The Peaceable Kingdom: A Primer in Christian Ethics*. London: SCM Press, 1984.
Hauerwas, Stanley. 'Time and History in Theological Ethics: The Work of James Gustafson'. *Journal of Religious Ethics* 13, no. 1 (1985): 3–21.
Hauerwas, Stanley. *Dispatches from the Front: Theological Engagements with the Secular*. London/Durham: Duke University Press, 1995.
Hauerwas, Stanley. 'Doctrine and Ethics'. In *The Cambridge Companion to Christian Doctrine*, edited by Colin Gunton, 21–40. Cambridge: Cambridge University Press, 1997.
Hauerwas, Stanley. *The Hauerwas Reader*, edited by John Berkman and Michael Cartwright. London/Durham: Duke University Press, 2001.
Hauerwas, Stanley. *Approaching the End: Eschatological Reflections on Church, Politics, and Life*. Grand Rapids: Eerdmans, 2013.
Hauerwas, Stanley and Jim Fodor. 'Remaining in Babylon: Oliver O'Donovan's Defense of Christendom'. *Studies in Christian Ethics* 11, no. 2 (1998): 30–55.
Hauerwas, Stanley and Charles Pinches. *Christians among the Virtues: Theological Conversations with Ancient and Modern Ethics*. Notre Dame: University of Notre Dame Press, 1997.
Hauerwas, Stanley and William H. Willimon, *Resident Aliens: Life in the Christian Colony*. Nashville: Abingdon Press, 2014.
Hays, Richard B. *The Moral Vision of the New Testament: A Contemporary Introduction to New Testament Ethics*. New York: HarperCollins, 1996.
Healy, Nicholas J. *The Eschatology of Hans Urs von Balthasar: Being as Communion*. Oxford: Oxford University Press, 2005.
Healy, Nicholas M. *Hauerwas: A (Very) Critical Introduction*. Grand Rapids: Eerdmans, 2014.
Healy, Nicholas M. 'Review of *Finding and Seeking*'. *Studies in Christian Ethics* 29, no. 3 (2016): 359–62.
Herdt, Jennifer. 'Oliver O'Donovan's *Ethics as Theology* and the Struggle for Communication'. *Modern Theology* 36, no. 1 (2020): 159–64.
Hittinger, Russell. 'Natural Law and Catholic Moral Theology'. In *A Preserving Grace: Protestants, Catholics, and Natural Law*, edited by Michael Cromartie. Grand Rapids: Eerdmans, 1997.
Hollinger, Dennis and David P. Gushee. 'Evangelical Ethics: Profile of a Movement Come of Age'. *The Annual of the Society of Christian Ethics* 20 (2000): 181–203.
Hollowell, Adam Edward. *Power and Purpose: Paul Ramsey and Contemporary Christian Political Theology*. Grand Rapids: Eerdmans, 2015.
Holmes, Christopher. *Ethics in the Presence of Christ*. London/New York: T & T Clark International, 2012.
Holmes, Christopher. *The Lord Is Good: Seeking the God of the Psalter*. London: Apollos, 2018.
Holmgren, Stephen. *Ethics after Easter*. Lanham: Rowman and Littlefield, 2000.
Hordern, Joshua, *Political Affections: Civic Participation and Moral Theology*. Oxford: Oxford University Press, 2013.
Horrell, David G. *Solidarity and Difference: A Contemporary Reading of Paul's Ethics*. 2nd edn. London/New York: Bloomsbury T & T Clark, 2016.

Hughes, John. 'After Temple? The Recent Renewal of Anglican Social Thought'. In *Anglican Social Theology*, edited by Malcolm Brown, with Jonathan Chaplin, John Hughes, Anna Rowlands and Alan Suggate, 74–101. London: Church House Publishing, 2014.

Hunsicker, David B. *The Making of Stanley Hauerwas: Bridging Barth and Postliberalism*. Downer's Grove: IVP Academic, 2019.

Hunsinger, George. *Disruptive Grace: Studies in the Theology of Karl Barth*. Grand Rapids: Eerdmans, 2000.

Hunsinger, George. 'The Daybreak of the New Creation: Christ's Resurrection in Recent Theology'. *Scottish Journal of Theology* 57, no. 2 (2004): 163–81.

Hütter, Reinhard. 'Creatio ex nihilo: Promise of the Gift. Remembering the Christian Doctrine of Creation in Troubled Times'. In *Some Christian and Jewish Perspectives on Creation*, edited by Robert A. Brungs and Marianne Postiglione, 1–12. St. Louis: ITEST Faith/Science Press, 1991.

Hütter, Reinhard. *Bound to Be Free: Evangelical Catholic Engagements in Ecclesiology, Ethics, and Ecumenism*. Grand Rapids: Eerdmans, 2004.

Hütter, Reinhard, *Dust Bound for Heaven: Explorations in the Theology of Thomas Aquinas*. Grand Rapids: Eerdmans, 2012.

Insole, Christopher. 'Discerning the Theopolitical: A Response to Cavanaugh's Reimagining of Political Space'. *Political Theology* 7, no. 3 (2006): 323–35.

Insole, Christopher. 'Seek the Wrong'. *Times Literary Supplement* 5427 (2007): 9.

International Theological Commission. *Some Current Questions in Eschatology* (1992), http://www.vatican.va/roman_curia/congregations/cfaith/cti_documents/rc_cti_1990_problemi-attuali-escatologia_en.html (accessed 26 April 2020).

Jackson, Timothy P. *Love Disconsoled: Meditations on Christian Charity*. Cambridge: Cambridge University Press, 1999.

Jenkins, Willis. *Ecologies of Grace: Environmental Ethics and Christian Theology*. Oxford/New York: Oxford University Press, 2008.

Jennings, Willie James. *The Christian Imagination: Theology and the Origins of Race*. New Haven: Yale University Press, 2010.

Jenson, Robert W. *Systematic Theology, vol. 1, The Triune God*. Oxford/New York: Oxford University Press, 1997.

Jenson, Robert W. *Systematic Theology, vol. 2, The Works of God*. Oxford/New York: Oxford University Press, 1999.

Jenson, Robert W. 'The Great Transformation'. In *The Last Things: Biblical and Theological Perspectives on Eschatology*, edited by Carl E. Braaten and Robert W. Jenson, 33–42. Grand Rapids/Cambridge: Eerdmans, 2002.

Jonas, Hans. *Philosophical Essays: From Ancient Creed to Technological Man*. Upper Saddle River, NJ: Prentice-Hall, 1974.

Jones, L. Gregory, Reinhard Hütter and C. Rosalee Velloso da Silva, eds. *God, Truth, and Witness: Engaging Stanley Hauerwas*. Grand Rapids: Brazos, 2005.

Jones, Paul Dafydd. 'Review of David Kelsey, *Eccentric Existence*'. *Journal of the American Academy of Religion* 80, no. 3 (2012): 787–800.

Joyce, A. J. *Richard Hooker and Anglican Moral Theology*. Oxford: Oxford University Press, 2012.

Jüngel, Eberhard. *Theological Essays II*, translated by Arnold Neufeldt-Fast and J. B. Webster. Edinburgh: T & T Clark, 1995.

Jüngel, Eberhard. *Theological Essays*, translated by John Webster. London/New York: Bloomsbury T & T Clark, 2014.

Jüngel, Eberhard. 'New – Old – New: Theological Aphorisms', translated by R. David Nelson. In *Theological Theology*, edited by R. David Nelson, Darren Sarisky and Justin Stratis, 131–5. London/New York: Bloomsbury T & T Clark, 2015.
Kant, Immanuel. *Religion Within the Boundaries of Mere Reason: And Other Writings*, edited and translated by Allen Wood and George di Giovanni. Cambridge: Cambridge University Press, 1998.
Katongole, Emmanuel. *Beyond Universal Reason: The Relation between Religion and Ethics in the Work of Stanley Hauerwas*. Notre Dame: University of Notre Dame Press, 2000.
Keenan, James. *A History of Catholic Moral Theology in the Twentieth Century: From Confessing Sins to Liberating Consciences*. New York: Continuum, 2010.
Keller, Catherine. 'Women against Wasting the World: Notes on Eschatology and Ecology'. In *Feminist Theological Ethics: A Reader*, edited by Lois K. Daly, 282–94. Louisville: Westminster John Knox, 1994.
Kelsey, David, *Eccentric Existence*, 2 vols. Lousville: Westminster John Knox Press, 2009.
Kerr, Fergus. *After Aquinas: Versions of Thomism*. Oxford: Blackwell, 2002.
Kerr, Nathan R. *Christ, History, and Apocalyptic: The Politics of Christian Mission*. Eugene: Wipf and Stock, 2009.
Kidwell, Jeremy and Sean Doherty, eds. *Theology and Economics: A Christian Vision of the Common Good*. New York: Palgrave MacMillan, 2015.
King, James. 'Moral Theory: Response to Chapter Four'. *Scottish Bulletin of Evangelical Theology* 33, no. 1 (2015): 86–91.
Kirk, Kenneth. *Some Principles of Moral Theology and their Application*. London: Longmans, Green, & Co., 1920.
Kroeker, P. Travis. *Messianic Political Theology and Diaspora Ethics: Essays in Exile*. Eugene: Cascade, 2017.
Laffin, Michael. *The Promise of Martin Luther's Political Theology: Freeing Luther From the Modern Political Narrative*. London/New York: T & T Clark, 2016.
Lamb, Matthew L. 'The Eschatology of St Thomas Aquinas'. In *Aquinas on Doctrine: A Critical Introduction*, edited by Thomas Weinandy, Daniel Keating and John Yocum, 225–40. London/New York: T & T Clark, 2004.
Lamb, Matthew L. 'Wisdom Eschatology in Augustine and Aquinas'. In *Aquinas the Augustinian*, edited by Michael Dauphinais, Barry David and Matthew Levering. Washington: Catholic University of America Press, 2007.
Lamb, Michael and Brian A. Williams, eds. *Everyday Ethics: Moral Theology and the Practices of Ordinary Life*. Washington: Georgetown University Press, 2019.
Leget, Carlo. 'Eschatology'. In *The Theology of Thomas Aquinas*, edited by Joseph P. Wawrykow, 44–9. Louisville: Westminster John Knox Press, 2005.
Lehmann, Paul L. *Ethics in a Christian Context*. London: SCM Press, 1963.
Levering, Matthew. *Biblical Natural Law: A Theocentric and Teleological Approach*. Oxford: Oxford University Press, 2008.
Levering, Matthew. *The Betrayal of Charity: The Sins That Sabotage Divine Love*. Waco: Baylor University Press, 2011.
Levering, Matthew. *Jesus and the Demise of Death: Resurrection, Afterlife, and the Fate of the Christian*. Waco: Baylor University Press, 2012.
Levering, Matthew. *Engaging the Doctrine of Creation: Cosmos, Creatures, and the Wise and Good Creator*. Grand Rapids: Baker Academic, 2017.
Lockwood O'Donovan, Joan. *George Grant and the Twilight of Justice*. Toronto: University of Toronto Press, 1984.

Long, D. Stephen. *Tragedy, Tradition, Transformism: The Ethics of Paul Ramsey*. Boulder: Westview Press, 1993.
Long, D. Stephen. *The Goodness of God: Theology, Church, and the Social Order*. Grand Rapids: Brazos, 2001.
Long, D. Stephen. 'Moral Theology'. In *The Oxford Handbook of Systematic Theology*, edited by John Webster, Iain Torrance and Kathryn Tanner, 456–75. New York: Oxford University Press, 2007.
Long, D. Stephen. *Christian Ethics: A Very Short Introduction*. Oxford/New York: Oxford University Press, 2010.
Long. D. Stephen. *Hebrews*. Louisville: Westminster John Knox, 2011.
Long, D. Stephen. *Saving Karl Barth: Hans Urs von Balthasar's Preoccupation*. Minneapolis: Fortress Press, 2014.
Long, D. Stephen. 'Protestant Social Ethics'. In *The Cambridge Companion to Christian Political Theology*, edited by Craig Hovey and Elizabeth Phillips, 88–108. New York: Cambridge University Press, 2015.
Lorish, Philip and Charles Mathewes. 'Theology as Counsel: The Work of Oliver O'Donovan and Nigel Biggar'. *Anglican Theological Review* 94, no. 4 (2012): 717–36.
Loughlin, Gerard. 'Being Creature, Becoming Human: Contesting Oliver O'Donovan on Transgender, Identity, and the Body'. *ABC Religion and Ethics* (2018), https://www.abc.net.au/religion/being-creature-becoming-human-contesting-oliver-odonovan-on-tran/10214276 (accessed 26 September 2019).
Löwith, Karl. *Meaning in History*. Chicago: Phoenix Books, 1949.
Macaskill, Grant. 'History, Providence, and the Apocalyptic Paul'. *Scottish Journal of Theology* 70, no. 4 (2017): 409–26.
MacIntyre, Alasdair. *Three Rival Versions of Moral Enquiry*. London: Duckworth, 1990.
MacIntyre, Alasdair. *After Virtue: A Study in Moral Theory*, 3rd edn. London/New York: Bloomsbury, 2013.
Mangina, Joseph L. *Karl Barth on the Christian Life: The Practical Knowledge of God*. New York: Peter Lang, 2001.
Marshall, Bruce D. '*Quod Scit Una Uetula*': Aquinas on the Nature of Theology'. In *The Theology of Thomas Aquinas*, edited by Rik Van Nieuwenhove and Joseph Wawrykow, 1–26. Notre Dame: University of Notre Dame Press, 2005.
Martens, Paul. 'With the Natural Grain of the Universe: Reexamining the Alleged Pacifist Rejection of Natural Law'. *Journal of the Society of Christian Ethics* 32, no. 2 (2012): 113–31.
Martyn, J. Louis, 'De-apocalyptising Paul: An Essay Focused on Paul and the Stoics by Troels Engberg-Pedersen', *Journal for the Study of the New Testament* 24, no. 4 (2002): 61–102.
Mathewes, Charles. 'Review of Hordern, *Political Affections*'. *Journal of the American Academy of Religion* 84, no. 1 (2016): 272–6.
Mathewes, Charles. 'A Response to Oliver O'Donovan's *Ethics as Theology* Trilogy'. *Modern Theology* 36, no. 1 (2020): 165–72.
Mattison, William C. *The Sermon on the Mount and Moral Theology: A Virtue Perspective*. New York: Cambridge University Press, 2017.
Mattson, Brian G. *Restored to Our Destiny: Eschatology and the Image of God in Herman Bavinck's Reformed Dogmatics*. Leiden/Boston: Brill, 2012.
McAdoo, Henry. *The Structure of Caroline Moral Theology*. London: Longmans, Green, & Co., 1949.
McCabe, Herbert. *God Matters*. London: Continuum, 1987.

McClendon, James Wm. *Ethics: Systematic Theology*, vol. 1. Nashville: Abingdon, 2002.
McDowell, John, *Hope in Barth's Eschatology: Interrogations and Transformations beyond Tragedy*. Farnham: Ashgate, 2000.
McIlroy, David. 'What's at Stake in Natural Law'. *New Blackfriars* 89, no. 1023 (2008): 508–21.
McGinn, Bernard. *The Calabrian Abbot: Joachim of Fiore in the History of Western Thought*. New York: MacMillan, 1985.
McGrath, Alister. 'Doctrine and Ethics'. *Journal of the Evangelical Theological Society* 34, no. 2 (1991): 145–56.
McGrath, Alister. *Scientific Theology: Nature*, vol. 1. London/New York: T & T Clark, 2002.
McGrath, Alister. *Science and Religion: A New Introduction*, 2nd edn. Chichester: Wiley-Blackwell, 2010.
McGuckin, John Anthony. *The Orthodox Church: An Introduction to Its History, Doctrine, and Spiritual Culture*. Oxford: Wiley-Blackwell, 2008.
McKenny, Gerald. *To Relieve the Human Condition: Bioethics, Technology, and the Body*. Albany: SUNY Press, 1997.
McKenny, Gerald P. 'Responsibility'. In *The Oxford Handbook of Theological Ethics*, edited by Gilbert Meilaender and William Werpehowski, 237–53. New York/Oxford: Oxford University Press, 2005.
McKenny, Gerald. *The Analogy of Grace: Karl Barth's Moral Theology*. Oxford: Oxford University Press, 2010.
McKenny, Gerald. 'Review of Brian Brock, *Christian Ethics in a Technological Age*'. *Studies in Christian Ethics* 25, no. 3 (2012): 372–5.
McKenny, Gerald. 'Evolution, Biotechnology, and the Normative Significance of Created Order'. *Toronto Journal of Theology* 31, no. 1 (2015): 15–26.
McKenny, Gerald. *Biotechnology, Human Nature, and Christian Ethics*. Cambridge: Cambridge University Press, 2018.
Meilaender, Gilbert. *The Theory and Practice of Virtue*. Notre Dame: Notre Dame Press, 1984.
Meilaender, Gilbert. *The Limits of Love: Some Theological Explorations*. University Park: Pennsylvania State University Press, 1987.
Meilaender, Gilbert. 'Ethics and Exegesis: A Great Gulf?'. In *A Royal Priesthood? The Use of the Bible Ethically and Politically: A Dialogue with Oliver O'Donovan*, edited by Craig G. Bartholomew, Robert Song, Jonathan Chaplin and Al Wolters, 259–64. Carlisle: Paternoster Press, 2002.
Meilaender, Gilbert. 'Divine Grace and Christian Ethics'. In *The Oxford Handbook of Theological Ethics*, edited by Gilbert Meilaender and William Werpehowski, 74–89. New York/Oxford: Oxford University Press, 2005.
Meilaender, Gilbert. 'Hearts Set to Obey'. In *I am the Lord Your God: Christian Reflections on the Ten Commandments*, edited by Carl E. Braaten and Christopher Seitz, 253–75. Grand Rapids: Eerdmans, 2005.
Meilaender, Gilbert. *The Freedom of a Christian: Grace, Vocation, and the Meaning of Our Humanity*. Grand Rapids: Brazos, 2006.
Meilaender, Gilbert. 'The Church: A Family of the Adopted'. In *Church, Society, and the Christian Common Good: Essays in Conversation with Philip Turner*, edited by Ephraim Radner, 131–45. Eugene: Cascade, 2017.
Meilaender, Gilbert and William Werpehowski, eds. *The Oxford Handbook of Theological Ethics*. New York/Oxford: Oxford University Press, 2005.

Melina, Livio. *Sharing in Christ's Virtues: For a Renewal of Moral Theology in Light of Veritatis Splendor*. Translated by William E. May. Washington: Catholic University of America Press, 2001.
Milbank, John. *The Word Made Strange: Theology, Language, Culture*. Oxford: Blackwell, 1997.
Milbank, John, Catherine Pickstock and Graham Ward, eds. *Radical Orthodoxy*. London: Routledge, 1999.
Miller, Colin D. *The Practice of the Body of Christ: Human Agency in Pauline Theology after MacIntyre*. Eugene: Pickwick Publications, 2014.
Mitchell, Basil. *How to Play Theological Ping-Pong: And Other Essays on Faith and Reason*, edited by William J. Abraham and Robert W. Prevost. Grand Rapids: Eerdmans, 1990.
Moberly, Jenny. *The Virtue of Bonhoeffer's Ethics: A Study of Dietrich Bonhoeffer's Ethics in Relation to Virtue Ethics*. Eugene: Pickwick, 2013.
Molnar, Paul. *Incarnation and Resurrection: Toward a Contemporary Understanding*. Grand Rapids: Eerdmans, 2007.
Moltmann, Jürgen. *Theology of Hope: On the Ground and Implications of a Christian Eschatology*. Translated by J. W. Leitch. London: SCM Press, 1967.
Moltmann, Jürgen. *The Trinity and the Kingdom*. Translated by Margaret Kohl. London: SCM Press, 1981.
Moltmann, Jürgen. *The Coming of God: Christian Eschatology*. Translated by Margaret Kohl. Minneapolis: Fortress, 1996.
Moltmann, Jürgen. *Ethics of Hope*. Translated by Margaret Kohl. Minneapolis: Fortress, 2012.
Moo, Douglas J. 'Nature in the New Creation: New Testament Eschatology and the Environment'. *Journal of the Evangelical Theological Society* 49, no. 3 (2006): 449–88.
Morse, Christopher. *The Difference Heaven Makes: Rehearing the Gospel as Good News*. London/New York: T & T Clark International, 2010.
Mühling, Markus. *T & T Clark Handbook of Christian Eschatology*. Translated by Jennifer Adams-Massmann and David Andrew Gilland. London: Bloomsbury T & T Clark, 2015.
Nation, Mark, ed. *Faithfulness and Fortitude: Conversations with the Theological Ethics of Stanley Hauerwas*. Edinburgh: T & T Clark, 2000.
Niebuhr, H. Richard, *Christ and Culture*. New York: HarperCollins, 1996.
Nimmo, Paul. *Being in Action: The Theological Shape of Barth's Ethical Vision*. London/New York: T & T Clark, 2007.
Nimmo, Paul T. 'The Law of God and Christian Ethics'. In *Christian Dogmatics: Reformed Theology for the Church Catholic*, edited by Michael Allen and Scott R. Swain, 291–310. Grand Rapids: Baker Academic, 2016.
Northcott, Michael. *The Environment and Christian Ethics*. Cambridge: Cambridge University Press, 1996.
Oakes, Edward. *A Theology of Grace in Six Controversies*. Grand Rapids: Eerdmans, 2016.
Oakes, Kenneth. 'Henri de Lubac and Protestantism'. In *T & T Clark Companion to Henri de Lubac*, edited by Jordan Hillebert, 373–92. London/New York: Bloomsbury T & T Clark, 2017.
O'Regan, Cyril. *The Heterodox Hegel*. Albany: SUNY Press, 1994.
O'Regan, Cyril. 'On Hegel, Theodicy and the Invisibility of Waste'. In *The Providence of God: Deus Habet Consilium*, edited by Francesca Aran Murphy and Philip G. Ziegler, 75–108. London/New York: Bloomsbury T & T Clark, 2009.

O'Regan, Cyril. *Theology and the Spaces of Apocalyptic*. Milwaukee, Marquette University Press, 2009.
O'Regan, Cyril. 'A Theology of History'. In *T & T Clark Companion to Henri de Lubac*, edited by Jordan Hillebert, 289–306. London/New York: Bloomsbury T & T Clark, 2017.
O'Regan, Cyril. 'Two Forms of Catholic Apocalyptic Theology'. *International Journal of Systematic Theology* 20, no. 1 (2018): 31–64.
Owen, John. *The Works of John Owen, vol. 1, The Glory of Christ*, edited by William H. Goold. London: Banner of Truth, 1965.
Pannenberg, Wolfhart. 'Constructive and Critical Functions of Eschatology'. *Harvard Theological Review* 77 (1984): 119–39.
Pannenberg, Wolfhart. *Systematic Theology*, vol. 3. Translated by Geoffrey W. Bromiley. Grand Rapids: Eerdmans, 1997.
Parry, Robin. 'Evangelicalism and Ethics'. In *The Futures of Evangelicalism: Issues and Prospects*, edited by Craig G. Bartholomew, Robin Parry and Andrew West, 164–93. Leicester: IVP, 2003.
Paul II, John. *Veritatis Splendor* (1993), http://www.vatican.va/content/john-paul-ii/en/encyclicals/documents/hf_jp-ii_enc_06081993_veritatis-splendor.html (accessed 26 April 2020).
Paul VI, *Optatam Totius* (1965), http://www.vatican.va/archive/hist_councils/ii_vatican_council/documents/vat-ii_decree_19651028_optatam-totius_en.html (accessed 26 April 2020).
Perry, John, ed. *God, the Good, and Utilitarianism: Perspectives on Peter Singer*. Cambridge: Cambridge University Press, 2014.
Perry, John. 'Jesus and Hume among the Neuroscientists: Haidt, Greene, and the Unwitting Return of Moral Sense Theory'. *Journal of the Society of Christian Ethics* 36, no. 1 (2016), 69–85.
Phan, Peter. 'Roman Catholic Theology'. In *The Oxford Handbook of Eschatology*, edited by Jerry L. Walls, 215–32. Oxford: Oxford University Press, 2008.
Pickstock, Catherine. 'The One Story: A Critique of David Kelsey's Theological Robotics'. *Modern Theology* 27, no. 1 (2011): 26–40.
Pinches, Charles. 'Principle Monism and Action Descriptions: Situationism and Its Critics Revisited'. *Modern Theology* 7, no. 3 (1991): 249–68.
Pinches, Charles, Kelly S. Johnson and Charles M. Collier, eds. *Unsettling Arguments: A Festschrift on the Occasion of Stanley Hauerwas's 70th Birthday*. Eugene: Cascade, 2010.
Pinckaers, Servais. *The Sources of Christian Ethics*. Translated by Mary Thomas Noble. Washington: Catholic University of America Press, 1995.
Pinckaers, Servais. *Morality: The Catholic View*. Translated by Michael Sherwin. South Bend: St. Augustine's Press, 2001.
Pieper, Josef. *On Hope*. San Francisco: Ignatius Press, 1986.
Poon, Michael Nai-Chiu. 'Recovering a Sense of Place'. *Living Church* (Spring 2012): 9–11.
Pope, Stephen J., ed. *The Ethics of Aquinas*. Washington: Georgetown University Press, 2002.
Porter, Jean. *The Recovery of Virtue: The Relevance of Aquinas for Christian Ethics*. Louisville: Westminster/John Knox, 1990.
Porter, Jean. *Natural and Divine Law: Reclaiming the Tradition for Christian Ethics*. Grand Rapids: Eerdmans, 1999.
Porter, Jean. *Ministers of the Law: A Natural Law Theory of Legal Authority*. Grand Rapids: Eerdmans, 2010.

Porter, Jean. 'Virtue Ethics'. In *The Cambridge Companion to Christian Ethics*, 2nd edn, edited by Robin Gill. Cambridge: Cambridge University Press, 2012.

Preston, Ronald H. *Confusions in Christian Social Ethics: Problems for Geneva and Rome*. London: SCM Press, 1994.

Radner, Ephraim. 'The Holy Spirit and Unity: Getting out of the Way of Christ'. *International Journal of Systematic Theology* 16, no. 2 (2014): 207–20.

Radner, Ephraim. *A Time to Keep: Theology, Mortality and the Shape of a Human Life*. Waco: Baylor University Press, 2016.

Radner, Ephraim. 'The Mystery of Christian Anthropology'. In *Anthropology and New Testament Theology*, edited by Jason Maston and Benjamin E. Reynolds, 243–62. London/New York: Bloomsbury T & T Clark, 2018.

Radner, Ephraim. *A Profound Ignorance: Modern Pneumatology and Its Anti-modern Redemption*. Waco: Baylor University Press, 2019.

Rae, Murray. 'Salvation and History'. In *God of Salvation: Soteriology in Theological Perspective*, edited by Ivor J. Davidson and Murray Rae, 89–103. Farnham: Ashgate, 2011.

Rasmusson, Arne. *The Church as Polis: From Political Theology to Theological Politics as Exemplified by Jürgen Moltmann and Stanley Hauerwas*. Notre Dame: University of Notre Dame Press, 1995.

Rasmusson, Arne. 'Not All Justifications of Christendom Are Created Equal: A Response to Oliver O'Donovan'. *Studies in Christian Ethics* 112, no. 2 (1998): 69–76.

Ramsey, Michael. *The Gospel and the Catholic Church*, 2nd edn. London: SPCK, 1990.

Ramsey, Paul. 'Human Sexuality in the History of Redemption'. *Journal of Religious Ethics* 16, no. 1 (1988): 56–84.

Ramsey, Paul. *One Flesh: A Christian View of Sex Within, Outside, and Before Marriage*, Grove Booklet E:8, edited by E. David Cook and Oliver O'Donovan. Nottingham: Grove Books, 1990.

Ramsey, Paul. *The Essential Paul Ramsey*, edited by William Werpehowski and Stephen D. Crocco. New Haven: Yale University Press, 1994.

Ratzinger, Joseph. *Eschatology: Death and Eternal Life*, 2nd edn. Translated by Michael Waldstein. Washington: Catholic University of America Press, 1988.

Ratzinger, Joseph. *'In the Beginning . . .': a Catholic Understanding of the Story of Creation and the Fall*. Translated by Boniface Ramsey. Grand Rapids: Eerdmans, 1995.

Reidy, Maurice. 'Review of O'Donovan, *Resurrection and Moral Order*'. *Scottish Journal of Theology* 42, no. 1 (1989): 131–4.

Rodenborn, Steven M., *Hope in Action: Subversive Eschatology in the Theology of Edward Schillebeeckx and Johann Baptist Metz*. Minneapolis: Fortress Press, 2014.

Rogers, Eugene F. *Sexuality and the Christian Body: Their Way into the Triune God*. Oxford/Malden, MA: Blackwell, 1999.

Rogers, Eugene F. *After the Spirit: A Constructive Pneumatology from Resources Outside the Modern West*. Grand Rapids: Eerdmans, 2005.

Rogers, Eugene F. 'Holy Spirit'. In *The Cambridge Dictionary of Christian Theology*, edited by Ian A. McFarland, David A.S. Fergusson, Karen Kilby and Iain R. Torrance, 220–2. Cambridge: Cambridge University Press, 2011.

Rose, Matthew. *Ethics with Barth: God, Metaphysics and Morals*. Farnham/Burlington: Ashgate, 2010.

Rosner, Brian. 'Paul's Ethics'. In *The Cambridge Companion to St Paul*, edited by James D. G. Dunn, 212–23. Cambridge: Cambridge University Press, 2003.

Rowland, Christopher. 'Response to *the Desire of the Nations*'. *Studies in Christian Ethics* 112, no. 2 (1998): 77–85.

Russell, Norman. 'The Work of Christ in Patristic Theology'. In *The Oxford Handbook of Christology*, edited by Francesca A. Murphy, 154–66. New York/Oxford: Oxford University Press, 2015.
Ryan, Mark. *The Politics of Practical Reason: Why Theological Ethics Must Change Your Life*. Eugene: Cascade, 2011.
Sauter, Gerhard. *What Dare We Hope? Reconsidering Eschatology*. Harrisburg: Trinity Press International, 1999.
Schaeffer, Hans. *Createdness and Ethics: The Doctrine of Creation and Theological Ethics in the Theology of Colin E. Gunton and Oswald Bayer*. Berlin/New York: Walter de Gruyter, 2006.
Schuurman, Douglas J. *Creation, Eschaton, and Ethics: The Creation-Eschaton Relation in the Thought of Emil Brunner and Jürgen Moltmann*. New York: Peter Lang, 1991.
Schuurman, Douglas J. 'Creation, Eschaton, and Social Ethics: A Response to Volf'. *Calvin Theological Journal* 30, no. 1 (1995): 144–58.
Schwartz, Hans. *Eschatology*. Grand Rapids: William B. Eerdmans, 2000.
Scott, Peter. 'Return to the Vomit of "Legitimation"?'. In *A Royal Priesthood? The Use of the Bible Ethically and Politically: A Dialogue with Oliver O'Donovan*, edited by Craig G. Bartholomew, Robert Song, Jonathan Chaplin and Al Wolters, 344–73. Carlisle: Paternoster Press, 2002.
Scott Smith, R. *Virtue Ethics and Moral Knowledge: Philosophy of Language after MacIntyre and Hauerwas*. Aldershot: Ashgate, 2003.
Scruton, Roger. *The Uses of Pessimism*. London: Atlantic Books, 2010.
Sedgwick, Timothy F. 'Revising Anglican Moral Theology'. In *The Future of Anglican Theology*, edited by M. Darrol Bryant, 131–41. New York: Edwin Mellon, 1984.
Sedgwick, Timothy F. 'Review of O'Donovan, *Resurrection and Moral Order*'. *Journal of the American Academy of Religion* 5, no. 2 (1989): 419–21.
Sedgwick, Peter. 'Anglican Moral Theology and Ecumenical Dialogue'. *Religions* 8, no. 9 (2017): 63–70.
Shanks, Andrew. 'Review of Bartholomew et al, eds., *A Royal Priesthood*'. *Theology* 107, no. 836 (2004): 145–6.
Sherwin, Michael. *By Knowledge and By Love: Charity and Knowledge in the Moral Theology of St. Thomas Aquinas*. Washington: Catholic University of America Press, 2005.
Shuster, Marguerite. 'The Redemption of the Created Order: Sermons on Romans 8: 18–25'. In *The Redemption: An Interdisciplinary Symposium on Christ as Redeemer*, edited by Steven T. Davis, Daniel Kendall and Gerald O'Collins, 321–42. Oxford: Oxford University Press, 2004.
Sider, J. Alexander. *To See History Doxologically: History and Holiness in John Howard Yoder's Ecclesiology*. Grand Rapids: Eerdmans, 2011.
Simmons, Frederick V. 'Eudaimonism and Christian Love'. In *Love and Christian Ethics: Tradition, Theory, and Society*, edited by Frederick V. Simmons, with Brian C. Sorrells, 190–209. Washington: Georgetown University Press, 2016.
Simpkins, Matthew. 'The Church of England's Exclusion of Same-sex Couples from Marriage: Some Problems with Oliver O'Donovan's Influence and Arguments'. *Theology* 119, no. 3 (2016): 172–84.
Smith, David H. 'Kenneth Kirk's *The Vision of God*'. In *The Oxford Handbook of Theological Ethics*, edited by Gilbert Meilaender and William Werpehowski, 449–65. New York/Oxford: Oxford University Press, 2005.
Smith, James K. A. *Awaiting the Kingdom*. Grand Rapids: Baker Academic, 2017.

Sonderegger, Katherine. '"Response", to Christopher Morse, *The Difference Heaven Makes*'. *Theology Today* 68, no. 1 (2011): 64–8.
Sonderegger, Katherine. 'Towards a Doctrine of Resurrection'. In *Eternal God, Eternal Life: Theological Investigations into the Concept of Immortality*, edited by Philip G. Ziegler, 115–29. London/New York: Bloomsbury T & T Clark, 2016.
Song, Robert. *Christianity and Liberal Society*. Oxford: Oxford University Press, 1997.
Song, Robert. *Human Genetics: Fabricating the Future*. London: Darton, Longman, and Todd, 2002.
Song, Robert. 'Knowing There Is No God, Still We Should Not Play God? Habermas on the Future of Human Nature'. *Ecotheology* 11, no. 2 (2006): 191–211.
Song, Robert. 'Bodily Integrity Disorder and the Ethics of Mutilation'. *Studies in Christian Ethics* 26, no. 4 (2013): 487–503.
Song, Robert. *Covenant and Calling: Towards a Theology of Same-Sex Relationships*. London: SCM Press, 2014.
Song, Robert and Brent Waters, eds. *The Authority of the Gospel: Explorations in Moral and Political Theology in Honor of Oliver O'Donovan*. Grand Rapids: Eerdmans, 2015.
Skrimshire, Stefan. *Politics of Fear, Practices of Hope: Depoliticisation and Resistance in a Time of Terror*. London/New York: Continuum, 2008.
Spaemann, Robert. *Persons: The Difference Between Someone and Something*. Translated by Oliver O'Donovan. Oxford: Oxford University Press, 2006.
Spaemann, Robert. *Essays in Anthropology: Variations on a Theme*, edited and translated by Guido de Graaff and James Mumford. Eugene: Cascade, 2010.
Spaemann, Robert. 'What Does It Mean to Say that "Art Imitates Nature"?'. In *A Robert Spaemann Reader: Philosophical Essays on Nature, God, and the Human Person*, edited by D. C. Schindler and Jeanne Heffernan Schindler. Oxford: Oxford University Press, 2015.
Spohn, William C. *Go and Do Likewise: Jesus and Ethics*. New York/London: Continuum International, 2007.
Stanley, Jon. 'Restoration and Renewal: The Nature of Grace in the Theology of Herman Bavinck'. In *The Kuyper Center Review, Vol. 2: Revelation and Common Grace*, edited by John Bowlin, 81–194. Grand Rapids: Eerdmans, 2011.
Stassen, Glen and Gushee, David. *Kingdom Ethics: Following Jesus in Contemporary Context*. Downers Grove: IVP, 2003.
Steck, Christopher. *The Ethical Thought of Hans Urs von Balthasar*. New York: Herder & Herder, 2001.
Stewart-Kroeker, Sarah. *Pilgrimage as Moral and Aesthetic Formation in Augustine's Thought*. Oxford: Oxford University Press, 2017.
Stott, John. *Issues Facing Christians Today*. Grand Rapids: Zondervan, 2006.
Stout, Jeffrey. *Democracy and Tradition*. Princeton: Princeton University Press, 2004.
Stringfellow, William. *An Ethic for Christians and Other Aliens in a Strange Land*. Eugene: Wipf & Stock, 2004.
Sugden, Chris and Oliver Barclay. *Kingdom and Creation in Social Ethics: Grove Booklet E:79*. Bramcote: Grove Books, 1990.
Swinton, John. *Critical Reflections on Stanley Hauerwas's Theology of Disability: Disabling Society, Enabling Theology*. Binghamton: The Howarth Pastoral Press, 2004.
Swinton, John. *Becoming Friends with Time: Disability, Timefullness, and Gentle Discipleship*. Waco: Baylor University Press, 2016.
Tanner, Kathryn, *Jesus, Humanity and the Trinity: A Brief Systematic Theology*. Minneapolis: Fortress Press, 2001.

Tanner, Kathryn. 'Eschatology and Ethics'. In *The Oxford Handbook to Theological Ethics*, edited by Gilbert Meilaender and William Werpehowski, 41–56. New York/Oxford: Oxford University Press, 2005.
Tanner, Kathryn. *Christ the Key*. Cambridge: Cambridge University Press, 2010.
Thiel, John E. *Icons of Hope: The 'Last Things' in Catholic Imagination*. Notre Dame: University of Notre Dame Press, 2013.
Thompson, John B. *The Ecclesiology of Stanley Hauerwas: A Christian Theology of Liberation*. Burlington: Ashgate, 2003.
Titus, Craig Steven. 'Servais Pinckaers and the Renewal of Catholic Moral Theology'. *Journal of Moral Theology* 1, no. 1 (2012): 43–68.
Tolonen, Miika. *Witness Is Presence: Reading Stanley Hauerwas in a Nordic Setting*. Eugene: Resource, 2013.
Torrance, T. F. *Kingdom and Church: A Study in the Theology of the Reformation*. Eugene: Wipf and Stock, 1996.
Townsend, Nicholas. 'Should Jesus Christ Be at the Centre of Introductions to Christian Ethics?'. *Studies in Christian Ethics* 33, no. 1 (2020): 95–106.
Tranter, Samuel and David Bartram Torrance. 'Ethnography, Ecclesiology, and the Ethics of Everyday Life: Introducing Michael Banner'. *Ecclesial Practices* 5, no. 2 (2018): 157–71.
Ulrich, Hans G. *Eschatologie und Ethik: die theologische Theorie der Ethik in ihrer Beziehung auf die Rede von Gott seit Friedrich Schleiermacher*. München: Kaiser-Verlag, 1988.
Ulrich, Hans G. 'Understanding the *Conditio Humana*'. In *Bonhoeffer and the Biosciences: An Initial Exploration*, edited by Ralf K. Wüstenberg, Stefan Heuser and Esther Hornung, 147–68. Frankfurt: Peter Lang, 2010.
Ulrich, Hans G. 'The Messianic Contours of Evangelical Ethics'. In *The Freedom of a Christian Ethicist: The Future of a Reformation Legacy*, edited by Brian Brock and Michael Mawson, 39–64. London/New York: T & T Clark, 2016.
VanDrunen, David. *Natural Law and the Two Kingdoms: A Study in the Development of Reformed Social Thought*. Grand Rapids: Eerdmans, 2010.
Van Leeuwen, Raymond C. 'Christ's Resurrection and the Creation's Vindication'. In *The Environment and the Christian: What Does the New Testament Say About the Environment*, edited by Calvin B. DeWitt, 57–72. Grand Rapids: Baker Book House, 1991.
Volf, Miroslav. 'Eschaton, Creation, and Social Ethics'. *Calvin Theological Journal* 30, no. 1 (1995): 191–6.
Volpe, Medi-Ann. *Rethinking Christian Identity: Doctrine and Discipleship*. Chichester: Wiley-Blackwell, 2013.
Vos, Geerhardus. *The Eschatology of the Old Testament*. Phillipsburg: P&R, 2001.
Wainwright, Geoffrey. 'The Holy Spirit'. In *The Cambridge Companion to Christian Doctrine*, edited by Colin Gunton, 273–96. Cambridge: Cambridge University Press, 1997.
Wannenwetsch, Bernd. *Political Worship*. Translated by Margaret Kohl. New York: Oxford University Press, 2004.
Wannenwetsch, Bernd. 'Creation and Ethics: On the Legitimacy and Limitation of Appeals to "Nature" in Christian Moral Reasoning'. In *Within the Love of God*, edited by Anthony Clarke and Andrew Moore, 198–216. Oxford: Oxford University Press, 2014.
Waters, Brent. *Reproductive Technology: Towards a Theology of Procreative Stewardship*. London: Darton, Longman, and Todd, 2000.

Waters, Brent. 'What Is Christian about Christian Bioethics'. *Christian Bioethics* 11, no. 3 (2005): 281–95.
Waters, Brent. *From Human to Posthuman: Christian Theology and Technology in a Postmodern World*. Aldershot: Ashgate, 2006.
Waters, Brent. *The Family in Christian Social and Political Thought*. Oxford/New York: Oxford University Press, 2007.
Waters, Brent. 'Review of Bennett, *Water Is Thicker than Blood*'. *Modern Theology* 29, no. 2 (2009): 341–3.
Waters, Brent. *This Mortal Flesh: Incarnation and Bioethics*. Grand Rapids: Brazos, 2009.
Waters, Brent. 'The Incarnation and the Christian Moral Life'. In *Christology and Ethics*, edited by Brent Waters and F. LeRon Shults, 5–31. Grand Rapids: Eerdmans, 2010.
Waters, Brent. 'Christian Ethics and Human Germ Line Genetic Modification'. *Christian Bioethics* 18, no. 2 (2012): 171–86.
Waters, Brent. *Christian Moral Theology in the Emerging Technoculture: From Posthuman Back to Human*. Farnham: Ashgate, 2014.
Waters, Brent. *Just Capitalism: A Christian Ethics of Economic Globalization*. Louisville: Westminster/John Knox, 2016.
Watson, Francis. 'Review of Hays, *Moral Vision*'. *Studies in Christian Ethics* 10, no. 2 (1997): 94–7.
Watson, Francis. '"America's theologian": An Appreciation of Robert Jenson's Systematic Theology, with Some Remarks about the Bible'. *Scottish Journal of Theology* 55, no. 2 (2002): 201–23.
Watson, Francis. '"Every Perfect Gift": James, Paul and the Created Order'. In *Muted Voices of the New Testament: Readings in the Catholic Epistles and Hebrews*, edited by Katherine M. Hockey, Madison N. Pierce, and Francis Watson, 121–37. London/New York: Bloomsbury T & T Clark, 2017.
Webster, John. 'Christology, Imitability and Ethics'. *Scottish Journal of Theology* 39, no. 3 (1986): 309–2.
Webster, John. 'The Human Person'. In *The Cambridge Companion to Postmodern Theology*, edited by Kevin Vanhoozer, 219–34. Cambridge: Cambridge University Press, 2003.
Webster, John. *Confessing God: Essays in Christian Dogmatics II*. London/New York: T & T Clark International, 2005.
Webster, John. 'Hope'. In *The Oxford Handbook to Theological Ethics*, edited by Gilbert Meilaender and William Werpehowski, 291–306. New York/Oxford: Oxford University Press, 2005.
Webster, John. 'One Under Authority'. *Living Church* (Spring 2012): 14–15.
Webster, John. 'Ecclesiocentrism'. *First Things* 246 (2014): 54–5.
Wells, Samuel. *Transforming Fate into Destiny: The Theological Ethics of Stanley Hauerwas*. Carlisle: Paternoster, 1998.
Wells, Samuel. *How Then Shall We Live? Christian Engagement with Contemporary Issues*. Norwich: Canterbury Press, 2016.
Wells, Samuel and Quash, Ben. *Introducing Christian Ethics*. Chichester: Wiley-Blackwell, 2010.
Werpehowski, William. *American Protestant Ethics and the Legacy of H. Richard Niebuhr*. Washington: Georgetown University Press, 2003.
Westberg, Daniel A. *Right Practical Reason: Aristotle, Action, and Prudence in Aquinas*. Oxford: Oxford University Press, 1994.
Westberg, Daniel A. 'Critic of Hubristic Modernity'. *Living Church* (Spring 2012): 16–18.

Westberg, Daniel A. *Renewing Moral Theology: Christian Ethics as Action, Character, and Grace*. Downers Grove: InterVarsity Press, 2015.
Westberg, Daniel A. 'The Influence of Aquinas on Protestant Ethics'. In *Aquinas among the Protestants*, edited by Manfred Svenson and David VanDrunen, 267–85. Chichester: Wiley-Blackwell, 2018.
Widdicombe, Peter. 'Patient Teacher to All'. *Living Church* (Spring 2012): 11–13.
Williams, Rowan. *On Christian Theology*. Oxford: Blackwell, 2000.
Williams, Rowan. 'Foreword'. In *The Authority of the Gospel*, edited by Robert Song and Brent Waters, viii–ix. Grand Rapids: Eerdmans, 2015.
Williams, Rowan. 'Review of John Milbank and Adrian Pabst, *The Politics of Virtue*'. *New Statesman* (2016), https://www.newstatesman.com/culture/books/2016/10/liberalism-and-capitalism-have-hollowed-out-society-so-where-do-we-turn-now (accessed 8 October 2019).
Williams, Stephen N. 'Outline for Ethics: A Response to Oliver O'Donovan'. *Themelios* 13, no. 3 (1988): 86–91.
Williams, Stephen N., with an essay response by Miroslav Volf. *The Limits of Hope and the Logic of Love: Essays on Eschatology and Social Action*. Vancouver: Regent College Publishing, 2006.
Wolters, Albert M. *Creation Regained: Biblical Basics for a Reformational Worldview*, 2nd edn. Grand Rapids: Eerdmans, 2005.
Wright, Christopher J. H. *Old Testament Ethics for the People of God*. Downers Grove: IVP, 2004.
Wright, Tom. *Surprised by Hope*. London: SPCK, 2007.
Yeago, David. 'Gnosticism, Antinomianism, and Reformation Theology'. *Pro Ecclesia* 2, no. 1 (1993): 37–49.
Zachman, Randall C. 'The Christology of John Calvin'. In *The Oxford Handbook to Christology*, edited by Francesca Aran Murphy, 284–96. Oxford/New York: Oxford University Press, 2015.
Zagzebski, Linda. 'Does Ethics Need God?'. *Faith and Philosophy* 4, no. 2 (1987): 294–303.
Zahl, Paul M. *Grace in Practice: A Theology of Everyday Life*. Grand Rapids: Eerdmans, 2007.
Ziegler, Philip G. '"To Pray, To Testify, and to Revolt"'. In Karl Barth, *The Christian Life*, translated by Geoffrey W. Bromiley, 1–16. London/New York: Bloomsbury T & T Clark, 2017.
Ziegler, Philip G. *Militant Grace: The Apocalyptic Turn and the Future of Christian Theology*. Grand Rapids: Baker Academic, 2018.

General index

Adam, Margaret   88, 89 n.245, 234 n.5
Adams, Nicholas   66 n.147, 233 n.2
Adams, Robert Merrihew   60–1, 63 n.129, 116 n.92, 120 n.110
Adams, Samuel V.   55 n.92, 237 n.6
Allen, Michael   83 n.223, 90 n.252, 136 n.190, 142, 179 n.69, 207 n.74
Anabaptist theology   47 n.56, 93, 122 n.112
Anglican theology   4, 27 n.55, 30 n.65, 43, 49 n.66, 58 n.103, 67, 86 n.232, 102–3, 106, 180 n.71
Apocalyptic theology   10, 63 n.128, 119 n.106, 173 n.46, 182 n.82, 207 n.76, 215 n.129, 237–41
apologetics   9, 52 n.79, 67 n.153, 215, 217–19
Aquinas, Thomas   37, 41 n.28, 106 n.45, 114, 116 n.96, 131, 134, 140 n.210, 151 n.277, 157–9, 188 n.109, 189, 228
   Thomist   14 n.2, 17, 24, 37, 40 n.27, 58 n.103, 83 n.223, 115–17, 119 n.108, 121 n.112, 128, 131, 143, 148, 158–9, 188, 198, 239 n.12, 241–2
Aristotle   39, 69, 102, 116 n.97
   Aristotelian   15, 45, 66, 69, 83 n.225, 116, 121, 167 n.17
Arner, Neil   120 n.110, 121 n.112, 130, 139 n.205
ascension   47, 109, 168, 216, 238
Augustine   23 n.40, 36, 45, 48, 62 n.120, 63 n.128, 83–4, 102, 117 n.97, 132–3, 140 n.210, 145, 152–5, 182 n.82, 183, 203, 234
   Augustinian   32, 123 n.120, 131, 148, 157–9, 185–90
Austin, Victor Lee   52 n.78, 102 n.22
authority   7, 100–9, 166, 195–6
   of the church   147, 171
   of created order   40, 99, 101, 103, 114, 118–19, 124–5, 152, 194–5

divine   55, 100–9, 113, 145, 167 n.17, 181
   political   8, 26, 175, 188–90
Ayres, Lewis   11, 112 n.72

Balthasar, Hans Urs von   112, 118 n.103, 119 n.107, 131 n.162, 227, 230 n.23
Banner, Michael   10–11, 42, 77 n.206, 146
Barclay, John   63 n.128, 77 n.203, 140 n.206, 219 n.143
Barclay, Oliver   27 n.55, 37 n.11, 52 n.79, 73 n.190
Barth, Karl   3 n.6, 6 n.15, 42, 44 n.45, 47 n.56, 55 n.88, 67, 81, 117–19, 131, 138, 142 n.218, 158, 168, 173 n.46, 192, 194, 202, 215, 236, 238
   Barthian   24, 32, 37, 67 n.153, 61, 106, 119 n.108, 120 n.110, 121, 158, 192, 204, 212, 218 n.140, 230, 239, 242
Bartholomew, Craig   68, 76 n.202
Bauckham, Richard   88 n.241, 201 n.51
Bavinck, Hermann   76 n.202, 81 n.214, 83 n.223
Bayer, Oswald   131 n.162, 159 n.305, 241
beatific vision   88, 90
Beiser, Frederick C.   59 n.104, 234 n.6
Benedict XVI   41 n.28, 58 n.103, 128 n.141, 157 n.296, 234 n.8, 236
Bennett, Jana   23 n.40, 63 n.128, 159 n.305
Berkman, John   69 n.161, 148, 156–7, 159
Biggar, Nigel   10 n.21, 27 n.56, 53, 117–18, 131, 140 n.209, 164 n.3, 189 n.117, 194 n.16, 202 n.60, 214 n.126
bioethics   16 n.14, 29, 96–7, 104 n.33
biotechnology   2, 6, 93–7, 194
Boersma, Hans   90 n.252, 192 n.8
Bonhoeffer, Dietrich   38 n.16, 96, 127, 134, 194, 215, 229 n.12

Bowlin, John   20 n.35, 40, 121 n.112, 234, 241
Bretherton, Luke   13 n.1, 159–61, 168 n.23, 220 n.147
Brock, Brian   3 n.6, 41 n.28, 49 n.65, 58 n.102, 131 n.164, 169 n.29, 184 n.92, 186 n.102, 187 n.104, 240, 241 n.21
Brown, Malcolm   146, 179 n.69
Brunner, Emil   75 n.201, 85 n.227, 131, 194
Bultmann, Rudolf   55, 194, 238, 240 n.18
Burger, Hans   50 n.69, 131 n.162
Burridge, Richard   77
Buttrey, Michael   69 n.161, 148, 156–7, 159

Calvin, John   38–9, 81, 83 n.223, 106 n.45, 120 n.110
Cameron, Andrew J. B.   16 n.11, 48 n.61
Carroll R., M. Daniel   170, 187 n.104
Catholic theology   18 n.24, 28 n.58, 37, 40, 41 n.28, 43, 49 n.66, 52, 58 n.103, 67 n.153, 83 n.223, 103 n.25, 105 n.37, 106, 116 n.96, 117, 119 n.108, 121, 123 n.120, 131, 134, 141–3, 157 n.296, 207, 212, 228 n.4
Cavanaugh, William T.   162 n.317, 182 n.82, 187 n.103
Cessario, Romanus   18 n.24, 58 n.103, 119 n.108, 135 n.184
Chaplin, Jonathan   27 n.55, 44 n.43, 69 n.155, 159 n.305, 185, 188 n.108, 189
character   7, 121 n.112, 123 n.120, 133–6, 144, 147, 149
Chester, Tim   65 n.143, 138 n.202
Christology   6 n.15, 7, 22, 35, 38 n.15, 43, 46–7, 50–4, 56, 64, 79–82, 85, 87–8, 99–101, 105–13, 115, 117 n.101, 119, 125, 129–30, 136, 139–40, 144, 149, 152, 155–6, 167, 169, 171, 173, 181, 188 n.105, 190, 193, 197–9, 201–4, 206, 211, 215–16, 218, 233 n.3, 238–40
church, *see* ecclesiology
Clough, David   87, 120 n.108
Coakley, Sarah   203 n.63, 218
Cole, Jonathan   189–90

Congar, Yves   23 n.41, 110 n.64, 112 n.74
consummation, eschatological   23, 26, 31, 46, 57, 63, 83 n.223, 85, 89, 92, 145, 169, 207 n.76, 235–7, 240–2
conversion   7, 72, 99, 103, 120, 133–6, 144, 150, 153, 194, 218–19
creation   1, 4–8, 13–14, 16–18, 20–33, 35–42, 44–54, 56–7, 59–65, 68–96, 99, 102–6, 108–9, 112–20, 124–32, 137, 142–3, 145, 148–79, 182, 185–90, 195, 202, 211, 213, 214–16, 219, 231, 235–41
creation ethics   4–5, 14, 27, 30, 33, 35, 37 n.11, 61, 73–9, 105, 143
cross, the   7, 46, 81 n.214, 99, 137–45, 166 n.16, 171–3, 194, 214 n.125, 216

Daley, Brian E.   228
Davidson, Ivor J.   111, 233 n.3
de Graaff, Guido   69 n.160, 184 nn.91–2, 189
de Lubac, Henri   25 n.47, 83 n.223, 112
divine command ethics   7, 46, 64, 72–3, 99, 103 n.30, 104, 114–23, 138–42
doctrine   1, 5, 9, 28, 31, 42, 133, 204–20, 227, 229–30, 235, 242
   and ethics   1, 5, 9, 28, 42, 92–3, 133, 193, 204–20, 227, 229–30, 242
doctrine of God   31, 154, 212, 214
dogmatic theology, *see* doctrine
Doherty, Sean   30, 180 n.72, 190 n.122
Dooyeweerd, Herman   159

ecclesiology   1, 3 n.5, 4, 7–8, 22, 44, 56, 79 n.205, 99, 110, 115, 135, 145–8, 161, 163, 166–74, 180–90, 193, 202, 208, 209, 215, 221–2, 224–5, 228, 231
ecological crisis, *see* environmental ethics
election   47 n.56, 72, 79–80, 206, 219
Elliot, David   1–2, 66 n.147, 143 n.222, 170 n.35, 198, 228 n.9, 229
environmental ethics   26, 28 n.58, 85–90, 93, 96, 237
epistemology   13, 17, 20, 23–5, 51, 53–4, 75–6, 124, 126–32, 155, 186
Errington, Andrew   49, 73, 102 n.22, 122 n.114, 127, 130, 157, 198 n.34

eschatology, *see* beatific vision;
consummation, eschatological;
Heaven; Kingdom of God;
resurrection, the
eudaimonism   120 n.110, 132,
138–43
evangelical theology   4–5, 13–14, 27–8,
32 n.70, 36–7, 42–4, 48 n.61, 49 n.66,
52 n.79, 67, 68 n.155, 73, 86, 133,
135, 138–9, 142, 160 n.307, 179 n.69,
180 n.71, 219, 221 n.153
evangelism   149, 219
Evans, C. Stephen   103 n.30, 116 n.92,
120 n.110

faith   7, 20, 26 n.50, 28 n.58, 29,
50 n.78, 70, 92, 107–8, 126,
132, 147, 148–52, 165, 170,
192, 194, 198, 201–3, 209,
211, 216, 221, 224, 228, 233,
240, 242
Fergusson, David   55, 89
Flipper, Joseph   25 n.47, 112 n.71
Forde, Gerhard   135–7
Forrester, Duncan   180, 214 n.126
Forsyth, P. T.   194–5
Francis, Pope   92
freedom, human   7, 40, 49, 51, 63 n.127,
69, 99–102, 107, 110–11, 145–6,
152, 193, 195–6, 206, 207 n.76

Gorringe, Timothy   65 n.139, 175 n.53,
179, 187–8, 190
grace   21, 23, 48, 70, 71, 72, 76 n.202,
81 n.214, 83 n.223, 78, 91, 116,
117 n.97, 119, 120 n.108, 135–6,
148, 150, 153, 158, 159 n.305, 168,
184–5, 219
and nature (*see* 'nature and grace')
Greer, Rowan   229, 234 n.5
Gregory, Eric   123 n.120, 139 n.205, 140,
183–7, 188 n.109, 190, 200 n.49,
225, 228 n.9
Gregory of Nyssa   32 n.69, 108 n.53, 111
Griffiths, Paul   87, 90 n.249
Gunton, Colin   236
Gushee, David   44 n.43, 200
Gustafson, James   38 n.15, 41–2, 46–7,
58, 75 n.201, 135, 138

Haas, Guenther   39
Hart, Trevor   88 n.241, 201 n.51
Hauerwas, Stanley   3, 23 n.40, 41 n.28,
53, 58 n.102, 75 n.196, 79 n.209,
82 n.217, 121, 128 n.140, 135 n.184,
136 n 192, 139, 142–3, 146, 161–2,
172, 173 n.46, 180 n.71, 182, 185 n.97,
187 n.103, 205, 208, 213, 214 n.126,
215 n.129, 220, 231, 237
Hays, Richard B.   66, 77 n.203, 166 n.16,
174 n.49
Healy, Nicholas M.   3 n.6, 192 n.9,
205, 208
heaven   19, 22–3, 64, 88–92, 104–6, 130,
145, 147, 150, 152, 155, 181, 186,
190, 193, 200 n.49, 203 n.62, 208,
216, 218, 220, 230, 234
Herdt, Jennifer   139 n.205, 203,
218 n.141, 234
historicism   5–6, 13, 21, 24–6, 57–66,
70–1, 80, 85 n.230, 93, 123, 128, 174
Hollowell, Adam Edward   81 n.216, 135
Holmes, Christopher   79–81, 238–9
Holy Spirit, *see* pneumatology
hope   1, 7–10, 19–20, 26, 51, 56–7, 62,
64–6, 69, 77–7, 85, 87–94, 100, 113,
126, 144, 148–52, 158–59, 168–70,
184, 192–201, 211, 221–4, 228–30,
233–7, 239–42
Hordern, Joshua   40, 155–6, 159,
160 n.307, 179–80, 187–8, 190,
200 n.49
Horrell, David   203–4
Hughes, John   180
Hunsinger, George   55
Hütter, Reinhard   83 n.223, 105,
119 n.108, 215 n.127, 240 n.20

incarnation, the   27 n.55, 46, 104, 110,
155–6, 166, 209, 216
Insole, Christopher   176, 182 n.82, 186
Irenaeus   83

Jenkins, Willis   86, 92–3
Jennings, Willie James   238
Jenson, Robert W.   68, 112 n.72, 124–5
Jesus Christ, *see* Christology
John Paul II   40, 43 n.38, 44 n.44,
58 n.103, 117, 127–8, 178, 219

joy 66, 124, 137–40, 143–5, 168–74, 201
Joyce, A. J. 103, 142 n.217
Jüngel, Eberhard 10, 112 n.72, 125, 135, 230
justice 8, 64, 65 n.142, 66, 171, 175, 183, 186, 200, 223
justification 103, 135, 150–1, 166, 215

Kant, Immanuel 102, 191, 208, 234 n.6
  Kantian 121
Kelsey, David H. 10, 102, 169, 192 n.10, 207 n.76, 230 n.18, 235–42
Kerr, Fergus 37, 40 n.24
Kerr, Nathan 173 n.46, 183 n.82, 239
Kierkegaard, Søren 71, 72 n.185, 103
  Kierkegaardian 50 n.72, 121
kingdom ethics 4–5, 14, 27, 30, 33, 35, 73–9, 105, 143, 178–9
kingdom of God 1, 9, 22–3, 28, 60–1, 63–4, 71, 73–5, 78, 93, 99, 103–9, 144–8, 151, 158, 160, 165 n.8, 167, 171, 174, 180–90, 193, 197–204, 217–18, 220, 222–5, 229–34, 239–40
Kirk, Kenneth 43, 58 n.103, 103 n.24, 142 n.217
Kroeker, P. Travis 38 n.15, 57 n.101, 167 n.18, 187 n.103, 239

Lacoste, Jean-Yves 11 n.26, 191–2
Laffin, Michael 240
Lamb, Matthew L. 157 n.296, 158 n.302
Levering, Matthew 88, 157 n.296, 228 n.9
liberation theology 3 n.6, 65 n 142, 138 n.201, 175–8, 234 n.8
Lockwood O'Donovan, Joan 3 n.5, 58 n.102, 129 n.148, 163 n.1, 164
Long, D. Stephen 41 n.28, 43, 119 n.108, 123 n.120, 141, 187 n.103, 239 n.12
Lorish, Philip 10 n.21, 11 n.23, 37, 154, 185–6
love 7, 18 n.24, 19–20, 29, 48, 60, 62, 99–102, 107, 111, 115, 136, 140 n.210, 141, 146, 148–52, 156–7, 169–70, 184, 190, 192, 198, 201, 203 n.62, 220–4, 228 n.9, 229, 242
Löwith, Karl 25 n.47, 110 n.64
Lutheran theology 10, 105–6, 135–6, 137 n.195, 140 n.210, 153 n.281, 194, 241–2
  law and gospel 105–7, 141, 183, 194

McAdoo, Henry 103 n.24, 142 n.217
Macaskill, Grant 119 n.106, 240
McCabe, Herbert 52, 116 n.97
McGrath, Alister E. 42
McIlroy, David 37
MacIntyre, Alasdair 3 n.6, 14 n.2, 16, 65, 135 n.184, 141, 159–61, 180 n.71
McKenny, Gerald P. 6, 16, 36, 45–7, 69, 94–7, 102 n.21, 130, 148, 156–7, 241 n.24
marriage 22–3, 49 n.65, 62–4, 78, 140, 157 n.294, 159 n.305
Marshall, Bruce D. 105 n.37, 228 n.8
Martyn, J. Louis 119 n.106, 240
Mathewes, Charles T. 10 n.21, 11 n.23, 37, 154, 160 n.307, 185–6, 190, 203, 217 n.135
Mattison, William C. 143 n.222, 144 n.228, 203 n.61
Maximus the Confessor 87
Meilaender, Gilbert 10, 41 n.28, 48 n.61, 54, 136 n.192, 153 n.281, 158–9, 242
Melina, Livio 103 n.25, 115 n.90, 117, 119 n.108, 141 n.211, 142 n.216, 144 n.246
Milbank, John 10, 39 n.18, 53, 57 n.99, 67 n.153, 143, 146, 180 n.71, 184 n.93, 190 n.120, 191
mission 28 n.58, 167 n.17, 172, 183
Mitchell, Basil 242
Moberly, Jennifer 134
Moltmann Jürgen 1–2, 3 n.6, 9, 55 n.88, 65–7, 75 n.201, 85 n.227, 112, 125, 178, 193, 199–201, 203, 223
moral reason, *see* practical reason
Morse, Christopher 238–39, 240 n.19
Mühling, Markus 228 n.6, 229

naturalism 21–5, 26–7, 43, 63, 103, 110, 176
natural law 5, 18, 20, 37–41, 43, 52–3, 57 n.99, 75, 77, 79, 88 n.243, 106, 117, 119 n.108, 119–23, 128, 130, 161–2, 188, 190, 214, 229, 237, 239
nature and grace 5 n.10, 76 n.202, 83 n.223, 117 n.97, 120 n.108, 159 n.305
Niebuhr, H. Richard 81 n.216, 101 n.9
Niebuhr, Reinhold 123 n.120, 140 n.210, 142 n.218, 194, 229

Nimmo, Paul T.   106 n.45, 118 n.102, 120 n.108
nominalism   16, 85 n.230, 121
Northcott, Michael   86, 96
Nygren, Anders   140 n.210, 153, 219

obedience   7, 15, 19, 47, 54, 99, 108, 111, 114, 119, 127–9, 139–45, 146, 196, 202, 209
O'Regan, Cyril   25 n.47, 26 n.50, 112, 230 n.24, 240
orthodox theology   47 n.56, 86
Outka, Gene   42, 141 n.210

Pannenberg, Wolfhart   55, 66–8, 80 n.211, 112 n.72, 125, 230
Parry, Robin   27 n.56, 42 n.36, 54, 73 n.190, 138 n.202
pastoral theology   1 n.1, 116, 121–2, 167 n.17, 192, 207, 210, 219, 230, 239
peace   66, 121 n.112, 171, 183 n.86, 186
Perry, John   123 n.120, 208 n.82
Pieper, Joseph   135 n.184, 198 n.30, 242
Pinches, Charles   120 n.109, 136 n.192, 143 n.225
Pinckaers, Servais   41 n.28, 58 n.103, 103 n.25, 142–3
Plato   39, 66
  Platonic   15, 45, 83 n.225, 133
pneumatology   6 n.15, 7, 81 n.214, 99–101, 107–13, 125–6, 145, 147, 151, 160, 166–7, 171, 181, 199, 216, 224, 233, 241
political theology   2–3, 7–8, 14, 18, 26–7, 29, 39 n.18, 50, 64, 79 n.209, 81 n.216, 89 n.244, 105 n.43, 123 n.120, 145–7, 156, 163–90, 196, 199–200, 203, 207, 209, 211, 218–19, 227, 234 n.8, 236–7, 239, 240, 242
Porter, Jean   37–8, 40, 75, 135 n.184
poverty   7, 9, 179–80, 201–3, 231
practical reason   49, 116–17, 178, 193, 195, 197–202, 207–8, 212–25, 234–5
praise, *see* worship
preaching   36, 79, 86 n.231, 109, 125–6, 139, 208, 236
Preston, Ronald   180, 200 n.50
protest   64–5

protestant theology   4, 10, 13–18, 32, 37 n.7, 38, 39 n.18, 40–3, 67, 71, 75, 106 n.45, 110, 112, 116, 120–2, 126–8, 130–1, 133–6, 139, 140–4, 212, 235–42
providence   1, 8, 16, 18, 22, 23 n.40, 24, 26, 29, 32, 70–1, 87, 89, 117 n.100, 119 n.106, 159, 163, 184–5, 188–90, 195, 238

Quash, Ben   53, 55, 130

Radical Orthodoxy   16 n.14, 67, 83 n.223
Radner, Ephraim   110, 112, 158 n.298, 237 n.4
Ramsey, Paul   2, 42–3, 58 n.103, 63 n.129, 81, 122, 123 n.120, 141 n.210, 191
Ratzinger, Joseph, *see* Benedict XVI
reformed theology   18 n.24, 38–40, 50, 81 n.214, 83 n.223, 86 n.234, 100 n.3, 106 n.45, 119 n.108, 159 n.305
resurrection, the   5–8, 35–41, 44, 46–57, 63, 65–6, 73–85, 87–90, 99–100, 103–4, 106–7, 109, 113, 137–40, 142, 150, 153, 155–62, 163, 167–74, 193–4, 200, 213, 216, 220, 224–5, 237–8
revelation, doctrine of   9, 18–21, 31, 38, 110, 118, 131–2, 215–16
Rodenborn, Steven   10 n.19, 65 n.142
Rogers, Eugene F.   6 n.15, 62 n.122, 109 n.58, 111 n.69

sacraments   54, 150, 166–7, 181
salvation, *see* soteriology
sanctification   103, 111, 135–7, 206–7
Schaeffer, Hans   131 n.162, 159 n.305
Schuurman, Douglas   65 n.143, 75 n.201, 85 n.227
secular, the   8, 181–5, 190
Sedgwick, Peter   58 n.103, 142 n.217
Sedgwick, Timothy F.   42, 58 n.103
sermons, *see* preaching
Simmons, Frederick   140–1
sin   7, 13, 23, 26, 32, 39, 47, 50, 57, 74, 75 n.201, 81, 89–91, 93, 99, 105, 111, 118, 126–32, 137, 139, 143, 146, 155, 156, 159 n.305, 161, 163, 173, 177–8, 182, 178 n.82, 184–7, 190, 202, 207, 214–15, 218–19, 236, 241–2

singleness 22–3, 59, 62–3, 159 n.305, 174 n.50, 231
Sonderegger, Katherine 233 n.4, 239 n.12, 240 n.19
Song, Robert 1 n.1, 49 n.65, 58 n.59 n.102, 63 n.129, 85 n.229, 160 n.307
soteriology 1, 5, 14, 21–3, 25–6, 31, 35 n.1, 43, 48, 56, 71–3, 81 n.214, 83–93, 100, 105–6, 110–12, 117 n.100, 118–20, 134–6, 144, 149, 153–4, 158, 163, 167–8, 170, 173, 178, 184, 187–9, 195 n.18, 206, 215–16, 219, 223–4, 236–40, 240, 242
Spaemann, Robert 11 n.26, 69 n.160
Spencer, Stanley 138
Steck, Christopher 118 n.103, 119 n.107, 218 n.142, 227 n.2
Stewart-Kroeker, Sarah 152, 190 n.120
Stott, John 4 n.7, 29 n.60, 48 n.61
Swinton, John 3 n.6, 237 n.4
Systematic Theology, *see* doctrine

Tanner, Kathryn 10, 219, 238, 240 n.16
Thielicke, Helmut 64, 104, 105–6, 229 n.15
Torrance, T. F. 21, 81 n.214
Townsend, Nicholas 53
trinity 107–13, 154, 156–7, 160, 213, 216

Ulrich, Hans G. 96 n.269, 240–1
utilitarianism 14, 123 n.120

virtue(s) 37 n.7, 50, 121 n.112, 134–5, 141–3, 149–50, 151, 184, 192, 197–8, 215, 222–4, 239
vocation 22–3, 59, 62– 4, 73–4, 107, 115–16, 118, 122, 146, 159 n.305, 171, 174 n.50, 181, 197, 209–10, 215

Volf, Miroslav 85 n.227, 139 n.205, 228 n.10
voluntarism 16, 71–3, 85 n.230, 114–17, 120 n.110

Wannenwetsch, Bernd 79 n.209, 127 n.137, 183 n.84, 184 n.92, 240
Waters, Brent 1 n.1, 22 n.39, 23 n.40, 29 n.63, 104, 155, 159, 160 n.307, 180 n.72
Watson, Francis 125 n.131, 174 n.49, 238
wealth 179–80, 201–3
Webster, John B. 57 n.100, 66, 97, 135–6, 148, 207, 208 n.80, 208 n.84, 230, 233, 239 n.12
Wells, Samuel 3 n.6, 53, 55, 63 n.129, 130, 142–3, 161 n.313, 182, 192 n.5, 214 n.126, 221
Werpehowski, William 41 n.28, 81 n.216, 213 n.120
Westberg, Daniel 49 n.66, 116 n.97, 117 n.97, 133–4, 139–43
Williams, Rowan 3, 39, 62, 179, 181 n.77, 217, 234 n.8
Williams, Stephen N. 90, 138, 228 n.10
Wolters, Al 76 n.202, 83 n.223
Wolterstorff, Nicholas 120 n.110, 163 n.1
worship 29, 79 n.209, 109, 128, 149, 206, 212, 227–8, 234, 242
Wright, N. T. 55, 80 n.211, 88–9, 157, 237

Yeago, David S. 105

Ziegler, Philip G. 77 n.203, 119 n.106, 128 n.139, 202 n.60, 239

Index of scripture references

Deuteronomy		17.1-9	107 n.51	5.5	224
32.36	48	19.12	22	6.4	130
		22.30	23, 159	6.12	130
1 Chronicles		24.13	144 n.229	6.17	140 n.206
29.10b-14	vi	24.42-51	199	8.2	106 n.45
				8.18-25	56, 86 n.231
Job		Mark		12.1	130
38–41	39	1.9-11	107 n.51	12.3	170
		1.15	222	14.17	171
Psalms		1.22	107 n.52	15.7	130
8	82	4.17	144 n.229	15.13	233–4
24.5	48	8.34	143 n.221		
37.6	48	9.2-8	107 n.51	1 Corinthians	
51.10-12	171 n.36	13.13	144 n.229	2.16	101
93.1	39	13.32-7	199	6.20	130
96.10	39			7	159 n.205
98.2	48	Luke		7.25-35	63
103.6	48	3.21-23	107 n.51	7.29	57
		4.18	107 n.51	12.3	126
Isaiah		4.32	107 n.52	13	221–2
40.31	233	9.23	143 n.221	13.12	132
43.19	115	9.28-36	107 n.51	15	156
61.1-2	48	12.35-48	199–200	15.44	88
		17.20	197	15.58	130
Jeremiah					
51.10	48	John		2 Corinthians	
		1.16	23	3.1	233
Amos		2	107 n.52	5.7	132
7.14	197	13.31	81	5.17	170
		13.34	149	9.13	140 n.206
Micah				13.13	224
7.9	48	Acts			
		2	109, 191	Galatians	
Matthew		2.11	215	5.1	130
3.11	167	2.37	206	5.7	140 n.206
3.13-17	107 n.51	3.21	88, 92 n.256	5.22	171 n.36
4.17	105–6	13.52	171 n.36		
7.1	136			Ephesians	
7.29	107 n.52	Romans		1.14	151
10.22	144 n.229	1.4	107	2.10	206
13.21	144 n.229	2.8	140 n.206	3.20	159 n.302
16.24	143 n.221	5.4	144 n.229		

5.1	130	2 Timothy		4.1-6	201
5.22–6.9	104, 174	2.12	144 n.229	5.1-6	201
		2.13	115		
Philippians				1 Peter	
2.2	224	Titus		1.3	77
2.12	130	2.13	234	1.5	56
4.1	130			1.13	78, 130, 168–9
Colossians		Hebrews		1.22	140 n.206
1.11	144 n.229	2.8-9	82, 211	2.13	78
1.15	169	5.8	143 n.224	2.13–3.7	104, 174
1.18	81, 169	5.9	140	4.1	130
2.6	130	6.19	234		
2.16	130	10.13	151	2 Peter	
3	156	10.23	144 n.229	1.16-18	107 n.51
3.3	151	10.39	144 n.229	3.10	90
3.5	130	11.1	151		
3.9-10	219	12.1	144 n.229	1 John	
3.11-15	219	12.2	139	3.2	88
3.18–4.1	104, 174	13.8	240		
				Revelation	
1 Thessalonians		James		4-5	129 n.148
1.6	171 n.36	1.12	144 n.229	15.4	172
4.18	130	1.25	144 n.229	21.1	88
5.11	130	2.4-7	201	21.2	145

www.ingramcontent.com/pod-product-compliance
Lightning Source LLC
Chambersburg PA
CBHW052112010526
44111CB00036B/1835